TAILORED DETERRENCE

Influencing States and Groups of Concern

Edited by

Barry R. Schneider

and

Patrick D. Ellis

USAF Center for Unconventional Weapons Studies

325 Chennault Circle

Maxwell Air Force Base, Alabama 36112-6427

First Edition, May 2011
Second Edition, March 2012*

*Michael Miller's chapter on "Nuclear Attribution as Deterrence" has
been removed from this edition

Disclaimer

The views expressed in this book are those of the authors and do not necessarily reflect the official policy or position of the U.S. government, Department of Defense, and the U.S. Air Force.

ISBN 978-0-9747403-8-6

Contents

Part Two - Deterrence Issues and Challenges: A Topical Approach

Acknowledgements

We thank Bonita Harris and Christy Truitt for their great work in processing and copy editing support in creating this book, and the contractor team at Northrop Grumman led by Michelle Spencer for securing access to seven of the key contributors of this volume. Thanks also go to Susan Fair, illustrator for the Air Force Research Institute, for the wonderful book cover, and to Technical Sergeant Wesley Powell for helping to coordinate the publishing of this book. Finally, we want to thank Headquarters Air Force, Office of Strategic Deterrence and Nuclear Integration, HQAF/A10, for their funding and support of this project.

ABBREVIATIONS

ALCM	Air-Launched Cruise Missiles
BMD	Ballistic Missile Defense
CBRN	Chemical, Biological, Radiological And Nuclear
CBW	Chemical And Biological Weapons
CD	Civil Defense
CENTCOM	Central Command
CEP	Circular Error Probable
CIKR	Critical Infrastructure And Key Resources
DCA	Dual-Capable Aircraft
DIME	Diplomatic, Intelligence, Military and Economic
DMZ	Demilitarized Zone
DPRK	Democratic Peoples' Republic Of Korea
EMT	Equivalent Megatons
EXCOMM	Executive Committee
FARC	Revolutionary Armed Forces Of Colombia
GLCM	Ground Launched Cruise Missile
GNP	Gross National Product
HML	Hardened Mobile Launchers
HEU	Highly Enriched Uranium
IAEA	International Atomic Energy Agency
ICBM	Intercontinental Ballistic Missile
IHO	International Humanitarian Organizations
INF	Intermediate-Range Nuclear Forces
IRGC	Islamic Revolutionary Guards Corps
IRGC-QF	IRGC Qods Force
IW	Information Warfare
JOC	Joint Operating Concept
KT	Kiloton
LTTE	Liberation Tigers Of Tamil Eelam
MAD	Mutual Assured Destruction
MAK	Maktab Al-Khidamat
MIRV	Multiple Independently Targetable Reentry Vehicle

NCA	Nuclear Command Authority
NIAC	National Infrastructure Advisory Council
NPR	Nuclear Posture Review
NPT	Nonproliferation Treaty
NSS	National Security Strategy
PAL	Permissive Action Link
PGM	Precision Guided Munitions
PNI	Presidential Nuclear Initiative
P.R.C.	People's Republic Of China
PSI	Proliferation Security Initiative
QDR	Quadrennial Defense Review
ROK	Republic Of Korea
SALT	Strategic Arms Limitations Talks
SDV	Strategic Delivery Vehicles
SIOP	Single Integrated Operational Plan
SLBM	Submarine-Launched Ballistic Missile
SOF	Special Operations Forces
SOP	Standard Operating Procedure
SORT	Strategic Offensive Reductions Treaty
SSBN	Ballistic Missile Submarine
START	Strategic Arms Reductions Talks
TLAM-N	Tomahawk Land Attack Missile-Nuclear
TRA	Taiwan Relations Act
UCAV	Unmanned Combat Aerial Vehicles
UNSCR	UN Security Council Resolution
USEUCOM	U.S. European Command
WMD	Weapons Of Mass Destruction

CHAPTER 1

New Thinking on Deterrence

Barry Schneider and Patrick Ellis

Deterrence thinking has evolved from the Cold War to the present. During the period from 1945-1991 when the United States sought to deter attacks by the U.S.S.R. and Warsaw Pact, U.S. nuclear forces were fielded primarily to prevent nuclear war or escalation of war. However, with the breakup of the Soviet Union, as an immediate threat to the United States, and the rise of lesser nuclear states proliferating nuclear technologies, deterrence is once again reexamined for newer solutions.

During the Cold War, deterrence strategy evolved over time as officials and defense strategists thought through the changes brought by nuclear weapons. Clearly after 1945, warfare had a new component. Long-range airpower gave states an intercontinental reach. The first A-bombs had an explosive power a thousand times more powerful than an equivalent weight of high explosive bombs like TNT. When thermonuclear weapons were created half a decade later, they, in turn, were a thousand times more powerful per unit weight than the A-bombs that destroyed Hiroshima and Nagasaki.

So in a period of four or five years, bomb explosive yields per unit weight increased a thousand times a thousand. This combination of long-range delivery vehicles coupled with warheads or bombs a million times more powerful than their World War II conventional counterparts led to a revolution in the way wars might be fought in the future if such weapons were employed.

In the nuclear era the homelands of the United States and other great powers are vulnerable to attack within a very short time. Everyone was now "at the front." The two great oceans had historically protected America, but now everyone was in the cross-hairs. There was no longer any delay in receiving or delivering absolutely devastating blows that could threaten the existence of a nation. A central nuclear war could start and be essentially over in a day. Indeed, nuclear weapons and long-range delivery opened up the possibilities that the populations and societies of a country might be destroyed even before their military forces were fully defeated – in just a few short minutes or hours.

Classic Cold War Deterrence

Because strategic defenses lagged so far behind bomber and missile-offensive forces, the United States came to embrace a Cold War deterrence strategy dependent upon several key elements including:

- Maintaining a retaliatory capability that could inflict what an adversary would clearly believe to be an unacceptable level of damage to their own country and regime.
- Having a "second-strike force" capable of such retaliatory power, even after the United States was attacked first in a surprise attack.
- Having the will to use such overwhelming force in retaliation, or, if necessary, in a first strike if war had begun and appeared heading toward Armageddon.
- Being able to clearly communicate the U.S. had such a retaliatory capability and the will to use it.
- Having a rational adversary that values its own leader and population survival, national power and key assets more than being able to inflict losses on the United States.
- Having the capability to identify the origins of any nuclear attack on the United States in a timely way, so as to remove doubt about the target of a U.S. retaliatory strike.
- Being able to hold at risk, locate and identify those assets that a rival leadership most values.

As long as these conditions held true, the U.S. leadership believed it could deter a Soviet attack on the United States and its declared allies. Even so, there were tense times when a wrong move might have triggered a nuclear war. The 1962 Cuban Missile Crisis is often cited as the event when we came closest to nuclear war with the U.S.S.R. and its allies.

Since the overthrow of the Communist Party in all eight past Warsaw Pact countries and 15 Soviet republics, a whole new set of nuclear rogue state and terrorist aspirants and powers have emerged on the world scene, each presenting their own unique threat and profile. Even Iraq, at one point before 1991, had a robust program to acquire nuclear weapons. Fortunately, this program was snuffed out by subsequent inspections and destruction of their capability.

For the most part, every country that embarks on nuclear weapons procurement presents dynamic challenges since there is no cookie cutter approach to deter any of them. North Korea, a rogue totalitarian state run by Kim Jong Il and a small group of family members presents its own unique set of problems. Other distinct problems are presented by Iran where the Ayatollah Khamene'i rules the Islamic Republic, a theocracy that is the leading state sponsor of terrorism in the world, and whose brand of Islamic revolution threatens everyone else in the region. Still another threat is posed by Syria, a state that appears to have collaborated with North Korea in pursuit of a nuclear weapon.

Rollbacks have averted some nuclear threats in Belarus, Kazakhstan, Ukraine and South Africa. Further, pressure or regime changes have terminated or temporarily blocked nuclear weapons research program in Taiwan, the Republic of Korea, Argentina, Romania and Brazil. Further, a nuclear Libya was narrowly averted by adroit U.S. negotiation with the regime of Muammar Qadhaffi, assisted by the interception of a shipment of A.Q. Khan black-market centrifuges bound for Libya.

And, alas, somewhere in the world, the al-Qaeda leaders still hide and still plot attacks on the "far enemy." They say they aspire to attack and are authorized to kill up to four million Americans using, if necessary, weapons of mass destruction. They are known to have sought nuclear, biological and chemical weapons, so far without result. At present, they have no known return address to retaliate against if they succeeded in acquiring and using a nuclear weapon. Such opponents may prefer martyrdom and "paradise" if they could strike a devastating nuclear blow against their declared enemy in the West.

Pakistan and India are recent entrants into the nuclear weapons state club. Still other states may start or re-start their nuclear weapons programs if the North Korean and Iranian nuclear programs are allowed to proceed unchecked.

The many new actors in the nuclear weapons arena mean that persons of very different cultures, languages, experiences, strategic situations and intentions must be deterred from using the ultimate weapon. This fact argues for a second approach to nuclear deterrence, namely tailored deterrence. Building on the deterrence elements of the Cold War and those assumptions, it can be argued that each regime, each leadership and each national situation is somewhat unique and therefore requires an approach to deterrence uniquely tailored to achieve maximum effect on that particular group of decision-makers.

Tailored Deterrence of New Actors

Tailored deterrence is, in the words of Dr. Jerrold Post, an actor-specific set of deterrence capabilities designed to influence a specific leader or leader's group.

Deterrence strategy may be tailored to the actors to be deterred, the capabilities needed to execute this strategy, and to the points in ongoing scenarios where there are opportunities to deter the adversary.[1]

This book looks at all three. We look at tailoring a deterrence strategy to Russia, North Korea, Iran and al-Qaeda. We discuss specific capabilities necessary to enhance deterrence like good strategic communications, attribution capability and programs to improve public resilience. In addition, we explore unfolding scenarios to look at decision points for deterring a conflict or escalation of a conflict such as in the example of the 1990-1991 Gulf War when Saddam Hussein's forces invaded Kuwait.

To increase the possibility of influence requires a full understanding of the enemy or potential enemy, and act accordingly. This means that one will have to develop an understanding of:

- Who in the regime is in charge of what kinds of national security decisions?
- Adversary decision-maker personalities, tendencies, views and experiences.
- Opponent leadership value hierarchy.
- Rival perceptions and knowledge of the situation, stakes and views of the U.S.'s willingness to use force in the scenario.

- The rival leadership's commitment to achieving particular outcomes in a given crisis or conflict.
- Past regime security decisions, decision processes and standard operating procedures.
- Regime behavior in past conflicts, crises and exercises.
- Regime history, strategic situation and strategic culture of the state.
- Regime military leaders, their unit capabilities, military doctrine and strategy.
- Regime internal and external allies, opponents and publics.
- Regime strengths: leaders, diplomatic, intelligence, military and economic.
- Regime weaknesses: leadership splits; any diplomatic, intelligence, military and economic (DIME) flaws; and their international rivals and borders.

Scenario Dependent Deterrence

In addition to these two views of what goes into effective deterrence, classic Cold War deterrence and tailored deterrence of a regime, it is important to mention the importance of context. Decision-makers can act very differently in different scenarios. These diverse scenarios give context to discussions about deterrence. Potential flashpoint scenarios must be anticipated and thought through ahead of time. This may allow the U.S. to take actions and communicate clearly in a timely way before events take on a life of their own. Just as a winning chess strategy requires the correct sequencing of moves to achieve a checkmate, the same is true of crisis and conflict decisions. Thinking through potential scenarios is an international chess match to be undertaken before the events take place so correct moves can be taken to prevent disastrous surprises and defeats. As the proverb says, an ounce of prevention is worth a pound of cure. Correct sequencing of moves can bolster deterrence, and scenario analysis may help inform such moves.

Tailoring Deterrence

This book was written with senior United States government leadership and decision-makers in mind as a key audience. It is meant to help them analyze the best means of deterring future conflicts with state and non-state adversaries in the 21st century. The central focus is on actor-specific tailored deterrence that influences force postures, communications and actions based on contextual and scenario considerations. Any top government decision-makers who formulate policy and strategy to counter nuclear and other WMD threats should read it. In addition, this volume would be instructive to interested national security experts, military officers and informed citizens.

This book addresses this series of deterrence questions:

- Why is it important to develop an actor-specific approach to deterrence of adversaries? Does one standard deterrence formula fit all adversaries and situations? Or must we craft a unique deterrence approach to each potential adversary?
- How do you deter a peer competitor like Russia, the only other nuclear superpower on the planet, and what is different about deterring Russian adventurism than any other state?
- How can we deter Iran, the leading state sponsor of terrorism in the world, after it achieves a nuclear weapons capability?
- Similarly, how can we influence North Korea's leaders to avoid war and spreading nuclear weapons to others now that they are a nuclear weapons state?
- What kind of extended deterrence policy is in the United States interest, and how much nuclear capability do we need to make an extended deterrent credible and capable?
- How can we deter non-state actors with no return address from using nuclear or other WMD weapons against us and our allies? How can we influence a terrorist leader's WMD acquisition and use calculus?
- How might the United States have better deterred the Iraqi invasion of Kuwait in 1990? To what degree did deterrence play in the decisions of both sides of the 1990-91 Gulf War as it unfolded?
- Why might the demonstrably weaker side sometimes attack much stronger opponents as has happened often in history? Why did or might deterrence fail in such cases of the weak attacking the strong?

- How might deterrence succeed or fail in a future Taiwan crisis that pits the People's Republic of China against the Taiwan government supported by the United States? What might be the role of asymmetric interests and asymmetric military power?
- How might deterrence work or fail to work during future crises in a world of zero nuclear weapons? Would the removal of nuclear weapons leads to a greater likelihood of conventional war?
- What United States strategic nuclear force structure will represent the strongest deterrent to war as deeper cuts are made by negotiated arms control treaties? Is a triad superior to either an ICBM-SLBM or Bomber-SLBM dyad? What are the deterrence tradeoffs?
- What is the role of strategic communications in transmitting our capability and will to potential adversaries and allies dependent on the U.S. nuclear extended deterrent? How can strategic communications be improved?
- Can the U.S. and allied publics be organized, trained and equipped to bounce back after a WMD attack and can the increased resiliency improve deterrence of adversary attacks? How might resilience be improved?
- What is the importance of being able to identify in a quick and sure way the identity of an adversary that has struck the United   States with a weapon of mass destruction? What impact can possessing a known nuclear attribution capability have in deterring such state and terrorist attacks on the United States?

It has been said if one wishes to keep the peace, prepare for war. Part of that preparation is to tailor the retaliatory threat to the specific potential enemy in such a way you maximize your influence on their decisions in all likely scenarios. This will require tailored deterrence that builds upon the elements of Cold War deterrence strategy and thinking through deterrence opportunities in future scenarios.

Notes

[1] See Elaine Bunn, "Can Deterrence be Tailored?" Strategic Forum No. 225, (January 2007), Institute for National Strategic Studies, National Defense University. Also, see Karl-

Heinz Kamp and David S. Yost, NATO and 21st Century Deterrence, (Rome: NATO Defense College, May 2009), 11-58.

Part One

Deterring State and Non-State Actors: Case Studies

CHAPTER 2

Actor-Specific Behavioral Models of Adversaries: A Key Requirement for Tailored Deterrence

Jerrold M. Post, M.D[1]

Deterrence theory makes assumptions about the nature of the adversary. Explicitly, or more often implicitly, how the adversary reasons and reacts to the prospect of violence as it considers pursuing a particular path is at the heart of deterrence theory. Thus the concept of deterrence is "primarily a psychological phenomenon, involving as it does calculations of the behavioral dispositions of an adversary state. In this sense, a complete understanding of the nation's security cannot be based solely on estimations of its military capability."[2]

Observing that deterrence theory is a sub-set of theories of rational choice, Janice Gross Stein characterizes deterrence as seeking "to prevent undesired action by convincing the party who may be contemplating such action that its cost will exceed any possible gain." She has emphasized there is no single theory of deterrence.[3] In reviewing the literature of deterrence, she observes that the first wave of deterrence theories, by scholars such as Schelling, were for the most part deductive in nature.[4] It emphasized the credibility of threats and commitments.

As observed by Keith Payne in his trenchant critique of deterrence theory, "the leaders are assumed to be rational and willing to engage in cost-benefit calculations when making policy decisions."[5] In her edited book, *Psychological Dimensions of War,* in a chapter on "Dilemmas of Deterrence: Rational and Irrational Perspectives," Glad has critiqued models of deterrence deriving from game theory, observing that "one assumes a certain rationality in both of the adversaries."[6] She then discusses multiple examples of misperceptions of adversary motivations.

But that assumption of rationality, as Keith Payne emphasizes, also assumes shared values and understandings. In his analysis of 20th century history, the political psychologist Ralph White coined the phrase "mirror imaging" to refer to the pre-war period leading up to conflicts, where each side resembled the other in its aggressiveness and in justifying the primarily defensive motivation of its own aggressiveness. He sees this as war-promoting motivation. He especially emphasizes the role of false attribution of motivations to escalating spirals of conflict.[7]

The underlying assumption of deterrence during the Cold War was indeed the rationality of the adversaries. Surely the Soviet leaders would not be so irrational as to risk assured destruction, strategists in the West reasoned. Surely, the United States leaders would not be so irrational as to risk assured destruction, reasoned the Soviet Union counterparts. Hence, Mutual Assured Destruction, suitably characterized by the acronym MAD, was the governing doctrine. But, proponents of MAD theory will note it worked. Whether the fact there were no nuclear conflicts during the Cold War era was a consequence of MAD doctrine is, however, a dubious, and ultimately improvable, proposition. For leaders are flesh and blood, and fall prey to the gamut of human emotions — pride, over-optimism, fear, insecurity — as the rest of us. And, as emphasized by Graham Allison in his analysis of the Cuban Missile Crisis, *Essence of Decision,* a hazard of the rational national actor level of analysis is it forecloses the ability to incorporate into analysis the impact of bureaucratic politics, what he termed the Organizational Process Model. Nor did it take into account the Governmental Politics Model which reflects the factional strivings and palace politics among leaders striving for influence.[8]

One of the puzzling aspects of the discovery of possible offensive missiles in Cuba by U-2 photography to the Executive Committee, President Kennedy's small advisory group, was the apparent absence of attempts to camouflage the sites under construction. Surely, the reasoning went, if the Soviet Union attempted to install offensive missiles in Cuba to close the missile gap, they would wish to accomplish this by a *fait accompli.* And yet the sites were not camouflaged. Therefore, the reasoning went, perhaps these were not offensive missile sites after all, delaying the conclusion of the gravity of the posed threat.

We now know from a series of meetings with Soviet interlocutors that gaining political-military advantage through a *fait accompli* was indeed the strategic goal of the Soviet politburo. But it turned the implementation of the decision over to the strategic rocket forces, which used the same standard operating procedure in establishing a missile site in Cuba that they had employed in the Warsaw Pact states. This conclusion required analysis at the level of bureaucratic politics and could not be discerned at the rational national actor level of analysis.

But in fact, organizations don't make decisions, policy-making groups do. Allison depicts the intense interplay among the participants in EXCOMM during the 13 days of the Cuban missile crisis. Three military options were under consideration: a surgical air strike, an invasion of Cuba and a military blockade. Demonstrating the power of analogy and framing, Attorney General Robert Kennedy framed the airstrike on the missile bases as analogous to Pearl Harbor and indicated history would view his brother as the Tojo of the Western world if he carried out this sneak attack. That was enough for JFK, who already had his eye on the history books, to take this quite sensible option off the table. As they were debating between an invasion and a blockade, U.N. Ambassador Adlai Stevenson indicated that it was unwise to push the Soviet into a corner. Since the missiles in Turkey were considered outmoded and needed to be removed anyway, why not offer the Soviets a face-saving way out of the dilemma, and offer to remove U.S. offensive missiles in Turkey in return for the Soviets removing their offensive missiles from Cuba? After raising this suggestion, he excused himself to go to the rest room. After he departed, a hawkish member of the Joint Chiefs made a derisive comment to the effect that Stevenson was a cowardly impotent old man. When he returned from the restroom, his idea had been discarded, and they were debating the merits of the two military options. [9] This is a classic example of "groupthink" as described by Irving Janis, where the general served as a "mindguard," making an *ad hominem* attack on the messenger, thus keeping his idea out of play. [10] Such a maneuver contributes to the so-called "risky shift" phenomenon, wherein social psychologists have found that groups of individuals can make riskier decisions than those individuals would if making the decisions on their own. [11]

But in fact, ultimately, groups don't make decisions, people do. And the retrospective analysis conducted by Sherman Kent, the father of national intelligence, of the intelligence failure during the Cuban missile crisis concerning the delay in understanding the gravity of the Soviet threat concluded insufficient attention was paid to the political personalities of the two principal actors, Nikita Khrushchev and Fidel Castro, who were uncritically assumed to be rational. This is not to say they were viewed as irrational. Rather, the nature of Krushchev's and Castro's decision-making, especially their risk-taking propensities, was insufficiently taken into account.

In fact, as Payne emphasizes, had Khrushchev followed the counsel of Castro and Che Gueverra, nuclear conflict might well have occurred with devastating consequences.[12] Payne quotes James Blight who was one of the negotiators in the historic meetings between U.S. and Soviet participants involved in the Cuban missile crisis.[13] Col. Viktor Semykin describes the Cuban leadership's extreme urgings of the Soviets to carry out a missile attack and reported they seemed heedless of the consequences: "The Cubans really insisted we use our weapons. 'Why else did you come here? Use your weapons. Fire.' They were ready for war. Maybe they believed so strongly, they were ready to sacrifice themselves." They would say, 'Cuba will perish, but socialism will win.' They were ready to sacrifice themselves." Che Guevara in particular expressed his willingness to sacrifice himself and Cuba for the cause of socialism. "If the rockets had remained, we would have used them all and directed them against the heart of the United States, including New York, in our fight against aggression." This "ultimate showdown" with the United States, in his view, was "the final aim of Communism."[14]

Reflecting a cooler disposition, and, as Payne notes, "a cost-benefit calculus more susceptible to deterrence threats," Soviet Deputy Premier Anastas Mikoyan is quoted as replying, "We see your readiness to die beautifully, but we believe that it isn't worth dying beautifully." Khrushchev himself was to remark later, "At that time he [Castro] was a very hot-tempered person.... He failed to think through the obvious consequences of a proposal that placed the planet on the brink of extinction."[15]

In discussions with Allison, I have observed that a fourth level of analysis is called for in that while his Governmental Politics Model does take individuals into account, it does so in the capacity as individuals, as rational actors, and as black boxes striving to maximize their interests. At this level, the individual is a coolly calculating Machiavellian. But this ignores the passions that drive men's souls. It ignores jealousy, suspiciousness, vengefulness, hubris and the gamut of emotions that drive men's actions. Thus, individual personalities and group dynamics both powerfully influence decisions.

The goal of the above discussion is to cast doubt on the assumption of rationality that governed deterrence theory during the Cold War. Even then, by no means were decisions the consequence of coldly calculated cost-benefit analysis. And if that was the case even then, what of the post-Cold War environment? Surely a requirement for deterrence in the post-Cold War environment is a nuanced understanding of the adversary in his cultural and political context. Optimally, to deter an adversary requires nuanced understanding of the adversary's psychology and decision-making. In his contribution to the Carnegie Commission on Preventing Deadly Conflict under the leadership of David Hamburg, Alexander George stressed in particular the need for accurate nuanced analysis of the adversary — what he called actor-specific behavioral models — as an indispensable requirement undergirding coercive diplomacy.[16] The report stressed the critical role of leadership both in promoting deadly conflict and in avoiding it.

This suggests that a required answer to the question posed by Elaine Bunn in her 2007 article in the *Strategic Forum*, "Can Deterrence Be Tailored?" is that *it must be*.[17] Bunn identifies three facets of tailored deterrence: first tailoring to specific actors and specific situations; second tailoring capabilities; and third tailoring communications.[18]

The end of the Cold War has been destabilizing, producing not a "peace dividend," but an unpredictable international climate in which major political crises have been produced by rogue leaders of outlaw nations. The relatively stable and predictable superpower rivalry has been supplanted by a series of regional conflicts often started by the actions of previously unknown or poorly understood leaders. Leaders of trans-national terrorist organizations must be added to the list of dangerous adversaries. There has been a proliferation of destructive power in the hands of nations and trans-national organizations with hostile agendas toward the United States.

There is "no one size fits all" deterrence, and what deters one adversary can be an incitement for another. Recognizing this, the 2006 *Quadrennial Defense Review (*QDR) *Report,* sets forth a concept of tailored deterrence with three classes of adversaries in mind: advanced military competitors, regional weapons of mass destruction (WMD) states, as well as non-state terrorist networks. It is interesting to observe the 2006 date, which is fully 17 years after the fall of the Berlin Wall and marked the end of the Cold War and the super-power rivalry. Yet the cold warrior mentality and attendant-deterrence strategy continued to dominate with a tendency to extrapolate uncritically deterrence theory established during the Cold War to new classes of adversaries. But to tailor deterrence to these new adversaries will in turn require a level of knowledge concerning the adversary which we often do not possess, and that is one of the dilemmas with which Bunn struggles in her essay; namely, we can never possess the degree of knowledge necessary to fully tailor deterrence to the adversary's unique psychology.

However, if we can never possess the full degree of knowledge of our adversaries' psychology, decision-making, and strategic calculus necessary to tailor deterrence with confidence that our policies will be perceived and our communications received in the desired fashion, we certainly can and must improve in our ability to accurately construct actor-specific behavioral models.

One of the first tasks is to define the locus of decision-making. Here the work of Hermann, Hermann and Hagan who have systematically studied how government makes decisions is particularly helpful.[19] They usefully distinguish among three types: first, the predominant leader, where a single individual has the power to make decisions and to stifle opposition; second, single group, a set of interacting individuals, all of whom are members of a single body, who have the ability to select a course of action and obtain compliance; and finally, multiple autonomous groups - the important actors are members of different groups or coalitions, no one of which has the ability by itself to decide or force compliance on the others and, no overarching body exists in which all the necessary parties are members.

Earlier, White had observed that both Hitler and Mussolini were "one-man dictatorships, and also aberrant personalities of an extremely macho and narcissistic if not also paranoid type." Observing that Stalin with his morbid suspicion of the West was also paranoid, he contrasts the Stalin period with the post-Stalin period of the Cold War.[20] The former was a leader predominant society, whereas the latter more closely resembled a single-group leadership, which to some degree guarded against a dominant aberrant personality. Within the Politburo, to be sure, the chairman was first among equals, but was indeed constrained by the dynamics of the politburo. Consider, for example, during the Cuban missile crisis that Khrushchev was compelled to resign after the forced Soviet withdrawal and humiliation in the crisis.

The balance of this chapter will focus on tailoring to specific actors, including trans-national terrorist organizations. The four examples chosen, Iraq, North Korea, Iran and al-Qaeda all were, or are of concern, with reference to weapons of mass destruction. This review of these four actor-specific behavioral models will also consider the importance of such models for coercive diplomacy. Several of the examples chosen will be from leader predominant states and will note the value of communications tailored to split the leader from his inner circle and/or followers.

Saddam Hussein of Iraq: "Saddam is Iraq, Iraq is Saddam"

Iraq under Saddam Hussein surely represents a leader predominant society, as reflected in the aphorism in the sub-head, "Saddam is Iraq; Iraq is Saddam." In the testimony I presented to the House Armed Services Committee and the House Foreign Affairs Committee in December 1990, a month before the outbreak of conflict, I summarized a political personality profile of Saddam I had developed after the invasion of Kuwait, depicting him as a malignant narcissist.[21] Indeed in his own mind, Saddam and Iraq were one and the same. He viewed himself as one of history's great leaders. He had a paranoid orientation, had no constraint of conscience, and was willing to pursue whatever aggression was necessary in pursuit of his goals.

In contrast to the wide-spread caricatures of Saddam as "the madman of the Middle East," closer analysis revealed him to be a rational calculator. He nevertheless often miscalculated because of his ethnocentric framework and because he was surrounded by a leadership circle composed of sycophants. For good reasons, they were reluctant to constructively criticize their leader, for to do so would result not only in losing their job, but could also lead to losing their life. Thus Saddam was in touch with reality psychologically, but could be out of touch politically because he was if he were only told what he wanted to hear rather than what he needed to hear.

Having traced a pattern of reversals during his career, Saddam could reverse himself and withdraw from Kuwait, only if he came to believe that he could do so without losing face and that he would retain his power — a double contingency. But if backed into a corner, he could lash out.

During the 1990-91 confrontation in the Gulf, President George H. W. Bush pounded on the table and said, "There will be no face saving." Moreover, a U.S. general had leaked contingency plans to remove Saddam. So, neither of the two contingent requirements was met, and Saddam felt no choice but to hunker down and attempt to survive the initial massive air campaign which had been well announced, hoping to engage the coalition in a ground campaign. Saddam believed the U.S. suffered from a Vietnam complex and could not tolerate again the spectacle of America's youth in body bags, which would lead to public protests. He believed given enough Iraqi resistance political impasse would result followed by a ceasefire. Thus Saddam also calculated he would win while losing by showing he had the courage to stand up to the mightiest military force on earth. Indeed, he held a press conference after five days of the massive air campaign, declaring victory. Since it had been predicted he could only withstand three days of aerial bombardment before crumbling, by holding out for five days he had already "won" and each additional day only further magnified the scope of his victory. The Mother of All Battles Mosque was erected to commemorate his great "victory." Here the attempt to coerce him with the threat of the massive battle looming failed because it did not take into account his political psychology, in particular, his need to save face and be guaranteed he would remain in power.[22]

In the run-up to the second Gulf War, two themes dominated the debate. One concerned administration contentions that Saddam Hussein and Osama bin Laden collaborated. The second involved the requirement to attack preemptively, lest Saddam Hussein provide nuclear weapons to terrorists. But careful analysis of political personalities of the principals would have cast serious doubt on both of these propositions. In the first place, there was considerable evidence that the committed Wahabi Sunni Muslim Osama bin Laden and the secular Saddam Hussein were bitter rivals, seeking support from the same constituency. Moreover, accepting the premise that Saddam was both a prudent decision-maker and risk averse, if he did have weapons of mass destruction, the likelihood he would give them to terrorists so they were out of his control was unlikely to the extreme, for the terrorists had no fixed address, whereas if the weapons were traced to him, he knew he would be incinerated. At a minimum, the conclusions springing from this level of analysis should have raised enough questions so as to prompt a Team B review.

In the second Gulf war, the administration of President George W. Bush was concerned with the possibility Saddam would use WMD. In the fall of 2002, it made use of tailored communications delivered publicly, in what could be characterized as public diplomacy or information operations. First, Secretary of Defense Donald Rumsfeld stated the Iraqi generals had an important role to play in the reconstruction of their country Iraq. Of course, he went on, if they became involved in weapons of mass destruction, all bets were off. Two weeks later, President Bush indicated President Saddam might order the use of weapons of mass destruction. If he did so, Bush went on, the Iraqi generals would be well advised to disobey those orders. Even though Iraq was clearly a leader predominant society, Saddam nevertheless required the loyalty of his generals. This double-barreled salvo of public diplomacy was designed to drive a wedge between Saddam and the generals and convince them to look out for their own welfare.

In the run-up to the 1990 invasion of Kuwait by Iraq with intelligence revealing a massive buildup of Iraqi troops on the Kuwait border, U.S. Ambassador April Glaspie was instructed to meet with Saddam Hussein. While she has been much criticized, the message she was instructed to deliver carefully avoided the threats of serious consequences should Iraq invade Kuwait. Referring to the massive deployment of troops in the South, she indicated she had received "an instruction to ask you, in the spirit of friendship — not confrontation —regarding your intentions."[23] Later she continued, "We have no opinion on your Arab-Arab conflicts, such as your dispute with Kuwait. Secretary Baker has directed me to emphasize the instruction, first given to Iraq in the 1960s, that the Kuwait issue is not associated with America." When this became public, it was widely assumed this explicitly non-confrontational language was taken as a go- ahead by Saddam, and in effect reassured him there would be no serious consequences for his planned invasion.

A subsequent profile characterized Saddam as a prudent decision-maker, who indeed was not prone to taking unnecessary risks. It further emphasized he tended to see the world through Arab eyes and take threatening language as hyperbole. In terms of coercive diplomacy, this emphasizes the importance in delivering an unambiguous demarche of the gravity of the consequences should Saddam proceed with what seemed to be preparation for an invasion of Kuwait.

Had Saddam already determined to go forward at that late hour? Perhaps. But as a prudent decision-maker who had often reversed himself in the service of "revolutionary pragmatism," Saddam might well have had his attention focused by a clear confrontational demarche in which it was made clear that an invasion of Kuwait would be met with force and avoided the destructive conflict that followed. Instead he took the explicitly non-confrontational language, coupled with statements from the Department of State that there were no security commitments to Kuwait, as reassurance that there would be no negative consequences.

President Mahmoud Ahmadinejad of Iran: Seeking Chaos?

Much of the provocative statements from Iran are from President Mahmoud Ahmadinejad. It was Ahmadinejad on April10, 2010, who revealed Iran had a centrifuge that would process uranium six times faster than the earlier models. Then on April19, Iran announced it would build a new uranium enrichment plant, giving emphasis to the memorandum from Secretary of Defense Bob Gates that starkly asserted the U.S. "does not have an effective long-range policy for dealing with Iran's steady progress toward nuclear capability."

Were he a predominant leader in the mode of Saddam Hussein of Iraq, there would be reason to be gravely concerned that Iran, under his leadership, as summarized in the following profile, was undeterrable. But, as Gregory Giles emphasizes in Chapter 5, "Deterring a Nuclear-Armed Iran from Adventurism and Nuclear Use," Iran is assuredly not a predominant leader state. Indeed, the national security decision-making is a very complex calculus, with many balancing factions, and the most important leader, Supreme Leader Khamenei, carefully balances out the often contradictory factions. This political personality profile of President Ahmadinejad is presented both as a profile of one of the important leaders, certainly the most vocal, but most importantly, to emphasize the importance of carefully analyzing the nature of the leadership and its decision-making and the constraints on any single leader.

Ahmadinejad's father, Ahmad Saborjhian, was a business failure, both as a barber and as a grocer. His name, signifying he was in the rug-weaving industry, suggested a peasant background. When he went to

Teheran in the construction boom, he changed his name to Ahmadinejad, "from the race of Prophet Muhammad." He sacrificed for his family, whose success would be his.

Young Ahmadinejad was known as an intelligent, diligent and studious child. He was excluded from Koran classes because he was too young, but insisted he could read the Koran and demonstrated such. He was an excellent student, who boasted to his fellow students that he would be in the top 10 nationally in the Concours university exams. (150,000 took the exam). He finished 132, which was in the top 1 percent, but this suggested a special sense of self.

Ahmadinejad started his university studies in civil engineering during the second half of the 1970s, a time of political turmoil in Iran. He was the founder of the Islamic Students Union and was involved in a radical anti-Shah student magazine. He was reportedly a member of the group that planned the takeover of the American embassy in Iran in 1979.[24]

Despite his cosmopolitan appearance and being at ease before international audiences, there is considerable evidence that Ahmadinejad is ideologically extreme. When Ayatollah Khomeini launched his human wave attacks of children, armed only with pink plastic keys to paradise around their necks, this terrifying tactic turned the corner in Iran-Iraq war. It was, according to some reports, Ahmadinejad that trained the children and purchased some 500,000 pink plastic keys from Taiwan.[25]

His comments on Israel have been extremely provocative and raised deep concerns, especially in Israel which felt existentially threatened. He spoke of the inequity of "the way the elected Government of the Palestinian people is treated" compared to the "support of the Zionist regime." In a conference in Teheran in October 2005 entitled "The World Without Zionism," he stated, "the establishment of the Zionist regime was a move by the world oppressor against the Islamic world," and that the state of Israel was illegitimate. Referring to Ayatollah Khomeini, he stated, "as the Imam said, Israel must be wiped off the map."

Ahmadinejad's statements concerning other nuclear powers have been equally provocative. Accusing them of using "the deadly weapons" as "instruments of coercion and threat against other peoples and governments," he stated they "consider themselves as the masters and rulers of the entire world and other nations as only second class in the world order." Between the provocative comments on Israel and his flaunting of

Iran's nuclear ambitions, which includes for nuclear enrichment, he seems to be pushing for confrontation and seeking chaos. Why?

To answer this question requires an understanding of Ahmadinejad's religious beliefs. There is a messianic tradition within Islam that believes the Mahdi (the "guided one"), who is a descendant of the prophet, will appear *at a time of chaos* just before judgment day and this will introduce a period of universal peace under the leadership of Shi'ite Muslims. The "Twelver" branch of Shia Islam refers to the Twelfth Imam, Muhammad al-Mahdi, in lineal descent from the prophet, who is said to have gone into a state of "occultation" in 874 A.D. According to legend, he is not dead, but will reveal himself in a period of chaos for a battle in the final days.[26] Most "Twelvers" are quietists, waiting for the arrival of the hidden imam. But there is a group of Mahdists who are religious belligerents, seeking to precipitate the final days by promoting chaos, "Twelvers" activists. There is persuasive evidence that Ahmadinejad is an activist "Twelver."

Ahmadinejad's mentor is Ayatollah Yazdi, a committed "Twelvers" activist, a supporter of the clerical regime of Ayatollah Khomeini, and a supporter of his successor Supreme Leader Khamenei. Yazdi is considered the most conservative member of Khamenei's inner circle. He is a member of the Council of Experts. It was Yazdi who persuaded the Supreme Leader, Ayatollah al-Khameini, to support Ahmadinejad's presidential candidacy, a crucial political act that paved the way for his electoral victory election.

During his tenure as mayor of Teheran Ahmadinejad made major investments in preparing the infrastructure for the arrival of the Mahdi, which he informed an Iranian journalist would be in two years. After his surprise victory in the presidential election, he gave $17 million to the Jamkaran mosque, which houses the well from which "Twelvers" believe the Mahdi will emerge. In November 2005, he said publicly the main mission of the Islamic Republic was to bring about the reappearance of the Twelfth Iman.

After the September 2005 address to U.N. General Assembly, he was caught on videotape telling a cleric that during the speech a halo appeared around his head on the podium. "I felt the atmosphere suddenly change. And for those 27 or 28 minutes, the leaders of the world did not blink…It seemed as if a hand was holding them there, and it opened their eyes to receive the message from the Islamic Republic."

So, if the apparent drive to develop a nuclear weapon and his calls to wipe Israel off the map seem designed to produce chaos, which may indeed be President Ahmadinejad's goal as a committed "Twelver" Muslim, a Mahdist religious belligerent, who apparently believes actions that produce chaos can help hasten the arrival on earth of the messiah.

This has major implications for deterrability. If Iran were a leader predominant state, one would have to conclude Iran was not deterrable.

But in presenting this profile to the annual security conference in Herzlea, Israel, on a panel entitled "Can a Nuclear Iran be Deterred?" an important distinction was made. In contrast to President Saddam Hussein of Iraq who assuredly ruled a leader-predominant state, despite being president, Ahmadinejad not only did not control the major resources of the state, in fact, he was not the main decision-maker. This was the role occupied by the Supreme Leader Ayatollah Khamenei, who has ultimate authority. As the Supreme Leader it is he who:

- determines the general policies of the Islamic Republic of Iran.
- has the power to declare war and peace and general troop mobilization.
- resolves differences and regulate relations among the three branches of the government.
- appoints and dismisses the:
  o Members of the Council of Guardians
  o Head of the Judiciary
  o Director of radio and television networks
  o Chief of staff of the armed forces
  o Commander-in-Chief of the Revolutionary Guards
  o Commander-in-Chief of the military and security services.

But Khamenei too is not entirely free to act, as he is constrained by a complex web of decision-making bodies, including the Assembly of Experts, the Council of Guardians and the Council of Expediency. So Iran, in vivid contrast to Iraq under Saddam Hussein represented the third type of state described by Hermann, Hermann and Hagan, one that is directed by multiple autonomous leader groups, with no one group having the sole authority.[27] So there is a complex matrix of competing forces, with pragmatists versus theocrats, and a Supreme Leader with ultimate authority and a President who is a religious conservative with a special sense of self, whose authority is constrained.

Moreover, it is important to take into account that 70 percent of the Iranian population under 30 years of age yearn to join the modern world. In contrast to North Korea, Iran is fully "wired" and connected to global connections networks. This restive population is actively informed through the internet. As a consequence, the reins of theocratic control are loosening.

Having a political personality profile of Ahmadinejad is necessary, but not sufficient in dealing with Iran as it pursues nuclear ambitions. A nuanced understanding of the complexities of Iranian decision-making, including profiles of the principal Iranian leaders and their complex interactions, is essential in attempting to influence Iran through coercive diplomacy.

Kim Jong-Il of North Korea: In the Shadow of His Father

One cannot understand the personality and political behavior of Kim Jong-Il without placing it in the context of the life and charismatic leadership of his father, Kim Il-Sung, North Korea's first leader. One of the difficulties in assessing the personality and political behavior of Kim Il-Sung has always been discerning the man behind the myth. The gap between the facts that scholars have been able to piece together and the hagiographic portrait presented to the people of North Korea is staggering.

Kim Jong Il was raised to succeed his heroic, charismatic father, Kim Il Sung. But, the present North Korean leader is no guerrilla fighter or nation builder. He inherited his charismatic image and national ideology of *Juche* and reunification from his father. As director of the Bureau of Agitation and Propaganda, he played a major role both in creating the cult of personality surrounding his father, but also in creating the existing myth that he is the "Man from Mt. Paektu," when in fact, he was raised in squalid circumstances under Soviet protection and is the boy from the U.S.S.R.

The disparity from his father contributes to profound insecurity in his son: "majesty sits uncomfortably on his shoulders." His father's giant shadow always looms over him. Succeeding a powerful father is a challenge. Succeeding a father of god-like stature is psychologically impossible. In many ways he is trapped by his father's ideology.

Malignant Narcissism

Kim Jong-Il's personality also reflects, in his cultural context, malignant narcissism. His extreme grandiosity and self-absorption overlay extreme insecurity about stepping into his father's god-like shoes. This insecurity is not just about his stature as a political leader, but also about his literal stature. Standing roughly 5 feet 2 inches tall, Kim Jong-Il reportedly has platform shoes custom built for him to enhance his height and weighs in around 175 pounds. Clearly his short stature is a long-standing issue for him; he reportedly was teased as a boy, called "Shorty." Upon first meeting the South Korean actress Choe Un-hui, whom he had kidnapped to help develop a North Korean movie industry, Kim reportedly asked, "Well, Madame Choe, what do you think of my physique? Small as a midget's droppings, aren't I?"[28] His hair is worn in a flamboyant style adding the appearance of additional height.

This long-standing insecurity leads him to be extremely sensitive to slights. He displays a lack of empathy for his own people, but this deficiency also leads him to not understand his adversaries. An aspect of his compensatory grandiosity is a tendency to be overly optimistic about himself and his nation and to underestimate his adversary. He has no constraint of conscience and has a paranoid orientation, and a tendency to find scapegoats when things do not go as he wishes.

Hedonistic Life Style

Kim has an extremely hedonistic lifestyle, especially striking, given the stark poverty in which most of his countrymen live. He lives in a seven-story pleasure palace in P'yong-yang, gives extravagant gifts to his senior leaders and likes to throw wild parties. Kim recruits young girls with clear complexions in junior high school for "joy brigades" to provide entertainment for his hard-working senior officials. During the 1990s, he spent between $650,000 and $800,000 annually on Hennessey Paradis

Cognac, their most expensive cognac at $630 a bottle, when the annual income of North Koreans was $900-$1000. Kim has a movie collection in excess of 10-20,000 titles.

Km Jong-Il's Vulnerabilities

It is official DPRK policy that maintaining the military is the foremost priority. Military spending has come first at the expense of the North Korean economy and the general population. But the economy is broken and cannot be fixed. Communist-style central control and disproportionate military spending is leading to the implosion of the D.P.R.K. As many as three million North Koreans starved to death in famines; hundreds of thousands lost lives in subsequent relocation to government-run camps. Yet Kim Jong Il asks the population to endure continuing hardships while the elite live in luxury.

What Kim Jong-Il Values

While he pays lip service to pursuing the ideology of self-reliance (*Juche*), in fact he often plays the role of mendicant, seeking aid to keep his impoverished nation afloat. Often these requests are accompanied by belligerent threats in terms of his nuclear capability. He explains this source of funding as representing the tribute from nations who admire his leadership. But analysis reveals what he truly values are the following: his safety and regime survival; P'yong-yang, which is an oasis in the impoverished desert of North Korea; his personal wealth; elite comfort; and total domestic control.

There is persuasive evidence that he cares not a whit for the North Korean peasant. He has lived an extravagantly luxurious lifestyle while tolerating starvation at home. In confronting North Korea's famine, saving lives has not been a top priority, and early in the famine cycle, Kim cut off nearly all food supplies to the four eastern provinces and denied these provinces access to international aid.[29] Large numbers of deaths also occurred when, between 1997 and 1999 on Kim's orders, several hundred thousand people displaced by the famine were herded into camps where conditions allowed few to survive.[30] Moreover, according to the testimony of eyewitnesses, Kim has ordered the systematic killing of babies born in North Korea's camps to political prisoners.[31]

This lack of concern for the Korean people is in contrast to the image of his father, Kim Il-Sung. Kim Jong-Il reportedly acknowledges the one occasion where he disobeyed The Great Leader and indeed seems to take pride in this incident:

> Only once have I disobeyed President Kim Il Sung. The President said, "Can you shave off some defense spending and divert it for the people's livelihoods?" I responded, "I am afraid not. Given the military pressure from the U.S., the Korean people must bear the hardship a little longer." How much pain I felt at my failure to live up to the expectations of the President who is concerned about raising the living standards of the people![32]

The gap between the self-indulgent hedonistic lifestyle of Kim Jong Il and his inner circle in P'yong-yang and the privation of his people, and, for that matter, the lower-level military, is extreme. Kim regularly calls for sacrifice from the Korean people in pursuit of the mission of reunification. But the lack of sacrifice in the life of Dear Leader and his inner circle is striking. While information is tightly controlled, penetrating the information barriers with stories concerned with the lavish self-indulgent lifestyle of Kim and his inner circle could significantly undermine the legitimacy of his leadership and his capacity to sustain the public psychology to maintain the nation on a continuing war footing.

The Role of Strategic Communication in Undermining Kim Jong-Il

As Bunn has emphasized, tailored communications are an important dimension of tailored deterrence. In vivid contrast to Iran, one of the most remarkable aspects of the Democratic Peoples' Republic of Korea is the control it maintains over information, so that defectors are regularly surprised when they make their way via China to South Korea with the quality of life they discover. Penetrating information control is key. The above values and vulnerabilities of the Kim Jong-Il regime suggest the utility of a program of strategic communications which:

- Identifies P'yong-yang as prime military target using extensive and overt surveillance,
- Counters the "one-a-match-for-one-hundred" military myth propagated by the DPRK by demonstrating US military capabilities, and
- "Educates" lower level military and the general population on the gap between their deprivation and the profligate hedonism of Kim Jong-Il and the national elites.

On the other hand, some believe undermining the regime might cause it to initiate hostilities with the U.S. and ROK to divert North Koreans and cause them to rally against an external enemy rather that focus on regime shortcomings. In short, efforts at regime change might increase the chance of war and reduce U.S./ROK deterrence effects on North Korean behavior.

In the foregoing sections, key aspects of the personality and political behavior of the leadership of the "axis of evil" have been presented; these are highlights of major political personality profiles. The intent is not to prescribe particular courses of deterrence for these nations, but rather to reflect the diversity of the leadership and decision-making of key adversaries; there cannot be a "one size fits all" deterrence strategy. Moreover, it is to make clear that in order optimally to develop deterrent strategies in the post-Cold world, it is imperative these strategies are tailored to fit the unique aspects of the leadership and strategic culture of the adversary in its unique political, cultural, historical and psychological context.

But in this age of terrorism, it would be remiss in reflecting on tailored deterrence not to consider how one might deter transnational terrorism, in particular, Osama bin Laden and al-Qaeda.

Osama bin Laden and al-Qaeda

In reflecting on deterrence and deterrability of a trans-national terrorist adversary, it is useful to consider the note that Mohammad Atta, the ringleader of Sept. 11, sent to the members of the four teams that would hijack the planes. Concerned they might betray their deadly mission with signs of facial anxiety, his notes communicated words to the effect of, *Be calm and serene. Have a smile upon your face, for soon you will be in Paradise.* But in his last will and testament, Atta prayed, quoting a *sura* from the Koran, *Spare me O Lord, a lifetime in shackles and irons.* While one should not uncritically extrapolate from Atta's words to the question of how to deter al-Qaeda from pursuing and employing weapons of mass destruction, it should give us pause to consider the prospect of death was considered calming for these potential martyrs, whereas life in prison was to be dreaded, suggesting that for Islamist fundamentalist terrorists, the death penalty was not a deterrent, but if anything an incentive, and a much more powerful deterrent would be life imprisonment without the prospect of release.[33]

In the following remarks on Osama bin Laden and al-Qaeda, a brief profile is presented; consideration is given to his interest in weapons of mass destruction, with implications for deterrence.[34]

Osama bin Laden was born in Jeddah, Saudi Arabia, in 1957, the 17th of 20-25 sons of Mohamed bin Laden, who had 52-54 children. Originally an immigrant from Yemen, Muhamed bin Laden, by befriending the royal family, had established a major construction company and had amassed a fortune of some $2-3 billion by the time of his death in 1967 in a plane crash. Although estimates range from $18 million to as high as $200 million, it is most commonly agreed that bin laden inherited approximately $57 million at age 16 from his father's estate.

Osama's mother, Hamida, a Syrian woman of Palestinian descent was the least favorite of Mohamed's 10 wives, and Osama was the only child of this marriage, perhaps the basis of Osama bin Laden's later estrangement from his family. Hamida was reportedly a beautiful woman with a free and independent spirit who, as a result, often found herself in conflict with her husband. Reportedly, by the time Osama was born, Hamida had been ostracized by the family and had been nicknamed "Al Abeda" (the slave). As her only child, Osama was referred to as "Ibn Al Abeda" (son of the slave). Hamida did not live on the compound with the larger bin Laden family and as a result, was virtually non-existent in her son's early life. When Mohammed bin Laden died, Osama, at the age of 10, for all intents and purposes, did not know his mother.

Osama bin Laden attended King Abdul Aziz University in Jeddah. He is a certified civil engineer, and worked toward a degree in Business Management (although it is not clear that he completed his course work), preparing him to play a leadership role in the family's far-flung business interests. These two skill areas would serve him in good stead in Afghanistan.

An important influence on bin Laden's political ideology was Abdullah Azzam, a radical Palestinian professor at the university who became an important intellectual mentor for bin Laden. It was Azzam, a noted Islamist, who provided the vision to bin Laden of what should be done in response to the invasion of the Muslim state of Afghanistan by the Soviet Union and what role bin Laden could play. In particular, he conveyed to bin Laden the importance of bringing together Muslims from around the world to defend the Islamic nation of Afghanistan against the godless Soviet Union.

Demonstrating his already blossoming management skills, Osama bin Laden assisted Azzam who founded the international recruitment network Maktab al-Khidamat (MAK - Services Office). MAK advertised all over the Arab world for young Muslims to fight the Afghan jihad. This massive international recruitment effort brought in Muslims from around the world who were to become the Afghan Arabs, the nucleus of bin Laden's loyal followership — 5,000 were recruited from Saudi Arabia, 3,000 from Algeria and 2,000 from Egypt. Recruitment booths were set up in the United States and Europe.

A leader is not formed until he encounters his followers, and bin Laden's leadership experience during the struggle in Afghanistan against the Soviet invasion was crucial in his psychological development which was transformational for him as a leader. He came to Afghanistan unformed and naïve. Generously using his own funds, he built clinics and hospitals. Eschewing an opulent lifestyle, he lived an ascetic life in the caves of Afghanistan with his followers. Regularly preaching about their holy mission and inspirational in his rhetoric, bin Laden inspired his followers who came to adulate him.

That they were able, with substantial American aid to be sure, to triumph over the Soviet Union in what was to become their Vietnam, surely confirmed the correctness of bin Laden's vision for him and his followers. Allah favored the weak and the underdog, and surely they could not have triumphed over the Soviet super-power unless God was on their side. This was the template of the destructive charismatic relationship between bin Laden and his religiously inspired warriors, the mujahedeen.

Bin Laden had not yet broken with the Saudi government, which after all, was the main foundation of his family's wealth. But he had successfully vanquished one of the three major enemies identified by Muhammad Abdel Salam Faraj, who wrote *The Neglected Duty: the existing Arab state, the Western-Zionist nexus, and the Communists.* Throughout the 1960s and 1970s, the critical enemy among this triad was the "near enemy," the Arab state, according to leading Islamists. In Faraj's manifesto, he argued, "We must begin with our Islamic country by establishing the rule of God in our nation...the first battle for jihad is the uprooting of these infidel leaders and replacing them with an Islamic system from which we can build."[35]

Bin Laden had come to see the Soviet super-power as a "paper tiger" that could be defeated, but also had already set his sights on the remaining super-power, the United States, as the next target. This represented a fundamental departure from the strategy of Faraj, in that it replaced 'the enemy that is near" with "the enemy that is afar," the super-powers.

With the victory in Afghanistan, bin Laden the warrior king and his loyal Afghan Arab fighters, were eager to continue to pursue the jihad. Bin Laden broadened his vision and decided to pursue the jihad on a worldwide basis, seeking to reconstruct the nation of Islam throughout the world, assisting Muslims who were in conflict in Algeria, Angola, Bosnia, Chechnya, Eritrea, Somalia, Sudan and so forth.

While bin Laden was committed to the international struggle, Abdullah Azzam believed in focusing all efforts on building Afghanistan into a model Islamic state. Following a split with Abdullah Azzam in 1988, with the nucleus of his loyal followers, bin Laden and Ayman al-Zawahiri, a founding father of the Islamic Jihad of Egypt, established al- Qaeda (The Base) as a direct outgrowth of MAK. The following year Abdullah Azzam died in a mysterious car bomb explosion. Although there has been suspicion of involvement by bin Laden, there has never been any proof linking him to the death of his one-time mentor.

But with the departure of the Soviet Union, in what was to become their Vietnam, the warrior-king bin Laden and his loyal warriors had lost their enemy. As Eric Hoffer observed, the power of a charismatic leader derives from his capacity to focus hatred against a single enemy, as Hitler did in the 1930s, unifying the German people in their hatred of the Jews. Bin Laden traveled to Sudan in 1999 and was distressed, indeed incensed, to find the United States with a military base on Saudi soil in the wake of the crisis in the Gulf, defiling the sacred Islamic land "of the two cities" (Mecca and Medina). Decrying this desecration of holy Saudi soil by the infidel Americans, bin Laden had seamlessly transferred his enmity from the first defeated super-power, the Soviet Union, to the remaining super-power, the United States, despite its aid in the struggle against the Soviet Union, which he dismissed.

Initially he sought only to expel the American military from Arab lands, but later in the 1998 fatwah, expanded the enemy to include all Americans, whether civilian or military, throughout the world. In the 1998 fatwa, Jihad Against Jews and Crusaders, bin Laden declared:

> In compliance with God's order, we issue the following fatwa to all Muslims: The ruling to kill the Americans and their allies -- civilians and military -- is an individual duty for every Muslim who can do it in any country in which it is possible to do it, in order to liberate the al-Aqsa Mosque and the holy mosque [Mecca] from their grip, and in order for their armies to move out of all the lands of Islam, defeated and unable to threaten any Muslim. This is in accordance with the words of Almighty God, "and fight the pagans all together as they fight you all together," and "fight them until there is no more tumult or oppression, and there prevail justice and faith in God." We - with God's help - call on every Muslim who believes in God and wishes to be rewarded to comply with God's order to kill the Americans and plunder their money wherever and whenever they find it.[36]

Note, in this message it is not bin laden but God who has ordered religious Muslims to kill all the Americans; God for whom bin laden speaks with authority. There is not an action bin Laden orders that is not couched and justified in language from the Koran.

Moreover, he actively criticized the Saudi royal family for apostasy, decrying the failure of stewardship of the land of the two cities, Mecca and Medina. The vigor of his criticism led Saudi Arabia to revoke his citizenship in 1994, and his family, which depended upon the Saudi leadership for their wealth, turned against him. This resembles the generational dynamics of social-revolutionary terrorists, such as the Red Army Faction and the Red Brigades, who attack the generation of their family which is loyal to the regime.[37]

Now bin Laden righteously attacked the other two enemies in the triad of enemies, the Western-Israeli nexus, and one of the newly designated apostate Arab nations, Saudi Arabia. But he maintained the primary focus on the external enemy, the United States. Yes, the leadership of the apostate nations had to be replaced, but the United States was the prime enemy, for America was responsible for propping up the corrupt leadership of these countries. Thus he continued the strategy born in Afghanistan of focusing on the enemy who is afar, the Zionist-Crusaders, rather than the enemy who is near, the *targhut* (oppressive domestic rulers).

There has been a series of triumphs for bin Laden—Khobar Towers , the first World Trade Center bombing, the bombings of the U.S. embassies in Kenya and Tanzania, the attack on the U.S.S. *Cole* in Yemen, and now, the most spectacular terrorist act in history, the events of Sept. 11. Osama bin Laden seems to be on a roll, speaking with messianic grandiosity, ever expanding his vision. The events of Sept. 11 were in many ways a "perfect storm." A destructive charismatic leader manipulated, in Eric Hoffer's words, "the slime of discontented souls"[38] to focus the hated and violence of his "true believers" against the identified enemy, the United States.

Al-Qaeda and the Threat of WMD Terrorism

Al-Qaeda and its allies have shown a willingness to perpetrate acts of mass casualty terrorism, as exemplified by the bombings of Khobar Towers in Saudi Arabia, the U.S. embassies in Kenya and Tanzania, and the Sept. 11 attacks on the World Trade Center and the Pentagon. Osama bin Laden, responsible for the embassy bombings and the attacks of Sept. 11, has actively discussed the use of weapons of mass destruction in public interviews. In an interview with Jon Miller of *ABC News* in May 1998, bin Laden first discussed such weapons.

In a follow-up interview with *TIME* magazine, in January of 1999, when asked, "The U.S. says you are trying to acquire chemical and nuclear weapons. How would you use these?" Bin Laden replied, "Acquiring weapons for the defense of Muslims is a religious duty. If I have indeed acquired these weapons, then I thank God for enabling me to do so... It would be a sin for Muslims not to try to possess the weapons."[39] Whether this was psychological warfare or represented genuine intent is not entirely clear. Bin Laden and al-Qaeda are not seen as constrained against carrying out chemical, biological, radiological or nuclear attacks, including attacks against the defined major enemy, the United States.

How does one tailor deterrence for an adversary whose members seek martyrdom? Is such an adversary deterrable? Not in the conventional sense. But let us rephrase the question: how can we reduce the threat of CBRNE terrorism?

It is difficult for the West to critique radical interpretations of Islamic doctrine which have been employed by bin Laden and his leadership to justify mass casualty terrorism. Moderate critics have until recently been muted. But, recently there have been cleavages in the ranks with internal critics of extremist violence beginning to speak out.

- Sayyid Imam al-Sharif (Dr. Fadl) who was a radical ideologue whose earlier work has set the template for al-Qaeda's violent jihad: "There is nothing that invokes the anger of God and his wrath like the unwarranted spilling of blood and wrecking of property," *The Rationalization of Jihad*
- Salman Al Ouda, a radical Saudi cleric, "My brother Osama, how much blood has been spilt?"
- Noman Benotman-Open letter rebuking Zawahiri.

The conflict initially was highly personalized focusing on Osama bin Laden, who, in President Bush's words, was "wanted dead or alive," with a $25,000,000 bounty on his head. Each personalized threat against bin Laden only served to magnify his stature among his constituents.

Moreover, there was an implication that the capture or death of bin Laden would mean the end of the threat. This assuredly is not the case, for al-Qaeda differs significantly from other terrorist groups and organizations, perhaps reflecting bin Laden's training in business management. Al-Qaeda was a loose umbrella organization of semi-autonomous terrorist groups and organizations. In effect, bin Laden was chairman of the board of radical Islam, Inc., a holding company, providing guidance, coordination, and financial and logistical facilitation, and expanded his corporation through mergers and acquisitions.

Unlike other charismatically led organizations, such as Guzman's Sendero Luminosa (Shining Path) of Peru, Ocalan's PKK of Turkey, and Prabhakaran's Tamil Tigers, all of which were mortally wounded when their leader was killed or captured, bin Laden designated Ayman al-Zawahiri as his successor and number two and has delegated significant authority and responsibility to other members of his organization. Should bin Laden be killed or captured, the reins of the organization would pass seamlessly to Zawahiri. Should the entire leadership echelon be eliminated, the threat, while diminished, would still remain. It is estimated al-Qaeda operates in 68 nations, and the semi-autonomous organizations under its umbrella would devolve and continue to pursue their terrorist mission.

President Bush and British Prime Minister Tony Blair took pains to clarify this is not a war against Muslims, but a war against terrorism. Seeking to frame this as a religious war, bin Laden has now laid claim to the title of commander-in-chief of the Islamic world, opposing the commander-in-chief of the corrupt, secular modernizing Western world; President George W. Bush is in a religious war. Alienated Arab youth find resonance in his statements, and see him as a hero.

And this is the real challenge. Osama bin Laden may be eliminated and the al-Qaeda network rolled up, but the path of anti-Western radical Islamist extremism is increasingly attractive to alienated Islamic youth. Terrorism, at heart, is a vicious species of psychological warfare; it is violence as communication. Smart bombs and missiles will not win this war. The only way to combat this vicious species of psychological warfare is with information warfare, countering the distorted extremist rhetoric of Osama bin Laden and radical Islamist clerics that rationalizes violence with verses from the Koran. This will be a long struggle.

One of the key tools in this struggle is tailored communications that accomplishes four goals.[40] First, inhibit potential terrorists from joining the group in the first place by de-romanticizing terrorists, providing alternate pathways to redress grievances, assisting in opening up autocratic societies and encouraging moderate secular education.

Secondly, it will be important to produce dissension in the terrorist group. The underground group is an emotional pressure-cooker, and it may be possible to foster paranoia by injecting rumors of traitors in the ranks. Also, a tailored communication plan should attempt to alienate followers from leaders and facilitate the cleavages in the ranks.

A third goal of anti-terrorist communications plan is to facilitate exodus from the group by its members. This can perhaps be accomplished by measures such as amnesty programs, offering reduced sentences for those who cooperate and using defector as a source of rumors to sow distrust.

Fourth and finally, the communications plan should try to reduce support for the group and delegitimize its leaders in society at large and in the recruitment pool. The program should seek to marginalize al-Qaeda and delegitimize bin Laden.

The alienated Islamic youth must not see violence as the only pathway. Most importantly, support for this dangerous movement must be reduced, so that radical Islamic extremism is marginalized, its leaders delegitimized. The program above summarizes a program of tailored communication designed to counter terrorism. What themes should be incorporated into such a tailored program to inhibit the development and use of weapons of destruction?

Let us turn to the terrorists for answers to this question. Among the incarcerated Islamist terrorists we interviewed, when asked about their views concerning weapons of mass destruction, most said something to the effect of *"just give me a good Kalashnikov."*[41]

While the majority was not averse to using a weapon that could kill 10,000 enemies, many had not even considered it. But some raised reservations. One spoke of his fear of "the silent death," concerns about dangers from handling poisons or bacteria. Another quoted the Koran and its prohibitions against poisoning the creatures of the earth.

In a focused program of psychological warfare, tailored communication designed to counter the development and use of weapons of mass destruction, these two themes should be prominently featured, i.e., the danger of the "silent death" and the prohibition in the Koran against poisoning the creatures of the earth.

Conclusion

In this post-Cold War era, given the variability of the leaders described above, deterrence must be tailored and based on nuanced actor-specific behavioral models. This in turn requires increased intelligence resources devoted to developing such models, for it is now more true than ever, in this era of rogue leaders of outlaw nations and transnational terrorism, there is no one-size-fits-all deterrence.

An important aspect of the analysis of adversary intentions is the locus of decision-making. When it is a leader- predominant society, such as Iraq under Saddam, and the leader is judged to not be deterrable, this calls for a tailored communications program designed to drive a wedge between the leader and his followers. This is also true for a more complex leadership society with multiple autonomous actors, such as Iran, where on the one hand President Ahmadinejad may not be deterrable, may indeed be seeking chaos, but he is not the sole or even principal actor.

A special dilemma is posed by transnational radical Islamist terrorism, many of whose members seek martyrdom. For this challenging target, a four-point program of tailored communications is proposed with the overall goal of reducing the ranks of terrorists by inhibiting potential terrorists from joining the group, producing dissension in the group, facilitating exit from the group, and reducing support for the group and delegitimizing its leaders. Messages designed to inhibit the development and uses of weapons of mass destruction are included in the suggested program.

Notes

[1] Jerrold Post is professor of Psychiatry, Political Psychology and International Affairs, and director of the Political Psychology Program, the Elliott School of International Affairs, The George Washington University, Washington, D.C.

[2] Han Park and Kyung Park, "Ideology and Security: Self Reliance in China and North Korea" in *National Security in the Third World,* Edward Azar and Chung-in Moon (eds.) (Hampshire, England: Edgar Elgar, 1988).

[3] Janice Gross Stein, "Deterrence and Reassurance" in *Behavior, Society and Nuclear War, Volume II,* Philip Tetlock, Jo Husbands, Robert Jervis, Paul Stern and Charles Tilly (eds.) (New York: Oxford University Press, 1991), 8-72.

[4] Thomas Schelling, *The Strategy of Conflict,* (Boston, Mass.: Harvard University Press, 1960); Arms *and Influence,* (New Haven, Conn.: Yale University Press, 1966).

[5] Keith Payne, "The Fallacies of Cold War Deterrence and a New Direction," *Comparative Strategy,* Volume 22 (2003), 411-428.

[6] Betty Glad, "Dilemmas of Deterrence: Rational and Irrational Perspectives" in Betty Glad *Psychological Dimensions of War'* (New York: Sage, 1990), 277-294.

[7] Ralph White, *Fearful Warriors: A Psychological Profile of US-Soviet Relations* (New York: Free Press, 1984), 256-257.

[8] Graham Allison, *Essence of Decision: Explaining the Cuban Missile Crisis* (Boston, Mass.: Little Brown, 1971).

[9] Jerrold Post, *Leaders and Their Followers in a Dangerous World* (Ithaca, N.Y. and London, UK: Cornell University Press, 2007), 15-16.

[10] Irving Janis, *Victims of Groupthink: A Psychological Study of Foreign Policy Decisions and Fiascos* (Boston, Mass.: Houghton-Miflin, 1972).

[11] Dorwin Cartwright, "Risk taking by individuals and groups: An assessment of research employing choice dilemmas, Journal *of Personality and Social Psychology,* Volume 20(3) (Dec. 1971), 361-378.

[12] Payne, *Comparative Strategy*, 418.

[13] James Blight, et al., *Cuba on the Brink: Castro, the Missile Crisis, and the Soviet Collapse,* (New York: Pantheon Books, 1993), 29.

[14] Ibid.

[15] Blight, ibid, as quoted by Payne, op cit.

[16] Hamburg, D. A., George A., and Ballentine, K., "Preventing Deadly Conflict: The Critical Role of Leadership," *Archives of General Psychiatry* 56.11 (1999), 971- 976.

[17] M. Elaine Bunn, "Can Deterrence be Tailored?," *Strategic Forum,* Volume 225 (Jan. 2007).

[18] Bunn, op cit.

[19] Margaret Hermann, C. Charles, F. Hermann, and Joe Hagan, "How Decision Units Shape Foreign Policy Behavior," Chapter 16, *New Directions in the Study of Foreign Policy* (New York: Harper Collins, 1991).

[20] White, op cit, 259.

[21] Jerrold Post, Congressional Record, testimony before House Armed Services Committee (Dec. 1990).

[22] Schneider, Barry R, *Deterrence and Saddam Hussein: Lessons from the 1990-1991 Gulf War*, USAF Counterproliferation Center, Future Warfare Series, No. 47 (August 2005), 19-24

[23] "Confrontation in the Gulf: Excerpts from Iraqi Document on Meeting With U.S. Envoy," *The New York Times* (Sept. 23, 1990).

[24] Al-Jazeera (June 19, 2005).

[25] "Ahmadinejad's Demons," *The New Republic* (April 25, 2006).

[26] This resembles messianic traditions of the "final days" in Christianity and in Judaism. The use of weapons of mass destruction by Shoko Asahara of the Japanese millenarian cult Aum Supreme Truth also was designed to precipitate the final apocalypse.

[27] Hermann, Hermann, and Hagan op cit.

[28] Elaine Sciolino, "Blurred Images of North Korea's 'Junior,'" *The New York Times* (July 17, 1994), Section 1, 1.

[29] Andrew S. Natsios, *The Great North Korean Famine: Famine, Politics, and Foreign Policy* (Washington D.C.: United States Institute of Peace Press, 2001), 106-107.

[30] Ibid., 73-74.

[31] "Defectors from North Korea Tell of Prison Baby Killings," *The New York Times*, (June 10, 2002).

[32] Kim Myong Chol, "Kim Jong Il's Military Strategy for Reunification," *Comparative Strategy*, Volume 20(4) (2001), 305.

[33] This consideration was introduced in testimony by the author during the death penalty phase of the 2001 trial of one of the al-Qaeda terrorists responsible for the bombing of the U.S. embassy in Dar es Salaan, Tanzania in 1998. The defendant was sentenced to life without parole in a super-max prison.

[34] This brief profile is drawn from the introductory chapter "The Explosive Force of Personality and Political Behavior" of *Leaders and their Followers in a Dangerous World* (Ithaca, N.Y.: Cornell University Press, 2004), 5-9.

[35] A. Hashim, "Osama bin Laden's World View and Grand Strategy," paper presented to conference at Navy War College (Nov. 19, 2001).

[36] World Islamic Front, "Jihad Against Jews and Crusaders," *Al-Quds al-Arabi* (Feb. 23, 1998).

[37] Post, (2007), op cit, 7.

[38] Eric Hoffer, *The True Believer* (New York: Harper and Row, [1951] 1966), 59-60.

[39] "Conversation With Terror," *TIME* (Jan. 11, 1999).

[40] For an extended discussion of the important role of psychological operations as a principal weapon in countering terrorism, see Jerrold Post, "Psychological Operations and Counter-Terrorism," *Joint Force Quarterly* (Spring 2005), 105-110.

[41] Jerrold Post, Ehud Sprinzak and Laurita Denny, "The Terrorist in Their Own Words: Interviews with 35 Incarcerate Middle East Terrorists," *Terrorism and Political Violence*, Volume. 15(1), (2003), 171-184.

CHAPTER 3

Tailoring U.S. Strategic Deterrent Effects on Russia

Franklin C. Miller

The concept of deterrence is not new. Presenting a potential enemy with major obstacles to achieving his aggressive military objectives by building a strong and credible defensive posture dates back at least to ancient Rome. As the fourth century Roman military writer Vegetius observed: *igitur qui desiderat pacem, praeparet bellum* (therefore, he who wishes peace, should prepare war). Indeed, in the infant United States, President George Washington, in his very first State of the Union Address on Jan. 8, 1790, told Congress (in the context of calling for a sufficient national military establishment and a domestic arms industry): "to be prepared for war is the most effectual mans of preserving peace." And yet, as history has demonstrated again and again, deterrence based on conventional military forces fails to deter military aggression.

Presented with strong defenses, aggressors have employed their military's creative genius to develop and devise plans and capabilities to guarantee—in their own minds—a sufficient chance of success to make the risk of war acceptable. In the 20th century, the Nazi campaign through the Ardennes which negated France's Maginot Line defenses and the Japanese surprise attack on the U.S. Pacific Fleet at Pearl Harbor (which had been forward deployed to demonstrate resolve in what we would call today a "flexible deterrent option") stand out.

All of this changed, however, in 1945. The U.S. development of the atomic bomb, the onset of the Cold War, and the U.S.S.R.'s subsequent acquisition of atomic weapons ushered in a new era. Nuclear weapons gave a state the ability, even as its conventional military forces were on the verge of defeat, to turn the aggressor's victory to ashes: nuclear retaliation could devastate the aggressor's homeland even as his armies won on the battlefield. War had suddenly become too dangerous for the nuclear-armed great powers. It took several decades, however, for this new reality to be absorbed by political and military leaders.

Deterring the Soviet Union: the Early Years

In the early years of the Cold War the United States adopted a relatively simple approach to deterring Soviet aggression. The U.S. government viewed nuclear weapons as more powerful versions of their conventional predecessors. At first, given the relatively small number of U.S. atomic weapons and our lack of intelligence information on the Soviet Union, the U.S. deterrent was conceived as an extension of the massive bombing raids against German and Japanese cities. We knew where Soviet cities were located, and, in the event of war, those cities and the political leadership, social infrastructure and industrial capacity which resided in them were targeted. When the United States joined with our European Allies to create NATO, we also planned to use nuclear weapons to defeat invading Soviet armies. And when, in August 1949, Russia demonstrated it too had developed an atomic weapon, destroying that nuclear capability became a priority U.S. goal.[1]

The Eisenhower administration, on entering office, was convinced one of the U.S.S.R.'s goals was to bankrupt the West by forcing it to spend enormous sums on building conventional forces; in response, the administration adopted a defense policy known as "the New Look" in which nuclear weapons would provide a cheaper alternative to building the massive conventional capabilities deemed necessary to defeat the Red Army.

The scientific prowess of U.S. nuclear weapons scientists allowed the Defense Department to field nuclear weapons to meet every need of the military. The Army even re-organized its force structure into "Pentomic Divisions" optimized to employ nuclear firepower and deployed nuclear artillery shells, nuclear landmines, nuclear-tipped short-range missiles, and nuclear surface-to-air missiles. The Navy had ship launched, submarine launched and air-dropped tactical nuclear anti-submarine warfare weapons, nuclear surface-to-air missiles, nuclear bombs for use by carrier air wings, and even nuclear shells for 16-inch battleship guns; the Air Force deployed nuclear bombs for use by strategic and tactical aircraft as well as nuclear-tipped air-to-air missiles.

As Henry Kissinger famously observed in his 1957 book *Nuclear Weapons and Foreign Policy*, "We added the atomic bomb to our arsenal without integrating its implications into our thinking."[2] U.S. deterrence policy was neither particularly sophisticated nor was it tailored. As annunciated by Secretary of State John Foster Dulles: "...there is no local defense which alone can contain the mighty land power of the Communist world. ... [The United States therefore has decided] to depend primarily upon a great capacity to retaliate instantly by means and at places of our own choosing"[3]

The challenge to the Soviet leadership was straightforward: attack the United States or our allies, and we will immediately launch an all-out nuclear response against the Soviet homeland and on its forward deployed military forces using all elements of our nuclear arsenal. As noted, this was neither tailored nor subtle.

As the U.S.S.R. began to mirror the United States' creation of a widely deployed nuclear arsenal, American strategists worried about two issues:

- Did the Soviet leadership, in the time-honored tradition of warfare, believe its military and scientific genius could devise a way to preemptively attack and destroy the U.S. capability to strike the Soviet homeland? Could the deterrent be negated?

- Would the Soviet leadership truly believe that in a crisis the United States would respond to any act of military aggression by initiating all-out nuclear war? In other words, was the deterrent threat in fact credible in Soviet eyes?

Tailoring U.S. Strategic Deterrence: the First Steps

The Kennedy administration leaders entered office convinced the answers to those two fundamental questions were (1) yes, and (2) possibly no. Accordingly, it quickly made major changes to U.S. war-planning policy and force structure.

To increase the survivability of the U.S. strategic deterrent the administration embarked on a major expansion of the Polaris-missile carrying submarine fleet and of the Minuteman ICBM force. The triad combination of (1) submarines designed to be invulnerable once at sea, (2) land-based missiles housed in silos designed to be resistant to nuclear attack by relatively inaccurate Soviet missiles, plus (3) the different strengths of the Strategic Air Command long-range bomber force, was judged sufficient to ensure a survivable and highly lethal U.S retaliatory threat credible to Soviet leaders.

Convinced the Soviet leadership would consider conducting limited conventional attacks unless confronted with tailored (as opposed to all-out) responses, the administration introduced the "Flexible Response" policy, premised on two concepts:

First, the United States and its allies would increase conventional force capabilities so that limited or small-scale Soviet attacks were unlikely to succeed. This would force the Soviet leadership to have to resort to major attacks, which in turn could credibly draw a nuclear response.

Second, the all-out, "one-shot" U.S. nuclear war plan was divided into multiple options so the president was given the choice of having U.S. regional commanders respond with variously-sized nuclear attacks, [4]

More significantly, the U.S. strategic war plan (the Single Integrated Operational Plan or SIOP introduced in 1960) would henceforth provide the president the option of ordering a retaliatory strike against three major target groupings: (1) Soviet military forces including military command and control targets; (2) of those forces and the Soviet political leadership and its command and control structures; (3) or those two target sets plus Soviet cities and industrial capacity. Secretary of Defense Robert McNamara, in a series of highly publicized speeches designed to influence the Kremlin leadership, made clear the United States now had powerful but less than all-out responses available to it.

In the event deterrence failed, the U.S. could exercise these more limited options if it chose not to strike Soviet cities – thereby explicitly suggesting to the Soviets their war plans should include a similar capability to halt a nuclear war short of destroying urban areas.

However, McNamara proceeded to muddy the signal within a relatively short period of time. In 1961 and 1962 he spoke publicly of the United States having both a "counterforce" (or "damage limiting") capability, (the option to strike against Soviet nuclear and conventional military forces) and also a "counter-value" capability, the option which expanded the counterforce strike to include cities and infrastructure. Shortly after the Cuban Missile crisis of October 1962, he ceased discussing counterforce publicly and instead spoke only of counter-value.[5]

This rhetorical shift, if nothing else, has completely confounded American scholarship of nuclear deterrence ever since. Several generations of professors and their students believe the two concepts competed rather than complimented, and the United States maintained a counterforce strategy (viewed by many academics as a "nuclear warfighting strategy") until 1963-1964, when it adopted a counter-value strategy (portrayed in academic circles as a "pure deterrent" approach). Nothing could be less accurate. The United States held at risk the full-target set developed by war-planners in the late 1940s and early 1950s: Soviet nuclear and conventional forces, Soviet political authorities and its control mechanisms, and urban population and industrial capacity.

McNamara was well aware of this, even if he misled Congress and the American public. In February 1966, in a meeting with NATO counterparts, long after "counterforce" had disappeared from his congressional testimony and public statements, McNamara engaged in the following colloquy with a NATO counterpart who asked "if in SIOP options the first launch covered only military targets."[6] McNamara replied:

This depended on the attack. Only in the event of an all-out Soviet attack would we make a total response. In the event the Soviets did not deliver an all-out attack, we would have the option of making a less than total response. The counterpart continued by "pointing out that a [Soviet] first strike hardly seemed rational...If the Soviets went all out we would have a surviving Assured Destruction capability. The refinements in SIOP options would be relevant only in the unlikely event of a limited Soviet nuclear attack." McNamara replied "Our first priority is Assured Destruction. This we have achieved....We have three times the forces needed to achieve Assured Destruction. However this 300 per cent excess is fundamental to the survival of the West...[7]

Tailoring U.S. Strategic Deterrence: One step forward and one back in the early 1970s

As the U.S.S.R.'s strategic arsenal grew throughout the 1960s and early 1970s, first reaching parity with the United States and then surpassing it, U.S. strategic planners sought additional means to influence the Soviet leadership. While McNamara had succeeded in providing options to allow a U.S. president to threaten limited responses, those "limited" options remained quite large. The smallest still involved employing thousands of nuclear weapons. Concern grew in the U.S. strategic community that all of the options were too massive, and therefore not a credible response, to Soviet limited aggression or attack. As a result, Secretary of Defense James Schlesinger directed the creation of a series of smaller strike options which might represent more credible deterrents to limited nuclear or conventional attack. The development of these plans was heralded in a series of speeches and public documents in an effort to ensure the Soviet leadership was aware of them.

U.S. planners also spent considerable time and energy analyzing whether the SIOP — which, as previously noted, was in fact a war plan rather than a plan to deter Soviet actions — presented the Kremlin leadership with sufficient disincentives to aggression. Deciding that it did not, they embarked on a study to determine what would convince the Soviets that the cost of aggression was unacceptable. Focusing unfortunately on American values, they concluded the nation which emerged from a nuclear war with sufficient resources to rebuild its economic infrastructure and economic–industrial capacity would be "the winner." The U.S. government then spent considerable energy in both seeking to convince the Kremlin the United States would "recover" faster and restructuring SIOP priorities so that Soviet "recovery targets" were covered.

Getting Tailored Deterrence Right

The Soviet build-up of its strategic nuclear forces continued unabated throughout the 1970s. The Soviet efforts emphasized fielding increasingly accurate ICBMs capable of destroying U.S. Minuteman silos. The Soviets also went to great lengths to "super-harden" their own ICBM silos. They were observed conducting exercises in which they re-loaded ICBM silos, thereby suggesting an interest in protracted nuclear war-fighting. Soviet writings and exercises also demonstrated an interest in launching SLBMs in so-called "depressed trajectories," flight-paths sufficiently low to escape detection by U.S. early warning radars. Such attacks, it was feared, were designed to destroy the U.S. bomber force on the ground, and, more importantly, to destroy Washington before the president could issue orders for a retaliatory strike. Additionally, the Soviets were observed to have begun construction covertly of a series of deep-underground command posts for their senior political and military leaders.

All of these developments convinced the U.S. government the Soviets had decided they might in fact "win" a nuclear war by emerging from the conflict with military forces and a command structure which would permit them to dominate the post-war world.

Accordingly, U.S. Defense Secretary Harold Brown ordered the initiation of a "Nuclear Targeting Policy Review" to determine if the focus of American deterrent policy needed to be changed. Based on extensive analysis of Soviet expenditures, force structure, exercises, classified and unclassified writings, and other all-source intelligence information, the study concluded the Soviet leadership had never bought into the "recovery paradigm."

To the contrary, it appeared they had concluded that a combination of pre-emptive capabilities, dispersed, buried and survivable command-and-control facilities, and reconstitutable strategic offensive forces would permit them to dominate a post-war world, and such a position would allow the U.S.S.R. to obtain the resources necessary to subsequently rebuild the Soviet economy.

This should not have been a major surprise given the Soviet experience in World War II, an experience which the Soviet leaders had lived through. The most important point made by the Nuclear Targeting Policy Review was that deterrence could only be achieved when the United States focused on what the Soviet leadership valued — and then threatened to destroy those assets if war occurred. "Mirror imaging," assuming that the Soviet leadership's outlook reflected US goals and values, was a dangerous self deception.

By 1980 Secretary Defense Harold Brown had brought about changes in U.S. targeting priorities and had put more resources behind programs to reinvigorate U.S. strategic programs which would undercut Soviet confidence in their ability to retain the assets they believed necessary to dominate the post-war world. This advertised to the Kremlin the United States leadership had understood them and was determined to deter them. In a speech at the Naval War College in August 1980 Brown made clear U.S. policy had embarked on a new course. Henceforth the United States would study what the Soviet leadership indicated — through its force developments, defense resource allocations, exercises and writings — what it valued most...and then would proceed to hold those at risk:

- "By definition, successful deterrence means, among other things, shaping Soviet views of what a war would mean..."
- "What we have done ... is to look more closely at our capabilities, our choices, our doctrine and our plans in light of what we know about Soviet forces, doctrine and plans. The Soviet leadership appears to contemplate at least the

possibility of a relatively [nuclear] prolonged exchange if war comes, and in some circles at least, they seem to take seriously the theoretical possibility of victory in such a war."

- "We cannot afford to ignore these views — even if we think differently, as I do. We need to have ... a posture – both forces and doctrine that makes it clear to the Soviets and to the world that any notion of victory in nuclear war is unrealistic."[8]

Brown had created the intellectual foundation of tailored deterrence. To deter successfully, the United States must understand an enemy (or potential enemy) leadership's value structure and then make clear, by policy, force structure and exercises, that the value structure would be destroyed — without question — should deterrence fail. Brown re-emphasized the point in his last Annual Report to Congress, sending a signal to the Kremlin as well as to the U.S. defense establishment. His words are worth reviewing carefully because they form the starting point of how the United States has practiced deterrence since 1980. The Secretary of Defense stated that:

"To the Soviet Union, our strategy makes clear that no course of aggression by them that led to the use of nuclear weapons on any scale of attack and at any stage of the conflict, could lead to victory. Besides our power to devastate the full target system of the U.S.S.R., the United States would have the option for more selective, lesser retaliatory attacks that would exact a prohibitively high price from the things the Soviet leadership prizes most — political and military control, nuclear and conventional military force, and the economic base needed to sustain war. ...Our planning must provide a continuum of options, ranging from small numbers of strategic and/or theater nuclear weapons aimed at narrowly defined targets, to employment of large portions of our nuclear forces against a broad spectrum of targets."[9]

Over the ensuing 12 years, the Reagan and George H.W. Bush administrations reinforced the credibility of this tailored approach by reaffirming the deterrent policy set forth by Secretary Brown, by aggressively pursuing a program to modernize U.S. strategic nuclear forces and their command and control backbone and by revising U.S. nuclear targeting plans.

Secretary of Defense Caspar Weinberger, in a widely publicized congressional testimony, made the retaliatory threat clear:

> "To deter successfully, we must be able – and we must be seen to be able – to retaliate against any potential aggressor in such a manner that the costs we will exact will substantially exceed any gains he might hope to achieve through aggression. We, for our part, are no under no illusions about the consequences of a nuclear war: we believe there would be no winners in such a war. But this recognition on <u>our</u> part is not sufficient to ensure effective deterrence or to prevent thc outbreak war: it is essential that the <u>Soviet</u> leadership understands this as well. We must make sure that the Soviet leadership, in calculating the risks of aggression, recognizes that because of our retaliatory capability there can be no circumstance where the initiation of a nuclear war at any level or of any duration would make sense. If they recognize that our forces can deny them their objectives at whatever level of conflict they contemplate and, in addition, that such a conflict could lead to the destruction of those political, military and economic assets which they value most highly, then deterrence is enhanced and the risk of war is diminished."[10]

The recapitalization of U.S. strategic forces — largely the product of the Kennedy administration's efforts — was designed demonstrably to offset any advantages the Soviets had sought to achieve through their own programs. The deployment of highly accurate systems such as air-launched cruise missiles, the MX (Peacekeeper) ICBM and, later, the Trident II SLBM offset Soviet silo-hardening efforts.

The U.S. early warning system and nuclear command and control network was upgraded. This made attacks far more survivable, and thereby resistant to pre-emption. The Trident II ensured a survivable hard-target capability invulnerable to pre-emption. Further the United States revealed (in an annual Defense Department publication entitled "Soviet Military Power") the U.S.S.R.'s covert efforts to build deep underground leadership command bunkers in sufficient detail to signal to Moscow those efforts had been detected, and the bunkers would not escape a retaliatory strikes.

The revision to planning was long overdue. Because, for bureaucratic reasons the link between policy makers and the war planners in Omaha (home to the Strategic Air Command and the Joint Strategic Target Planning Staff) was weak, the latter never fully comprehended the intent behind the smaller strategic options which Secretary Schlesinger had directed in the early 1970s. As a result, the implementation of Schlesinger's policy failed to provide what was needed: the options were still too large and were designed in such a manner the Soviet warning systems — and therefore the Soviet leadership — could not have determined the combined signal of determination and restraint the options were intended to send. By the latter part of the 1980s, these and other targeting issues had been corrected, and the White House had a war plan which was both a deterrent plan and which conformed to the policy requirements set by the United States' political leadership.[11]

The Cold War Ends

In an ironic and not altogether unrelated series of developments, as the United States finally established and deployed a highly credible and tailored deterrence policy against the U.S.S.R., the Soviet Union collapsed. The emergence of Russia and 14 other countries — four of which (Russia, Ukraine, Kazakhstan and Belarus) possessed former Soviet nuclear weapons – created new challenges for the United States. The most pressing task was not deterring Russian attack, since Russia had become inwardly focused and was consumed with establishing its emerging democracy.

The greatest danger was the possibility that former Soviet weapons would fall into the hands of terrorists or other illegal groups. Closely tied to this was the possibility that Ukraine, Kazakhstan or Belarus might decide to retain possession of resident nuclear weapons and become recognized nuclear weapons states. As a result, while Cold War era contingency plans remained in place in Omaha, the United States devoted its main efforts to ensuring Russia would be the only nuclear state to spring from the ashes of the U.S.S.R. and to helping Russia safeguard or destroy the inherited nuclear weapons.

As Russia's infant democracy battled coup attempts by dissident parliamentarians, as dissatisfaction with Russia's course arose within both the elites and the Russian population more generally, and as the Russian economy threatened to implode, Russian President Boris Yeltsin plucked an obscure former KGB colonel named Putin to serve first as his prime minister and then, in 1999, as his successor.

Russian Nuclear Policy under Putin and Medvedev

As is well known now, Vladimir Putin was not committed to democracy. Rather, he was and remains an authoritarian who has worked to crush democratic reformers and to re-establish state control over most areas of Russian life. As a result, the Russian security services regained much of the authority they had lost during the Yeltsin years. With the Russian government's coffers newly replenished thanks to the dramatic rise in oil and gas prices in the first decade of the 21st century, and Russian petro-diplomacy providing a coercive tool against Russia's neighbors, Putin embarked on an aggressive foreign policy which was, in some respects, reminiscent of Soviet efforts to intimidate nations on its borders.

With his conventional military forces capability greatly reduced from that once possessed by the Soviet armed forces, Putin has engaged from time to time in nuclear saber-rattling. He authorized Russian strategic bombers to violate Norwegian, British, Icelandic, Japanese and American airspace.[12] He stated Poland and the Czech Republic would be subject to nuclear strikes if they hosted elements of a U.S./NATO missile defense shield;[13] and Russian spokesmen announced that Russia could potentially use nuclear weapons in "local or regional wars."[14]

Having served his statutory time as president of Russia, in May 2008 Putin orchestrated a succession arrangement in which his protégé Dmitry Medvedev succeeded him as president while Putin became prime minister.

The nuclear saber-rattling has continued unabated. Russian bombers continued to fly near and into Western airspace;[15] the Russian government announced a new nuclear doctrine which asserted the right to attack preemptively with nuclear weapons those threatening Russian security;[16] and, in the fall of 2009, Russian forces conducted an exercise simulating conventional and nuclear strikes against Poland.[17]

Deterring Russia (and from what)

The question which must confront U.S. policymakers today and in the future is the degree to which the evolution of Russian nuclear policy represents an active threat to be deterred, a latent threat to be watched carefully, or simply the pronouncements of a leadership determined both to warn the West against aggression and to reassure the Russian public the government's failure to modernize Russian conventional forces is compensated for by Russian nuclear forces.

It appears fairly clear at this point in time (2010) that Putin and Medvedev are different from their Soviet predecessors and they do not believe nuclear war is "win-able" as did the Soviet leaders. Yet, it is also clear they still place a very high reliance on nuclear weapons particularly to threaten and intimidate the governments of former Soviet and former Warsaw Pact states.

In the same period of time the Obama administration has reduced the role of nuclear weapons in U.S. national strategy (and aims at a very long-term goal of eventually eliminating nuclear weapons altogether) the two Russian administrations have taken a very different point of view, placing nuclear weapons at the very center of Russian national security policy. Some of this may be attributable to classic Russian paranoia, fueled by the many advantages which U.S. conventional forces today enjoy over their Russian counterparts. But it stretches credulity to believe the Russian leadership seriously fears a U.S. attack.

A more reasonable explanation is the Russian leadership believes its nuclear saber-rattling provides some degree of cover for the aggressive foreign policy for which the Putin-Medvedev team has shown a penchant. Whether cutting off energy supplies to neighbors, assassinating a former

KGB official in London, poisoning a Ukrainian presidential candidate or continuing to occupy Georgian territory after the 2008 border conflict, Russia has engaged in activities which would under other circumstances draw, at minimum, international sanctions and condemnation. So too should the nuclear saber-rattling, so redolent of the Cold War and so seemingly out of place in our view of the 21st Century. The absence of such international reaction suggests the fear with which other nations view Russia and reinforces, therefore, the Russian government's penchant for continuing to play the nuclear card.

Are Putin and Medvedev foolish enough to contemplate military confrontation with the United States? The answer is probably not, but America's NATO allies, particularly the Baltic States but also others whose borders touch Russia's can draw no comfort from the Russian intervention in Ossetia.

Tailoring Deterrence against Russia Today

In the unlikely event the Russian leadership at some point in a crisis contemplated conducting a limited military attack against the United States or against one of the allies over whom we have placed a "nuclear umbrella. U.S. policymakers would do well to recall points made by Caspar Weinberger in his 1982 Senate testimony.

He said, "…in order for our retaliatory threat to be seen as credible, we must be able, and be seen to have the means, to respond appropriately to a wide range of aggressive actions. If our threatened response is perceived as inadequate or inappropriate, it will be seen as a bluff and ignored."

Further Weinberger argued,"…deterrence is a dynamic effort, not a static one. In order to continue to deter successfully, our capabilities must change as the threat changes and as our knowledge of what is necessary to deter improves."[18]

A successful U.S. deterrent policy must have identified in advance those assets the Russian leadership values most, it must make obvious to that Russian leadership the consequences of aggression, and those statements will need to be reinforced by capable nuclear forces and command and control capabilities which we are confident can make the deterrent threat credible in Russian eyes.

As to what the Russian leadership might value, this could change each time the leadership changes hands. Putin/Medvedev presumably place high value on the nuclear forces they employ to intimidate their neighbors, on the security services which permit them to exercise their authoritarian style of government, on their ability to control Russia, and on the petroleum and gas infrastructure which provides the economic support the Russian government requires.

Their successors may or may not share the same values. To the degree Russia evolves in a democratic manner, as we hope it does, the tools of intimidation of neighbors and of Russian citizens presumably will be of less and less interest to future Russian leaders. To the degree Russia becomes even more authoritarian then those same elements of power and intimidation may be of equal or greater value to the leadership. The U.S. government needs to place considerable emphasis on understanding who the future leaders will be and what they value; scholarship and intelligence need to be brought together to create a coherent and accurate picture. This applies, of course, to the leadership of any nation whom we believe we may need to deter, now or in the future.

Once the United States has identified what it might need to hold at risk, it must ensure it has deployed the appropriate mix of forces to ensure the leaders of the government we seek to deter understand clearly and unequivocally we possess the means necessary to back up our threats. The U.S. nuclear force of 2010 is largely a product of the Reagan-"Bush 41" strategic modernization plan.

The Minuteman force is aging and will require some kind of replacement in the next 10-15 years. The Trident II missiles will continue to be operational for several decades, but the submarines which carry them will need to be replaced beginning in another 15-20 years. The air-launched cruise missiles carried by the B-52 bombers are 30 years old; they need to be replaced soon or the decision needs to be made to remove the B-52s from a nuclear role.

The nuclear weapons infrastructure — and indeed some of the nuclear weapons types in the U.S. inventory — also needs to be modernized. If we lost confidence in the weapons we deploy or the delivery systems that would become known to our potential adversaries, and our deterrent effect would be the weaker for it. And, additionally, in the case of Russia, the

United States will need to maintain parity in strategic nuclear capabilities with Moscow in order to prevent misperceptions from arising in Russian calculations. Finally, the Department of Defense must be a good and faithful steward with respect to our nation's nuclear forces. The department must display the utmost competence in carrying out all aspects of its nuclear responsibilities.

Notes

[1] For an excellent discussion of the origins of U.S. nuclear targeting policy see David Allen Rosenberg, "The Origins of Overkill: Nuclear Weapons and American Strategy, 1945-1960 International Security (Spring 1983).

[2] Henry A. Kissinger, *Nuclear Weapons and Foreign Policy* (New York, 1957), 8.

[3] John Foster Dulles, *U.S. Department of State Bulletin*, Volume XXX, No. 761 (Jan. 25, 1954).

[4] While completely overlooked by historians, in November 1957 NATO Commander (and U.S. General) Lauris Norstad delivered a speech which modified Dulles "Massive Retaliation" policy by stating that in the event of a Soviet attack against NATO the first U.S. response would be massive use of nuclear weapons by theater-based forces against the invading Red Army; only if that failed, he suggested there would be a massive attack on the USSR itself. Flexible Response required however that theater commanders develop nuclear war plans which featured multiple options. See David N. Schwartz, NATO's Nuclear Dilemmas (Washington, 1983), 58.

[5] In part, this was a bureaucratic attack against the U.S. military regarding any further expansion of nuclear forces, which McNamara believed were sufficiently sized. Counter-value capability, which he defined as being able to destroy 25 percent of the USSR's population and 50 percent of its industry, was a relatively small target set, and the number of weapons required to meet this goal was easily calculable. Counterforce requirements, on the other hand, were more open-ended, and "damage limitation" called for further investment in an anti-ballistic missile system, with which McNamara had become disenchanted.

[6] From unpublished and declassified minutes from the February 1966 NATO Nuclear Planning Group Ministerial meeting in the author's possession.

[7] Ibid.

[8] Harold Brown, speech at the U.S. Naval College (Newport, R.I., Aug. 20, 1980).

[9] Secretary of Defense Harold Brown, *Annual Report to Congress Fiscal Year 1982* (January 1981), 40-41.

[10] Secretary of Defense Caspar Weinberger's testimony before the Senate Foreign Relations Committee (Dec. 14, 1982).

[11] Because these changes were corrective rather than intended to create new policy, and because they were highly classified at the time, none of this was discussed publicly.

[12] See for example: Richard Norton-Taylor, "Typhoons scrambled to intercept Russian aircraft," *Guardian* (Aug. 22, 2007); Matthew Hickley and David Williams, "RAF fighter jets scrambled to intercept Russian bombers," *Daily Mail* (Aug. 22, 2007); Erik Holmes, "More Russian bombers flying off Alaska," *Air ForceTimes* (April 8, 2008), article notes: 'there have been 16 such [incidents] since July [2007]'; Wojocieh Moskwa, "Russian Bombers fly unusual N. Sea sortie: Norway," *Reuters* (July 20, 2007).

[13] See for example: Bronwen Maddox, "Putin raises spectre of nuclear war in Europe," *Times*, (June 4, 2007); Nicole Winfield, "Putin: Russian missiles will be aimed at U.S. bases," *Independent* (June 4, 2007).

[14] See for example, Nikolai Sokov, "Russian Ministry of Defense's New Policy Paper: The Nuclear Angle," James Martin Center for Nonproliferation Studies, (October 2003).

[15] See for, example, Mike Wade, RAF Intercepts Russian bombers over Stornoway, *The Times* (March 25, 2010). The article notes 20 such violations have occurred since January 2009.

[16] See for example: Fred Weir, "Would Russia really use nuclear weapons against neighbors?," *The Christian Science Monitor* (Nov. 15, 2009); "Russia may revise use of nuclear weapons in new military doctrine," *RIA Novosti* (Oct. 8, 2009); "Russia to Allow Preventative Nuclear Strikes," CBSNews.com (Oct. 14, 2009).

[17] Matthew Day, "Russia Simulates Nuclear Attack on Poland", *Telegraph* (Nov. 1, 2009).

[18] Secretary of Defense Caspar Weinberger's testimony before the Senate Foreign Relations Committee (Dec. 14, 1982).

CHAPTER 4

Crisis Deterrence in the Taiwan Strait[*]

Douglas McCready

Despite the warming of Chinese-American relations, the Taiwan Strait remains a potential flash point between the People's Republic of China (P.R.C.)[1] and the United States.[2] Although Taiwan is only one aspect of the complex relationship between the United States and China, it remains the most volatile part. The U.S. *National Defense Strategy* for 2008 describes China as an ascendant state with the potential for competing with the United States. It continues to modernize and develop military capabilities, primarily focused on a Taiwan Strait conflict and is developing technologies to disrupt traditional American advantages.[3]

A recent report from the Center for Strategic and International Studies concluded, "Unless China renounces the use of force as a possible avenue for reunification, the possibility of conflict with China over Taiwan will remain a central feature in American contingency planning."[4] Similarly, in 2001, a Chinese official described Taiwan as the most sensitive issue in Sino-American relations.[5]

These somber conclusions reflect the overwhelming view of American and Chinese specialists in Sino-American relations. More broadly, "the challenge presented by a rising China is the principal issue facing American policy."[6] Denny Roy puts this into regional perspective: "Taiwan's security problem is Asia's security problem: cross-Strait conflict would disrupt regional trade and force other Asian states to side with or against the People's Republic of China. Taiwan's security problem is also America's: one likely consequence of such a conflict would be

---

[*] This chapter was originally published as a Strategic Studies Institute (SSI) monograph, U.S. Army War College, Carlisle, Pa., in November 2003. The author has updated and revised it to reflect changes since its initial publication.

unambiguous Chinese opposition to, and corresponding action against, the U.S. military presence in Asia."[7]

The challenge facing the U.S. is to convince both the P.R.C. and Taiwan to refrain from precipitous action toward unification and independence respectively. This will be much less difficult with respect to Taiwan than the P.R.C. Roy explains the situation with regard to the P.R.C. thus: "Taiwan remains the substance of a classic security dilemma between China and the United States: one country sees its own actions as justifiably self-defensive, but these same actions appear aggressive to another country. Beijing views itself as trying to preserve the status quo and Chinese national territory … against the threats of [Taiwanese] separatism and U.S. intervention to prevent unification. In America's view, however, China is a large authoritarian country menacing a small democratic polity and trying to change the status quo by building up a military imbalance in China's favor."[8]

For almost 60 years, the American policy of strategic ambiguity has successfully prevented a major conflict. Domestic developments in both the P.R.C. and Taiwan require all three parties to reevaluate their policies. The continued success of American deterrence has become questionable. The stated American position that resolution of the conflict, whatever the result, must be by peaceful means appears increasingly unlikely and does not adequately address U.S. interest in the region. That the U.S. can delay Chinese actions is almost certain; that it can indefinitely deter China is unlikely.[9]

This study considers the Taiwan situation in terms of deterrence theory and its application across cultures to see under what conditions the P.R.C. might be convinced not to use force to resolve the Taiwan situation to its satisfaction. This study also examines the perceptions and misperception of each of the parties involved; their interests, capabilities and possible intentions; and how the P.R.C. intends to deter U.S. intervention in the Taiwan Strait.

An examination of the options available to each party concludes by suggesting likely courses of action and ways to increase the likelihood of successful U.S. deterrence in the Taiwan Strait. There is no presumption China will soon become a peer competitor to the United States. Chinese decision-making and actions regarding Taiwan will be driven by what the P.R.C. – but not necessarily other nations – views as domestic concerns.

Unlikely to defeat the U.S. in a direct military confrontation in the near term, China seeks to develop "niche weapons" and strategies that would make U.S. intervention too difficult or too costly, especially anti-access and area denial measures. Cliff notes, however, as serious as the threat is, the U.S. can do much to lessen it.[10]

The complexity of the Taiwan Strait situation suggests any future American attempt at crisis deterrence will be exceedingly difficult, and long-term success is unlikely unless at least one party to the conflict makes significant concessions to the others. The tangled relationship involves a combination of deterrence and coercive diplomacy. As the U.S. seeks to deter Chinese military action and Taiwanese provocation, the P.R.C. seeks to deter U.S. intervention and formal Taiwanese independence.

A dangerous aspect of the relationship is the confrontation between an inconsistent U.S. policy regarding Taiwan and the P.R.C., and a P.R.C. that exhibits simultaneous characteristics of paranoia, entitlement, victimization and arrogance arising out of its history. The paranoia leads China to view all actions of potential adversaries as directed primarily against China. Its historical self-image as the paramount state in Asia causes China to view the behavior of regional rivals, the U.S. and Japan, as intended to weaken or marginalize China and deny its rightful place in the international community.[11]

The complexity of China's self-image can be seen in its simultaneous expectation of receiving the prestige and authority of a permanent member of the United Nations Security Council with the right to a decisive say on events in Asia, the expectation of the preferential treatment given to developing nations, and opposition to any modification of the U. N. Charter to give Japan a permanent Security Council seat because this would dilute Chinese primacy as the spokesman for Asian interests.

Both the U.S. and the P.R.C. see themselves as occupying the moral high ground in their international dealings.[12] This makes compromise and communication difficult because each presumes it is in the right while the other acts wrongfully and must be brought around to its way of thinking. This moral self-image is deeply ingrained in both Chinese and American culture.

The most desirable outcome would be for China to transform into a pluralistic, democratic society where Taiwan could be accommodated and feel comfortable, but not necessarily required to integrate politically with the Mainland. This is highly unlikely in the short-term, so the U.S. needs to plan now for alternatives. This study explores a range of alternative courses of action with the intent that good crisis management will make a long-term peaceful solution possible.

History of the Conflict

Without a sense of the post-World War II history of the region, nothing else about its potential for crisis makes sense. Historically, Taiwan's relationship to the mainland was tenuous, but Japan claimed the island after defeating China in 1895. After World War II, the island was returned to China, and the Chinese Nationalists fled there after their defeat in the Chinese civil war. Although the Chinese Communists had expressed little interest in Taiwan previously, the island now became a symbol of the incompleteness of the communist victory in the civil war. Plans to invade the island were stymied by U.S. actions at the outbreak of the Korean War.

Thus, since 1950, the Taiwan Strait has been a source of international tension. After the warming of U.S.-P.R.C. relations, China seemed willing to live with the status quo for decades. Taiwan's move to democratic government since 1987, however, renewed earlier tensions. Democracy seemed to imply a move toward *formal* independence and a denial of the one-China policy that both the P.R.C. and the Chinese Nationalists had affirmed since 1949. This led to military confrontation between the P.R.C. and the U.S. in 1995-96 and periods of tension during the summer of 1999 and in early 2000.

Repeated conflict in the Taiwan Strait during the past 60 years has resulted in a variety of mutual perceptions and misperceptions on the part of each of the parties involved. China and Taiwan have images of each other that do not adequately reflect their history and aspirations. The P.R.C. ignores that Taiwan has had a separate history and developmental path for more than a century.

Both the P.R.C. and the U.S. view each other through the lens of their participation in conflicts going back to the Korean War. Some of these perceptions are well grounded, but others are simply wrong. Both lack of understanding and misunderstanding can spark a new Taiwan Strait crisis as easily as can irreconcilable national interests.

A residue of bitterness remains among Chinese leaders toward the U.S. dating back to the Chinese civil war, when the U.S. sided with the Chinese Nationalists.[13] This distrust prompted P.R.C. intervention in the Korean War. Believing war with the U.S. was inevitable, P.R.C. leaders decided their best hope lay in choosing the time and place for that war.[14]

Perceptions and Misperceptions in International Relations

Wars result most often from real conflicts of national interest. They may also, and too often do, arise from misunderstandings and misperceptions between nations. John Stoessinger considers misperception the most important single precipitating factor in the outbreak of war.[15] Misunderstanding and misperception often exacerbate the clash of national interests. The situation becomes more complicated when adversaries have different cultural backgrounds and different histories, as do China and the U.S.

This does not mean there is no conflict of national interest. For China, the U.S., Taiwan and even Japan, the resolution of Taiwan's international status involves important, even vital, national interests. Probably the most dangerous misunderstanding is the belief, prevalent in both the U.S. and China, that the U.S. has no significant national interest at stake. Therefore, it is imperative that U.S. political leaders define and explain, both to the American public and Chinese decision-makers, its interests, why they are important, and to what extent the U.S. is prepared to defend them.

What could possibly be so important about Taiwan that U.S. leaders should speak and act as forcefully as they have on several occasions? The U.S. has a legal commitment under the Taiwan Relations Act to support Taiwan in defending itself against forcible integration into China; it also has a moral obligation going back more than half a century to provide for Taiwan's defense. This moral obligation has only increased in the two decades since Taiwan has taken the path of democracy. American failure to keep its word to Taiwan would cause regional allies to doubt U.S. commitment to them.

In Japan's case, this could lead to rearmament and even development of a nuclear capability backed up by a missile-delivery system.

This would be in no one's interest, least of all China's. Finally, "a China that is conventionally predominant along the East Asian littoral could pose a direct, difficult, broad and enduring challenge to the U.S. position as guarantor of regional stability and security, a challenge that could extend well beyond Taiwan."[16] Some who do not consider Taiwan's democratic society, the security of Japan, and the credibility of U.S. commitments as vital interests, still view conflict in the Taiwan Strait as a danger to the peace and stability of the region, which does constitute a vital American interest.[17] In any case, what happens in the Taiwan Strait concerns the United States, and it needs to understand and proclaim this interest.

In the Taiwan Strait case, the problem of misperception and misunderstanding includes a difference of cultures and for the U.S. disagreement about what constitutes the relevant Chinese culture. Alistair Iain Johnston has challenged the conventional wisdom about China by suggesting modern Chinese strategic thinking is not simply a repetition of the ancient classics such as Sun Tzu's *Art of War*. Instead, China's strategic culture resembles much more the hard *realpolitik* of western international relations theory albeit with a greater potential for flexibility.[18]

Johnston found the P.R.C. has been much less reluctant to use force in strategic concerns involving territory than have other major powers.[19] This contrasts with the Chinese image (which is promoted by the P.R.C.) of China as a gentle Confucian nation that must be sorely provoked before it will resort to force. Andrew Scobell has taken this a step further in suggesting China has a dualistic strategic culture comprising Confucian-Mencian and Realpolitik elements which he calls a "Cult of Defense."[20] In practice, this means "Chinese elites believe strongly that their country's strategic tradition is pacifist, non-expansionist, and purely defensive but at the same time able to justify virtually any use of force – including offensive and preemptive strikes – as defensive in nature."[21]

Which interpretation is correct makes a difference in how the U.S. should approach the possibility of conflict in the Taiwan Strait. Chinese misperceptions of the world around it are affected by its history of xenophobia, a sense of having been humiliated by the West and Japan, a measure of paranoia, and a sense of moral and cultural superiority (which is not unique to China). No matter which interpretation of Chinese strategic culture is correct, domestic concerns will always influence how it operates in specific situations (especially Taiwan).

Misperceptions come in several varieties. The one that comes most naturally to mind is when the other party incorrectly interprets what *we* have said or done. No less serious, although much more difficult for us to understand, is the misperception where we communicate with the other party in ways it cannot understand or finds unconvincing because we do not see that party as it really is. This happens when we fail to understand the other party's culture and history, when our actions and words appear to conflict, or when our message seems unbelievable. The second kind of misperception frequently leads to the first kind. A third kind of misperception involves how each party sees itself. Few nations see themselves as others see them, yet most are prone to believe everyone else sees them as they see themselves. Each of these forms of misperception has occurred more than once in the century and a half relationship between China and the United States – the 1949 communist revolution in China only made it more acute.

Those unfamiliar with their adversary's culture often presume their adversary looks at the world and at the issues being contested in the same way they do.[22] They tend to project their own cultural values and historical experiences on to their adversary. In a conflict situation, this means each side misjudges the price its adversary is willing to pay, the suffering it is willing to endure, and what constitutes a compelling deterrent or reward to that adversary. They have difficulty seeing how their actions will affect their adversary domestically,[23] regionally and internationally. They also believe their own actions are as transparent to their adversary as to themselves and do not understand why their adversary would look for a hidden agenda. They forget people see what they expect to see and interpret the unfamiliar in terms of the familiar. This means they interpret our actions in terms of their expectation, not our intention. People also are prone to see as intentional what in reality is an accidental, unintended consequence or is just plain muddling through.[24]

Neither the U.S. nor China has considered sufficiently how the other country views it in terms of their relationship over the past 150 years. Each country knows what the other has done to it, but thinks much less about what it has done or what the other thinks it has done to the other country.

Each sees itself in terms of its intentions and interests – which it puts in the best light – not the other country's perceptions and experience of it.[25] This does not mean we need to agree with the other country's actions or beliefs, only that it is essential we try to understand the other country on its terms.[26] Then we can predict better how it will interpret and respond to our words and actions and craft our messages in a way more likely to be understood by the Chinese in the way we intend them to be understood.

There are at least four areas of mutual misperception whose correction is necessary for peace in the Taiwan Strait. Although their revision will not remove the conflict of national interests involved, it will enable us to see that conflict more clearly. These areas are the nature of the national interest involved, the level of commitment to that interest, the governmental decision-making process, and the attitudes that drive each nation's international behavior. American China watchers and Chinese America watchers now have a good sense of the other nation in each of these areas, but they appear to have had less success in communicating this to their national leadership. Due to the nature of the regime, the problem is greater on the part of Chinese leaders. Correcting these misperceptions and misunderstandings is difficult because people tend to see what they want to see, especially when they have made an investment in that conclusion.

Chinese leaders appear not to understand how the U.S. government is organized and how it makes policy. They do not appear to understand the balance of power among the branches of government, particularly the limits to presidential authority. They also have a hard time understanding American idealism and a political system so complex even the president cannot ignore special interests.[27] Thus, Chinese leaders do not understand the Taiwan Relations Act directs American policy despite the communiqués signed by American presidents and Chinese leaders.

One Chinese analyst complained, "Many Chinese analysts don't understand the domestic political and bureaucratic motivations" underlying U.S. policy. They see a coherent, hostile, anti-China strategy, not a series of ad hoc decisions made in response to competing interests.[28] They may also misinterpret the open debate in the U.S. media as expressions of U.S. government policy, particularly the hostile portion. This could lead China into precipitous action in response to what it sees as hostile U.S. intent. Additionally, Chinese leaders appear not to fully appreciate the influence of public opinion on American foreign policy.[29] Swaine notes that China has repeatedly been unable to correctly predict U.S. responses to its military initiatives.[30]

Possibly the most dangerous Chinese misperception is the oft-stated belief the United States lacks the political will to fight. This derives from the U.S. interventions in Somalia and Haiti during the 1990s. China's perception is eerily reminiscent of Japanese leaders in 1941, who believed a devastating surprise attack against U.S. forces would destroy the American will to fight without regard to American capacity to ultimately defeat Japan. This is, however, a flawed reading of American history and ignores those wars where the U.S. was prepared to sustain heavy casualties.

Richard Halloran comments on this misperception. "A careful reading of U.S. history in the 20th century… shows that Americans will fight for causes they understand to be vital to their principles or national interest."[31] Richard Sobol agrees the American public will make sacrifices when its leaders explain the cost and benefit of a policy to them.[32] Should China act on the basis of this misperception, it risks unleashing what some have called the American "crusade mentality." China likewise views Taiwan as a "soft" society where people would sooner flee overseas than fight to defend their island.[33]

This means China views the American will to fight as our weakest link. So it will threaten casualties in an effort to break that will early in any confrontation. One scenario would have China sink a U.S. aircraft carrier. The most powerful threat would be one that placed the continental U.S. at risk.

One serious American misunderstanding of China involves the matter of "face." The U.S. does not appreciate the impact of its behavior on China's sense of public honor. Given the disparity between the two nations' military powers, this can be serious. In 1996, the U.S. was slow to appreciate that the Chinese missile tests and war games required some reaction from the United States. When that reaction finally came, it signaled clearly and overpoweringly the U.S. was still supreme in Asian waters. One well-publicized deployment of a carrier battle group and a firm public diplomatic warning would have sufficed. Two carrier battle groups was overkill and a public humiliation administered to the P.R.C. leadership. Chinese military leaders have vowed this will never happen again.

Another problem lies in the different ways the U.S. and China perceive their own and the other's actions. For example, the U.S. tends to separate the military and political in such a way it often ignores the political implications of its military actions. China, however, sees political implications behind every military decision (even when none is intended).[34] In part, this may result from the different relationship that exists between civilians and the military in American and Chinese society, but there is also a cultural element. Where the U.S. mandates a clear separation and subordination of the military to the civilian, China has emphasized a close inter-relationship between the two.[35]

Chinese have described the most dangerous American misperception as our failure to understand the seriousness of their intent to regain Taiwan. This leads the United States to interpret Chinese warnings as "mere rhetoric," to conclude China is bluffing, and to underestimate the price China is willing to pay to achieve its aim. It also leads American policymakers to conclude if China has no reasonable hope of victory, it would not use force against Taiwan because "people don't start wars they expect to lose." Chinese leaders respond that, quite to the contrary, Taiwan is such a serious matter of regime legitimacy that any government would sooner fight a war it knows it would lose than allow Taiwan to go its own way unchallenged.[36]

Chinese have stated repeatedly no cost is too great if the issue is political control of Taiwan. In 2001, a People's Liberation Army (PLA) colonel told a group of visiting American academics China is willing to suffer a 20-year or 30-year setback to its economy in order to gain control of Taiwan.[37] The flip side of this American misperception is China's failure to recognize the U.S. may have interests related to the status of Taiwan it considers no less important than China's.[38]

Another crucial difference seems to lie in how the U.S. and China understand victory. For the U.S., victory is measured in military terms. For China, the political and psychological (and moral) are at least as important. The U.S. should have learned this from the Vietnam War.

China, with its fundamentally *realpolitik* approach to international relations, does not understand American foreign policy is an often inconsistent blend of realism, idealism, naiveté and ad hoc solutions. Instead, it sees American behavior as carefully thought out, devious and always directed toward some strategic interest.[39] Thus, it was incomprehensible to the Chinese the U.S. could have bombed their embassy in Belgrade by accident. Likewise, U.S. humanitarian intervention must have an ulterior motive. China described NATO intervention in Kosovo as a warm up for intervention in China's domestic affairs.[40]

The second aspect of China's *realpolitik* approach is its belief the costs to the U.S. of challenging China over Taiwan so outweigh any possible gain as to make such a challenge unlikely.[41] Nonetheless, Chinese America-watchers believe the U.S. will intervene in any military confrontation the P.R.C. initiates against Taiwan, although China seeks to influence American behavior so as to avoid a confrontation.[42]

China's fixation on Japan is the one great exception to its realist approach, but given the recent history between the two countries, it is understandable and not unique to China. Nonetheless, China has an exaggerated picture of Japanese interest and involvement in the Taiwan area and invariably interprets Japanese actions alone and in conjunction with the United States as threats to Chinese interests and sovereignty. At the same time, it is unable to understand how Japan can interpret threatening Chinese behavior negatively. This reflects a pattern where China's focus on bilateral relations prevents it from seeing how its actions appear to other nations. The 1996 missile firings near Taiwan's ports are an example of this. China was shocked that countries around the world reacted unfavorably to China's coercive diplomacy. It had expected they would ignore its effort to punish Taiwan.[43]

Closely associated with this is what Johnston calls Chinese leaders' failure to understand the security dilemma: "where a defensive action taken by one status quo actor is interpreted as threatening by another; the second actor then takes what it believes are defensive counteractions that, in turn, are interpreted by the first actor [as threatening]."[44]

The Chinese, in particular, seem not to understand the unintended impact of their military actions on others and are prone to misinterpret their responses.[45] This was clear in 1997, when Chinese leaders described Japan's willingness to establish new security guidelines with the United States (apparently in response to China's actions against Taiwan) as part of a new U.S.-Japan conspiracy to prevent Chinese control of Taiwan.

A final misperception is China's failure to understand the history and perceptions of those living on Taiwan. P.R.C. leaders appear predisposed to view apparently innocuous actions and statements by

Taiwan's leaders as covert moves toward independence. The result has been a Chinese loss of patience, setting of time and behavioral limits, and coercive actions.

Since the late 1980s, native-born Taiwanese have increasingly taken political control from the Mainlanders who arrived after World War II. Taiwanese public opinion now limits the options of the island's leaders, but China does not appear to understand or appreciate this (just as it discounts American public opinion). Taiwanese public opinion is overwhelmingly opposed to union with Mainland China. [46]

The 1996-1996 Crisis

The 1995-96 Crisis in the Strait shows how cumulative misperceptions and miscommunication can create and then exacerbate a crisis. The crisis is important because it led the P.R.C. to a reassessment of its military structure and doctrine to which the U.S. and Taiwan have not yet fully responded. The proximate cause of the crisis was Taiwan President Lee's visit to Cornell University, where he delivered a speech lauding the achievements of a democratic Taiwan.

China responded by staging missile tests in the sea off Taiwan's two main ports during July and August 1995. This was to show China's displeasure with U.S. actions and teach Taiwan a lesson, said Chinese spokespersons. The U.S. and other major states showed little response although the test areas endangered commercial shipping.

Both Taiwan and the U.S. ignored China's sensitivity about its sovereignty claims over Taiwan. China viewed Lee's trip as an attempt to gain international standing for an independent Taiwan. China's anger at American "duplicity" resulted from its inability to understand how the U.S. government works, especially the relationship between the executive and legislature. U.S. failure to respond vigorously to China's missile diplomacy led Beijing to believe the U.S. wouldn't get involved. This would come back to haunt both countries six months later.

In December 1995, China decided to use coercion to influence the outcome of Taiwan's presidential and legislative elections. This included military exercises and more missile tests. The tests were close enough to Taiwan's major ports to affect ship traffic and cause panic in Taipei's financial markets. This time, the U.S. dispatched two carrier battle groups to the scene. The Chinese were publicly outraged at what they saw as an American overreaction. China threatened war in order to avoid the need to go to war and expected the U.S. would understand. China was also publicly humiliated because it was obvious to all it could do nothing about the presence of the carriers.

On Taiwan, candidates favoring independence expressed their views without considering how China would respond. China considered coercion to be a matter solely between itself and Taiwan, somewhat like the relationship between the U.S. Government and Rhode Island. It misread the Clinton administration's previous inaction as signaling a lack of interest. China believed the U.S. would understand the missile tests and invasion exercises posed no immediate threat to Taiwan. It also believed Japan and other regional states would not interpret China's actions as potentially threatening even though many of them also had territorial disputes with the P.R.C. The United States waited too long after China announced its exercises to respond. Following the weak response to the first set of exercises, this delay signaled American indifference to Beijing.

When the U.S. did respond, it overreacted. The American response highlighted China's relative military weakness in contrast to American ability to operate in the area virtually unimpeded. China probably learned from this crisis the U.S. will respond forcefully should China attempt to use overt military force against Taiwan, but if China opts for a less confrontational approach, the U.S. will be unsure how and when to react.

While the crisis is over, the consequences are not. A series of basic misperceptions, and the actions and communications based on them, led to a crisis that could have resulted in war. Clearing away misperceptions and miscommunications is no guarantee the crisis would not have occurred, but it makes the possibility of crisis less likely and less serious.

As Scobell warns, P.R.C. behavior during the crisis offers four reasons for concern. It reminds us China is serious about using force to gain control of Taiwan if necessary. It warns China finds the possibility of a first strike against Taiwan attractive. It shows China's preference for using missiles against Taiwan, emphasizing China's deployment of these weapons and Taiwan's impotence against them. It also demonstrated a "dangerous lack of clear communications" between the U.S. and China.

Although each thought the signals it sent were clear, the other side misinterpreted them.[47]

Interests

Each of the parties involved – China, Taiwan, the United States, even Japan – has important national interests at stake in the Taiwan Strait conflict. The situation is complicated because not every party recognizes the intensity or validity of the others' interests. China has expressed its interests in terms of national sovereignty, territorial integrity and the respect due a major state. A 2000 White Paper listed a number of basic interests including: desire for settlement of the Taiwan issue and reunification of China, affirmation Taiwan is an inalienable part of China, resolution of the Taiwan issue is an internal Chinese affair, desire for peaceful reunification, use of force is a last resort, no one must attempt to change Taiwan's status by referendum, and the U.S. must deal with China and Taiwan on the basis of the Three Communiqués of 1972, 1979 and 1982.[48] China's unstated interests are no less important. Chinese leaders fear if Taiwan becomes independent, this will encourage separatists in Tibet, Xinjiang and Mongolia. Taiwan also threatens the Chinese Communist regime because it offers a successful political alternative to the Mainland in a Chinese cultural setting.

To achieve what it views as its proper role as the paramount state in Asia, China needs to remove American power and presence from the region. It sees regaining Taiwan as essential to achieving this. China believes the U.S. is a state in long-term decline.[49] When China talks about a multi-polar world, it appears to see itself as the preeminent (Asian) state in that world. The P.R.C. is more like the "Middle Kingdom" of Chinese history than a Marxist-Leninist-Maoist state. So, having discarded their Marxist ideology, China's communist leaders are increasingly dependent on the theme of national unification to legitimize their rule, as reflected in their playing the nationalism card in times of crisis.

Taiwan has no incentive to unite with the Mainland. It would prefer to remain free to continue its development as a democratic society and economically successful state. Anything China might interpret as a move toward independence would jeopardize everything Taiwan has gained because of the likelihood of war, but union would inhibit Taiwan's economic development and political freedom.

Taiwan desires international recognition and membership in international organizations commensurate with its democracy and economic power, but China opposes both and has been able to enforce this opposition through diplomatic and economic coercion.[50] Taiwan faces a conflict between promoting its status and survival. Taiwan has the greatest stake in maintaining the status quo, but its slow drift away from China presents the greatest threat to status quo – and the P.R.C. appears to understand this better than anyone else.[51]

The United States, consistent with its policy of strategic ambiguity, has been vague about its interests in the P.R.C.-Taiwan situation. The 2010 National Security Strategy (NSS) said an American goal in the region is encouraging "continued reduction in tension between the People's Republic of China and Taiwan." Also, the U.S. "will encourage China to make choices that contribute to peace, security, and prosperity as its influence rises."[52] The previous NSS was similarly ambiguous but did define several kinds of U.S. interests. Although few would describe Taiwan itself as a vital national interest, it can be linked to vital interests. Taiwan's existence as a democratic society is the result of American encouragement, so U.S. acquiescence in any solution to the Taiwan Strait situation that ignores or rejects the views of Taiwan's population would be inconsistent with the stated American goal of supporting democracy around the world.

P.R.C. leaders appear convinced the U.S. is committed to Taiwan's security such that a P.R.C. attack on Taiwan would result in American military intervention. Taiwan's leaders seem less confident.[53] American failure to act would cause allies in the region who have treaty commitments with the U.S. to reconsider those treaties.

Soon after passage of the Taiwan Relations Act (TRA), Sen. Jacob Javits explained his understanding of the TRA's impact on American commitments to Taiwan: "I was particularly concerned with other dangers which in fact seemed more realistic than an outright invasion from across the Strait. The language finally adopted ... referred to U.S. concern for activities which jeopardized not only the security, but also 'the social and economic system, of the people on Taiwan.'"[54] Similarly, Ralph Clough describes Taiwan as an important economic partner that "has been linked to the United States for many years by a diverse and growing web of interrelationships."[55] Despite this history, it is important to remember U.S. and Taiwanese interests are not identical.[56]

The United States has at least three basic interests in how the Taiwan Strait situation is resolved. The United States has been a Pacific power for more than a century. For it to allow another state to dominate the East Asia-Pacific region contradicts not only current U.S. policy, but also American grand strategy since the late 1800s.[57] The United States has security commitments to several key East Asian and Pacific states. It also has a legal, and many would argue moral, obligation under the TRA to assist Taiwan in defending itself against forcible assimilation by the P.R.C. Regional states view the U.S.-Taiwan relationship as a significant commitment; the consequences of U.S. failure to support Taiwan would be more far reaching than the defeat of South Vietnam in 1975,[58] causing American allies in the region to rethink their relationship with the U.S.

It is unclear that the U.S. should find acceptable even a peaceful assimilation of Taiwan to the P.R.C. This would provide China with the technology the U.S. has given Taiwan, and that Taiwan has developed itself. It would also project P.R.C. military power eastward into the Pacific with naval and air bases on Taiwan controlling the sea lanes vital to the Japanese and South Korean economies. The U.S. also has a longstanding "soft" interest in encouraging and supporting democracy, and ignoring American idealism is not realistic.[59] Taiwan is an example of democratic transformation as the P.R.C. is not. Abandonment of Taiwan would contradict values enshrined in America's founding documents. So while the U.S. has stated an interest in the peaceful settlement of the conflict between Taiwan and the P.R.C., this not necessarily reconcilable with other U.S. interests.

Japan also has interests in the situation. It wants to retain its relationship with the U.S. without antagonizing China. Any basing or logistical support for U.S. assistance to Taiwan could result in military retaliation and certainly in economic retaliation. Refusal to assist the U.S., however, could be the end of the mutual security relationship. Japan also has an interest in China not becoming so powerful that it could threaten Japanese security. This includes P.R.C. control of the sea lanes east of Taiwan that are vital to the Japanese economy. Balancing these interests will require Japan to walk a fine line. This is especially the case because Japan has a strong pacifist element, and the countries of East and Southeast

Asia have unpleasant memories of the Japanese occupation during World War II.

There is a clear conflict among the interests of the parties involved. The danger is the parties do not fully recognize or acknowledge the interests of the others. China does not believe U.S. interests relating to Taiwan justify going to war. The U.S. is skeptical about China's territorial claim, may not fully appreciate its regime-survival concern, and probably has concerns about how resolution of the Taiwan situation would affect China's standing as a rising power.

Capabilities

Most studies of the situation compare the relative military capabilities of the P.R.C. and Taiwan (and sometimes the U.S.). This is necessary because intentions and capabilities are related, but by itself it can be misleading. Capabilities and intentions influence each other, but neither determines the other. Different viewers evaluate capabilities differently, so what we see as capabilities do not necessarily limit our adversary's intentions. In the Taiwan Strait case, this comparison is usually of a conventional military confrontation. But, as the U.S. learned in Vietnam, military capability is only one consideration for engaging in or winning a war. Also, military confrontations need not be purely conventional.

The P.R.C. says assimilation of Taiwan would signal the end of China's civil war. China would prefer to resolve the situation peacefully, but, failing that, is willing to resort to force to gain its end. Chinese leaders have said repeatedly they would fight rather than allow China to be permanently divided. That they might not win does not preclude their use of force.[60] For domestic reasons, China appears willing to use force even when defeat is certain. Many western analysts find this incomprehensible, but they shouldn't. They conclude such a course of action is irrational, so China wouldn't follow it. But, in doing this, they impose their sense of rationality and values on the Chinese, who may have their own reasons for reaching a different conclusion.

There are historical precedents for this "irrational" course of action. In 1941, Japan initiated a war against the U.S. it doubted it could win because every other option seemed worse than war. Japan's leaders had concluded the nation's survival was at stake.[61] In 1973, the Arab states attacked Israel although they knew Israel was militarily more powerful than they were. Achieving surprise, they almost won, but they understood a military defeat could still be a political victory. China's perspective appears little different.

The difficulty in planning for a Taiwan Strait crisis arises from disagreement about China's capabilities, intentions, goals and strategy. This includes the P.R.C.'s regional and international goals and where Taiwan fits into them, whether the P.R.C. and the U.S. are on an inevitable collision course in East Asia, whether the P.R.C. will be subtle or heavy-handed in its dealings with Taiwan, how much the P.R.C. is willing to pay to gain control of Taiwan and where nuclear weapons fit into the P.R.C.'s strategy.

Comparisons of the military capability of the P.R.C. and Taiwan usually begin with the major weapons systems each side has or plans to purchase. They also analyze the parties' strategic doctrine and public statements. Occasionally, they probe behind the numbers to ask if the military has integrated the weapons systems in its arsenal; if there are sufficient trained personnel to maintain, operate and support the systems; which systems can be employed in the Taiwan area; and what other threats or responsibilities the military must be prepared to handle.[62] Questions about joint operations and command and control reflect unfavorably upon both the P.R.C. and Taiwan. The 2000 Department of Defense report on Taiwan and the P.R.C. listed significant U.S. intelligence gaps regarding logistics, maintenance and training of both militaries.[63] Michael Pillsbury adds command and control,[64] doctrine, special operations and mine warfare to the list.[65] More important than how these militaries function in peacetime is their ability to increase their tempo in a combat environment and maintain it for the duration of a war.

As capability affects intentions, so intentions influence capability. Analysts who look at the structure of the P.R.C. military, Taiwan's geography and Taiwanese airpower generally conclude an invasion of Taiwan would be unsuccessful. P.R.C. leaders have likely reached the same conclusion and decided to configure their military accordingly.[66] Thus, China has chosen to concentrate on weapons that will enable it to intimidate Taiwan and deter U.S. intervention. This is a situation where intentions help determine capability. Some Chinese strategists believe a multifaceted surprise attack could so demoralize Taiwan's population that an invasion would be unnecessary.

The different cultures involved in the Taiwan Strait conflict make more difficult an accurate assessment of military capabilities because of differing attitudes toward public disclosure. American capabilities, apart from classified details of weapons systems, are widely available in open-source materials. The U.S. seeks to deter opponents by letting them know how powerful it is.[67] In contrast, the P.R.C. attempts to deter potential adversaries by denying them knowledge of its military organization, doctrine, plans and capabilities.

This lack of transparency is a part of Chinese strategic culture. As Jason Ellis observes, "Significant information gaps have intensified the effects of Chinese deception, internal debate and lack of transparency, which have further hampered the U.S. ability to discern the nature, purpose and likely extent of Chinese plans in this area and to craft an appropriate policy response."[68] The U.S. has stated officially P.R.C. lack of transparency is destabilizing and increases the likelihood of misperception and miscalculation.[69]

It is one thing to have modern weapons. It's another matter to be able to maintain these weapons and use them to their full potential. It is even more difficult to employ them in a combined arms scenario where communications and coordination are essential. It is doubtful the P.R.C. has sufficient training or experience to mount major combined arms operations.[70] The Secretary of Defense's 2009 report on China said, "The content of Integrated Joint Operations has yet to be formally defined, remains largely an aspiration, and will likely continue to be so until at least 2010.... China's military leaders recognize and acknowledge that one of the primary obstacles to Integrated Joint Operations is that many PLA commanders have little or no training for, or experience operating in, a joint environment."[71]

An additional difficulty regarding the P.R.C. is although the U.S. knows where it is focusing its weapons development and acquisition, it is unclear how well the P.R.C. can integrate its various systems into a coherent war-fighting force, implement its doctrine for joint operations, and sustain its forces in a combat environment. American analysts have a better idea of Taiwan's general capabilities because P.R.C. pressure has made the U.S. into Taiwan's only major source of arms. But Chinese pressure also means the U.S. no longer has the relationship with Taiwan to enable it to evaluate Taiwan's military readiness, maintenance, command and control, and weapons survivability. The quality and quantity of Taiwan's domestic arms production are likewise unclear.[72]

The consensus is the conventional military balance is shifting in the P.R.C.'s favor, but is at the same time becoming more complex. Assessing China's efforts toward employing asymmetrical warfare against Taiwan, Stokes says, "Emphasis on preemptive, long-range precision strikes, information dominance, command and control warfare, and integrated air defense could enable the PLA to defang Taiwan's ability to conduct military operations."[73] Kaplan adds the P.R.C. is developing niche capabilities in submarines, missiles and space technology "that will allow them to potentially embarrass us at sea ... or to lock us out of the Taiwan Strait."[74] This could also seriously degrade U.S. capability for military action in the region, especially the mobilization and deployment necessary to support Taiwan against attack.

China is also developing a cyber warfare capability to attack Taiwanese, Japanese, and American command and control centers, financial markets and other key electronic facilities so essential to the functioning of modern society.[75] The P.R.C. has repeatedly tested its cyber war capability against U.S. government and civilian computer networks.[76] Yet, as Mulvenon has pointed out, while we know the extent and direction of China's interest in cyber war because they are discussed in open-source literature, we do not know Chinese capabilities in the field because that information is highly classified.[77]

Richard Clarke warns although P.R.C. offensive cyber war capabilities may be less than those of the U.S., China has superior defensive capabilities (including the ability to quickly disconnect the entire country from the Internet). Clarke describes the U.S. cyber war defense as minimal, enabling an enemy to take down both the military and civilian infrastructure in a first strike.[78] Mulvenon, however, suggests the P.R.C. tends to overestimate the U.S. military's reliance on computers.[79]

China lacks sufficient sealift capacity to successfully invade Taiwan, although it probably can achieve air superiority over the Taiwan Strait. [80] The west coast of Taiwan is notoriously unsuited to amphibious operations – and the east coast is worse.[81] The P.R.C. has shown no intention of improving its amphibious capability, but has focused on anti-access weapons whose greatest utility would be in deterring U.S. intervention. It is improving the quality and accuracy of its ballistic and cruise missiles, expanding and modernizing its submarine fleet,[82] developing its cyber war capability, and developing other asymmetrical capabilities to degrade Taiwan's defenses and hinder U.S. intervention.

China's large inventory of short- and medium- range ballistic missiles can quickly reach neighboring states and its ICBMs can reach the continental United States. With the mobile solid fuel and submarine-launched ICBMs being deployed, the P.R.C. has a limited second strike capability. Chinese officers have threatened to use nuclear weapons against American cities if the U.S. intervenes to defend Taiwan. It remains unclear whether this was more than bravado.

Chinese ballistic missiles are being configured to enable terminal precision guidance so they can damage Taiwan's major airfields, ports, and key infrastructure, degrading Taiwan's ability to launch fighter aircraft and coordinate air defense, and possibly putting U.S. carriers at risk. The P.R.C. is also developing cruise missiles with an over-the-horizon capability that to fly under current and projected missile defense systems. The P.R.C. has also purchased advanced anti-ship cruise missiles and torpedoes from Russia.

The U.S. technological warfare in the Persian Gulf and Kosovo shocked and impressed China. It decided it needed to develop at least some of these capabilities itself. Pillsbury says some Chinese strategists want the P.R.C. to leapfrog American technology by investing in exotic weapons systems, developing new doctrines and deploying new organizations.[83] The same technological prowess the Chinese want for themselves they also believe they can turn against the United States. Because the U.S. military has built information technology into every aspect of war-fighting, disrupting that technology would have devastating consequences on American ability to use its military. Chinese military leaders believe if they disable these high-tech systems, they can keep the U.S. out of the fight or defeat it when it engages.[84]

Interestingly, China considers the U.S. vulnerable because of its dependence on technology yet believes it can exploit technology to deter or defeat the U.S. in a regional conflict without exposing itself to the same vulnerability. China seems to understand technology instrumentally without necessarily understanding the organizational elements required and believes technology can quickly and inexpensively transform China's offensive military capability to enable a weaker nation to defeat a stronger one. These ideas go by the names Assassin's Mace and "Inferior Defeats the Superior" in the Chinese military literature.[85]

Chinese military authors have written extensively on the potential of Information Warfare (IW) to enable China to bypass several generations of technology to defeat a more powerful and advanced adversary. They believe many aspects of IW can be found in embryonic form in the Chinese military classics. Drawing on these for inspiration, China is likely to develop innovative IW strategies that will look nothing like American IW programs.[86] To the extent they are different and the U.S. fails to recognize the differences, they will be difficult for U.S. forces to counter.

The United States has the most powerful military in the world. This is not the same, however, as being able to concentrate that power in support of Taiwan. U.S. forces are deployed around the world, limiting their ability to focus on any one place, whereas, as a regional power, China can focus on its immediate vicinity. In the future, the U.S. is likely to need more than carrier battle groups. American ability and willingness to support Taiwan militarily will depend on the magnitude of the crisis; whether other international situations require a U.S. presence; the willingness of allies, especially Japan, to allow the U.S. to use bases on their territory and even to provide some direct assistance; American public support;[87] and the nature of Chinese deterrence.

The most important factor for America's regional allies will be how China threatens to respond. Robert Kaplan, who doubts a war will ever be fought in the Taiwan Strait, warns that even the perception the U.S. couldn't win such a war would change the entire balance of power in Asia.[88]

American support to Taiwan can range from political and diplomatic intervention, through provision of replacement and supplementary weapons systems and intelligence, to direct military involvement with naval and air forces. Deployment of American ground forces is unlikely. The U.S. stations one carrier battle group in the region and has land-based aircraft in Japan. Anti-submarine warfare and minesweeping might require Japanese assistance if the political climate permits.

Taiwan would have difficulty defending itself against a coordinated attack by P.R.C. conventional air and naval forces, especially if softened up by a missile barrage. Taiwan cannot defend itself against ballistic or cruise missile attack and likely would face difficulty in responding to a concerted special operations or cyber attack. Taiwan's anti-submarine warfare capability is limited. Its submarines are obsolete. Thus, Taiwan has virtually no self-defense capability against a first strike of the sort China has been talking about.[89] It could defeat many of the individual parts, apart from ballistic missiles, but a coordinated, multifaceted surprise attack would overwhelm it. Stokes notes that, absent a viable defense against Chinese ballistic missiles, Taiwan may consider such counterforce operations as preemptive strikes on missile sites.[90]

Taiwan needs to refocus away from ground forces toward air and naval forces. The battle will be at least half lost if the PLA secures a beachhead on Taiwan. Historically, the army has been the most powerful of Taiwan's armed forces. It is skeptical the air force and navy can prevent an invasion, so it wants weapons able to defeat the PLA on the beach. Thus, until recently, anti-submarine ships and helicopters have not been high on Taiwan's list of desired purchases, and no one has been willing to sell it modern submarines. Taiwan also needs to upgrade its air force to include fourth-generation fighters if it is to maintain air superiority.[91] China has effectively used the threat of economic retaliation to deter countries other than the U.S. from selling weapons to Taiwan, but remains frustrated by its inability to make the U.S. stop selling weapons to Taiwan.[92]

As important as acquiring new weapons are integrating current systems, improved pilot and crew training, hardened airfield facilities, improved air defense command and control, and better interoperability with U.S. forces.[93] These are less glamorous than some of the new weapons systems Taiwan would like, but they are more essential to a successful defense of the island.

Because it cannot defend against Chinese ballistic missiles, Taiwan risks losing the air superiority over the Strait necessary to defeat any P.R.C. invasion attempt.[94] This assumes China attains sufficient precision with its missiles that it can render runways at least temporarily inoperable, slowing the Taiwan air force's sortie rate, decreasing the number of defensive aircraft that can be in the air at any one time and destroying AWACS aircraft on the ground.[95]

With its modern, technological economy and educated population, Taiwan's capacity for offensive cyber warfare probably exceeds the P.R.C.'s. But Taiwan's defenses against a computer network attack are inadequate. As a technologically advanced and open society, Taiwan is more vulnerable to cyber warfare than the P.R.C. Taiwan is also concerned by the P.R.C.'s declared interest in developing an electromagnetic pulse weapon. Detonated high over Taiwan, such a weapon could destroy all unshielded electronics on the island without causing any direct casualties.

Taiwan has the know-how to develop nuclear weapons and delivery systems. It halted its nuclear program more than 30 years ago because of U.S. pressure. China has threatened Taiwan's development of nuclear weapons now would constitute grounds for war. Stokes notes, however, should Taiwan doubt U.S. support, it might try to develop nuclear weapons and delivery systems.[96]

Intensions

The only party to make its intentions clear is the P.R.C. It wants to integrate Taiwan with the Mainland, and is willing to use force to achieve this goal. In various public pronouncements, the P.R.C. has stated conditions that would cause it to use force against Taiwan and nations aiding Taiwan and has drawn a firm line on acceptable international and domestic behavior by Taiwan, the intent of which is to isolate Taiwan internationally. Taiwan has refused to accept P.R.C. conditions for negotiations because it believes they would predetermine the outcome,[97] but it has carefully avoided statements hinting at *formal* independence.

The U.S. has sought to leave unclear to both Taiwan and the P.R.C. its willingness to intervene in cross-Strait conflict, saying only that it expected a mutually agreeable, peaceful resolution of differences between Taiwan and the P.R.C. In part, this strategy results from U.S. uncertainty about what it would do in various contingencies.

Japan is the fourth actor which must be considered. Despite P.R.C. complaints, it is unclear how supportive Japan would be of U.S. military assistance to Taiwan. The preference of all four parties involved appears to be a continuation of the status quo, but this may not be a viable option.

China believes Taiwanese separatism encourages separatists on the Mainland. For the current generation of Chinese leaders, who lack the revolutionary legitimacy of Mao and Deng, the final unification of China that began with Hong Kong and Macao must include Taiwan (this legitimacy concern is also likely to make them less willing to compromise if a crisis does arise). The P.R.C. considers political control of Taiwan a vital national interest. It is not clear that the U.S. recognizes the emotional and nationalist depth of Beijing's interest or the widespread support of the Chinese public for unification.

Because China considers Taiwan a "renegade province," it does not consider its dealings with Taiwan to be a matter of concern to other nations. This includes weapons sales, visits by government officials, and Taiwan's participation in international organizations and defense arrangements. The P.R.C. reserves the right to treat Taiwan as it does Mainland provinces. But to many Americans, what China considers quelling domestic disturbance or concluding a civil war appears as aggression and evidence of P.R.C. belligerence. As a firm supporter of the Westphalian view of national sovereignty, the P.R.C. has consistently opposed international interventions in what it considers domestic matters of other countries. The primary reason for this is China fears a similar argument could be used to justify intervention in what China considers its domestic concerns.

Traditionally, China has seen itself as a nation that prefers to settle disputes peacefully. This is called the Confucian-Mencian strategic culture. Johnston has challenged this self-image. He says China's dispute behavior in some cases has been "higher risk, more militarized, and less connected to specific limited political demands than was once believed." He suggests China will be "more likely to resort to force – and relatively high levels of force – when disputes involve territory and occur in periods when the perceived gap between desired and ascribed status is growing or large."[98]

Many Chinese believe Americans see a rising China as a threat to the United States that must be countered with political, economic and military measures.[99] This affects their perception of U.S. actions with regard to Taiwan and other regional states and potential deployment of any missile defense system. China considers including Taiwan in any missile defense a political statement and sees the existence of any missile defense as intended to intimidate what it considers legitimate Chinese action in the region and deny it a credible nuclear deterrent.

Taiwan's ability to defend itself against P.R.C. attack is becoming increasingly problematic.[100] It can probably repel an invasion if it maintains air superiority over the Taiwan and the Strait. Its ability to control the sea east of Taiwan is doubtful because it lacks blue water navy, and it lacks the resources to defend against P.R.C. submarines or sweep mines from its ports and their sea approaches. If the P.R.C. gained air superiority over the Strait, it likely could coerce Taiwan into submission.

Taiwan has become a lively, even raucous, democracy. The governing party has changed peacefully twice in the past decade. The downside of this interparty conflict has stymied military modernization.[101] Rapid economic growth has improved the Taiwanese standard of living far beyond that of the average Mainlander.

As the relationship between the P.R.C. and Taiwan has improved, visiting across the Strait has begun. This has decreased Taiwanese interest in incorporation into the P.R.C. Taiwanese are willing to construct factories, do business, and even live on the Mainland, but most don't want to become part of it. Extensive economic investment on the Mainland has given Taiwanese businessmen an interest in peaceful and expanding cross-Strait relationships, and their political clout has impacted the government's ability to set policy. The P.R.C. believes increasing economic integration with Taiwan has given it both a carrot and a stick to achieve unification, but Roy suggests the situation is more complicated than the P.R.C. believes.[102]

Crisis Deterrence and Coercive Diplomacy

Deterrence theory is part of western international relations theory, developed primarily in a Cold War setting. Thus, there is some question about applying it cross-culturally and in non-western settings. Apart from the Taiwan Strait, the United States has had limited success in deterring Asian adversaries. We hope with a proper understanding of ourselves and our adversary and openness to solving our disagreements we can achieve either a peaceful resolution or successful deterrence, but this is not always the case.[103]

Deterrence theory presumes our adversary is rational, reasonable and generally predictable. It also presumes each side knows its own and the other side's interests. Only when we know our interests can we know what we are trying to deter, and only when we know the other side's interests can we know what deterrence is likely to cost. The problem is adversaries frequently misunderstand one another and act in ways the other considers irrational, making it hard for us to know our adversary.

What we often miss in all this is our standard of rationality does not necessarily apply to our adversary's situation, especially in the interplay between domestic and international concerns.[104] The adversary we call irrational might only be "crazy like a fox." When the adversary has a different culture and history, the gap only increases unless each party makes a determined effort to understand the other.

According to classic deterrence theory, successful deterrence requires threatening to exact a cost greater than any potential gain the adversary might achieve or removing a benefit the adversary currently enjoys.[105] It can also mean reducing the expected benefit the adversary hopes to gain,[106] a course of action too rarely considered. Thus, successful deterrence requires understanding how the adversary measures the value of gains and losses. It also means convincing that adversary the deterrent threat is credible. Thus, the threat should be relevant to the subject of the dispute and proportional to the value of the gain sought.[107] The deterrent threat must be understandable, believable and certain to the adversary.[108]

In 1950, China's threat to intervene militarily in Korea was unconvincing to the U.S. because the messenger was a known P.R.C. sympathizer, the U.S. believed China incapable of intervention to the extent required for success, and Chinese intervention in the face of overwhelming U.S. power appeared irrational.[109] From a Chinese perspective, all three perceptions were wrong. Yet, in making its threat, China failed to consider the difference between American and Chinese perspectives. The result was a deterrence failure and three more years of war.

American efforts to deter Chinese intervention were equally unsuccessful. Neither side understood what motivated the other, but thought it did. For the P.R.C., intervention was a regime survival issue of paramount importance. Chinese leaders thought that the U.N forces' attempt to occupy North Korea was directed at China.[110]

The problem is not merely that the U.S. and China have different cultures, but the leaders of both nations have acted as if they do not. Moreover, deterrents may not have the same meaning in Washington and Beijing.[111] Effective deterrence requires understanding our adversary's thought processes and preferred way of behaving. This information is both difficult to obtain and, once obtained, to interpret and apply to specific situations.

Not every adversary can be deterred. Sometimes the value to be gained or maintained is greater than any threat we can credibly make. This would be true in the case of national and possibly regime survival. It would also be true if the adversary believes it can evade the conditions of the threat, considers any condition better than the status quo, or cannot evaluate the threat for cultural, domestic or psychological reasons.[112] Potential aggressors do not always recognize credible deterrent threats. This is a real danger with regard to Taiwan. The U.S. has not articulated its tangible interests as clearly as the P.R.C. and its intangible interests do not impress China as commensurate with its own.

Further, the formal U.S. position regarding resolution of the issue conveys no strategic American interest in the continued existence of a Taiwan separate from Mainland China – it merely says the U.S. expects both sides to settle the conflict peacefully. Rightly or wrongly, this signals a low level of interest in the situation. Successful deterrence, however, requires a credible (to the intended audience) reason why the deterring power opposes the intended action.

Even when threats are clearly and deliberately communicated, the opponent may engage in wishful thinking, distort information about the deterrer, or ignore or twist the evidence it has in order to make the evidence fit its desires. The opponent may be too occupied with domestic concerns to pay sufficient attention to the international environment.[113] In the post-Cold War environment, potential conflicts are likely to involve intrinsic interests for the regional state and non-intrinsic interests for the U.S. This means the U.S. commitment will appear less credible.[114]

The most effective deterrent appears to be convincing potential aggressors they will not be able to achieve a quick victory or maintain control of the situation.[115] China has said that if using force becomes necessary, it intends to defeat Taiwan before the United States can intervene. The most effective deterrent threats are issued before one's adversary has committed psychologically and physically to act. Even tentative decisions are difficult to reverse.[116] For many Asians, involuntarily halting an action would involve loss of face.

Getting our adversary's attention can be difficult. States tend to focus on their own domestic political pressures and their strategic and domestic interests rather than on the interests and capabilities of those trying to deter them. The U.S. historically has sought to deter P.R.C. action against

Taiwan by deploying carrier battle groups to the area as a show of commitment. Rhoades suggests this ploy is usually unproductive despite American belief to the contrary.[117]

No matter how well thought out and appropriate to the situation, deterrence is always in the eye of the beholder, the adversary we are attempting to deter.[118] This means it is not our perception of the issues involved, relative strength, or potential gain or loss that matters, but our adversary's. At least as important as interests and capability is our adversary's perception of relative will: will we actually carry out the threat? When it comes to Taiwan, China believes it may be able to deter the U.S. from intervening militarily in support of Taiwan.

Conventional deterrence theory usually operates with a "one size fits all" model. Most theorists developed their ideas during the Cold War confrontation with the Soviet Union. Today, they tend to act as if the theory is universal in application. We cannot apply Soviet deterrence theory to China without major modifications. Both the U.S. and the Soviet Union found successful deterrence of China required threatening much higher levels of violence than required against each other. It is unclear the United States can morally and credibly threaten China with the use of force sufficient to deter action against Taiwan in every case. [119] And the U.S. is unlikely to risk a Chinese nuclear response directed against the continental United States to any action it might take in the case of deterrence failure. Or, as the Chinese general put it, would we sacrifice Los Angeles for Taiwan? Would U.S. leaders be willing to risk finding out if that would be the true cost?

Shulsky notes, "The historical record indicates that China's adversaries often misunderstand its motives and willingness to use force, which affects their ability to deter the Chinese use of force." He says China has been willing to use force because it can use the resulting tension to its own advantage. As long as China can control the tension level and escalation process, it believes the tension helps China and hurts its adversary.[120]

Possibly the greatest obstacle to successful crisis deterrence in the Taiwan Strait is neither the U.S. nor the P.R.C. sufficiently recognizes the other side believes it has important national interests at stake. In part, this is because the basic P.R.C. and U.S. interests involved are qualitatively different. China's interests are more obvious: national sovereignty, territorial integrity and regime legitimacy. It is also a matter of national pride.

For the U.S., credibility of commitments and support for democratic governments are more central than traditional security interests, although these are not absent. The credibility of U.S. commitments to Asian allies may be more important than China realizes. U.S. leaders have neither clearly nor convincingly articulated American interest in the situation and doubt China is as committed as it claims to be.

If the U.S. attempts to predict P.R.C. actions using conventional deterrence theory without considering China's national self-image, it will seriously underestimate the cost China is willing to pay to gain Taiwan.[121] In part, this is because China in the past used bombastic rhetoric that significantly exceeded its capabilities and adversaries could too easily dismiss. This is no longer the case.

An additional problem for the United States is Chinese strategic thought emphasizes achieving surprise and inflicting psychological shock on its adversary. This is especially important when facing a more powerful adversary such as the United States.[122] Should China conclude resort to force is its only option; a surprise attack would be very difficult to deter. China has suggested such an attack would include not only Taiwan, but also Japan and American bases in East Asia and the Pacific. It probably would combine asymmetric and conventional attacks. Shlapak suggests making clear the escalatory consequences to the P.R.C. of attacking U.S. bases in the region could enhance deterrence.[123]

Closely linked with crisis deterrence is coercive diplomacy. Because it seeks to make a state undo a successful action instead of trying to convince that state not to attempt an action that may or may not be successful, coercive diplomacy is more difficult than deterrence. Since the early 1990s, however, the P.R.C. has used coercion successfully to rein in Taiwan's attempts to acquire international space through informal diplomacy. The P.R.C. also has successfully coerced the U.S. to modify its Taiwan policy and its general policy toward China, including human rights, trade and technology transfer.[124]

Should Taiwan move toward formal independence, the P.R.C. likely would attempt coercive measures before resorting to military force. Should the P.R.C. successfully conquer Taiwan before the U.S. could intervene militarily, the U.S. would face the prospect of attempting coercive diplomacy before having to decide on a military response. Domestic and allied support for the latter is unlikely.

What the U.S. is unable to deter, it may be able to delay. The difference between deterring and delaying is a function of China's willingness to pay the costs of military action. If forced to choose between Taiwanese independence and using force, China will use force. There is no credible threat serious enough to deter China. But as long as there is the likelihood of settling the conflict peacefully, it is less costly for China to delay acting.

The likelihood of American intervention, the fear of failure, domestic and international consequences of military action, increased economic leverage over Taiwan, and belief in an improvement in the relative military balance over time may encourage China to delay action against Taiwan. One long-term concern for Taiwan is the large number of Taiwanese businessmen residing and educating their children on the Mainland. This is more important than it might appear. A delay measured in decades rather than years would allow for changes in both China and Taiwan that could lead to a peaceful resolution of the conflict in a way few may even be considering now. While long-term indicators, apart from Taiwanese public opinion, appear to favor the P.R.C., it is unclear that the P.R.C. leadership sees things that way due to its fixation on "Taiwanese independence."

Options

Crisis deterrence requires knowing what one is trying to deter. In the Taiwan Strait situation, it also means the U.S. needs to consider P.R.C. efforts to deter U.S. intervention. The latter is the more difficult task due to the nature of the P.R.C.'s deterrent threats and the secretiveness of its decision-making process. It will only become more difficult as the P.R.C. increases the quality, quantity, and survivability of deterrent assets.

Each party involved in the Taiwan Strait has a range of options. Which option each will or should choose depends on what that party hopes to accomplish and the resources it has available. China has a wide range of options, and this creates a problem for U.S. policymakers because different options require different forms of deterrence. The cost of trying to deter all the possible Chinese options would exceed the resources and time available.

Thus, the first task is to evaluate the P.R.C.'s options in terms of likelihood. The key determinants are Chinese capabilities and weaknesses and the risk to China involved in each course of action (China's interest in Taiwan is clear). The less spectacular and blatant courses minimize the risk of international and domestic repercussions and can be tried more than once.

A failed invasion would harm the P.R.C. economy, weaken the armed forces, probably delegitimize the Chinese Communist Party and topple the government, and irrevocably alienate the people of Taiwan from the Mainland. That would be a high price to pay for an action with little likelihood of near-term success.

The P.R.C.'s minimal goal is to prevent Taiwan from becoming formally independent.[125] China has stated clearly and repeatedly the behaviors by Taiwan and its allies that would provoke a P.R.C. military response. Most American analysts believe China is serious about its readiness to back its claim with force.[126]

No Chinese government can hope to survive if it allows Taiwan to gain its independence without a fight. Even war with the United States would be a lesser evil. It is equally doubtful the people of Taiwan would agree freely to assimilation apart from a drastic deterioration in the military balance or major improvements in the political and economic conditions in the P.R.C. China's leaders need the support of the PLA, which sees itself responsible for successfully concluding China's civil war, unifying the country, and defending its proper borders. For the PLA, Taiwan is non-negotiable.

Unfortunately, Taiwan, the U.S. and Japan are less clear about their goals. Taiwan's desire to remain separate from Mainland China does not currently include a plan for formal independence. The stated American goal is for the P.R.C. and Taiwan to settle their differences peacefully. This would not necessarily advance American interests, however. Any result that limited U.S. freedom of movement and action in East Asia and the western Pacific would be unacceptable.

Japan's goal or goals are even more unformed because of constitutional constraints, residual fears on the part of its Asian neighbors, and domestic political and generational differences. Japan doesn't want to have to choose between the U.S. and China. Japan is concerned, however, about Chinese aspirations to regional hegemony and claims to the Senkaku or Diaoyutai Islands.[127]

Continuation of the status quo would be the best short-term solution. Although it is no one's ideal (least of all the P.R.C.'s), there appears to be no alternative acceptable to all. China, however, looks at Taiwan's democratic society, the growing Taiwanese sense of identity, and negative political attitudes toward the P.R.C. with concern. The P.R.C. fears the status quo is shifting subtly but steadily toward Taiwanese separatism.[128] If so, coercion or direct military action will be required to achieve the P.R.C.'s goal.

Despite China's sovereignty claims, it is likely to prefer options least confrontational internationally and least likely to result in outside intervention. Shulsky says history suggests any Chinese military action against Taiwan is likely to occur at the lower end of the scale in terms of force.[129] Whether he is right will depend on what precipitates P.R.C. military action, the window of opportunity before an American response, and the perceived likelihood of American action given the international situation at the time.

China's Options

China has two deterrence concerns. First is preventing Taiwan from taking steps toward formal independence and deploying weapons that would make P.R.C. actions against Taiwan more difficult or most costly. Second is deterring the U.S. from providing encouragement and support to Taiwan and from intervening militarily in support of Taiwan should a crisis lead to war. China has shown little reluctance to replace failed deterrence with coercive actions directed at both Taiwan and the United States, but it has also demonstrated a willingness to negotiate or compromise with regard to objectives.[130] China also uses the lure of its potential market and trading relationship to discourage American support for Taiwan, even having U.S. business lobby in its behalf. It is doing the same with Taiwanese business and industrial leaders. When this fails, China has not hesitated to use trade as a form of coercive diplomacy.

The P.R.C. and Taiwan have become increasingly economically interdependent. Much of this is the result of Taiwanese investment in and exports to the Mainland. Some have suggested this is causing Taiwan to be pulled increasingly into China's orbit with inevitable unification; China certainly hopes so. Taiwan's leaders have recognized this danger and encouraged businesses to diversify their investment into other parts of Asia. This cross-Strait economic relationship would make conflict extremely costly for both parties. Both stand to suffer enormous economic loss in the case of war.

An underlying difficulty with the absorption theory, however, concerns China's economy. Economists have suggested China's rapid economic growth masks serious weaknesses in its banking system, state-owned enterprises, and other parts of the economic infrastructure.[131] Chinese have actually expressed concern that Taiwan might see a Chinese economic crisis as an opportunity to declare independence because China would be too distracted and disorganized to respond. Non-Chinese analysts have expressed concern the P.R.C. might use military action against Taiwan to divert domestic attention from a domestic political or economic crisis.

Some China specialists have suggested that in the P.R.C. decision-making process good analysis and creative options are unlikely to survive the bureaucratic gauntlet and gain the attention of the actual decision-makers.[132] This would mean any easing tensions in the Taiwan Strait are unlikely to come from China. Additionally, the PLA may keep Taiwan a matter of concern for budgetary reasons, to maintain a sense of mission, and to reinforce its nationalist self-image.

Chinese strategic culture differs significantly from the American way of war – use of these two different terms is intended to demonstrate this, although that oversimplifies matters. China's strategic concept is broader than the American, more multidimensional and integrated. Well before conflict begins, China begins an integrated psychological, political, diplomatic, economic and military offensive intended to isolate and unsettle its potential adversary.

Following Sun Tzu's famous (and widely misunderstood) adage,[133] China attempts to achieve victory without war, but, because this rarely happens, it also aims to shape the multidimensional battlefield to its advantage before the adversary even realizes there is a battlefield. So, Chinese goals are more complex than Americans recognize. They are often unsure what is at stake and what counts for victory or defeat. In any Taiwan Strait crisis, China probably will be engaged strategically before the U.S.

realizes a crisis exists, hoping to outmaneuver the U.S. and foreclose options *before* any combat.

China would prefer to deter Taiwan from taking any step toward greater independence than it already enjoys. It can attempt this using military threats, psychological warfare and economic pressures. Because of domestic changes on Taiwan, China does not appear to consider this a long-term option, although its economic leverage over Taiwan continues to grow. China's concern should not prevent American and Taiwanese policymakers from seeking innovative ways of maintaining the current situation acceptable to China. Although most long-term indicators favor the P.R.C. over Taiwan, it is uncertain whether China's leaders are inclined to wait as long as might be required.

China has a history of provoking crises in order to test its adversaries' reactions and show them the political and possible military costs of pursuing policies antagonistic to China.[134] Because China views crises as opportunities, not only dangers, it is willing to create a sense of crisis for its adversary and historically has been successful in evaluating risk. China might use a series of carefully orchestrated crises to try to unsettle the U.S. and Taiwan publics, divide the two parties, and damage their will to fight. While this is a low-risk strategy, it is not risk-free. The possibility of miscommunication and misperception raises the risk of unintended escalation.

In seeking to deter the U.S. from responding militarily to Chinese initiatives to gain control of Taiwan, the P.R.C. has a range of options. China's most likely courses of action, in terms of its strategic culture – and assuming non-military measures are unsuccessful – are those that could be accomplished before the U.S. could respond or those that never rise to a level that would trigger a U.S. military response. The latter includes a low-intensity, unconventional attack on Taiwan's economic infrastructure and a long-term obstruction of Taiwan's sea lines of communication, disrupting the trade that is the island's lifeblood. So China's best options are a quick, intense, surprise attack and a slow, low-intensity strangulation campaign.

Because Taiwan is resource poor and has one of the world's densest populations, its survival depends on a thriving export economy supplied by a steady flow of oil and raw materials.[135] During the 1995-96 Crisis, the P.R.C. learned it can disrupt Taiwan economically and possibly destabilize it politically at an acceptable cost and without the need for direct confrontation.[136] This would both make it difficult for the U.S. to decide if or when to intervene and could wear out both the U.S. and Taiwan. This is a situation where a dictatorship has the advantage over democracies with limited tolerance for long-term conflicts.

Presenting the U.S. with a *fait accompli* would be the most advantageous military course for China,[137] although it would have serious political and diplomatic consequences – consequences China says it is willing to accept. P.R.C. success means the U.S. would have to counter P.R.C. action with its own invasion of the island to restore Taiwan's independence. Gaining public support for this would be far more difficult than for assisting Taiwan in its own defense – as would the counter-invasion itself be – unless the P.R.C.'s quick strike included first strikes on U.S. forces in East Asia that caused heavy casualties, something PLA writers have discussed.

Unfortunately, the Chinese discussion has emphasized U.S. timidity in Somalia, Haiti and Kosovo, concluding the U.S. is so averse to casualties it might be deterred from acting. Chinese writers have apparently ignored Pearl Harbor and forgotten American willingness to suffer major casualties in the Persian Gulf in 1991. Chinese belief the U.S. is casualty-averse could lead it to take provocative actions that would almost certainly result in war in the Taiwan Strait.

Thus, one crucial aspect of crisis deterrence must be to disabuse the P.R.C. of this dangerous misperception about American casualties. The P.R.C. leaders' view that Taiwan is much more important to them than to the U.S. joined with the (mis)perception that the U.S. is casualty-averse creates precisely the condition for unintended war between China and the United States.

A second difficulty for the U.S. in the face of a swift P.R.C. conquest of Taiwan would be the response of America's Asian allies. The U.S. would require, at a minimum, use of regional bases and local logistical support to mount a military response to the P.R.C. In the face of a *fait accompli*, regional allies would be unlikely to provide such support. This would be the result of limited domestic public support coupled with fear of P.R.C. retaliation. Japan, the only nation with first-hand experience of nuclear attack, would have to provide most of the support for such an operation. A credible Chinese threat, coupled with doubt the U.S. would be willing to suffer a nuclear attack in Japan's defense, almost certainly would mean Japanese refusal to assist the U.S. in supporting Taiwan.

One form of the *fait accompli* the Chinese have discussed is a surprise attack on Taiwan, Japan and U.S. military facilities in the East Asia-Pacific region. Some Chinese believe this would render all three unable to respond militarily to China before it could gain control of the island and would so shock the populations psychologically they would not permit their governments to act. Classic Chinese military writers emphasize the use of surprise and shock to gain strategic advantage.[138] Few American analysts and decision-makers take this as seriously as Chinese military history would seem to warrant, and Taiwan is unprepared militarily or psychologically for such an eventuality.

Such a first strike could be a conventional attack on Taiwanese, American and Japanese military assets in the region coupled with one or more high altitude electromagnetic pulses in the upper atmosphere. This would have the advantage of devastating high-tech weaponry without the provocation of a nuclear attack. Computer network attacks could degrade command and control, logistics and counterstrike assets.

The least risky option for the P.R.C. would be a computer network attacks against Taiwan's banking system, stock market, communications system, electrical grid, transportation network and early warning system. This is within the P.R.C.'s current capabilities. The P.R.C. has discussed openly using cyber warfare not only to damage Taiwan's economy and communications, but also the U.S. information and financial infrastructure, which it considers vulnerable.

Such serious disruption would devastate the economy and defense system and possibly panic the populace. If applied only to Taiwan, this course of action has the advantage it is unlikely to rise to the level where the U.S. could justify responding or to determine an effective way to intervene. It might even be carried out covertly.

An attack on this same scale on American government and civilian computer networks probably would result in a public outcry for retaliation. While such an operation might be deniable, detection would expose the P.R.C. to a devastating response. The *threat*, however, to use cyber war is the one Chinese weapon that could affect the entire continental United States and place at risk essential infrastructure.

This option becomes increasingly attractive as Taiwan becomes more democratic. The P.R.C. fears this democratic trend for four reasons: it means the P.R.C. cannot reach an agreement with leaders over the heads of the people of Taiwan (as happened to Hong Kong and Macao), the people of Taiwan find political union with the repressive P.R.C. increasingly unattractive, a democratic Taiwan demonstrates democracy and Chinese culture are not incompatible, and the continued existence of a democratic Taiwan makes easier for western democracies to justify defending it.[139]

A second course of action would be an attack by precision guided ballistic and cruise missiles against Taiwan's air force bases, radar installations, and command and control centers. If successful, The P.R.C. could achieve air superiority over the Strait and Taiwan itself. This would allow the air drop of troops, capture of Taiwan's ports, and the movement of large numbers of soldiers quickly across the Strait, followed by occupation of the island.

This scenario assumes the P.R.C. can keep its preparations hidden from U.S. and Taiwan intelligence, that a missile attack followed by aircraft attacks would rapidly destroy Taiwan's air force, P.R.C. troops delivered by aircraft could defeat Taiwan's army on the ground, that the P.R.C. has accurate terminal guidance systems for its missiles, and – most important – that the P.R.C. could synchronize such an operation – all of this before the U.S. could react. Although P.R.C. writers have mentioned this course of action, each element is problematic. RAND analysts have concluded a missile attack, especially if China can argue it was directed exclusively against military targets, might not receive as serious an international response as would an invasion or an indiscriminate missile attack. They also suggest such an attack might seriously affect Taiwanese morale.[140]

A third option is some form of blockade. This would cripple Taiwan's economy and further isolate it diplomatically. Chinese leaders appear to consider this less provocative than missiles or an invasion, but it would tax China's naval forces to enforce a full blockade. Anything less than a full blockade would take so long to be effective Taiwan and its friends could develop countermeasures.

Michael O'Hanlon says, "Even a limited blockade effort conducted by China's modern submarine force could stand a reasonable chance of dragging down Taiwan's economy – and keeping it down for a prolonged period. U.S. military intervention might be needed to break the blockade quickly."[141] Current and proposed improvements to China's navy are intended to inhibit U.S. Navy access to the area, hampering its ability to break blockade.[142] Any U.S. effort would probably require the assistance of Japanese minesweepers.

A variation on this would involve using submarines to lay minefields outside Taiwan's main harbors and even threatening to sink commercial vessels that entered an exclusion zone outside Taiwan's main ports. This could be part of a larger blockade or implemented on its own. The sinking of one merchant ship would virtually halt seaborne commerce and devastate Taiwan's economy. This is within the P.R.C.'s capabilities, but could provoke U.S. intervention. But if the operation spread over a sufficiently long period, the U.S. might tire of involvement and Taiwan become too worn down to continue resistance. The result, again, would be disruption and collapse of Taiwan's economy with a probable capitulation by Taiwan.

The P.R.C.'s "one China" claim provides legal cover for this option. Blockades are acts of war under international law, but because it considers Taiwan a part of China, the P.R.C. asserts any blockade is solely a domestic matter. When considered in conjunction with China's self-understanding as a moral actor, the domestic claim points in the direction of some form of blockade if the other relevant factors are conducive.

The least likely scenarios involve an amphibious assault across the Taiwan Strait or a nuclear attack on Taiwan. The first is impossible without P.R.C. air superiority over the Taiwan Strait, additional sealift capacity, and a combined arms capability the PLA has yet to demonstrate. In any case, it would be a formidable task and the cost of failure would be high, including almost certainly the *de jure* independence of Taiwan. This would be the last resort of a desperate Chinese government.

The second course would produce a hollow victory with Taiwan's economy destroyed, its surviving population forever alienated, and the P.R.C. an international pariah. China has stated repeatedly that it will not use nuclear weapons against other Chinese; the threat of their use appears directed at American and Japanese intervention.

Distinct from actual use of nuclear weapons would be the threat to use such weapons against the continental U.S. or forward deployed U.S. forces in East Asia and the western Pacific. A U.S. president would have to consider carefully how the crisis appeared to the Chinese leadership before deciding whether the threat was serious or a bluff. There are no adequate historical analogies to help in making this decision.

The threat to use nuclear weapons is the most powerful deterrent the P.R.C. has to discourage American involvement in any Taiwan conflict, but actual use of such weapons would invite a massive retaliatory response. The P.R.C. currently has more to lose to such retaliation than at any time in its history, so nuclear threats likely will be used to deter conventional U.S. intervention.

Currently, the P.R.C. believes it can achieve its goal without resorting to force. It is convinced that if it does use force, the U.S. will intervene on the side of Taiwan. China also recognizes the U.S. is greatly superior to China militarily. So if the day ever comes that China believes war is inevitable, it will seek to choose the time, place (or places), and nature of the conflict so as to overcome the American material advantage through strategic and tactical surprise. The China Security Review Commission warns, "China's leaders believe that the United States, although technologically superior in almost every area of military power, can be *defeated*, most particularly, in a fight over Taiwan in which China controls the timing."[143] China's targets will be those Taiwanese, American and Japanese assets most able to respond to China militarily and those whose destruction will deliver the sharpest psychological blow to China's potential adversaries. Chinese suggestions that the most effective action would be a powerful surprise attack inject an inherent instability into the situation.

Taiwan's Options

Taiwan's best option is to lay low and maintain the status quo. This leaves the initiative with China. The people of Taiwan do not want to become part of the P.R.C., and they now have a say in the matter. "There is strong popular opposition to China's coercive diplomatic and military moves, little support for China's position on unification, and strong support for maintaining Taiwan's current status in the face of Chinese pressure. However, the public also wants to benefit from cross-strait economic and other exchanges and to avoid confrontation with China and tensions in relations with the U.S."[144]

Taiwan's political development precludes a simple unification with the Mainland. Events in China have done nothing to ease Taiwanese reluctance. Taiwan's safest path is to maintain a low profile internationally while highlighting its democratic political system and thriving economy, improve its defensive capability by buying the weapons systems it really needs, developing or improving informal relationships with the United States and other regional actors, and doing nothing the P.R.C. could construe as steps toward *formal* independence.

Taiwan needs to prepare its citizens for the domestic impact of P.R.C. action, coercion as well as attack, and make critical improvements to its defenses against surprise attack and cyber warfare. Taiwanese leaders should also develop unconventional options that respond to P.R.C. concerns and preserve P.R.C. "face" while preserving a separate existence for the island and its population. A moderate improvement in Taiwan's defensive capability could help stabilize the situation as well as enhance deterrence.

U.S. Options

The United States has a range of options, not all of which are equally attractive. Actually, there are two sets of options regarding Taiwan. The first concerns U.S. actions when the situation is relatively calm and aims to maintain that calm. The intent is good decision-making and execution will prevent crises from developing. The second concerns U.S. actions when a crisis occurs. The purpose is two-fold: to prevent the crisis from becoming a shooting war and to prevail should war break out. The former includes unofficial travel between the U.S. and Taiwan, types of weapons sold to Taiwan, unofficial military exchanges and coordination with Taiwan, official military exchanges with the P.R.C., deployment of a national or theater missile defense system, and similar actions whose cumulative effect will influence U.S.-China-Taiwan relations. The latter involves trying to persuade both China and Taiwan not to choose a military solution or provoke the other party to do so. This could mean naval deployments, political and economic sanctions, breaking a blockade, or direct military intervention. Deterrence must be matched by reassurance. For both the P.R.C. and Taiwan, this means a strong reaffirmation of U.S. support for the status quo, as the Bush Administration did in reining in Taiwan's President Chen.

American policymakers have not tried to use China's stated fear of a resurgent Japan to encourage China to moderate its international behavior. One benefit China gains from the U.S. presence in East Asia is a Japan whose military capability does not match its economic and political strength. Although China professes not to understand why Japan might have any reason to fear it, an American departure from East Asia or failure to keep its commitments is likely to cause Japan to consider rearming. Were Japan to apply its technological and industrial capability to military development, China would have grounds for concern. When China complains about a forward American presence in East Asia, the U.S. can remind China's leaders this is a cheap price to pay for not having to worry about a militarized Japan.

The U.S. remains obligated under the Taiwan Relations Act to provide Taiwan with adequate weaponry to defend itself. The emphasis should be on low-profile, defensive weapons Taiwan needs to counter areas of current and expected P.R.C. advantage. The greatest needs are for anti-submarine and mine-clearing capabilities, a more flexible command and control system, missile defense, and modern fighter aircraft.

China also needs to be aware it does not have veto power over U.S. weapons sales. American weapons sales to Taiwan must walk the fine line of providing those items Taiwan needs for self-defense without providing systems or quantities that embolden Taiwan or cause the P.R.C. to react militarily.

Economic threats have often been proposed as a way to deter Chinese action. Actually, the only successful economic threats have been those China has made to the United States. Threatening sanctions has only turned China to alternate suppliers and led to vigorous lobbying by American businesses fearful of being shut out of the China market. Given the size of the U.S.-China trade imbalance and the P.R.C.'s creditor status regarding U.S. debt, the U.S. can take few economic measures within WTO rules.

Crisis-related options include withdrawing from the situation, seeking to maintain the status quo, or taking a clear position in support of the P.R.C. or Taiwan.[145] Much more than for China, American options must be evaluated in the context of domestic public opinion. A poll by the Foreign Policy Association questions the likelihood of public support for

American military intervention if the P.R.C. invades Taiwan, the most blatant option Beijing has.[146]

A second limit to action is that as a superpower the U.S. has many interests other than Taiwan. One or more of those may already be claiming American attention and resources when a Taiwan crisis develops. Also, U.S. action in one area affects relations with nations in other areas. China could use American commitments to instigate a crisis in some other part of the world to divert American attention and resources as it prepared to act against Taiwan. This would fit neatly into the classic Chinese approach to warfare.

The foundation of U.S. policy for the past half century has been "strategic ambiguity." This has left both the P.R.C. and Taiwan unsure of how the U.S. would respond to conflict in the Taiwan Strait – and that is how U.S. leaders have wanted it. This policy should be retained. It may not be the best policy, but none of the alternatives is better.

Strategic ambiguity's great advantage is it gives the U.S. room to maneuver. It also encourages caution on the part of both China and Taiwan because neither can ever be quite sure how the U.S. will act in a particular situation. The policy reflects the reality the U.S. cannot be sure how it will act in a crisis until one actually occurs.

Too much of a shift in either direction is liable to tempt the gaining party to take destabilizing risks. The U.S. can always fill in details quietly to each party within the overall policy. The policy does not prevent the U.S. from telling Taiwan and the P.R.C. it views particular actions by each to be out of bounds and automatically precluding or mandating U.S. military intervention.

Probably the greatest advantage in an age of media-driven foreign policy is everyone knows the U.S. probably will act, but no one is quite sure how. The imprecision of strategic ambiguity provides U.S. leaders with flexibility and time to think if crisis arises. The U.S. response can be tailored to the particular crisis and not constrained by previous public statements. If the U.S. does decide it must act to prevent Chinese action against Taiwan, it should do so early and delicately enough to permit China a way out that doesn't cause it to lose face – as happened in 1996.

Withdrawal would have the same practical result as openly supporting the P.R.C.'s claim to Taiwan. Both courses would have domestic U.S. and regional repercussions. Domestically, there could be a revival of the "Who lost China?" debate of the 1950s, exacerbated by the fact Taiwan is a democracy in a way Nationalist China never was. Regionally, the action would undercut the credibility of U.S. commitments to allies, who likely would seek alternate security means or cut a deal with China.[147] Here, Japan with military and technological potential and regional history becomes a matter of concern. According to Charles Freeman, "A U.S. failure to respond to a P.R.C. attack on Taiwan would so devalue the U.S.-Japan relationship that Japanese would feel even more impelled to develop a military capable of independent action to defend their strategic interest."[148]

Open U.S. support for Taiwan might not lead to a formal declaration of independence, but certainly would encourage Taiwan in that direction. Such support would require a clear American security commitment. This would be unacceptable to the P.R.C. and would result in Chinese coercion against the U.S. and Taiwan. A declaration of independence or Taiwan's obstinacy in the face of P.R.C. coercion probably would result in war.

Open U.S. support of Taiwan would mean U.S. facilities in the region could be targeted as well as the Taiwan military. P.R.C. military have threatened this, and the missiles that can reach Japan and other U.S. allies are nuclear-capable.[149] Chinese military history demonstrates readiness to use surprise attacks, especially against more powerful foes.[150]

During earlier crises, the U.S. was able to plan a response without needing to consider China's capability to harm American forces in the region, much less the continental United States. For any future crisis involving the P.R.C., the U.S. must consider China's potential use of conventional, cyber and nuclear weapons against U.S. forces in East Asia and the Pacific and targets in the continental United States.

While many consider the statement by a Chinese general that the P.R.C. could act militarily against Taiwan without fear of U.S. intervention because U.S. leaders "care more about Los Angeles than they do about Taiwan" to include a great deal of bluff, it would be foolish to ignore such threats. It is not clear the P.R.C. leadership understands the seriousness of using nuclear weapons against another nuclear power, especially first use.[151] In any case, all future U.S. planning regarding Taiwan must include the remote possibility it could escalate into a nuclear war.[152]

Current U.S. doctrine includes attacking the enemy's command and control system, strategic weapons, airfields, and communications and utilities infrastructure, but the U.S. has never fought even a regional war against another nuclear power. American war planning for the Taiwan Strait should consider potential consequences of striking Mainland Chinese facilities – or allowing Taiwan to do so – and consider options that do not risk escalation to nuclear war.[153]

The U.S. must also plan for a protracted crisis. Democracies do not handle long-term conflicts well, and the U.S. is known for its desire to get in, get done and get out. The P.R.C. would be at an advantage if the U. S. had to deploy resources to the region over an extended period, without the crisis ever rising to a level that would require military intervention. How the American public, Congress and American allies would respond to the expense, stress and impact on the U.S. to meeting its responsibilities in other areas is unclear, but history is not encouraging.

One possibility relates to China's self-image as a moral exemplar. This both places a limit on how the U.S. can deal with China and opens a door. The limit is the U.S. should neither put China in a place where it is forced to see itself or allow others to see it as acting immorally nor use language that portrays China's behavior toward Taiwan as immoral.

At the same time, it might be possible to portray to China what could constitute a settlement of the Taiwan situation that leaves Taiwan separate from China (but not formally independent) and puts China in a morally favorable light. This would have to be approached cautiously because of China's sovereignty concern and fear of internal instability, but as a long-term process, it might offer the greatest prospect of enduring peace.

Taiwan would have to be encouraged at the same time to accept the status quo with its lack of "international space" for the foreseeable future in order to ease domestic pressure on Chinese leaders. To be successful, this policy would have to maintain the status quo for several generations in hope Chinese irredentism would moderate over time.

Deterrence theory suggests effective deterrence requires understanding the motivation and degree of determination of our adversary. Ellis says the U.S. should "determine the pressure points to which Chinese leadership will respond."[154] Applying this to China's expressed concerns about national sovereignty and territorial integrity, the threat to encourage separatist movements within Mainland China would strike at a matter of expressed Chinese interest and concern. It would also be relatively inexpensive and unlikely to result in a direct U.S.-P.R.C. military confrontation.

The downside is being able to turn the threat off as readily as one turns it on. This option would require major preparation, and it could easily outpace U.S. ability to control or halt it. This option would also be constrained by both American law governing covert operations and domestic opinion when the operation became public knowledge (as it surely would).

A final possibility, one whose application in this case is unclear, would be to make conquering Taiwan appear much less valuable to China than it now does. This seems to be difficult to implement because China's greatest perceived benefits are self-image and prestige, not economic resources or strategic position.

Given Taiwan's rugged interior and history of guerrilla activity against occupiers, well-publicized preparations for such operations and a discrete American expression of readiness to encourage and even assist them would warn China it could be entering into a situation that could slowly bleed its resources in the way Vietnam did the U.S. and Afghanistan did the Soviet Union. But would this threat deter China? Probably not.

Japan's Role

More than half a century after its defeat in World War II, Japan remains in an awkward position in East Asia. Despite its peace constitution, relatively small military and weakened economy, Japan's neighbors have not forgotten its imperialist history and continue to fear the possibility of a remilitarized Japan. Japan has the strong scientific and economic foundation to quickly develop a powerful military. Japan has its own regional concerns, not the least of which is a potentially powerful China. Chinese success against Taiwan would only increase the P.R.C.'s regional power and the danger to Japan. Control of Taiwan would put the P.R.C. astride the sea lanes through which passes much of Japan's commerce.

For Japan, the best option is continuation of the status quo, both in the China-Taiwan relationship and in the Japanese-American relationship. While the mutual security treaty and more recent security guidelines create obligation on Japan's part, they also protect Japan from the need to create a powerful military with the regional reaction this would engender. If it so decided, Japan could quickly become the peer (other than in size) of any regional power except the United States.

Conflict in the Taiwan Strait would be a nightmare for Japan. Japan would have to choose between its U.S. alliance and the strategic benefit of a non-hostile relationship with China. Freeman believes this dilemma would lead many Japanese to advocate developing an independent defense force to pursue Japan's strategic interests.[155] Because of lingering anti-Japanese feelings in China, any direct Japanese involvement in a Taiwan crisis would likely exacerbate the crisis and even provoke escalation.[156]

Japan's current leaders are disinclined to accept guilt for Japan's imperial past and are also taking a close look at the U.S.-Japan security alliance. While the alliance is less costly to Japan and less threatening to Japan's neighbors than other options, it brings with it the domestic consequences of having American military bases in Japan and is a source of contention on Okinawa where most of the U.S. bases are located.

Conclusions

The Taiwan Strait remains a potential flash point between the United States and China. This is not only because the U.S. has interests in the East Asia-Pacific region that conflict with China's, but also because the current status of Taiwan focuses those interests in a way that demonstrates their incompatibility. The tension has existed for 60 years without war, but the past is no guarantee of the future. The leaders of the P.R.C. appear to take the possibility of war more seriously than do American leaders and are preparing for that eventuality. There is the distinct possibility the U.S. and Taiwan are preparing for a different type of military crisis than the P.R.C. may be planning. The more this is true, the less successful will be deterrence efforts.

Part of the complexity the U.S. faces is historical attachment to Taiwan, but "Taiwan is a place that Americans ought to like."[157] In a part of the world populated by dictatorships and failed democracies, Taiwan has progressed in less than 20 years from a reactionary dictatorship to a vibrant, if rowdy, democracy. It has a strong economy, vibrant society and a range of freedoms. Taiwan offers a model for other Asian states, and that makes China uncomfortable.

All parties would prefer the status quo continues. This worked well through the late 1980s, but political and economic developments have frayed it. So China and Taiwan no longer understand the status quo in precisely the same way. The new dynamic threatens regional stability because China faces the possibility of Taiwan following a separate path. Acquiescing in this would be political suicide for China's leaders.

Most discussion of the Taiwan situation emphasizes the military elements. These are important, but not the most important. The P.R.C.-U.S.-Taiwan relationship is fundamentally political and can only be settled politically. The military emphasis avoids the hard work of developing non-military options acceptable to all. Just as strategists attempt to "think outside the box" to develop better military solutions, so too must policymakers think unconventionally about Taiwan to find creative possibilities short of war.

The U.S. military has planned and war-gamed conflict in the Taiwan Strait. The question is whether it has been preparing for the right conflict. When deterrence breaks down, the course of action the U.S. has been preparing for may not be the one China chooses – and China is likely to strike first in case of war. China would prefer to gain control of Taiwan in a way that provides the U.S. no rationale for intervening and every incentive not to. American leaders should consider now how they might respond then, instead of waiting for a *fait accompli*. It is essential to convince Chinese decision-makers to remember Pearl Harbor and not "Blackhawk Down" when they think about American willingness to fight. At the same time, U.S. and Taiwanese leaders should remember other, no less crucial lessons of Pearl Harbor.

China brings many advantages to conflict in the Taiwan Strait. Geography is obvious, but probably even greater is timing. Unless Taiwan for some reason decides to strike first, China can decide when, how and even where to act. The ideal time for China would be when the United States is distracted by another part of the world and has deployed significant forces there.

In a war over Taiwan, everyone will lose, but some more than others (Taiwan the most). The military, political and economic cost will be high. The consequence of the P.R.C. forcibly gaining control over Taiwan without an American response would probably be even more serious because of the regional military and political repercussions. China's stated interests are such that, apart from an unexpected resolution, deterrence will almost certainly fail in the long run.

The U. S. can delay Chinese action against Taiwan, but cannot deter China indefinitely. At least in part, this is because China does not believe American interests and commitment match those of China. The U.S. needs to clearly define and explain its interests relating to Taiwan, both to the American public and to China's leaders.

The best situation would be an indefinite continuation of the status quo and of the American policy of strategic ambiguity. The former is unlikely, but the latter is possible. It will require close coordination within the U.S. government, careful consideration of the military and political impact of deploying a missile defense system to the region, continued visible American military presence in the region, and encouragement to the P.R.C. and Taiwan to explore unconventional options for settling the future status of Taiwan.

The United States should begin by gaining a better understanding of how China sees itself and its place in the world. U.S. policymakers also need to consider how their words and actions appear to Chinese and Taiwanese leaders. What they intend from their historical and cultural perspective is not necessarily what the Chinese see from theirs.

Equally important is recognizing the many Chinese misperceptions about the United States and working to correct them. Planners will have to take these misperceptions into account because they can increase political friction and lead to military conflict. The most serious misperception is the U.S. actively seeks to weaken China and block its rise and every U.S. action in the region is directed toward this end.[158]

Apart from a Taiwanese misstep, the crucial variable is the perception of China's leaders. While recognizing Chinese interests regarding Taiwan, the U.S. must clearly state its interests in the area and a willingness to use force to defend them – without compromising the strategic ambiguity that has been central to U.S. policy. This should be balanced by encouraging China and Taiwan to see the advantages, especially economic, that derive from the status quo.

The greatest danger is if China's leaders come to believe they have more control over the situation than they actually do or they become convinced they have run out of options. There will be some situations where China believes the time is right for action, and it has the advantage, but can be convinced otherwise. Under other conditions, however, the cost becomes irrelevant and nothing will deter China from taking military action against Taiwan.

Notes

[1] In this study, People's Republic of China (P.R.C.) or China designates the nation the United States, the United Nations and most of the world's countries recognize as China. The government of the Republic of China and the island it is primarily located on will be called Taiwan. While this study focuses on the U.S.-P.R.C.-Taiwan relationship, it is important to remember Taiwan is not the only point of disagreement between the P.R.C. and the U.S.

[2] Denny Roy, *Taiwan Strait Update: Crisis Deferred* (Honolulu: Asia-Pacific Center for Security Studies, February 2006), 2.

[3] Department of Defense, *National Defense Strategy* (June 2008). The 2010 National Security Strategy, however, describes the military situation more indirectly and encourages development of a cooperative relationship between the U.S. and the P.R.C. See Barak Obama, *National Security Strategy* (Washington: The White House, May 2010), 43.

[4] Michael McDevitt, "For Taiwan, the Best Defense Is Not a Good Offense" (Pacific Forum CSIS, PacNet Number 9, Feb. 22, 2007). See also Kenneth Lieberthal, "Preventing a War over Taiwan," *Foreign Affairs* 84/2 (March/April 2005), 53.

[5] Su Ge, "Sino-American Relations: Climbing High to See Afar," *Xiandai Guoji Guanxi,* (September 2001), as found on the U.S.-China Commission web site, http:www.uscc.gov (Nov. 6, 2002).

[6] Richard K. Betts and Thomas J. Christensen, "China: Getting the Questions Right," *National Interest* 62, (Winter 2000/2001), p.17.

[7] Denny Roy, "Tensions in the Taiwan Strait," *Survival* 42 (2000), 78.

[8] Roy, *Taiwan Strait Update: Crisis Deferred*, p. 8.

[9] I am indebted to Alan Wachman for the language to make this distinction between delaying and deterring clear.

[10] Roger Cliff, et al, *Entering the Dragon's Laire: Chinese Antiaccess Stretagies and Their Implications for the United States,* "Some of the measures are relatively low cost, but others will require additional capabilities and still others may require a fundamental reassessment of operational doctrine and plans" (Santa Monica: Rand, 2007), xix.

[11] See, for example, Gao Fuqiu, "The Real Purpose of the American March into Central Asia," *Liaowing* (May 10, 2002), as found on the US-China Commission web site, http:www.uscc.gov (Nov. 6, 2002). Su warns the P.R.C. will not permit Taiwan's status as part of China to change.

[12] I am indebted to Andrew Scobell for emphasizing to me the P.R.C.'s self-image as an international moral leader.

[13] Wang Jisi and Xu Hui, "Pattern of Sino-American Crises: A Chinese Perspective," in Michael D. Swaine, et al. (editors). *Managing Sino-American Crises: Case Studies and Analysis* (Washington, DC: Carnegie Endowment for International Peace, 2006), 135

[14] Hao Yufan and Zhai Zhihai, "China's Decision to Enter the Korean War: History Revisited," *China Quarterly* 121 (1990), 115.

[15] Cited in Jaw-ling Joanne Chang, "Lessons from the Taiwan Relations Act," *Orbis* 44, (2000), 69.

[16] David A. Shlapak, et al., *A Question of Balance: Political Context and Military Aspects of the China-Taiwan Dispute* (Santa Monica: Rand, 2009), 141.

[17] Alan Wachman, *Challenges and Opportunities in the Taiwan Strait: Defining America's Role*, China Policy Series Number 17 (New York: National Committee on United States-China Relations, 2001), 27.

[18] Alastair Iain Johnston, *Cultural Realism: Strategic Culture and Grand Strategy in Chinese History* (Princeton: Princeton University Press, 1995). Scobell suggests both the Confucian-Mencian and *realpolitik* approaches are operative and interactive, combining dialectically. This could explain how China can display realism while at the same time claiming the moral high ground. Scobell made this suggestion at a conference on "The Rise of China: Security Implications" in Chapel Hill, N.C. (March 2-3, 2001).

[19] Ibid., 256-257.

[20] Andrew Scobell, *China and Strategic Culture,* (Carlisle, Pa.: Strategic Studies Institute, 2002), 3.

[21] Ibid, 3. What Scobell calls preemptive is better described as surprise attacks. See also Michael D. Swaine, "Chinese Crisis Management: Framework for Analysis, Tentative Observations, and Questions for the Future," in Andrew Scobell and Larry M. Wortzel (editors.), *Chinese National Security Decisionmaking under Stress* (Carlisle, Pa.: Strategic Studies Institute, 2005), 36.

[22] In his *China Debates the Future Security Environment* (Washington: National Defense University, 2000), xv and 39. Michael Pillsbury applies this to the U.S.-P.R.C. relationship and comments in particular that China seems to assume other nations share its view about the future use of military force. Interestingly, however, while the P.R.C. sees itself as a peace-loving nation, it views the United States as guided by *realpolitik*. This makes it very difficult for China to take "soft" American interests regarding Taiwan seriously. It also means not only that China sees itself as peace-loving, but also expects other nations to see it this way despite any actions to the contrary.

[23] Swaine in Scobell and Wortzel, *Chinese National Security Decisionmaking under Stress*, 23. "In China, domestic factions often are critically important in a political-military crisis, and, in some instances, arguably more important than external factors.... Both elite and popular views and actions involving internal issues and concerns can limit options, increase rigidity, slow response times, and distort signals in a crisis."

[24] Most of the insights in this paragraph come from Robert Jervis, *Perception and Misperception in International Politics* (Princeton: Princeton University Press, 1976).

[25] Michael D. Swaine, "Conclusion: Implications, Questions, and Recommendations," in Michael D. Swaine, *Managing Sino-American Crises,* 436.

[26] Susan L. Craig, *Chinese Perceptions of Traditional and Nontraditional Security Threats* (Carlisle, Pa.: Strategic Studies Institute, 2007), 1.

[27] Ezra F. Vogel, "Current U.S.-China Relations," *Harvard China Review* 2 (Spring/Summer 2000), 21-22.

[28] Phillip C. Saunders, "China's America Watchers: Changing Attitudes towards the United States," *China Quarterly* 161 (2000), 50-51.

[29] John W. Garver, *Face Off: China, the United States, and Taiwan's Democratization* (Seattle: University of Washington Press, 1997), 150-151.

[30] Michael D. Swaine and Oriana Skylar Mastro, "Assessing the Threat," in Swaine, et al. (editors), *Assessing the Threat: The Chinese Military and Taiwan's Security* (Washington, DC: Carnegie Endowment for International Peace, 2007), 351.

[31] Richard Halloran, "Who's the Sleeping Tiger Now? U.S.?" *Boston Globe* (Sept. 10, 2000), F2. Halloran was specifically addressing the U.S.-China-Taiwan relationship and challenging the widespread misperception that the U.S. is afraid to suffer casualties under any circumstance.

[32] Richard Sobol at a discussion of his book, *The Impact of Public Opinion on U.S. Foreign Policy Since Vietnam,* at the Harvard COOP Bookstore (March 12, 2001).

[33] Statement of Zhu Xianlong in *Zhongguo Pinglun* (March 5, 1999), quoted in Roy, "Tensions in the Taiwan Strait," 88. See also Andrew J. Nathan "China's Goals in the Taiwan Strait," *China Journal* 36 (1996), 90; James Mulvenon, "P.R.C. Information Operations: Myths, Trends, and New Opportunities," 246, in Swaine, *Assessing the Threat*; Denny Roy, *Taiwan's Threat Perceptions: The Enemy Within*, Occasional Paper Series (Honolulu: Asia-Pacific Center for Security Studies, March 2003), 2.

[34] See Phillip C. Saunders, "Project Strait Talk: Security and Stability in the Taiwan Strait," Center for Nonproliferation Studies (Monterey: Monterey Institute of International Studies, July 2000), 5, 6.

[35] Desmond Ball, "Strategic Culture in the Asian-Pacific Region," *Security Studies* 3 (1993), 63-64.

[36] Saunders, 9.

[37] Interview with Alan Wachman at the Fletcher School of Law and Diplomacy (Feb. 8, 2001). Dr. Wachman was one of the academics involved in the conversation.

[38] Alan D. Romberg, "Future East Asian Security Architecture: Implications for the PLA," in Swaine, *Assessing the Threat,* 319.

[39] Craig, *Chinese Perceptions of Traditional and Nontraditional Security Threats*, p. 47; Richard E. Nisbett, *The Geography of Thought: How Asians and Westerners Think Differently ... and Why* (New York: Free Press, 2003), 45.

[40] Vogel, 21-22.

[41] Garver, 147; Wang and Xu, in Swaine, *Managing Sino-American Crises*, 139.

[42] Robert D. Kaplan, "The Geography of Chinese Power: How Far Can Beijing Reach on Land and at Sea?," *Foreign Affairs* 89/3 (May/June 2010), 38.

[43] Garver, 147.

[44] Alastair Iain Johnston, "China's Militarized Interstate Dispute Behaviour 1949-1992: A First Cut at the Data," *China Quarterly* 153 (1998), 2.

[45] Lonnie D. Henly, "Evolving Chinese Concepts of War Control and Escalation Management," in Swaine, *Assessing the Threat,* 97. "One finds little consideration of the possibility that what China considers a resolute response to maintain the political initiative, the opponent might misconstrue as alarming preparations for aggressive military action. Chinese military authors seem to be unable to get outside of their own subjective view of

china's innocent intentions and righteous principled stance to see China as others might view it."

[46] See Global Views Survey Research Center, *Survey on Signing of Economic Cooperation Agreement with Other Countries, People's Views on Unification with China and Independence and President Ma Ying-jeou's Approval Rating* (March 23, 2010), 3, http://taiwansecurity.org/2010/GVMaApproval_ECFA-032310.pdf, (May 31, 2010).

[47] Andrew Scobell, *Show of Force: The PLA and the 1995-96 Taiwan Strait Crisis* (Carlisle, Pa.: Strategic Studies Institute, 1999), 16.

[48] Taiwan Affairs Office and Information Office of the P.R.C. State Council, "The One-China Principle and the Taiwan Issue," (issued Feb. 21, 2000,) *Asian Affairs* 27 (2000), 37-53.

[49] Banyan, "Bottoming out," *The Economist* 395/8678 (April 17-23, 2010), 50. It has been suggested the P.R.C. has overstated U.S. decline and the P.R.C.'s rise, emphasizing U.S. weakness while minimizing Chinese weaknesses and greatly overrating China's economic leverage over the U.S.

[50] David A. Shlapak, et al., *A Question of Balance: Political Context and Military Aspects of the China-Taiwan Dispute* (Santa Monica: RAND, 2009), 12. Shlapak says the P.R.C. has found economic coercion a potentially powerful weapon, but one difficult to use effectively.

[51] Shlapak, *A Question of Balance,* 16.

[52] *National Security Strategy* (2010), 43.

[53] Denny Roy, *Taiwan's Threat Perceptions: The Enemy Within*, 8.

[54] Jacob K. Javits, "Congress and Foreign Relations: The Taiwan Relations Act," *Foreign Affairs* 60 (Fall 1981), 59.

[55] Ralph N. Clough, *Reaching Across the Taiwan Strait: People-to-People Diplomacy* (Boulder: Westview, 1993), 187. See also Denny Roy, "Rising China and U.S. Interests: Inevitable vs. Contingent Hazards," *Orbis* 47/1, (Winter 2003), 136.

[56] Denny Roy, "U.S.-Taiwan Arms Sales: The Perils of Doing Business with Friends," *Asia-Pacific Security Studies* 3/3 (April 2004), 4.

[57] Aaron L. Friedberg, "The Struggle for Mastery in Asia," *Commentary* 110 (November 2000), 17. At an IFPA-Fletcher-USMC Security Conference in 2001, Ambassador Stephen Bosworth said if an East Asian state achieved regional hegemonic status, U.S. vital interests would be very much affected. William Perry, then-Secretary of Defense, says in March 1996, then-National Security Advisor Anthony Lake told a delegation of senior Chinese officials the U.S. has vital national security interests in the western Pacific and the ongoing Chinese missile firings threatened those interests. See Ashton B. Carter and William J. Perry, *Preventative Defense: A New Security Strategy for America,* (Washington: Brookings Institute, 1999), pp. 96-97.

[58] Kurt Campbell, in a luncheon presentation at MIT's Security Studies Program (Nov. 1, 2000).

[59] Sandy Berger, National Security Adviser during the Clinton administration, at Harvard's JFK School of Government (March 12, 2001). Governments like that of the P.R.C. often find it difficult to understand and respond to the American habit of making its national values part of its international relations – especially when these would appear to

detrimental to U.S. national interest narrowly defined. Yet given the right set of circumstances, the P.R.C. would respond to Taiwan in a way other nations might consider irrational and contrary to its national interest.

[60] Douglas Porch, "The Taiwan Strait Crisis of 1996: Strategic Implications for the United States Navy," *Naval War College Review* 52 (1999), 29.

[61] Ephraim Kam, *Surprise Attack: The Victim's Perspective* (Cambridge: Harvard University Press, 1988), 71.

[62] Recent reports suggest neither the P.R.C. nor Taiwan has integrated the weaponry it possesses. In addition, the P.R.C. pilots do not appear to be well trained or to receive sufficient flying hours each year to maintain proficiency. Taiwan has been reported to suffer a lack of pilots for its latest generation fighters because many pilots leave the air force to fly for the airlines.

[63] Department of Defense, "Report to Congress Pursuant to Public Law 106-113" (Dec. 18, 2000), DefenseLink at http://www.defenselink.mil/twstrait_12182000.html, (Dec. 20, 2000).

[64] Michael D. Swaine, "Chinese Crisis Management: Framework for Analysis, Tentative Observations and Questions for the Future," in Scobell and Wortzle, *Chinese National Security Decisionmaking Under Stress,* 28. "This critical set of variables influencing China's crisis management behavior is very poorly understood in the West, and even, it seems, within much of the Chinese political system."

[65] Michael Pillsbury, "China's Military Strategy toward the U.S.: A View from Open Sources" (Nov. 2, 2001), 4, U.S.-China Commission website http://www.uscc.gov, (Nov. 5, 2002).

[66] Swaine and Mastro, "Assessing the Threat," 346, in Swaine, *Assessing the Threat.* See also Shlapak, *A Question of Balance, passim.*

[67] Mark A. Stokes, *China's Strategic Modernization: Implications for the United States* (Carlisle, Pa.: Strategic Studies Institute, 1999), 145.

[68] Jason D. Ellis and Todd M. Koca, "China Rising: New Challenges to the U.S. Security Posture," Strategic Forum number 175, Institute for National Security Studies (Washington: National Defense University, 2000), 7.

[69] Office of the Secretary of Defense, *Annual Report to Congress: Military Power of the People's Republic of China 2009* (March 2009), I.

[70] Swaine and Mastro, 345. See also Eric Hagt and Matthew Durnin, "China's Antiship Ballistic Missile: Developments and Missing Links," *Naval War College Review* 62/4 (Autumn 2009), 93, 95. They note hitting a moving ship with an antiship ballistic missile requires synchronizing a lot of very advanced technology and are skeptical that China has all the technology, much less the ability to synchronize it.

[60] Office of the Secretary of Defense, *Annual Report on the Military Power of the People's Republic of China* (March 2009), 15.

[72] Richard A. Bitzinger, "Taipei's Arms Procurement Dilemma: Implications for Defending Taiwan," *Asia-Pacific Security Studies 3/4*, (April 2004), 2.

[73] Stokes, 137.

[74] "Q&A with Robert Kaplan on China," n.p., *Foreign Affairs* (May 7, 2010), http://www.foreignaffairs.com/discussions/interviews/qa-robert-kaplan-on-china, (May 14, 2010).

[75] For an excellent overview of China's Information Warfare program, see Toshi Yoshihara, *Chinese Information Warfare: A Phantom Menace or Emerging Threat?* (Carlisle, Pa.: Strategic Studies Institute, 2002).

[76] Timothy L. Thomas, "Like Adding Wings to a Tiger: Chinese Information War Theory and Practice" (Ft. Leavenworth, Kansas, Foreign Military Studies Office, 2001), 2, http://call.army.mil/ call/fmso/fmsopubs/ issues/China, (Feb. 1, 2001).

[77] James Mulvenon, "The PLA and Information Warfare," 176, in James Mulvenon (ed.), *The People's Liberation Army in the Information Age,* (Santa Monica, Calif.: RAND, 1999), 183, Mulvenon also notes P.R.C. military planners tend to view IW as a preemptive weapon, which would make it especially attractive in a Taiwan scenario. Actually, we know something about Chinese cyber war capabilities because they have been used in various ways against the U.S. since 1999.

[78] Richard A. Clarke and Robert K. Knake, *Cyber War: The Next Threat to National Security and What to Do about It* (New York: HarperCollins, 2010). See especially Chapter 6. See also Wesley Clark and Peter Levin, "Securing the Information Highway," *Foreign Affairs* 88/6, (November/December 2009), 2-10.

[79] Mulvenon, in Swaine, *Assessing the Threat*, 256.

[80] Shlapak, *A Question of Balance*, p. 118, "An invasion of Taiwan would, in the face of properly prepared defenses, remain a bold and possibly foolish gamble on Beijing's part."

[81] See Yu Chuanxin, "A Few Issues Concerning Logistic Support for the Cross-strait Amphibious Landing Operation," *Journal of Military Economics Studies* (Jan. 15, 2001), 1, as found in translation on the U.S.-China Commission website, http://www.uscc.gov, (Nov. 6, 2002).

[82] Steven M. Goldstein, "China's Taiwan Strategy: Status Quo or Disequilibrium?" p. 186, in Jonathan B. Pollock (ed.), *Strategic Surprise? U.S.-China Relations in the Early Twenty-first Century* (Newport, R.I., Naval War College Press, 2003). "All these trends suggest that submarines will form the centerpiece of a gradual Chinese strategic reorientation toward maritime priorities." Robert Kaplan notes that a Chinese attack submarine tracked a U.S. carrier strike group in the Pacific undetected, finally surfacing within five miles of the carrier itself.

[83] Pillsbury, "China's Military Strategy toward the U.S.," 4. As Pillsbury notes, it is unclear how much influence this group has on P.R.C. military policy making.

[84] Pillsbury, "China's Military Strategy toward the U.S., 10-11. Pillsbury notes a People's Liberation Army Navy (PLAN) officer as writing that instead of going head-to-head with U.S. Navy combatants, the PLAN should concentrate on attacking American naval command and control, information systems, and logistics because these are the minimally protected weak links in the system.

[85] Pillsbury, "China's Military Strategy toward the U.S.," 9-10.

[86] Tim Thomas, "China's Technological Stratagems," *Jane's Intelligence Review* 12 (December 2000), 39.

[87] Pew Research Center for the People & the Press, *America's Place in the World 2009: An Investigation of Public and Leadership Opinion About International Affairs*, (Dec. 2009), 2-3. A recent Pew survey found both that half of Americans believe the U.S. should "mind its own business and let other countries get along the best they can on their own," and that the public views a rising China as more worrisome than do opinion leaders.

[88] "Q&A with Robert Kaplan on China," n.p.

[89] Tom Donnelly, "Dire Strait," *Jane's Defense Weekly* 35 (March 14, 2001), 26.

[90] Mark A. Stokes, "China's Military Space and Conventional Theater Missile Development: Implications for Security in the Taiwan Strait," 151, in Susan M. Puska (ed.), *People's Liberation Army after Next* (Carlisle, Pa., Strategic Studies Institute, 2000). Roy, *Taiwan's Threat* Perceptions, 5. Taiwan's population apparently supports a force structure that would enable punitive strikes against the P.R.C. if it launched a missile attack on the island.

[91] This has become a political and security issue in the U.S. because compromise of the technology of the latest version of the F-16 fighter would harm U.S. airpower as well as Taiwan's.

[92] Drew Thompson, "China's Temper Tantrum," *The National Interest Online* (Feb. 2, 2010), http://www.nationalinterest.org/PrinterFriendly.aspx?id=22832, (March 22, 2010).

[93] David A. Shlapak, David T. Orlesky, and Barry A. Wilson, *Dire Strait? Aspects of the China-Taiwan Confrontation and Options for U.S. Policy* (Santa Monica: RAND, 2000), 51-54. Shlapak's 2009 update to the study, *A Question of Balance*, does not change this conclusion.

[94] Thomas J. Christensen, "Theater Missile Defense and Taiwan's Security," *Orbis* 44 (2000), 83.

[95] See Schlapak, *A Question of Balance, passim*, for a current assessment of Chinese capabilities.

[96] Stokes in Puska, *People's Liberation Army after Next,* 151.

[97] Richard Bush, "Chinese Decisionmaking under Stress: The Taiwan Strait, 1995-2004," 150, "As part of its negotiations playbook, Beijing seeks to get it adversary's acceptance of basic principles at the outset, which it manipulates to its advantage thereafter."

[98] Johnston, "China's Militarized Interstate Dispute Behaviour 1949-1992: A First Cut at the Data," 6-7, 28-29.

[99] See *NSS,* (2010), 43. The 2010 National Security Strategy seeks to counter this: "We welcome a China that takes on a responsible leadership role in working with the United States and the international community to advance priorities like economic recovery, confronting climate change, and nonproliferation."

[100] Swaine and Mastro, "Assessing the Threat," 346. McDevitt says the only way Taiwan can deter the P.R.C. militarily is to convince it that it cannot seize the island. This would require hard economic decisions in order to create a military that could do this. Also, "many observers assert that Taiwan is not improving its own military capabilities in many areas to a level and at a pace sufficient to ensure the maintenance of a credible deterrent against Chinese coercion or a PLA attack."

[101] Roy, *Taiwan's Threat Perceptions*, 8. "Ultimately much of Taiwan's insecurity stems from sources within Taiwan itself.... Taiwan in some instances lacks a mature democracy's capacity for serious, rational debate on important questions."

[102] Roy, *Taiwan's Threat Perceptions*, 5.

[103] Ken Booth, *Strategy and Ethnocentrism,* (New York: Holmes & Meier, 1979), 55. "'Reasonable Western thinking finds it very difficult to accept that there are some conflicts which cannot be 'settled' other than by brute force."

[104] Americans forget other countries have the same problem in dealing with the United States, where domestic concerns often take priority over what would otherwise be pressing foreign policy matters and can lead to foreign policy decisions that make no sense if one does not know the domestic influences at work.

[105] I have drawn much of what I say about deterrence theory from Edward Rhoades, "Conventional Deterrence," *Comparative Strategy* 19 (2000), 221-253, Keith B. Payne, *Deterrence in the Second Nuclear Age,* (Lexington: University of Kentucky Press, 1996), and Michael S. Gerson, "Conventional Deterrence in the Second Nuclear Age," *Parameters* 39/3, (autumn 2009), 32-48. For attempts to apply deterrence theory to China, I am indebted to Robert S. Ross, Shu Guang Zhang and Abram N. Shulsky, among others. For an application of this to the Taiwan Strait, see Shlapak, *A Question of Balance*, 141-142. The conclusions with respect to China, however, are my own.

[106] Abram N. Shulsky, *Deterrence Theory and Chinese Behavior* (Santa Monica: RAND, 2000), 17.

[107] This is not solely a matter of applying moral standards to deterrence; a grossly disproportional threat is likely to lack credibility. Such a threat would be neither moral nor a deterrent. My assumption here is we should apply Just War criteria to deterrence in the same way we do (or should do) to war itself. After all, when deterrence fails, war is usually the result. I recognize for many this assumption creates a difficulty in regard to nuclear deterrence, but that is all the more reason to inject moral criteria at the beginning of the process instead of appending them as an afterthought.

[108] Gerson, 40. "The credibility of conventional deterrence – and execution of the threat if deterrence fails – requires convincing potential aggressors the United States can and will rapidly respond to aggression against its global interests, and there is nothing the regime can do to prevent or hinder the response."

[109] Allen S. Whiting, *China Crosses the Yalu: The Decision to Enter the Korean War* (Stanford: Stanford University Press, 1960), 109-110.

[110] Gerson, 42. "Leaders motivated by the necessity to prevent losing something of value, however, may be willing to engage in a long and expensive conflict, especially if the stakes are deemed critical to national security or domestic political survival."

[111] Shu Guang Zhang, *Deterrence and Strategic Culture: Chinese-American Confrontations, 1949-1958* (Ithaca: Cornell University, 1992), 272, 4.

[112] Rhoades, 222, 228.

[113] Ibid., 234-238.

[114] Payne, 79.

[115] Rhoades, 243.

[116] Robert Jervis, quoted in Rhoades, 238.

[117] Rhoades, 239.

[118] Payne, 121. "Because it is the challenger who ultimately chooses whether to be deterred but who cannot be controlled predictably, no deterrer, including the United States, can establish deterrence policies that it can be confident are 'ensured' or 'conclusive.'"

[119] Shulsky, 36.

[120] Shulsky, 35, 38, 39.

[121] Denny Roy, *China's Foreign Relations* (Lanham, MD: Rowman & Littlefield, 1998), 217.

[122] See Zalmay Khalilzad, et al., *The United States and a Rising China*, (Santa Monica: RAND, 1999), 85, and Alistair Iain Johnston, "China's New 'Old Thinking,'" *International Security* 20 (Winter 1995/96), 21.

[123] Shlapak, *A Question of Balance*, xix.

[124] Robert S. Ross, "The 1995-96 Taiwan Strait Confrontation: Coercion, Credibility, and the Use of Force," *International Security* 25 (2000), 104.

[125] I agree with Betts and Christensen, page 28, about this. China will use all available military, economic and political options to achieve its goal.

[126] See, for example, Roy, "Tensions in the Taiwan Strait," 78.

[127] Eric A. McVadon, "The Chinese Military and the Peripheral States in the 21st Century: A Security *Tour d'Horizon*," 34, in Larry M. Wortzel (ed.), *The Chinese Armed Forces in the 21st Century* (Carlisle, Pa.: Strategic Studies Institute, 1999).

[128] Bernice Lee, *The Security Implications of the New Taiwan*, Adelphi Paper 331, International Institute for Strategic Studies (New York: Oxford University Press, 1999), 53. "Taiwan's domestic political development is gradually pulling the island away from reunification with China. Leaders in Beijing remain uncertain as how to respond, but know their nationalist agenda gives them little scope for compromise."

[129] Shulsky, 46.

[130] *Taiwan News*, (Nov. 22, 2002), Taiwan Security Research website (Nov. 30, 2002). "Top Envoy Says China Willing to Disarm: Proposal Hinges on U.S. Reduction of Military Assistance."

[131] Roy, "Tensions in the Taiwan Strait," 90, and interview with Dr. Leif Rosenberger at CINCPAC headquarters, (Nov. 13, 2000). But the often-predicted Chinese economic collapse has yet to happen.

[132] Wachman, 17-18. See also Banyan, 50.

[133] Sun Zi, *The Art of War*, trans. by Samuel B. Griffith (New York: Oxford University Press, 1963), 77. "To subdue the enemy without fighting is the acme of skill." Those who understand this as the essence of Sun Zi's advice forget that it is surrounded by several hundred other sentences about how to fight wars, campaigns and battles.

[134] Mark Burles and Abram N. Shulsky, *Patterns in China's Use of Force: Evidence from History and Doctrinal Writings* (Santa Monica: RAND, 1999), 17.

[135] Maria Hsia Chang, "The Future of Taiwan-Mainland Relations," 212, in Bih-jaw Lin and James T. Myers (eds.), *Contemporary China and the Changing International Community* (Columbia: University of South Carolina Press, 1994). The 2002 China Security Review Commission report says Taiwan officials estimate the island could last only 120 days before it would require resupply of essential materials.

[136] Robert S. Ross, "The 1996 Taiwan Strait Crisis: Lessons for the United States, China and Taiwan," *Security Dialogue* 27 (1996), 468.

[137] Gerson, 33-34. Gerson says preventing this is central to modern conventional deterrence.

[138] Jianxiang Bi, "Managing Taiwan Operations in the Twenty-first Century: Issues and Options," *Naval War College Review* 52 (1999), 38.

[139] See Andrew J. Nathan and Bruce Gilley, *China's New Rulers: The Secret Files,* (New York: New York Review of Books, 2002), 216 f. In *China's New Rulers*, however, Andrew Nathan quotes three members of the fourth generation of P.R.C. leaders as believing growing economic and cultural ties will inevitably draw Taiwan to the Mainland, the Democratic Progressive Party is passing phenomena, and the language of Taiwanese independence is an American plot. In a September 2002 study, the Atlantic Council reached much the same conclusion. It said China's leaders now believe that the rapidly increasing investment in the Mainland by Taiwanese businessmen is the first step toward the eventual incorporation of Taiwan into China. See also Charles Snyder, "Beijing Now Thinks Time on its Side, Report Says," *Taipei Times* (Sept. 6, 2002), Taiwan Security Research website, (Dec. 2, 2002).

[140] Shlapak, Orlesky, and Wilson, p. 60.

[141] Michael O'Hanlon, "Why China Cannot Conquer Taiwan," *International Security* 25, (2000), p. 83.

[142] Jim Yardley and Thom Shanker. "Chinese Navy Buildup Gives Pentagon New Worries," *New York Times* (April 8, 2005), A3. "America's carriers responding to a crisis would now initially have to operate at least 500 miles from Taiwan" due to the threat of China's submarine fleet.

[143] China Security Review Commission, Report to the Congress of the U.S. (July 2002), Chapter 1, http://www.uscc.gov, (Oct. 28, 2002).

[144] International Crisis Group, *China and Taiwan: Uneasy Détente,* Asia Briefing No. 42 (Sept. 21, 2005), 5.

[145] Both China and Taiwan recognize American intervention almost certainly would be in support of Taiwan, the only questions being the nature and extent of intervention.

[146] Central News Agency (Taipei), "Poll Shows Americans Would Oppose Using Troops to Defend Taiwan," (Feb. 14, 2001), Taiwan Security Research homepage (Feb. 22, 2001). Other reports have suggested greater American support, especially if the P.R.C. attack were unprovoked and the U.S. president offered a clear and compelling statement of American interest in the outcome.

[147] Tucker, 153. "Even without formal obligations, many in the region think of Washington as Taipei's friend and patron, and might question their own relations with the U.S. if it stood aside."

[148] Charles W. Freeman, Jr., "Same Strait, Different Memories," 59, in Gerret W. Gong (ed.), *Remembering and Forgetting: The Legacy of War and Peace in East Asia,* (Washington: Center for Strategic & International Studies, 1996).

[149] China Security Review Commission, Report to the Congress of the U.S. (July 2002), Chapter 8, http://www.uscc.gov, (Oct. 28, 2002).

[150] Burles and Shulsky, vii.

[151] Brad Roberts, "The Nuclear Dimension: How likely? How Stable?" in Swaine, *Assessing the* Threat, 234. China appears to believe "the asymmetry of stake and interest between China and the United States in a Taiwan contingency would only be magnified in a war that crosses the nuclear threshold."

[152] An attendee at a March 2001 conference on "The Rise of China," afraid China shows insufficient responsibility in the way it uses its nuclear status, commented that during the Cold War, no Soviet leader ever threatened nuclear attack on specific American cities if the U.S. intervened conventionally in a conflict the Soviet Union was interested in.

[153] See Shlapak, Orlesky and Wilson, xxi.

[154] Ellis and Koca, 7.

[155] Freeman, "Same Strait, Different Memories," 59.

[156] Thomas J. Christensen, "China, the U.S.-Japan Alliance, and the Security Dilemma in East Asia," *International Security* 23 (1999), 67.

[157] Richard Bernstein and Ross H. Munro, *The Coming Conflict with China* (New York: Vintage, 1998), 149.

[158] Michael Pillsbury, "Dangerous Chinese Misperceptions: The Implications for DOD" (Washington: Department of Defense Office of New Assessment, 1998), 2, 4.

CHAPTER 5

Deterring a Nuclear-Armed Iran from Adventurism and Nuclear Use

Gregory F. Giles

Introduction

U.S. policy is to deter four kinds of Iranian behavior: (1) Iranian acquisition of nuclear weapons; (2) Iranian adventurism abetted by such nuclear acquisition, (3) direct military conflict with Iran's armed forces, and (4) escalation of U S.-Iranian military conflict to the use of nuclear weapons.

By definition, the advent of a "nuclear-armed Iran" means the failure of one form of U.S. deterrence strategy — the deterrence of proliferation. Both the Obama administration and its predecessor publicly committed the United States to keeping Tehran from acquiring nuclear weapons. So in postulating a nuclear-armed Iran, we must accept up front that U.S. credibility – a key component of deterrence – had suffered a serious blow, one that will generally make it harder subsequently to deter various threats from the Islamic Republic.

Of particular concern is nuclear-backed "adventurism," defined here as more risk-acceptant Iranian challenges to regional and global order than currently exist. Examples include heightened levels of: political-military-economic intimidation, support for terrorism and insurgency, clashes with U.S. naval forces in the Gulf, and the proliferation of weapons of mass destruction (WMD) to others. At the end of this spectrum is the potential for direct combat with U.S. forces and Iranian nuclear use, most likely arising from conflict escalation.

As a Shi'a revolutionary regime, it is not clear how readily Tehran will accept the same nuclear "rules of the road" that governed the Cold War. Therefore, checking Iranian nuclear adventurism and use will hinge, in part, upon our ability to adapt traditional deterrence concepts to the idiosyncrasies of this increasingly militarized theocracy.

As this chapter contends, the United States has a poor track record of deterring the Islamic Republic, and the regime itself seems ill-suited to the demands of nuclear crisis management. These factors pose fundamental challenges to reliably establishing and maintaining deterrence of a nuclear-armed Iran.

With All Due Modesty: The U.S. Track Record in Deterring Iran

In thinking through how to deter a nuclear-armed Iran it is essential to recognize we do not begin with a clean slate. The United States and the Islamic Republic have been locking horns ever since 1979. How Tehran has perceived American motivations and resolve in past confrontations will inevitably color how much credibility it places in U.S. deterrent threats once it acquires the bomb. Two such episodes are instructive in this regard: U.S.-Iranian naval clashes in the late-1980s and ongoing Iranian lethal support for the insurgencies in Iraq and Afghanistan.

U.S. Convoy Operations in the Persian Gulf, 1987-88

By the late 1980s, U.S. relations with the fledgling Islamic Republic of Iran were bitter. From the 1979-1981 U.S. embassy hostage crisis, to the 1983 U.S. Marine Corps barracks bombing in Lebanon, to the embarrassing Iran-Contra scandal of 1986, Washington had found itself burned time and again by the mullahs in Tehran.

While the United States would have preferred to distance itself from the Iran-Iraq war, Iranian attacks on merchant shipping drew Washington deeper into the conflict in early 1987. At the request of Kuwait, America agreed to reflag a number of Kuwaiti tankers and provide naval escort protection for them.

Deterrence was at the heart of the U.S. escort plan, as it was assumed by U.S. military planners at Central Command (CENTCOM) and the Pentagon that Tehran would not dare risk war with America by directly challenging the escort operations. "CENTCOM had contingency plans should Iran attack a convoy, but U.S. military leaders remained convinced that the presence of a U.S. aircraft carrier in the region would discourage such attacks."[1] For good measure, the United States issued a stern warning in June 1987 to Tehran via the Swiss embassy that the use of Silkworm cruise missiles against the Kuwaiti convoys would be tantamount to a declaration of war.[2] Tehran did not respond to the warning.

With the *USS Kitty Hawk* carrier battle group on station in the Arabian Sea, the first U.S. escort mission passed through the Silkworm-ringed Strait of Hormuz unmolested the following month. Further up the Persian Gulf, however, one of the reflagged tankers, the *Bridgeton,* struck a mine laid by Islamic Revolutionary Guards Corps (IRGC) naval forces. In essence, U.S. assumptions about deterrence failed before the first convoy even reached its destination. Iran, for its part, denied any involvement, calling the mine attack the act of angels. Based on the limited damage and lack of casualties from the attack, Washington decided not to retaliate.[3] Because U.S. naval forces were unprepared for mine warfare, the convoys were suspended until mine clearing assets could be brought to bear. The following month, Iran extended its mine laying to the Gulf of Oman, where the convoys formed up.

In September 1987, U.S. forces caught IRGC naval forces in the act of laying mines from the deck of the *Iran Ajr*. Tehran maintained its denials, despite the capture of the *Iran Ajr,* its crew and a load of Iranian-manufactured mines, as well as other indisputable evidence. Within days, Iran resumed its attacks against merchant shipping, using missiles and gunfire against a Greek tanker despite the nearby presence of two U.S. warships. In October, Iran used its vaunted Silkworm missile to attack a U.S.-flagged tanker, *Sea Isle City*, wounding 18 sailors. The ship was in Kuwaiti waters and therefore not under the protection of the U.S. Navy at the time.

In contrast to the *Bridgeton* attack, the United States struck back. In Operation Nimble Archer, U.S. forces attacked two oil platforms the Iranians had used to track the *Sea Isle City* and relay targeting data. U.S. warships warned the IRGC crews to abandon the platforms before they commenced firing. Back in Washington, the Reagan administration emphasized this was a "prudent yet restrained response." Asked if the attack meant the United States and Iran were at war, President Reagan replied, "No, we're not going to have a war with Iran. They're not that stupid."[4] While another administration official cautioned, "In no way do we want this to be interpreted as an escalation," Defense Secretary Caspar

Weinberger warned "stronger countermeasures" would be taken if Iranian attacks continued.[5] Then-Vice President Bush remarked, "Nobody thinks that this will end it."[6] Within days, Bush had his confirmation as Iran fired another Silkworm missile into Kuwait's Sea Island Oil Terminal on Oct. 22, 1987. The following month, Iran launched another mining operation.

In February 1988, the U.S. Navy executed a more aggressive strategy to harass Iran's naval forces and disrupt its attacks on merchant shipping. Iran countered with another mining operation that hit the *USS Samuel B. Roberts*, causing extensive damage but only minor crew injuries. Washington debated retaliation. The State Department emphasized any retaliation had to be proportionate. U.S. military planners considered a range of responses up to an attack on the Iranian naval base at Bandar Abbas. In the end, two oil platforms that had been used by the Iranians to monitor the convoys and a major surface combatant were approved as targets.[7]

On April 18, 1988, the United States launched Operation Praying Mantis. At the end of it, Iran suffered the loss of a number of ships, including the *Sahand*, which went down with most of its 135 men. The operation marked the end of Iranian mining operations. It did not, however, halt Iranian attacks against merchant shipping, with two more vessels being struck the following week. By month's end, the United States expanded its protection scheme to include "friendly, innocent neutral vessels flying a nonbelligerent flag outside declared exclusion zones that are not carrying contraband or resisting legitimate visit and search by a Persian Gulf belligerent."[8]

Flushed with the success of the Praying Mantis operation and coincidental Iraqi battlefield advances at the time, the Reagan administration hoped a more aggressive U.S. naval posture in the Gulf would push Iran to accept a cease-fire to end the war.[9] It seems Washington achieved that goal, although not without tragedy.

On July 3, 1988, U.S. warships operating under the new rules of engagement came to the defense of neutral merchant shipping. During the ensuing firefight with IRGC naval forces, the *USS Vincennes* mistook an Iranian airliner flying overhead for an Iranian fighter, shooting it down with the loss of all 290 civilians on board. While having pledged to fight until Saddam Hussein was vanquished, Ayatollah Khomeini suddenly announced to the Iranian nation on July 20 that he had agreed to a cease-fire with Iraq "…based only on the interest of the Islamic Republic."[10]

As a test case of American deterrence, the reflagging episode demonstrated a U.S. pattern of misreading Iran. Washington failed to appreciate that because Kuwait underwrote the Iraqi war effort, Tehran would view the U.S. naval escort of Kuwaiti tankers not as the defense of neutral shipping, but as a hostile act against the Islamic Republic. U.S. military planners compounded this misperception by assuming that sheer American "military might" would deter Iran from attacking the convoys. Iran disproved that notion with the very first escort mission. As the U.S. naval commander in the Gulf at that time observed, "The day [the *Bridgeton*] hit the mine was very important because it meant that deterrence would not succeed and the Iranian leadership had decided to take their chances by directly challenging the U.S. The threat of the carrier was not enough — deterrence failed."[11]

The failure of the United States to retaliate for the *Bridgeton* mining underscored American reluctance to antagonize Iran for fear it would escalate terrorist attacks against Americans abroad.[12] In hoping to demonstrate restraint to Tehran, however, Washington likely only convinced Iranian hard-liners that, as with the U.S. withdrawal from Beirut after the bombing of the Marine barracks three years prior, America lacked the stomach for a fight. Two more mining operations followed. By the same token, U.S. retaliation for the October 1987 *Sea Isle City* attack *also* failed to deter further Iranian mining operations. The mixed messages emanating from Washington at the time probably did not help, with the Pentagon warning of more serious consequences if Iranian attacks continued while the White House emphasized it was not seeking to escalate.

In any event, it was not until Iran suffered major naval losses during Operation Praying Mantis in April 1988 that Tehran finally ceased mining and other attacks against the U.S. convoys. Iran continued attacking non-U.S. flagged merchant shipping (with guns and missiles) despite the extension of U.S. naval protection to them in late April, albeit with declining frequency. In short, Tehran made tactical adjustments in response to U.S. military pressure, but defiantly continued to attack merchant shipping until the July 1988 cease-fire.

Iran also demonstrated a proclivity for keeping its attacks just under the threshold of a devastating U.S. response. It studiously avoided use of its Silkworm missiles against the U.S. convoys as they transited the Strait of Hormuz where they were most vulnerable, an indication that Tehran took seriously the U.S. warning of June 1987. However, Iranian military planners exploited a loophole by using the Silkworm to attack a reflagged tanker once it was in Kuwaiti territorial waters and unprotected by U.S. naval escorts. Iran's navy paid a stiff price for that strike, but the Iranian homeland remained untouched by the U.S. military.

An important dimension of the American deterrence dynamic with Iran was the extent to which U.S. military operations influenced the Iranian leadership debate about courses of action. Throughout the war, pragmatists within the regime, such as then-Parliament Speaker Hashemi Rafsanjani and then-President Ali Khamenei, were constantly at odds with extremist clerics and the IRGC.

To underscore this point, the IRGC launched the *Iran Ajr* mining operation just before President Khamene'i was due to speak at the U.N. General Assembly to complain about the U.N. Security Council's unfair treatment of Iran in its war with Iraq. While the embarrassing U.S. capture of the *Iran Ajr* should have been a boon to Iranian pragmatists, it "actually allowed the radicals to prevail again by arguing that Iran needed to show the Americans that it would not be so easily deterred."[13]

In an apparent compromise, the IRGC launched its Silkworm missile attack against the *Sea Isle City* the next month while further mining operations were suspended.

In early 1988 the mining debate resumed in Tehran. The pragmatists sought to avoid provoking the United States which, in their view, would only increase the American military commitment to the region. Extremists insisted Iran needed to deal a decisive blow against the U.S. Navy.[14] The extremists prevailed although not without further challenge. The regular Iranian navy opposed the resumption of mining and actually tried to sweep the mines laid by the IRGC just before the *USS Samuel B. Roberts* was struck.[15] The heavy U.S. retaliation that followed led to the discrediting of the mining advocates within the top leadership circle and an end to the practice for the remaining three months of the war.[16]

In 2005, Mohsen Rezaie, the overall IRGC commander during the mining operations shed further light on the leadership's deliberations over the 1987 U.S. naval intervention in the Gulf. According to Rezaie, Supreme Leader Ayatollah Khomeini personally advocated attacking U.S. warships as they moved through the Strait of Hormuz, although he left the issue to the military to decide.[17] This fascinating footnote underscores Khomeini was not the least bit deterred by the U.S. warning of June 1987 and apparently had utter disregard for the consequences of attacking U.S. warships. It also highlights the important role regime pragmatists played in attenuating the extremist tendencies of Khomeini and the IRGC and brokering a compromise attack plan – the equivalent of a "guerrilla war at sea" – that would inflict costs on America but remain below its threshold of devastating retaliation against the Iranian homeland.

In the end, the regime came to believe the downing of the Iranian airliner by the *USS Vincennes* was a deliberate signal by the United States it was about to unleash its full power to bring down the Islamic Republic, a factor that weighed heavily in the monumental decision days later to accept the UN cease-fire with Iraq.[18]

Iranian Lethal Support to Insurgencies in Iraq and Afghanistan, 2003 to Present

As they had with respect to deposing the Taliban in 2001, American and Iranian interests converged up to a certain point as the Bush administration prepared to topple Saddam Hussein the following year. While a U.S. invasion of Iraq would remove another of Tehran's sworn foes, it would also complete the virtual encirclement of Iran by U.S. military forces. Having recently been lumped in with Iraq as part of the "Axis of Evil," Iran's ruling mullahs had reason to suspect they might be next on the Bush administration's regime change list.

Against this backdrop, Supreme Leader Khamene'i convened Iran's Supreme National Security Council in early September 2002, concluding, "It is necessary to adopt an active policy in order to prevent long-term and short-term dangers to Iran."[19] That active policy entailed a range of diplomatic, military and paramilitary moves to safeguard Iran's western flank.

Operating under the cover of the Geneva Contact Group on Afghanistan, Iranian diplomats engaged their American counterparts to assess U.S. intentions vis-à-vis Iraq. For American officials, the Contact Group provided an opportunity to elicit Iranian cooperation in the forthcoming invasion, akin to what had been achieved in Afghanistan.[20] Specifically, in early 2003 White House special envoy Zalmay Khalilzad "asked Iranian officials in Geneva to pledge Tehran's assistance for any American pilots downed in Iranian territory. Khalilzad also sought assurances that Iran's armed forces would not join the fighting at any time. According to Iranian sources familiar with the meeting, Tehran agreed to both, but asked for a promise of its own: that the United States would not set its sights on Iran after the U.S. Army toppled Saddam Hussein's regime. American officials reportedly equivocated..."[21]

Evidently still wary of U.S. intentions, Iran strengthened its military deployments in the West, moving up some 40 infantry and missile brigades.[22] The regime's security organs also began to build up networks of Shi'ite militias inside Iraq. By the spring of 2004, the decision to activate those networks appeared to have been made, with the commander of the IRGC Quds Force (IRGC-QF), Brigadier General Suleiman, reportedly instructing the proxy militias that "any move that would wear out the U.S. forces in Iraq should be done. Every possible means should be used to keep the U.S. forces engaged in Iraq."[23]

Before long, lethal Iranian involvement in the unfolding Iraqi insurgency was detected. The initial U.S. response was to lodge a diplomatic protest with Tehran, via the Swiss embassy, in July 2005. The demarche took note of Shi'ite militants that had been trained in Iraq by the IRGC and Iranian-backed Lebanese Hezbollah and supplied with bomb-making equipment. It further noted one of these bombs had now killed a coalition soldier. The protest concluded the United States "will continue to judge Iran by its actions in Iraq." Iran's response the following month flatly denied the allegations.

Having been rebuffed privately, U.S. officials took their case public, with National Security Advisor Stephen J. Hadley noting that bombs used against allied forces, "seem to have a footprint similar to that of devices used by groups that have historically had Iranian support." Despite the public attention, U.S. casualties in Iraq from Iranian bombs, so-called explosively formed penetrators (EFPs) continued to mount, accounting for about 30 percent by the end of 2006.[24]

Increasingly frustrated with Tehran, the Bush administration adopted a more aggressive strategy. In a speech to the nation on January 10, 2007, President Bush announced:

...Succeeding in Iraq also requires defending its territorial integrity and stabilizing the region in the face of the extremist challenge.

This begins with addressing Iran and Syria. These two regimes are allowing terrorists and insurgents to use their territory to move in and out of Iraq. Iran is providing material support for attacks on American troops. We will disrupt the attacks on our forces. We will interrupt the flow of support from Iran and Syria. And we will seek out and destroy the networks providing advanced weaponry and training to our enemies in Iraq.

Behind the scenes, the Bush administration had already been employing a program to "catch and release" Iranian operatives in Iraq. With no attenuation of EFP attacks, however, in late-2006 the administration decided to escalate the pressure by authorizing the U.S. military to kill or capture Iranian operatives in Iraq. Within hours of the President's speech, U.S. forces apprehended five members of the IRGC-QF in the Iraqi city of Irbil.

That month also saw a drop in the number of U.S. casualties from explosively formed penetrators, leading some U.S. officials to suggest that the decline was due to American efforts to publicly highlight Iran's involvement.[25]

Whatever satisfaction that decline might have provided, Iran's response to the seizure of the "Irbil 5" was swift. On January 20, an attempt to kidnap U.S. servicemen in a raid on the Karbala provincial headquarters resulted in five American fatalities. The following week, President Bush warned, "If Iran escalates its military action in Iraq to the detriment of our troops and/or innocent Iraqi people, we will respond firmly...we will do what it takes to protect our troops."[26]

At the same time, the President announced he had no intention of making an incursion into Iran. In March, Iran was hit with a U.N. Security Council resolution on its nuclear program, banning it from exporting arms, a provision directed at its arming of insurgents in Iraq.[27]

The following month, the Chairman of the Joint Chiefs of Staff, General Peter Pace, announced that Iranian arms (including explosively formed penetrators) were now being supplied to the Taliban in Afghanistan.[28]

On the diplomatic front, the United States engaged Tehran in direct talks on the security situation in Iraq. In May 2007, U.S. Ambassador Ryan Crocker confronted his Iranian counterpart with "a number of our direct specific concerns about their behavior in Iraq, their support for militias that are fighting both the Iraqi security forces and coalition forces, the fact that a lot of the explosives and ammunition that are used by these groups are coming in from Iran, that such activities, led by the IRGC Qods Force needed to cease, and that we would be looking for results." Iran's Ambassador Kazemi-Qomi, himself an IRGC Command officer, denied the U.S. allegations. Neither Ambassador Crocker nor Iranian officials publicly indicated whether the United States warned Iran of any consequences if it failed to halt its lethal support.

At a second round of talks in July 2007, after the U.S. military publicly announced that the IRGC-QF had helped plan the deadly Karbala raid, Ambassador Crocker pointed out to his counterpart that Iranian-backed attacks had only increased since the initial meeting:

> We made it clear to the Iranians that we know what they're doing. It's up to them to decide what they want to do about it because a point we have made previously is that Iran's stated policy of…support for a stable democratic Iraq is not only consistent with U.S. policy. It makes sense in terms of Iran's own interests…

Crocker also informed the Iranians that IRGC-QF operatives and their surrogates "are not going to be safe in Iraq."[29] Once again, the Iranian delegation denied the U.S. allegations. In a meeting with Iraqi Prime Minister Maliki the following month, Iranian officials were more forthcoming, reportedly pledging to curb their aid to Shiite militias in Iraq.[30]

To help stem the flow of explosively formed penetrators from Iran, the U.S.-led coalition built up its bases and patrols near the Iraqi border in the fall of 2007. In the following months, U.S. officials noted a decline in the use of EFPs. A senior U.S. military spokesman in Iraq and an Iraqi official suggested that Tehran seemed to be holding up its pledge to Prime Minister Maliki.

State Department officials were inclined to see the drop as the result of direct engagement with Tehran, whereas Defense Department officials attributed the decline to U.S. counter-measures rather than a strategic decision by Iran to alter its behavior.[31] Any sense of optimism was short-lived, however, with explosively formed penetrator attacks in January 2008 rising to the highest level in a year.

By spring, General David Petraeus, the overall U.S. commander in Iraq, Ambassador Crocker and CIA Director Michael Hayden had all publicly concluded Iran was waging a proxy war against the United States in Iraq. Petraeus' successor, General Ray Odierno, noted in June 2009, "Iran is still supporting, funding, training surrogates who operate inside of Iraq — flat out…They have not stopped. And I don't think they will stop."[32] The following month, the Obama administration, which was committed to engaging Iran, released the "Irbil 5" to the Iraqi government which promptly turned them over to Tehran.

As a test case for U.S. deterrence of Iranian adventurism, Iran's lethal support for anti-American insurgents ranks as a near total failure. The failure is largely attributable to a misplaced American faith in common objectives with Iran. Iranian assurances in early 2003 not to intervene militarily in Iraq seem to have been accepted at face value without any indication from the United States there would be potentially serious consequences for welshing.

Perhaps the U.S. failure to issue a clear deterrent warning was appropriate in 2003 given Tehran's prior cooperation in Afghanistan, but this faith in common purposes was still evidenced by Ambassador Crocker in the July 2007 round of talks with Iran, which he himself pointed out were being conducted against a backdrop of *increased* Iranian-backed attacks.

Even then, the strongest deterrent threat the United States could seem to muster in those direct talks was a warning that IRGC operatives in Iraq would not be safe. The continued use of explosively formed penetrators and other forms of lethal support for the insurgency indicate what little credibility Tehran placed in that threat.

In essence, Washington failed to anticipate the consequences of not adequately reassuring Iran it would not be invaded next. This is where common American and Iranian interests in deposing Saddam Hussein diverged. For Tehran, bloodying U.S. forces in Iraq under the guise of a Shi'ite insurgency helped ensure the country could not be used as a spring board for an American invasion of Iran. The United States also seemed to underestimate Iran's ability to "split hairs," that is, sticking to the letter of its pledge not to intervene in Iraq with its armed forces while instead employing the IRGC-QF, a military unit the regime does not acknowledge even exists, to train and direct proxies in Iraq.

Washington's deterrence potential was also greatly diminished by self-imposed constraints. Having failed to deter the initiation of Iranian covert support for the Iraqi insurgency, the United States fell back on a posture of deterrence by denial, that is, it aimed to deny Iran the gains it sought from the insurgency by disrupting its networks *inside* Iraq and applying greater force protection measures. In reality, this was part of a wider Bush administration effort begun in late-2006 to confront Iran's growing influence in the region, so as to press Tehran into giving up its nuclear ambitions,[33] an effort which yielded equally dismal results.

In any event, the path of deterrence by punishment was effectively undercut when President Bush took military options against Iranian territory off the table in January 2007, leaving an unenforceable U.N. ban on Iranian arms exports and rather weak U.S. economic sanctions against some IRGC-QF officials.[34] Even the dispatch of a second U.S. carrier battle group to the Persian Gulf in April 2008 seemed half-hearted; with Secretary Gates observing the deployment was a "reminder" to Iran, not an escalation.[35]

The constraints themselves reflected wariness by many U.S. officials to confront Iran while American forces were already overstretched in Iraq and Afghanistan. To Tehran, it must have appeared as an unmistakable lack of U.S. resolve. Thus hampered, Washington had to look elsewhere for influence over Iranian behavior. This led Secretary of Defense Gates in April 2008 to publicly encourage the Iraqi government to "...bring some pressure to bear on Iran" to stop the insurgents' attacks.[36]

Perhaps the most troubling aspect of the insurgency debacle was the American reluctance even to attribute Iran's covert activities to its top leadership. In April 2007, Joint Chiefs Chairman Gen. Pace observed:

> "We know that there are munitions that were made in Iran that are in Iraq and in Afghanistan. And we know that the Quds Force works for the IRGC. We then surmise from that one or two things. Either the leadership of the country

knows what their armed forces are doing, or that they don't know. And in either case that's a problem."[37]

Shortly thereafter, Gen. Petraeus remarked:

> "With respect to how high does it go and, you know, what do they know and when did they know it, I honestly cannot – that is such a sensitive issue that – and we do not – at least I do not know of anything that specifically identifies how high it goes beyond the level of the Qods Force, Commander Suleiman. Beyond that, it is very difficult to tell – we know where he is in the overall chain of command; he certainly reports to the very top – but again, nothing that would absolutely indicate, again, how high the knowledge of this actually goes…"[38]

In essence, top U.S. military commanders publicly connected the provision of explosively formed penetrators and other lethal support to the IRGC-QF and its commander, who they acknowledged reported to the Supreme Leader, but they would not affirmatively tie the activity to the Supreme Leader himself.

This reluctance extended elsewhere. In claiming IRGC-QF operatives helped plan the January 2007 raid in Karbala in which five U.S. soldiers were killed, Brig. Gen. Kevin Bergner noted, "Our intelligence reveals that the senior leadership in Iran is aware of this activity." When asked if Iran's Supreme Leader Khamene'i could be unaware of the activity, Bergner said, "That would be hard to imagine."[39]

Commenting on Iran's lethal support to the Taliban in June 2007, Secretary Gates observed, "…given the quantities [of Iranian weapons] we are seeing, it is difficult to believe it's associated with smuggling or the drug business or that it's taking place without the knowledge of the Iranian government."[40] Indeed, it was not until April 2008 that C.I.A. Director Hayden remarked, "I will share with you my view that it is the policy of the Iranian government, approved to the *highest levels of that government*, to facilitate the killing of Americans in Iraq, okay? So just make sure there's clarity on that."[41]

Some of this reluctance could be attributed initially to a simple lack of incriminating intelligence. However, the American reticence to finger publicly Iran's Supreme Leader endured even as the picture came into focus. The overriding U.S. concern appears to have been not inflaming the conflict further. Indeed, Washington may have been trying to leave the regime a face-saving "exit ramp," namely, the top leadership could act as if it had been unaware of the lethal support and put a stop to it without appearing to have been cowed by "the Great Satan."

Alternatively, U.S. officials may have concluded that to publicly accuse the Supreme Leader for the ongoing killing of U.S. soldiers would have only increased pressures for escalation, something they studiously sought to avoid. In the end, the only exit ramp Tehran was interested in was the complete withdrawal of U.S. forces from Iraq and Afghanistan. It never wavered from its denials of U.S. allegations or strategically altered its lethal support for the insurgents.

The U.S. failure to hold Iran's top leaders publicly accountable for this lethal support has set a dangerous precedent for deterrence of a nuclear-armed Iran. It needlessly raised doubts at home and abroad that Iran's top leaders might not be cognizant of hostile cross-border acts by their security forces. As explained further below, the Supreme Leader is, in fact, tightly coupled to all sensitive security matters. The episode also has taught Iran's rulers that in the future they can hope to exploit this window of uncertainty over so-called rogue operations and make quick gains before the U.S. builds its case for regime culpability.

Indeed, the implicit potential for Iranian nuclear escalation will naturally extend that window of opportunity by raising the standard of evidence that the top leadership in Iran is, in fact, responsible for a given provocation. Even then, U.S. public diplomacy seems to be easily checked with persistent Iranian denials of any wrongdoing, helping to delay and deflect pressure on the regime.

Where U.S. deterrence registers with Iran is in the broader sense; as with the mining of the Persian Gulf in 1988, Iran remains wary of engaging American forces in direct conventional combat. This has driven Tehran to rely on asymmetric warfare and plausible deniability. Indeed, the manner in which Iran prepared the Iraq insurgency indicates that the regime does not perceive itself as completely invulnerable to outside scrutiny or pressure. From the outset, Iran adopted a "train the trainer" approach, whereby selected insurgents would receive advance instruction in Iran and then return to Iraq to train others. This was done in anticipation that coalition forces would tighten up the border with Iran and to avoid unwanted attention directed at Tehran.[42]

At the same time, Iran indicated once again it was quite willing to engage in tit-for-tat retaliation, if not escalation, with the United States; in this case planning the Karbala raid that killed five American servicemen. In the end, what Iranian hard-liners are likely to take from this conflict is that even though America's diplomats, generals and spymasters, not to mention its hawkish president, all publicly conceded Iran was fighting a proxy war against it – with hundreds of American soldiers killed by explosively formed penetrators – the United States was neither prepared to hold the Supreme Leader accountable nor shed Iranian blood to stop it.

Is the Ruling Regime Rational?

The foregoing case studies highlight a key question for future U.S. deterrence planning; namely, can we count on Iran's rulers to rationally calculate when it is in their best interest to avoid conflict with the United States? Expert opinion on this issue is roughly divided into two camps, deterrence optimists and pessimists.

Generalists among the Iran deterrence camp contend if the United States could successfully deter a nuclear-armed Soviet Union and China, two other "revolutionary" states, it could certainly deter a nuclear-armed Iran as a "lesser included case."[43] Iran experts in this camp point to various examples of the regime's rationality. Among them, Ayatollah Khomeini's dictum that survival of the state supersedes religious considerations, his acceptance of the cease-fire with Iraq in 1988, and more recently, the growing economic interests of the IRGC, which presumably give the Corps more to lose in a conflict with the United States.

In contrast, Iran deterrence skeptics tend to worry about Iran's capacity for irrational behavior. Indeed, such behavior can be gleaned from the foregoing case studies. For example, Tehran insisted on attacking U.S. convoys in 1987-1988 despite the fact the broader campaign against merchant shipping had no diminishing effect on the Iraqi war effort, while the mining of international waters only served to coalesce the West against Iran, increase the U.S. military presence in the Gulf, and invite the destruction of Iran's navy. Tehran had so badly played its hand by 1988 that the only international condemnation of the *USS Vincennes'* downing of the Iranian airliner came from Syria.[44]

As we have seen, extremist clerics, including Ayatollah Khomeini himself and their equally zealous comrades in the IRGC have shown little to no regard for the consequences of their actions – a key assumption in the rational actor model and deterrence theory. In short, they seemed to discount earthly costs for heavenly gains. While Khomeini is long gone from the scene, religious extremism has not subsided in Iran. Indeed, concern is mounting that an apocalyptic Shi'a sect, the Hojjatieh, is gaining influence in the regime through the efforts of Ayatollah Mesbah Yazdi and President Mahmoud Ahmadinejad. Given the shadowy nature of the Hojjatieh sect, it is difficult to assess the group's potential impact on the regime's cost-benefit calculus once it acquires nuclear weapons. What is clear is that Iranians themselves express concern today that religious extremists within the leadership, referred to as the "Shi'a Taliban," should not be trusted with an atomic bomb.[45]

The reality is that the Iranian regime is capable of both rational and irrational behavior, a reflection of the enduring internal struggle for power between pragmatists and extremists. The latter are devoted to metaphysical concepts. They see ideological and armed "resistance" as an end to itself. Once committed, the regime's extremists will stubbornly adhere to a course of action beyond the point where it proves counter-productive and risks self-preservation. Of particular concern in the event Iran acquires nuclear weapons is that these extremists are disproportionately represented in the regime's intelligence, military and security organizations.

Regime pragmatists play an important role in restraining the irrational tendencies of the radicals. Yet, because the two camps are semi-autonomous, Iran can demonstrate rational and irrational behavior simultaneously, confounding outsiders with such contradictory behavior. Thus, for example, the IRGC with Khomeini's blessing undertakes a risky mining operation in September 1987 that undercuts a concurrent attempt by Iran's president to generate greater international sympathy for Iran before the United Nations. Likewise, in 1994, Iran supports a terrorist attack against the Jewish center in Buenos Aires at the same time it seeks nuclear cooperation with the Argentine government.

Compounding this schizophrenic behavior is a deep-seated religious and cultural predisposition in Iran not to knuckle under to illegitimate power, which, in the regime's world view, means any government besides the Islamic Republic. Refusing to have terms "dictated" to it by "arrogant" powers, Tehran is thus balking at an international offer to convert its low-enriched uranium into fuel rods for the Tehran research reactor, which makes radioisotopes to treat cancer patients but is running out of fuel.

Notably, President Ahmadinejad favors this deal but is being thwarted from within by his political opponents in the traditional conservative, pragmatic conservative and reformist camps. The episode underscores that Iran's extremists do not necessarily have a monopoly on irrational behavior. Indeed, such behavior can be tactically employed for over-arching rational goals (e.g., undermining one's political opponent).

Iranian National Security Decision Making

How rational Tehran's behavior seems to outsiders will also be a function of how well its decision makers hold up under the stress of a crisis. Intra-group dynamics and psychological predispositions have been known to distort rational thinking. Therefore, the resiliency of Iranian decision making processes and key players merits careful consideration.

Processes and Institutions

In terms of processes, Iranian national security decision making reflects the broader distribution of political power. At the top is the Supreme Leader, former-President Khamene'i, who is constitutionally designated as the commander in chief of the armed forces with the power to declare war. He does not wield absolute power, however, in that he lacks the personal charisma and religious credibility of the Islamic Republic's founder, Ayatollah Khomeini. Therefore, Supreme Leader Khamene'i must balance various other semi-autonomous power centers, grouped into major factions.

Since the end of the Khatami presidency in 2005, the reformist faction has essentially been excluded from national security decision making, leaving Khamene'i to balance the views of pragmatic conservatives like Rafsanjani with those of traditional conservatives such as Ali Larijani, and extremists like Ahmadinejad.

After the disputed re-election of President Ahmadinejad in June 2009, Iranian politics has become increasingly polarized, with the Supreme Leader leaning more in favor of Ahmadinejad, leaving many to speculate how much influence the pragmatists continue to wield. This is an important development, bearing in mind the pragmatists' role in attenuating the regime's more extreme tendencies.

The overall national security decision making process therefore operates on a consensus basis with the Supreme Leader as the highest decision authority. Outwardly, the regime likes to portray the process as one of elite solidarity. Behind the scenes, the intense factionalism translates into a tendency to adopt lowest common denominator policies.[46] Those policies are constantly subject to renegotiation, moreover, as factions challenge decisions not to their liking. This helps explain the on-again, off-again mining operations of 1987-1988 and may also help account for the dialing up and down of lethal support to the Iraqi insurgency since 2003.

The Supreme National Security Council (SNSC) is the highest constitutionally sanctioned deliberative body on national security affairs. It is headed by the President and represents the heads of the ruling system, as well as the IRGC. Decisions of the SNSC do not take effect, however, until they are approved by the Supreme Leader. More secretive sub-groupings of the SNSC and the Supreme Leader have been publicly reported for particularly sensitive operations, such as cross-border terrorism.[47]

Other institutions also likely play a significant role in Iranian national security decision making, including the Supreme Leader's Office. Among its staff are Ayatollah Khamene'i's most trusted foreign policy and military advisors, such as former-Foreign Minister Ali Akbar Velayati and former IRGC commander Rahim Safavi.

The Leader's Office is also responsible for the network known as the Supreme Leader's Representatives. These "clerical commissars" are embedded in all major security institutions. The Leader's Representatives ensure the political reliability of the armed forces but can also intervene in operations at will, thereby superseding the bureaucracy's chain of command. The Supreme Leader also maintains direct ties to military officers and officials, routinely meeting with them privately on a weekly basis or as events warrant.[48]

These sessions provide another oversight mechanism for the Leader, as well as an opportunity for the officers and officials involved to influence the Leader's views. According to opposition sources, Iran's intelligence apparatus spies on top regime officials and officers, providing tape recordings to the Supreme Leader on a routine basis, further keeping Ayatollah Khamene'i apprised.[49]

In the event Iran acquires nuclear weapons, these mechanisms and processes will provide a basis from which to construct a Nuclear Command Authority (NCA). Undoubtedly, the Supreme Leader will be the ultimate decider on questions of nuclear use. Equally certain is that the IRGC, as the most trusted of security organs, will play a leading role in the control of Iranian nuclear weapons. How widely an Iranian NCA would consult with other heads of the ruling system is an open question.

In peacetime, top regime officials may well be invested with an advisory role on the development of nuclear forces, akin to the Nuclear Development Committee of Pakistan's NCA.[50] An Iranian NCA might also make provisions for consulting the state president on questions of nuclear use, as does Pakistan's NCA Employment Control Committee – time and communication links permitting. It is also possible that Iranian nuclear control arrangements would allow for delegation of nuclear launch authority to IRGC commanders under certain conditions, such as the incapacitation of the Supreme Leader.

Key Decision Makers

As for the psychological dispositions of the regime's top leaders, a good deal can be gleaned from their tenures in office. Ayatollah Khamene'i generally has proven to be a cautious Supreme Leader. His measured approach to most policy matters probably reflects his diminished authority compared to his predecessor. He simply cannot impose his will in the way Khomeini did. In turn, his questionable religious credentials have forced Khamene'i into an alliance with those most supportive of the concept of a Supreme Leader, militant extremists.

More recently, Khamene'i has acted hastily and clumsily, exacerbating the disputed re-election of President Ahmadinejad by pre-empting the constitutionally mandated three-day waiting period before endorsing Ahmadinejad's supposed victory. This pre-emption helped solidify the views of the Green movement that the electoral "fix was in."

At other times, Khamene'i can be indecisive.[51] Perhaps to break this indecisiveness, Khamene'i reportedly resorts to estekhareh, an Islamic form of fortune-telling, to make critical decisions for the country.[52] In the most common form of estekhareh, a cleric takes the Koran in both hands, says some prayers, then opens the book and reads the first line of the page on the right. The cleric then offers his impressions of what God recommends a person should do.[53] A relative of Khamene'i's speculates the Supreme Leader is especially prone to use estekhareh when he is depressed,[54] in part the result of listening to the recordings of officials who pledge their loyalty to him face-to-face but berate him behind closed doors.[55]

Publicly, Khamene'i maintains that nuclear weapons are against Islam and has issued a fatwa, or religious edict, prohibiting their development, possession or use by Iran. Behind the scenes, however, he has been a staunch advocate of acquiring the bomb. According to an investigation by the International Atomic Energy Agency, as president in 1984, Khamene'i pushed for nuclear weapons, saying, "A nuclear arsenal would serve Iran as a deterrent in the hands of God's soldiers."[56]

Khamene'i is able to reconcile this duplicity under the Shi'a practice of taqiyya, whereby it is not only morally acceptable but obligatory to lie to one's enemies if that will avert harm. Because it can be practiced collectively, taqiyya makes it difficult to place much stock in the public utterances of Khamene'i or other members of the ruling regime. Likewise, Khamene'i is deeply distrustful of the United States, believing it is intent on regime change in Iran, President Obama's offer of engagement notwithstanding.

President Mahmoud Ahmadinejad in many ways represents the future of the Islamic Republic. He embodies the so-called "second generation" of Islamic revolutionaries, having come of age in the late-1970s and fighting in the Iran-Iraq War as a member of the IRGC. As a university student leader, he advocated the seizure of the U.S. embassy in 1979 and remains committed to the teachings of Ayatollah Khomeini. This helps explain his anti-American and anti-Israeli tirades.

As an IRGC veteran, Ahmadinejad has supported the political and economic ascendancy of the Guards Corps. Although he is not in the operational military chain of command, as state president and chair of the Supreme National Security Council, Ahmadinejad has asserted himself as the face and voice of the Iranian government.

Ahmadinejad's decision-making style has a certain "shoot first, ask questions later" quality to it. He is widely criticized within Iran for his arrogance and disdain for expert opinion. He regularly invokes conspiracy theories to explain world events, including the assertion that America staged the 9/11 attacks itself so it would have a pretense to invade Muslim lands,[57] a view publicly shared by Rahim Safavi, the Supreme Leader's military advisor.[58] Ahmadinejad is widely seen as being "...susceptible to neither offers of incentives nor threats of force."[59]

Although not a cleric, Ahmadinejad harbors extremist religious views. He is widely suspected of belonging to a secret apocalyptic society, such as the Hojjatieh. Ahmadinejad routinely invokes the Shi'a messiah, the so-called Hidden Imam or Mahdi, and asserts his return is imminent.

In Shi'a eschatology, when the Mahdi returns he will impose universal Islamic Government and many infidels will be massacred. In contrast to mainstream Shi'a who believe it is impossible to know when the Mahdi will return, Ahmadinejad seems to believe that his return can be hastened by creating chaos and conflict.[60]

Ahmadinejad's public diatribes closely link the killing of Jews and the Imam's return,[61] an incendiary combination in the event Iran acquires nuclear weapons. In critical situations, Ahmadinejad also reportedly resorts to estekhareh to help him decide on a course of action.[62]

Hashemi Rafsanjani is the antithesis of Ahmadinejad. Rafsanjani is one of the clerical founding fathers of the Islamic Republic, having worked closely with Ayatollah Khomeini. After serving as speaker of the Iranian Parliament and two-terms as president, today Rafsanjani simultaneously chairs two key regime institutions, the Assembly of Experts, which has the power to elect or remove the Supreme Leader, and the Expediency Council, which arbitrates disputes between the Parliament and the Guardian Council.

Rafsanjani is known as the regime's top pragmatist. He was largely responsible for persuading Khomeini to end the war with Iraq in 1988. Politically, he lacks conviction and seems to be motivated by whatever cause will best enhance his personal power and wealth, the latter being quite considerable. In the past Rafsanjani opposed the reformists but since the rise of Ahmadinejad and the extremists, he has found common cause with the Green movement. In addition to being a consummate opportunist, Rafsanjani is a pivotal coalition builder. He has tried to bridge the chasm between reformists and extremists in the wake of the disputed re-election of President Ahmadinejad. His lack of progress in this endeavor has led to speculation that his influence, and those of his fellow pragmatists, may be waning in the regime.

In the late-1980s, Rafsanjani publicly advocated that Iran acquire WMD, a key lesson of the war with Iraq. He has been a long-time proponent of Iran's nuclear program, which secretly engaged in cooperation with the A.Q. Khan nuclear proliferation network during his presidency. He supports better ties with the United States, presumably from a position of nuclear strength.

Another key leader of the system is Ali Larijani, the current Speaker of Parliament. Larijani is a sophisticated intellectual, with a Ph.D. in Western philosophy. A traditional conservative, Larijani served in the IRGC and was the Secretary of the Supreme National Security Council from 2005-2007 when he resigned amid a dispute with President Ahmadinejad.

Ali Larijani is often mentioned as a likely successor to President Ahmadinejad when the latter's term of office ends in 2013. If so, we should not expect the substance of the regime's policies to change. As Larijani has remarked, "Ideologically, I have no differences with Ahmadinejad, but we indeed have differences in style, approach and management."[63]

Scions of a prestigious religious family, Larijani and his brothers have long held special positions of trust with the Supreme Leader. Ali's brother Sadeq previously served as a clerical member of the Guardian Council and was recently appointed head of Iran's judiciary. Brother Mohammad Javad has long been a foreign affairs advisor to Khamene'i. Ali Larijani proved to be pivotal in winning the release of British sailors detained by Iran in 2007, demonstrating greater personal influence within the regime than the Foreign Minister, Manouchehr Mottaki,[64] who has since been fired by Ahmadinejad.

While Supreme National Security Council Secretary, Larijani was the regime's lead negotiator with the West on Iran's nuclear program, and he steadfastly refused to accept limits on it. More recently, Larijani has opposed President Ahmadinejad on the aforementioned deal with the West to exchange Iran's enriched uranium for research reactor fuel. This opposition stems from an opportunistic desire to undercut a political rival, as much as his staunch nuclear nationalism.

Larijani is thought to favor Iran's acquisition of nuclear weapons, recently claiming the Nuclear Non-Proliferation Treaty, to which Iran is a State Party, should simply be ignored.[65] His pro-nuclear stance seems to be influenced by the trauma of the Iran-Iraq War: "We witnessed the effect of WMDs when the Americans and the Europeans provided Saddam with them and he used them, in places like Halabja. I was there when he attacked and I can't wipe the images from my mind. Everything and everyone – children, men, women and animals were exterminated."[66] In effect, while WMD are heinous, acquiring nuclear weapons would deter their use against Iran in the future. As noted further below, Larijani also believes nuclear weapons will give Iran greater freedom of action.

Crisis Management

In terms of crisis management, the ruling regime has demonstrated it can perform reasonably well where there is a build-up of tensions that measures weeks or longer. In the 1998 near-war crisis between Iran and Afghanistan's Taliban, Supreme Leader Khamene'i proved he was capable of resisting domestic pressures for a war that he deemed not to be in Iran's interest. By contrast, Tehran seems less capable of performing under the stress of fast-breaking crises. In both the 2005 false report of an attack on the Bushehr nuclear reactor and the more recent demonstrations against Ahmadinejad's re-election, the regime demonstrated poor situational awareness.

Key leaders were unavailable publicly and lesser officials gave conflicting accounts of events. The leadership also seemed to face difficulty in building a consensus on the proper course of action. As an exalted religious figure, Khamene'i frequently will not even comment publicly on controversial topics for weeks, if then. This can lead to improvisation that carries unintended consequences (e.g., the abuse of protestors in an ad-hoc detention center became a major embarrassment and liability for the regime).

These facets of Iranian decision making under stress will be an obvious and potentially disastrous liability in the event Iran becomes nuclear-armed, setting the stage for the failure of deterrence.

The Potential for Deterrence Failure

There are essentially two modes of deterrence failure pertinent to Iran; instances where regime decision making is not constrained by rationality and cases where rationality is otherwise impaired. In terms of the former, the regime may deliberately undertake a course of action that, by Western standards, seems utterly reckless because it all but assures harsh consequences for itself.

Such would be the case, for example, where the regime discounts costs and focuses primarily or even solely on prospective gains, or where the bearing of costs itself is considered a virtue. The regime demonstrated its capacity to act in such a manner during its war with Iraq. In short, the regime locked itself into an eight-year-long conflict that nearly brought about its collapse by extolling the virtues of suffering in the name of "justice," as well as large-scale martyrdom.

It is said that 30 years past the revolution, the regime can no longer inspire such mass martyrdom. Since June 2009, however, the eagerness of Iran's Basij militia to torture, rape and kill fellow citizens in the name of loyalty to the Supreme Leader should serve as a timely reminder the regime still has a large base of fanatical devotees and a willingness to exploit them. Left to their own devices, apocalyptically-inspired Hojjatieh and other radicals could likewise prove to be undeterrable since conflict with the United States, possibly including even the use of nuclear weapons, serves their agenda.

The latter form of deterrence breakdown involves cases where rationality is impaired by the stress of crisis decision making. This could stem from an inadequate understanding of U.S. national security interests, resolve, and decision-making processes. Here, it is noteworthy that despite top priority access to information, Supreme Leader Khamene'i has acknowledged he does not understand how foreign policy decisions are made in the United States.[67]

Cultural influences could further skew rational decision making in Tehran, given the aforementioned presence of conspiracy theorists among the top leadership, as well as the high political costs of backing down under U.S. pressure. Decisions for war or peace may well hinge on the advice top leaders receive from their estekhareh religious advisors, who likely will have no appreciation for the stakes involved or the implications of their advice.

Bureaucratic politics and standard operating procedures, while certainly not unique to Iran, could similarly lead to a breakdown of deterrence. For instance, Iran's ability to signal to Washington its intent to de-escalate a confrontation could be compromised by IRGC commanders who countermand orders to stand down, as they have done in the past. Compounded by the lack of diplomatic relations and interaction between Washington and Tehran since 1979, such mixed messaging could well be interpreted by the United States as a deception intended to mask Iranian preparations to initiate nuclear use.

In essence, the seeds for deterrence failure have already been sown in Tehran. The regime's highly stylized form of decision making seems ill-suited to the demands of fast-breaking crises where the potential for nuclear escalation exists. Depending on circumstances, there may not be enough time for the regime to achieve consensus on a course of action among the heads of the system. This would tend to shrink the circle of advisers in proximity to the Supreme Leader, probably in favor of hard-liners, who are his natural constituency and are disproportionately represented in that circle.

The results could be skewed in favor of escalation, or if the Supreme Leader is unable to decide, paralysis at the top. The latter outcome carries risks of its own, since a lack of responsiveness may be misinterpreted as non-compliance with U.S. demands. Paralysis at the top might also afford more radical Iranian commanders, including in the nuclear forces, an opportunity to escalate a crisis on their own. U.S. deterrence planning must contend with both potential failure modes.

Increasing the Prospects of Deterring a Nuclear-Armed Iran

As we speculate about the steps necessary to deter a nuclear-armed Iran it is important to set realistic expectations. It should be clear that a Cold War, cookie-cutter approach to nuclear deterrence will find itself out of step with the complex and confounding idiosyncrasies of the Islamic Republic.

U.S. deterrence planning therefore needs to be more culturally attuned and tailored to Iran's decision-making environment if we hope to influence leadership calculations about the wisdom of challenging U.S. interests. Even under ideal circumstances, deterrence is an uncertain business. Despite our best efforts it can fail at different points on the spectrum of conflict and for a variety of reasons.

Along these lines, various forms of adventurism could be quite difficult to deter once Iran gets the bomb. As we have already seen, the Reagan administration was reluctant to confront Iran for fear it would retaliate with terrorist attacks against *Americans abroad*. The George W. Bush and Obama administrations have likewise been reticent to use military force against Iran for fear Tehran would retaliate against *American soldiers* in Iraq and Afghanistan.

Arguably, we are already self-deterred when it comes to Iran. Why would we be any more willing to confront the Islamic Republic once it acquires nuclear weapons and the ability to hold *American cities* at risk?

This is a conundrum that Iranian leaders seem to understand quite well. As Parliamentary Speaker Ali Larijani remarked, "If Iran becomes atomic Iran, no longer will anyone dare challenge it, because they would have to pay too high a price."[68] We should therefore expect that a nuclear-armed Iran will be even more prone to engage in terrorism and insurgency in the heady days following nuclear weapons acquisition since the leadership's greatest perceived cost of doing so – U.S. retaliation against the homeland – will likely shrink to zero.

U.S. nuclear superiority is plainly understood in Tehran.[69] American conventional military superiority is likewise acknowledged, though the regime contends asymmetric warfare can neutralize it. What Iran sees as lacking is America's will to confront it. Indeed, as noted at the outset, Iranian leaders will point time and again to their acquisition of nuclear weapons as proof that American threats have no credibility.

All of this suggests the single most important step the United States can and must take to enhance the prospects for successfully deterring a nuclear-armed Iran is to restore the credibility of its threat to use force against the Islamic Republic.

To rebuild the credibility of its deterrence strategy, the United States must begin by clearly delineating unacceptable red lines for the most threatening aspects of potential Iranian behavior, namely nuclear weapons-related transfers and use. It will be necessary to put the regime on notice publicly and privately that the United States will hold it accountable for transferring nuclear weapons-related technology, materials and the like to others.

Washington should further make clear such transfers to non-state actors will be deemed a direct threat to U.S. national security, subjecting the regime to the full range of military responses. To lend credence to these deterrent warnings, the United States could consider overt or covert operations to interdict other types of Iranian weapons smuggling, as a surrogate demonstration of American resolve.

Deterring Iranian nuclear use is a multi-faceted challenge. To deter such use against the United States, it will likely be necessary to dampen Iran's initial nuclear euphoria with sober reminders that America's nuclear arsenal was now specifically targeted against the ruling regime, that America had missile defenses while Iran did not, and that if Tehran was nonetheless foolish enough to use nuclear weapons against the United States, American nuclear retaliation would ensure Shi'a clerical rule and influence in Iran and within Islam more broadly would come to an abrupt end.

For those among the ruling elite who may be apocalyptically-minded, a slightly more tailored message through an appropriate medium would be in order, namely that far from hastening the return of the Shi'a messiah, the initiation of nuclear weapons use by Iran would only insult God by disgracing Shi'ism and triggering the destruction of His Islamic Republic.

Deterring Iranian nuclear use against U.S. allies, in particular Israel, raises challenges of its own. While Iranian leaders routinely castigate Israel for its presumed nuclear weapons stockpile, they nonetheless perceive the Jewish states as particularly vulnerable to nuclear destruction given its lack of strategic depth and concentrated population.

As Hashemi Rafsanjani remarked in 2001, "...the use of a nuclear bomb in Israel will leave nothing on the ground, whereas it will only damage the world of Islam."[70] The issue of a future Iranian nuclear attack against Israel was debated during the Democratic presidential primary campaign in 2008. Then-Senator Hillary Clinton took a decidedly hard line on the issue. Speaking to *ABC News*, Clinton explained:

> Well, the question was, if Iran were to launch a nuclear attack on Israel, what would our response be? And I want the Iranians to know that if I am president, we will attack Iran. And I want them to understand that. Because it does mean that they have to look very carefully at their society. Because whatever stage of development they might be in their nuclear weapons program, in the next 10 years during which they might foolishly consider launching an attack on Israel, we would be able to totally obliterate them. That's a terrible thing to say, but those people who run Iran need to understand that. Because that, perhaps, will deter them from doing something that would be reckless, foolish and tragic.[71]

Iran responded to Clinton's remarks by filing a protest at the United Nations. President Ahmadinejad brushed off the comments by claiming that neither Clinton nor her opponent, then-Senator Obama, could ever get elected president.

Obama took a more circumspect stance than Clinton. He acknowledged Israel was America's "most important ally" in the Middle East, and Washington would respond "forcefully and appropriately" to any attack. "But it is important that we use language that sends a signal to the world community that we're shifting from the sort of cowboy diplomacy, or lack of diplomacy, that we've seen out of George Bush. And this kind of language is not helpful." In Obama's view, "When Iran is able to go to the United Nations complaining about the statements made and get some sympathy, that's a sign that we are taking the wrong approach."[72]

Should Iran acquire nuclear weapons during the Obama administration, it will be necessary for the President and Secretary of State Clinton to revisit their respective campaign remarks. Inevitably, the President would be asked by the press if he now endorses the more hawkish views expressed by Clinton in 2008. At a minimum, the President will need to commit explicitly U.S. nuclear forces to the defense of America's allies in the region.

More careful deliberation will be needed as to whether Washington should then also specify that the societal destruction of Iran will be the price Iran's leaders pay for attacking Israel or another U.S. ally with nuclear weapons. It may be the case that most of the deterrence burden can rest on a narrower target set linked to the personal and corporate interests of the ruling elites. In this regard, it will be important to identify those values (e.g., personal wealth; societal control mechanisms such as state-run media, the IRGC and Basij; avoidance of diplomatic isolation, etc.) and how best to imperil them. In many, if not most, cases nuclear weapons will be overkill.

Given the short missile flight times involved, it will also be necessary to beef up the forward presence of U.S. forces in the region in order to: present the President with viable pre-emption options in the event Iran begins preparations for a nuclear attack, otherwise blunt such an attack with integrated and layered missile defenses, and rapidly hold Iran's leaders and military chain of command accountable for initiating nuclear weapons use.

Such forward basing carries risks, however, in exposing U.S. forces to attacks, from Iranian-backed terrorists and IRGC special forces to nuclear-armed ballistic missiles. Therefore, great attention will need to be devoted to U.S. force protection measures, as well. More intense security cooperation with our regional allies, including arms sales and counter-terrorism/counter-insurgency training, will help boost their confidence in resisting Iranian intimidation.

As in other cases of extended deterrence, we should expect Tehran to seek to undermine our allies' confidence in American security guarantees. Firm, consistent, and authoritative declaratory policy backed by the right force posture to implement it, as well as enhanced allied cooperation, should help parry Iran's rhetorical jabs.

To lend further credibility to its red lines, the United States must demonstrate a greater willingness to fight "in the shadows," as Iran does. Even after it acquires nuclear weapons, Tehran can still be expected to probe and exploit loopholes in U.S. deterrent warnings, employing lethal force either overtly or covertly in a manner designed to stay below the U.S. threshold for retaliation. Convincing Iran we will fight below that threshold can only help bolster our deterrence of conflict above it. In short, the demonstrated willingness to hold Iran accountable for lower levels of violence could have a credibility "multiplier effect."

This is not to suggest, however, that a greater U.S. willingness to fight Iran at lower levels of the conflict spectrum will immediately put an end to Iranian adventurism. As we have seen in the Persian Gulf and in Iraq, the IRGC in particular has demonstrated its willingness to engage in tit-for-tat retaliation against U.S. forces. We should therefore expect Iran to reply in-kind to demonstrate that *Tehran* will not be so easily deterred.

How this cycle has been broken in the past is for the United States to inflict major losses on Iran's military capabilities. We will need to be prepared to do so again in the future. Moreover, since we are postulating that Iran would have recourse to nuclear weapons, we will need to act a little Iranian ourselves, modulating our application of force to remain under Tehran's threshold for nuclear use. This will require careful consideration, as Tehran itself may not have a clear sense of when it would use nuclear weapons. In any event, to help keep a lid on the action-reaction cycle, we will also likely need to remind Iran of our escalation dominance.

Lastly, we should expect recurring crises with a nuclear-armed Iran. Indeed, the period immediately after nuclear weapons acquisition could be particularly perilous as Iranian historical grievances, insecurity, ambition and nuclear chauvinism all combine into a volatile mixture. In time, Iran will learn, as all previous nuclear powers have, that nuclear weapons have very limited utility. The question then becomes whether it will take a limited conventional conflict like the Pakistan-India clash over Kargil in 1999 to bring that lesson home to Tehran or will it require a near nuclear war like the 1962 Cuban missile crisis. In either case, we can be sure the United States will be involved.

Therefore, we must be prepared to defuse nuclear crises with Iran. This will likely require greater agility and flexibility on the part of Washington. It will entail careful messaging to the right audiences, a major challenge for our Intelligence Community and our diplomats. It will also likely require us to make important trade-offs.

For example, will it be more important to hold Tehran strictly to a given deadline – which it will be predisposed to defy – or can we allow a deadline to pass if, in doing so, it enables Iran to save face and both sides to defuse a given crisis? Moreover, will we be prepared to accept Iranian proclamations of "victory" over the United States if that helps to achieve our objectives? These are complex and challenging issues that should be explored by our policy and military planners in crisis simulations and exercises.

Conclusions

Deterrence will have to bear a very heavy load in the event Iran acquires the bomb. The regime's idiosyncrasies, including intense factionalism, belief in conspiracy theories, apocalyptic messianism and superstitious reliance on fortune telling, all seem destined to impair rational behavior under the intense stress of a nuclear crisis. Add to this environment intent to spread the Islamic revolution and a perception that the United States lacks the will to confront it and the stage seems set for deterrence to fail.

To decrease the risks of deterrence failure, much work will need to be done by U.S. military and policy planners. To begin, they must recognize America's track record of deterring the Islamic Republic since 1979 is rather poor and they must understand why that has been the case. They will need to tailor deterrence strategy and tactics to Iran's unique decision-making environment. Above all, they will need to rebuild the credibility of U.S. deterrent threats. This will require a greater willingness to employ limited force against Iran despite its possession of the bomb while maintaining U.S. escalation dominance to discourage Iran from initiating nuclear use.

Given the potential for nuclear chauvinism in Tehran, especially in the heady days following acquisition of the bomb, U.S. planners and decision makers should also use simulations and exercises to explore various means by which a nuclear crisis with Tehran could be defused. Even after making these investments, deterrence of a nuclear-armed Iran may still fail. We should also hedge against that possibility by buttressing the full panoply of offensive and defensive capabilities to limit their capacity to inflict damage and to defeat Iranian adventurism and nuclear use.

Notes

[1] David B. Crist, *Gulf of Conflict: A History of US-Iranian Confrontation at Sea,* Policy Focus No. 95 (June 2009), Washington Institute for Near East Studies, 3, http://www.washingtoninstitute.org/templateC04.php?CID=313.

[2] Ibid., 10.

[3] Stephen Andrew Kelley, "Better Lucky Than Good: Operation Earnest Will As Gunboat Diplomacy," U.S. Naval Postgraduate School Thesis (June 2007), 57. http://www.nps.edu/Academics/Centers/CCC/research/StudentTheses/kelley07.pdf .

[4] Steven V. Roberts, "U.S. Ships Shell Iran Installation in Gulf Reprisal," *New York Times* (Oct. 20, 1987), http://www.nytimes.com/1987/10/20/world/us-ships-shell-iran-installation-in-gulf-reprisal.html?pagewanted=1.

[5] Ibid.

[6] Ibid.

[7] Kelley, *op cit.,* 67-68.

[8] Ibid., 73.

[9] Ibid., 74.

[10] Kenneth M. Pollack, *The Persian Puzzle* (New York: Random House, 2005), 233.

[11] Crist, *op cit.,* 4.

[12] Pollack, *op cit.,* 226.

[13] Ibid., p. 227.

[14] Crist, *op cit.,* 13.

[15] Kelley, *op cit.,* 67.

[16] Crist, *op cit.,* 13.

[17] According to Rezaie, Khomeini said, "'If I was in your place, I would attack the [U.S.] warship just as it entered the Strait of Hormuz,' but he left the final decision to the officials. Later, we arrived at the conclusion that this approach was not wise, and the imam easily accepted our argument." See, "Iran: Former IRGC Commander Reza'i Narrates Memoirs of Iran-Iraq War," Open Source Center, IAP20051002011015 (Sept. 25, 2005).

[18] Pollack, *op cit.,* 232. Among the reasons cited by Hashemi Rafsanjani for Iran's decision to accept the ceasefire was, "The Americans had blatantly intervened on Iraq's side..." See "Former Iran President Comments on the End of the 1980s War with Iraq," Open Source Center, IAP20060928950007 (Sept. 26, 2006).

[19] Michael Ware, "Inside Iran's Secret War for Iraq," *Time* (Aug. 15, 2005).

[20] Ibid., p. 354.

[21] Afshin Molavi, "Iran-US Relations: A Cold, Fragile Peace," *Eurasia Insight* (April 7, 2003), http://www.eurasianet.org/departments/insight/articles/eav040703.shtml.

[22] Ware, *op cit.*

[23] Ibid.

[24] Information in this paragraph is drawn from Michael R. Gordon and Scott Shane, "U.S. Long Worried That Iran Supplied Arms in Iraq" *New York Times,* (March 27, 2007), http://www.nytimes.com/2007/03/27/world/middleeast/27weapons.html.

[25] Gordon and Shane, *op cit.*

[26] "Full Transcript: NPR Interview with President Bush," *National Public Radio* (Jan. 29, 2007), http://www.npr.org/templates/story/story.php?storyId=7065633.

[27] Kenneth Katzman, *Iran's Activities and Influence in Iraq,* Congressional Research Service (Dec. 26, 2007), 5, http://www.comw.org/warreport/iraqarchiveregion.html.

[28] Michael R. Gordon, "U.S. Says Iranian Arms Seized in Afghanistan," *New York Times* (April 18, 2007),
 http://www.nytimes.com/2007/04/18/world/middleeast/18military.html?pagewanted=print.

[29] "On-the-Record Briefing: US Ambassador to Iraq Ryan C. Crocker on His Meeting With Iranian Officials," U.S. Department of State (July 24, 2007), http://merln.ndu.edu/archivepdf/iran/State/88999.pdf.

[30] Katzman, *op cit.*

[31] Ibid.

[32] Steven Lee Myers, "Americans Release Iranian Detainees to Iraq," *New York Times,* (July 9, 2009), http://www.nytimes.com/2009/07/10/world/middleeast/09release.html.

[33] Dafna Linzer, "Troops Authorized to Kill Iranian Operatives in Iraq," *Washington Post* (Jan. 26, 2007),
 http://www.washingtonpost.com/wp-dyn/content/article/2007/01/25/AR2007012502199.html.

[34] Washington designated the IRGC-QF as a supporter of terrorist organizations in late-2007, but pulled its punches and has yet to designate the IRGC-QF as a foreign terrorist organization.

[35] "Gates: 2nd Carrier in Gulf a 'Reminder' to Iran," *MSNBC* (April 29, 2008), http://www.msnbc.msn.com/id/24377396/.

[36] Lolita C. Baldor, "Gates: Iran Boosts Support for Militias," *Washington Post* (April 11, 2008).

[37] Michael R. Gordon, "U.S. Says Iranian Arms Seized in Afghanistan" *New York Times,* (April 18, 2007),
 http://www.nytimes.com/2007/04/13/world/middleeast/18military.html?pagewanted=print.

[38] "DoD News Briefing with Gen. Petraeus from the Pentagon" (April 26, 2007), http://www.defense.gov/transcripts/transcript.aspx?transcriptid=3951.

[39] Michael R. Gordon, "US Ties Iran to Deadly Iraq Attack," *New York Times* (July 2, 2007), http://www.nytimes.com/2007/07/02/world/middleeast/02cnd-iran.html.

[40] Thom Shanker, "Iran May Know of Weapons for Taliban, Gates Contends" *New York Times,* (June 14, 2007),
 http://www.nytimes.com/2007/06/14/world/middleeast/14gates.html.

[41] "Transcript of Remarks by Director of the Central Intelligence Agency Gen. Michael V. Hayden at the Landon Lecture Series, Kansas State University April 30, 2008," Central Intelligence Agency, https://www.cia.gov/news-information/speeches-testimony/speeches-testimony-archive-2008/landon-lecture-series.html. Emphasis added.

[42] Joseph Felter and Brian Fishman, *Iranian Strategy in Iraq: Politics and "Other Means,"* Combating Terrorism Center at West Point (Oct. 13, 2008), 64, http://www.ctc.usma.edu/Iran.

[43] This assumes deterrence actually worked during the Cold War, a proposition Keith Payne and others have called into question. See, for example, Keith B. Payne, *Deterrence in the Second Nuclear Age* (Lexington, Ky.: University Press of Kentucky, 1996), 37-60.

[44] Kelley, *op cit.,* p. 83.

[45] Jackson Diehl, "In Iran, Apocalypse vs. Reform," *Washington Post* (May 11, 2006), http://www.washingtonpost.com/wp-dyn/content/article/2006/05/10/AR2006051001791.html. See also, Karl Vick, "In Iran, Even Some on Right Warning Against Extremes," *Washington Post* (March 27, 2006), http://www.washingtonpost.com/wp-dyn/content/article/2006/03/26/AR2006032600755.html.

[46] Daniel Byman, Shahram Chubin, *et al, Iran's Security Policy in the Post-Revolutionary Era*, (Washington, DC: RAND, 2001), 21-23, http://www.rand.org/pubs/monograph_reports/MR1320/.

[47] Anthony H. Cordesman, *Iran's Developing Military Capabilities* (Washington, DC: CSIS Press, 2005), 47.

[48] Mohsen Makhmalbaf, "The Secrets of Khamene'i's Life: Part I – His Interests" (Dec. 29, 2009), http://homylafayette.blogspot.com/2009/12/makhmalbaf-secrets-khameneis-life.html. Makhmalbaf is the Iranian opposition's main spokesman abroad and claims to have compiled this information from former staff members of the Supreme Leader's Household and the Intelligence Ministry who have fled abroad.

[49] Mohsen Makhmalbaf, "The Secrets of Khamene'i's Life: Part II – His Entourage and Household Operations" (Dec. 30, 2009), http://homylafayette.blogspot.com/2009/12/makhmalbaf-secrets-of-khameneis-life.html.

[50] "Pakistan Establishes Nuclear Control Body," *Arms Control Today,* (March 2000), http://www.armscontrol.org/node/2899.

[51] Pollack, *op cit.,* 359.

[52] Mehdi Khalaji, *Apocalyptic Politics: On the Rationality of Iranian Policy,* Policy Focus No. 79, Washington Institute for Near East Policy (Jan. 2008), 19, http://www.washingtoninstitute.org/templateC04.php?CID=286.

[53] Ibid., 16.

[54] Ibid., 19.

[55] Makhmalbaf, "The Secrets of Khamene'i's Life: Part II – His Entourage and Household Operations."

[56] Julian Borger, "IAEA Secret Report: Iran Worked on Nuclear Warhead," *Guardian* (Sept. 18, 2009), http://www.guardian.co.uk/world/2009/sep/18/iran-nuclear-warhead-iaea-report.

[57] According to Iranian state media, Ahmadinejad described the destruction of New York's twin towers on Sept. 11, 2001 as a "complicated [U.S.] intelligence scenario and act," adding, "The September 11 incident was a big fabrication as a pretext for the campaign against terrorism and a prelude for staging an invasion against Afghanistan." See "Iran's Ahmadinejad Calls Sept. 11 'Big Fabrication,'" *Reuters* (March 6, 2010), http://www.reuters.com/article/idUSTRE6251AO20100306.

[58] According to Safavi, "The events of September 11 were ordered by US officials and Mossad [Israeli intelligence] so that they could carry out their strategy of pre-emption and warmongering and unipolarisation in order to dominate the Middle East." See "Iran says U.S., Israel Ordered September 11 attacks," *Iran Focus* (Sept. 6, 2006), http://www.iranfocus.com/en/special-wire/iran-says-u.s.-israel-ordered-september-11-attacks-08512.html.

[59] Ray Takeyh and Joseph Cirincione, "ElBaradei is Quietly Managing to Disarm Iran," *Financial Times* (Feb. 26, 2008), http://www.ft.com/cms/s/0/06a1fa90-e4d7-11dc-a495-0000779fd2ac.html.

[60] Khalaji, *op cit.,* 32.

[61] Ibid., 24-25.

[62] Ibid., 16.

[63] Sami Moubayed, "'President' Larijani: A Star is Born," *Asia Times* (June 21, 2008), http://www.atimes.com/atimes/Middle_East/JF21Ak02.html.

[64] Paul Reynolds, "Ahmadinejad's Final Flourish," *BBC News* (April 4, 2006), http://news.bbc.co.uk/2/hi/middle_east/6526359.stm.

[65] "Larijani Sees Ulterior Motives Behind West N-hype," *PressTV* (Dec. 5, 2009), http://www.presstv.ir/pop/Print/?id=112902.

[66] Amira Howeidy, "Taking Matters in Hand," *Al Ahram Weekly,* Issue No. 791 (April 20-26, 2006), http://weekly.ahram.or.eg/print/2006/791/re6.htm.

[67] For example, in his 2009 New Year's address, Khamene'i remarked, "I do not know who is making the decisions in America. Is it the President? Is it the Congress? Or is it the unknown people who pull the strings?" See, "Supreme Leader's Speech in Mashhad," (March 21, 2009), The Center for Preserving and Publishing the Works of Grand Ayatollah Sayyid Ali Khamenei,
 http://english.khamenei.ir//index.php?option=com_content&task=view&id=1076&Itemid=4.

[68] Larijani's 2005 remarks to IRGC commanders quoted in Shahram Chubin, *Iran's Nuclear Ambitions*, (Washington, DC: Carnegie Endowment for International Peace, 2006), 33.

[69] As noted by Iran's ambassador to the IAEA, "…But let's suppose that Iran would go for nuclear weapons. How many warheads do you think Iran would have? In a couple of years, let's say one or two. If we were to get a nuclear weapon we would be at a disadvantage, competing with the United States, which has thousands of warheads. It would be a tactical mistake for our country to do that, and our leaders are clever enough not to do it…" See, "Interview Excerpts: Iran Ambassador Ali Asghar Soltanieh," *Washington Post* (Sept. 17, 2009), http://www.washingtonpost.com/wp-dyn/content/article/2009/09/17/AR2009091703072.html.

[70] "Former Iranian President Rafsanjani on Using a Nuclear Bomb Against Israel," *Special Dispatch Series*, No. 325, (Jan. 3, 2002), Middle East Media Research Institute (MEMRI), http://www.memri.org/report/en/0/0/0/0/0/0/582.htm.

[71] "Iran: Considering Hillary Clinton's 'obliterate' remarks," *Los Angeles Times*, (April 24, 2008), http://latimesblogs.latimes.com/babylonbeyond/2008/04/iran-considerin.html.

[72] "Obama: Clinton's 'obliterate' Iran statement too much like Bush," *CNN* (May 4, 2008), file:///C:/Documents%20and%20Settings/gilesg/My%20Documents/Iran/US%20Policy/Obliterate%20Iran/5-5-08_Obama_Clinton%27s%20%27obliterate%27%20Iran%20statement%20too%20much%20like%20Bush_CNN.htm.

CHAPTER 6

Deterring North Korea from Using WMD in Future Conflicts and Crises

Bruce W. Bennett

For nearly 60 years, North Korea has determinedly pursued the development of weapons of mass destruction (WMD) usually defined as involving chemical, biological, radiological and nuclear (CBRN) weapons. In recent years, North Korea has used its nuclear weapons to deter action against it and to coerce its neighbors in crises. As the North Korean regime continues to suffer many failures, it may someday lash out and cause a major war in Northeast Asia or the North Korean government may collapse into civil war and anarchy. With almost no chance of winning a conflict limited to conventional weapons, and having invested so much of their limited resources in WMD, North Korean leaders are likely to use these weapons in conflicts or further crises. North Korean WMD could cause immense damage to the populations and economies in Northeast Asia, potentially destabilizing the region for many years.

It is therefore incumbent on the United States and its allies to develop means to deter North Korean use of WMD. But doing so is not easy. The United States and the Republic of Korea (ROK) have clearly failed to deter multiple North Korean provocations associated with WMD. Moreover, the North Korean leaders appear insensitive to the kind of "assured destruction" nuclear weapon retaliatory threats against cities and industry that were the major basis for Cold War deterrence. Instead, deterrence of North Korean WMD use needs to be based more on the ability to defeat that use and deny its objectives, while still threatening retaliation that would undermine or destroy the North Korean regime.

This chapter describes such a deterrent approach. It first characterizes North Korea as a failing state, one which has used crises and may yet try to use conflict to strengthen the regime. It then addresses the nature of the North Korean WMD threat, how North Korea might use that threat, and the damage it could cause. This chapter concludes by discussing how the United States and the ROK might deter the North Korean WMD threats in conflict and crisis.

"Know Thy Enemy"

The ancient Chinese philosopher/strategist, Sun Tzu, urged, "Know thy self, know thy enemy. A thousand battles, a thousand victories." The situation in North Korea is serious, complicating efforts to deter North Korean use of WMD.

The Situation in North Korea

North Korea is a failing state. Its economy has had many failures. Its agricultural production is usually much less than its subsistence food requirements.[1] As a result, many North Koreans starve to death, while the rest of the population survives in part because of substantial foreign aid and in part because of market activities. But the North Korean regime fears that North Korean merchants are beyond the regime's control, especially given the merchants' extensive use of bribery. The regime therefore carried out a currency revaluation in late-2009 that allowed only minimal currency exchange and prohibited the use of foreign currency, seeking to wipe out the merchants' capital. This currency revaluation also took away the savings of many North Korean elites, caused hoarding of goods (especially food) and resulted in hyperinflation.

Despite the North Korean efforts to control people's lives, North Korea sees a lot of rebellious behavior. This includes refugee flows into China,[2] major black market activities, graft and corruption by North Korean authorities[3] and even reported attacks on the North Korean leaders.[4]

Social unrest appears to be spreading in North Korea. The North Korean regime has tried to maintain its control of the country through the heavy use of propaganda. But "there is mounting evidence that Kim Jong Il is losing the propaganda war inside North Korea, with more than half the population now listening to foreign news, grass-roots cynicism undercutting state myths and discontent rising even among elites."[5]

Meanwhile, North Korea's leader, Kim Jong-Il, is in bad health, may die, and his succession is not clearly resolved. His apparently designated successor, his third son Kim Jong-Un, is young and inexperienced. Trying to build his image, the regime credited him with the December 2009 currency revaluation, in the end making him appear to have caused a disaster.

The U.S. commander in South Korea, General Walter L. Sharp, has summarized this situation as the following: "Combined with the country's disastrous centralized economy, dilapidated industrial sector, insufficient agricultural base, malnourished military and populace, and developing nuclear programs, the possibility of a sudden leadership change in the North could be destabilizing and unpredictable."[6]

How Is North Korea Coping?

The North Korean leadership has a culture of empowerment to justify its legitimacy. As the regime has faced the many failures described above, it has used provocations to demonstrate it is still empowered and to create a diversionary conflict effect: the North Korean regime seeks to unify its elites against the common external adversaries, mainly the ROK and the United States, trying to steer the elites' displeasure away from the regime.

For example, in 2006 North Korea faced serious U.S. economic sanctions imposed because of illegal North Korean activities such as counterfeiting U.S. currency and goods. North Korea could have reversed these sanctions by admitting its illegal activities, apologizing for them and promising to stop them. But in the culture of empowerment, such North Korean action would make the leadership appear weak and subject to overthrow.

Instead, the leadership prepared for, and carried out, a series of provocations, including missile launches on July 4 (U.S. time), and escalating to a nuclear weapon test on October 8 (U.S. time). Kim Jong-Il had demonstrated his empowerment, and by February 2007, he had concluded an agreement with the United States and the other regional powers that reversed the U.S. economic sanctions and otherwise proved very advantageous to North Korea.

North Korea has continued its pattern of escalating brinksmanship to deal with its many challenges. North Korea used missile launches and a nuclear test again in 2009 to demonstrate Kim Jong-Il's continued empowerment despite his very poor health, to support regime succession, to continue his use of diversionary conflict and to achieve other objectives discussed below. And in 2010 North Korea sank a ROK warship, escalating its pattern of provocations.

North Korean Asymmetric WMD Threats

As ROK and U.S. conventional military superiority developed over several decades, the North Korean economy could not keep pace. Instead, North Korea opted to pursue various asymmetric threats, especially WMD. This was a natural evolution from Kim Il-Sung's emphasis on special operations forces in World War II. This section describes the North Korean WMD component of its asymmetric capabilities.

How Much WMD Might North Korea Have?

Most experts in the United States assume North Korea has developed its nuclear weapon capabilities independently. For example, the CIA said North Korea produced enough plutonium by 1994 for one to two weapons,[7] and North Korea did not produce any more plutonium until 2003. These experts typically argue North Korea could have roughly five to 10 nuclear weapons today,[8] though given the limited testing of the weapons and their delivery means like missiles, only two to six of these would likely be deliverable and reliable.

However, a number of stories suggest North Korea has had external help. For example, in 1999 Dr. AQ Khan of Pakistan said he went to North Korea and was shown three plutonium weapons that could be assembled for use on ballistic missiles in one hour.[9] If he was right, North Korea must have had an external source of plutonium.

Moreover, North Korea would not likely have put all of its weapons in one place at one time and shown them to a foreigner, as a security failure could have led to U.S. preemption. North Korea may thus have had at least five to six nuclear weapons in 1999, consistent with what the defector Hwang Jong-Yup said he was told in 1996.[10]

If these stories are correct, North Korea may have developed more than 10 nuclear weapons. In particular, one story from Russian intelligence claimed that in 1992, North Korea got 56 kilograms of plutonium from the former Soviet Union.[11] If so, North Korea could have enough fissile material today for perhaps 20 nuclear weapons. And if some organizations risked giving North Korea fissile material, they may have also provided the technical expertise necessary to make ballistic missile warheads, as Dr. Khan asserted.

There are many reports on North Korean chemical and biological weapons. "We also assess Pyongyang has an active biological weapons research program, with an inventory that may include anthrax, botulism, cholera, hemorrhagic fever, plague, smallpox, typhoid and yellow fever."[12] "North Korea has an assessed significant chemical agent stockpile that includes blood, blister, choking and nerve agents."[13] "In the assessment of U.S. intelligence services, their reserves, accommodated in perhaps half a dozen major storage sites and as many as 170 mountain tunnels, are at least 180 to 250 tons, with some estimates of chemical stockpiles run as high as 2,500-5,000 tons."[14] "In May 1996 ROK Foreign Minister Yu Chong-ha reported to the National Assembly that it was estimated that North Korea possessed approximately 5,000 tons of biological and chemical weapons. Given the extensive production facilities, this later estimate may constitute the low end of the actual stockpile."[15]

In terms of delivery systems, "chemical weapons can be delivered by virtually all DPRK fire support systems. This includes most artillery, multiple rocket launchers (including those mounted on CHAHO-type boats), mortars, FROG and SCUD missiles, and some bombs."[16] "The North has about 600 SCUD missiles capable of hitting targets in South Korea, and possibly also of reaching Japanese territory. There are a further 200 Nodong-1 missiles which could reach Tokyo."[17] North Korea would likely use its special operations forces (SOF) to deliver biological weapons. "Military authorities in Seoul estimate that North Korea's special operations forces currently exceed 200,000 soldiers."[18] "North Korea has recently deployed about 50,000 special forces along its border with South Korea."[19]

Potential North Korean Uses of WMD

In peacetime, North Korea regularly uses its nuclear weapons to threaten neighbors, hoping to coerce them and/or deter their actions. For mainly internal purposes, North Korea has used nuclear weapon possession and tests to illustrate the strength or formidability of its regime and to claim

North Korea is one of the most powerful (and respected) countries in the world. It has also used nuclear weapons as a bargaining chip to secure goods and agreements from other countries. North Korea generally does not use chemical and biological weapons for these strategic purposes.

It is less clear how North Korea would use WMD in wartime. North Korea has threatened to use nuclear weapons against the cities and military facilities of neighbors. An "unofficial spokesman" talks of North Korea using nuclear weapons to: (1) create electromagnetic pulse (EMP) effects to disable electronic systems, (2) attack nuclear power plants (causing widespread nuclear fallout), and (3) attack cities in various ways.[20]

While the use of nuclear weapons against cities would be horrific, the United States planned a similar concept during the Cold War with its so-called "assured destruction" concept of threatening Soviet cities. As early as 1945, the U.S. Joint Chiefs of Staff explained the concept of targeting Soviet cities: "The atomic bomb, in the foreseeable future, will be primarily a strategic weapon of destruction against concentrated industrial areas vital to the war effort of an enemy nation. In addition, it may be employed against centers of population with a view to forcing an enemy state to yield through terror and disintegration of national morale."[21]

North Korea is likely to view the survivability of its nuclear forces as limited, pushing it to use them relatively early in a conflict. This attitude would be strengthened by a belief the United States will use nuclear weapons early,[22] and nuclear weapons would provide greater, potentially conflict winning leverage early on. For example, North Korea might hope appropriate nuclear weapon use would convince Japan to not become involved in the conflict, and thereby deny the United States the use of Japan to support U.S. deployments and operations.[23]

North Korea might alternatively wait until an invasion of the ROK fails and the ROK/U.S. start a counteroffensive before using North Korean nuclear weapons. The North Korea regime would know it had to stop the counteroffensive or not survive, and would be prepared to take very risky actions to survive, including nuclear attacks on cities. Many analysts argue this would be the most likely kind of North Korean nuclear weapon use.

North Korea is more likely to use its chemical and biological weapons to achieve specific operational objectives. These objectives would likely include causing breakthroughs on the battlefield, disrupting airfield and port operations and disrupting the flow of US forces into Korea. Such attacks would most likely support North Korean objectives if done very early in a conflict. Given the potency of biological weapons, North Korea may prefer to use them at some significant geographical distance from the Korean peninsula, such as in Japan or the United States.

Nuclear Effects on People and Things

Table 1 evaluates the *expected* effectiveness of North Korean nuclear attacks delivered by ballistic missiles against ROK ground forces, airfields and population centers. This analysis assumes an airburst weapon to maximize prompt effects and eliminate most fallout. The Republic of Korea today, in peacetime, has 47 Army divisions, 15 major military airfields and a population of 48,500,000.

Table 1
Approximate North Korean Nuclear Weapon Effects
on ROK Target Types

Weapon Performance (60 % delivery)	Weapons Launched Per Target	Army Divisions Lost to Prompt Casualties	Airfields Lost to Prompt Casualties	ROK City Prompt Casualties*
10 Kt, 1.5 km CEP	20	1.40 of 47	5.7 of 15	3,100,000
10 Kt, 1.5 km CEP	15	1.05 of 47	4.7 of 15	2,400,000
10 Kt, 1.5 km CEP	10	0.70 of 47	3.1 of 15	1,700,000
10 Kt, 1.5 km CEP	6	0.42 of 47	1.9 of 15	1,100,000
10 Kt, 1.5 km CEP	3	0.21 of 47	0.93 of 15	600,000
10 Kt, 1.5 km CEP	1	0.07 of 47	0.31 of 15	200,000
50 Kt, 0.5 km CEP	1	0.25 of 47	0.70 of 15	850,000

*Expected casualties, including reliability/delivery probability. Thus a 10 Kt weapon launched at a city like Seoul will cause an expected 200,000 fatalities and serious casualties (assuming a baseline reliability/delivery probability of 60 percent); if it actually detonates in the middle of the city, it will cause an expected 340,000 fatalities and serious casualties.

Thus, if North Korea uses one 10 kiloton (Kt) weapon against a ground force division (the second to last row), prompt effects would cause an expected 7 percent attrition, whereas the same weapon would cause an expected attrition of 31 percent at a typical airfield or nearly 200,000 expected casualties in a city like Seoul. A high effectiveness warhead (the last row) with higher explosive yield (50 Kt), accuracy (0.5 km CEP), and delivery probability (70 percent) would cause several times as much damage, depending upon the target type, suggesting the value North Korea might place on improving nuclear weapon capabilities.

The earlier rows of Table 1 show multiple nuclear weapons would do even more damage. For example, if North Korea uses (launches) three nuclear weapons against ground forces, 21 percent of a division would be damaged, while three weapons (spread across three airfields) would create an expected damage of 31 percent at each of three airfields, or casualties equivalent to 93 percent for a single airfield. At the extreme, 20 nominal

North Korean nuclear weapons launched against these targets would affect about 3 percent of the ROK ground forces, or almost six ROK major airbases, or about 3 million ROK civilians. The very high potential damage to the civilian population suggests why North Korea might focus its attacks on cities as targets.

The Effects of Chemical and Biological Weapons

Chemical and biological weapons (CBW) can also cover large areas with their effects. Consider a 12.5 Kt nuclear air burst will cause fatalities over perhaps 8 km^2, a large area in a city. In contrast, chemical and biological weapons are carried by the wind; their effects are a function of the original dispersal pattern, wind direction and speed, and atmospheric conditions. If dispersed across a wide base, 1,000 kgs of sarin might cause lethal effects over 0.7 to 8 km^2, depending upon these various factors. Similar dispersal of 10 kgs of anthrax might cause lethal effects over 5 to 30 km^2.[24] These areas suggest that possible quantities of chemical and biological weapon could affect similar areas to those shown for nuclear weapons in Table 1.

The other key difference between the chemical and biological weapons and nuclear weapons is the fraction of people in these areas most likely affected. With an airburst nuclear weapon, most people in the lethal area would be affected. Even those inside buildings would see their buildings collapse or seriously damaged, contributing to the injuries the people would suffer. With chemical and biological weapons, the buildings in these areas may provide some degree of shelter from weapon effects. This would be especially true of buildings without central air conditioning and having many floors, as is typical in Seoul. Thus, only a fraction of the people in these areas would be affected depending upon the time of year and building ventilation, leading to somewhat fewer casualties if a similar area is affected. Still, even if the casualties are only half or a quarter as much as with nuclear weapons over a similar amount of area, these quantities of chemical and biological weapons could cause tens of thousands of casualties or more in ROK cities.

Against military targets, chemical and biological weapons would tend to cause far less damage than is shown for nuclear weapons in Table 1. Military personnel tend to have protective clothing, medicines and other counters to chemical and biological weapons, protections that would significantly reduce casualties. Still, these military forces would need timely warning to apply many of these protections, and thus warning of WMD use would become a key determinant of the damage North Korean chemical and biological weapons could do to military forces.

Deterrence Theory

Deterrence occurs when an adversary expects the benefits of an action are less than the costs. The *Deterrence Operations Joint Operating Concept* (JOC) is the official Defense Department statement on deterrence. It says: "Deterrence operations convince adversaries not to take actions that threaten U.S. vital interests by means of decisive influence over their decision-making. Decisive influence is achieved by credibly threatening to deny benefits and/or impose costs, while encouraging restraint by convincing the actor that restraint will result in an acceptable outcome."[25]

Basic Deterrence Concepts

The *Deterrence Operations JOC* uses a rational deterrence theory framework.[26] This theory examines the adversary's perception of the net benefits (benefits minus costs) of any action as well as the probabilities of these net benefits to determine the utility of the action. It then compares the utilities of the alternative actions; if the utility of restraint (the status quo) is greatest, then deterrence is achieved.[27] This assessment does not require an adversary to find an action that is clearly beneficial. In some situations, all of an adversary's choices (even the status quo) may have negative utility, as appears to be the case with North Korea. In such cases, the adversary looks for the "least miserable option." Said differently, a noted deterrence expert, Robert Jervis, has argued, "It is rational to start a war one does not expect to win ... if it is believed that the likely consequences of not fighting are even worse."[28]

Rational deterrence theory assumes the adversary is risk neutral: The adversary's decision is based upon expected value calculations, and neither takes nor avoids risk.[29] The alternative theory considered by the *Deterrence Operations JOC* is called prospect theory, which assesses risk differently. It argues that when an adversary faces serious losses, as in the North Korean conditions described above, the adversary becomes a risk taker, ready to try actions that avoid or reduce its losses even if there is serious risk in those actions. Deterrence of risk takers is a much more difficult effort, as US experience with North Korea has illustrated.

Understanding Deterrence Leverage

As suggested, deterrence is achieved by affecting the benefits and costs perceived by an adversary, as well as the adversary's perceptions of the probabilities it will experience these costs and benefits. The literature talks about two kinds of deterrence efforts: deterrence by threat of punishment and deterrence by threat of denial.[30]

Deterrence by threat of punishment usually seeks to increase the costs an adversary will suffer from an unwanted action, while deterrence by denial seeks to reduce the benefits the adversary hopes to achieve. For example, if the United States wants to deter a North Korean missile test, it could threaten economic sanctions if North Korea proceeds with the test (punishment) or it could threaten to preemptively destroy the missile on the launch pad (denial).

Deterrence is in the eye of the adversary. What does he perceive to be the benefits and costs of particular actions, and what does he believe the probabilities of each outcome are? Those perceptions are in turn based on U.S. capabilities for denial and punishment and U.S. will to impose denial and punishment. When adversaries perceive the U.S. lacks will (e.g., the U.S. fails to act against the bad behavior of an adversary), they may discount other U.S. denial and punishment threats (they perceive lower probabilities of costly outcomes, and higher probabilities of beneficial outcomes).

Each U.S. deterrent action has consequences for both sides. For example, a U.S. preemptive attack on a missile launch pad could destroy the missile and potentially embarrass the North Korean leadership, contributing to deterrence. But this action would likely lead to further escalation, something the United States would usually prefer to avoid but which North Korea may be prepared to accept to rally its military and other elites around a failing regime. North Korea's escalation might be to an artillery attack on the ROK, an attack the ROK would want to avoid. Thus, the ROK might pressure the United States not to carry out a preemptive attack to avoid this escalation.

Many in the international community would also likely communicate their view that U.S. preemptive action was unnecessary and inappropriate, hence reducing the probability of such U.S. action. If the United States has strong incentives not to carry out a preemptive attack, the adversary may conclude that the probability of such a U.S. action, despite U.S. capabilities, is extremely low.

In addition, if the United States cannot fully prove bad behavior by an adversary, it will normally be reluctant to take action. For example, despite assertions by then-President Bush in 2006 he would hold North Korea accountable for nuclear proliferation, no serious US action was taken against North Korea when its assistance in building a Syrian nuclear reactor was discovered the following year, assistance the United States could not prove beyond a reasonable doubt.

To the extent that U.S. adversaries can keep their WMD activities covert, the United States will have difficulty responding against them. Adversaries may thus feel undeterred from pursuing covert WMD development and proliferation efforts.

Finally, there is a difference between U.S. efforts to deter an attack upon the United States and U.S. efforts to deter attacks on U.S. allies. Most adversaries will perceive the United States would respond very seriously to an attack on the United States. But deterrence that supports U.S. allies—so-called extended deterrence—often appears less probable to draw a serious U.S. response, given the lower level of U.S. interest. To counter this concern, the U.S./ROK Presidential Summit in June 2009 declared a *Joint Vision for the Alliance of the United States of America and the Republic of Korea*. This *Joint Vision* said in part, "The Alliance is adapting to changes in the 21st century security environment. We will maintain a robust defense posture, backed by allied capabilities that support both nations' security interests. The continuing commitment of extended deterrence, including the US nuclear umbrella, reinforces this assurance."[31]

Applying the Theory

In practice, few decision makers explicitly calculate the costs and benefits of each possible outcome, estimate the probability of that outcome and calculate the preferred action based on precise calculations. Instead, consideration of these factors is more subjective and approximate. Moreover, it is difficult to estimate these factors for Kim Jong-Il and his regime, given how the regime strives to deny information on its attitudes and decision making to the outside world. Nevertheless, North Korean behavior does give some baselines against which to examine this framework and at least try to understand the tradeoffs North Korea might perceive.

Consider the case of the April 2009 North Korean missile test provocation.[32] Why did Kim Jong-Il select this action? To keep this example simple, assume there were three alternative North Korean courses of action at that time: (1) restraint (the status quo), (2) the use of artillery to fire into the ROK, and (3) the North Korean missile test.

The long-range missile launched on April 5, 2009, was likely seen as Kim Jong-Il's best course of action for creating the appearance of regime empowerment, while not causing much chance of retaliatory actions that could threaten regime survival nor giving the appearance of weakness to his internal or external enemies. Doing nothing in his regime's deteriorating position was likely seen as unhelpful, and doing too much—such as a North Korean artillery attack on Seoul—was likely viewed as unleashing a concatenation of escalation responses that could destroy the Pyongyang regime.

With the missile test Kim Jong-Il probably hoped to counter the appearance of regime weakness associated with its many failures and his recent illnesses. He likely also hoped to create a "diversionary conflict" where his military and other elites focused on the United States and the ROK as their enemies, responsible for North Korea's problems, thereby creating an environment where his son had the best chance to succeed him. While his past provocations have invariably led to the United States and the ROK imposing some form of costs in return, usually economic sanctions, Kim Jong-Il has turned these costs to political benefit by unifying his military and other elites against their external enemies and in support of the regime.

Kim's missile test in April 2009 might have backfired if the United States had shot down the missile during the boost phase, preventing Kim Jong-Il from demonstrating his missile capability.[33] Alternatively, a North Korean artillery fire provocation could have failed due to effective ROK counter battery fire that quickly silenced the North Korean artillery, demonstrating North Korean weakness rather than strength. Further, North Korean artillery fire into the ROK was clearly too escalatory and dangerous, and thus an unacceptable action.

The United States might have deterred a second North Korean missile launch if it had prepared to intercept the missile. The United States could have announced that it would not allow North Korea to launch another intercontinental-range ballistic missile.[34]

The U.S. announcement could have said, "If North Korea launches, the U.S. will use the opportunity to test its missile defenses against the target missile kindly provided by North Korea. Of course, since this would be an initial ballistic missile defense (BMD) test against this kind of threat, there would be a significant potential that the missile intercept would fail. But even then, the United States would gain significant experience in, and data about, intercepting real North Korean missiles."[35]

Kim Jong-Il might have viewed such a U.S. BMD threat as posing a good probability of making the regime look weak (by successfully intercepting the missile), plus some chance the launch episode could have escalated out of control toward full-scale war if the United States was prepared to be so aggressive. Under those conditions, Kim Jong-Il could have preferred the status quo to the outcome of a second missile launch.[36]

This simple example illustrates many of the characteristics of deterrence. In particular, it suggests Kim Jong-Il might be deterred by U.S. efforts to deny his provocations. Historically, much of the deterrence literature, and especially the nuclear deterrence literature, has focused on deterrence by the threat of punishment: An adversary could be deterred from taking an action because of the punishment threatened if it takes the action. But the United States and the ROK also need to apply denial threats and find punishments that deter North Korean provocations like missile launches.[37]

Deterring WMD Use

When trying to deter North Korean WMD use, what is the relative utility of deterrence by denial and deterrence by punishment? Is there sufficient leverage in these two approaches combined to somehow control or prevent North Korean WMD use?

Options for Deterrence by Punishment Threats and Deterrence by Denial Threats

During the Cold War, the United States focused its deterrence of the Soviet Union on punishment. Deterrence by the threat of punishment can be achieved by threatening various assets of an adversary. Early in the Cold War the United States recognized nuclear weapon attacks against adversary cities were a serious deterrent threat (as noted above). The United States also discussed targeting adversary military forces and/or adversary leadership to achieve deterrence by threat of punishment (and also a significant level of deterrence by denial).

There are four basic actions that support deterrence by denial: counterforce, active defense, passive defense and consequence management. Counterforce attacks seek to destroy adversary WMD forces (both weapons and delivery means) to prevent their use, and may also target command and control capabilities as well as adversary leaders to prevent WMD launch. Active defenses seek to intercept WMD when en route to targets, and include air and missile defenses as well as border control against Special Operations Forces. Passive defenses seek to protect people and assets from WMD effects once the weapons detonate or are otherwise released. Consequence management seeks to deal with the effects of WMD after people/assets have been exposed, providing medical care and other kinds of damage recovery.

These denial means provide different levels of leverage against WMD use. Counterforce can be powerful if preemptive action is possible and if the locations of the WMD forces are known. Active defense can be technologically challenging but potentially very effective as technologies mature. Passive defenses are relatively more effective against chemical, biological and radiological weapons, having a more limited role against nuclear weapons (though sheltering and evacuation/dispersal can still be important). And consequence management is important for dealing with WMD effects, but consequence management capabilities have generally not been considered very effective in achieving deterrence of WMD use.

The Historical Approach to Deterrence by Punishment

Nuclear deterrence was a major international issue during the Cold War. For much of the period, the United States talked about strategic nuclear deterrence almost interchangeably with the concept of assured destruction: The United States deterred Soviet nuclear attacks on the United States by threatening to destroy Soviet cities with their associated population and industry (imposing a high punishment cost). Many in the United States felt that if the Soviet cities were destroyed then most of their society would also be destroyed, and the risk averse Soviet leadership would not take that chance since their power flowed from the talents and productivity of their people.

In the 1970s, the abilities of the United States and the Soviet Union to destroy each other's cities were assessed in the terms shown in Figure 1.[38] At the time, both the United States and the Soviets had thousands of equivalent megatons (EMT) of nuclear weapons,[39] as suggested by the "capability" mark at the right.

Figure 1
Deterring Nuclear Weapon Use: Cold War vs. North Korea

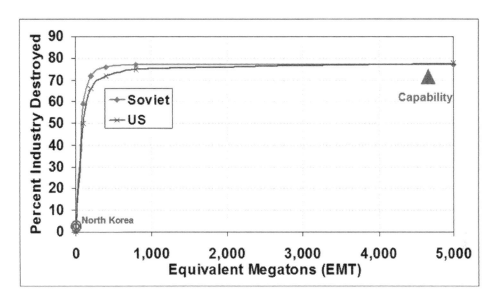

The curves in Figure 1 indicate even if the Soviets could have somehow destroyed most of the U.S. nuclear forces, the United States could still have destroyed most of the Soviet industrial capacity,[40] since even a "small" city attack (a few hundred EMT) would have been devastating.[41] And the same was true for the Soviets: They also deterred U.S. nuclear attacks by threatening U.S. cities. Moreover, the cost of adding one more warhead to the attack to insure damage would always be much less than the adversary's cost of destroying one more warhead. Thus, there was little leverage achieved by the capability for counterforce attacks or active defenses: Not enough of the opposing threat could be denied to make a difference.

But the North Korean nuclear threat is a different problem because it is on the part of the curve with steep returns. A North Korean force of five to 20 nuclear weapons of 10 Kt yield each would amount to about 0.25 to 1 equivalent megatons (EMT). Because North Korea has relatively few nuclear weapons, serious US/ROK efforts to destroy those weapons combined with effective active defenses could significantly reduce the damage North Korea could cause against its possible nuclear targets in ROK and Japanese cities and elsewhere.

Deterring of Chemical and Biological Weapon Use

During the Cold War, the U.S. approach to deterring chemical and biological weapon use was less clear. The United States carried out a serious chemical and biological weapons defense program (passive defenses), seeking protection against the use of these weapons and deterrence of their use by being able to deny their effects. U.S. counterforce and active defense capabilities would also have helped deny chemical and biological weapon effects and thereby had some role in deterrence.

Early in the Cold War, the United States developed its own chemical and biological weapons to allow it to retaliate in kind against any Soviet chemical or biological weapon attack. Effectively, the United States was prepared to use these weapons to deny the Soviets any advantage from having employed similar weapons; in addition, research on offensive chemical and biological weapon capabilities significantly aided passive defense efforts against those threats.

Eventually, the United States joined the Biological and Toxin Weapons Convention (BWTC) in 1972 and the Chemical Weapons Convention in 1993 in the hopes of precluding these weapons from future conflicts. But toward the end of the Cold War, the United States learned that the Soviet Union had not given up its biological weapons efforts despite having joined the BWTC. Lacking biological weapons at that point, the United States implied it would employ nuclear retaliation against the use of these weapons.

But in the 2010 *Nuclear Policy Review Report* (*NPRR*), the United States declared, "With the advent of U.S. conventional military preeminence and continued improvements in U.S. missile defenses and capabilities to counter and mitigate the effects of CBW, the role of U.S. nuclear weapons in deterring non-nuclear attacks – conventional, biological or chemical – has declined significantly. The United States will continue to reduce the role of nuclear weapons in deterring non-nuclear attacks."[42] This statement does not preclude a nuclear response to adversary chemical and biological weapon use, but it makes such a response unlikely (a low probability), potentially reducing the deterrence of such attacks unless highly effective conventional force responses are guaranteed.

Deterring North Korean Use of WMD in a War

Deterrence of North Korean WMD use in war requires understanding what North Korea would think it could gain from war and from using WMD. Given North Korea's circumstances, a North Korean invasion of the ROK would most likely be an act of desperation for a regime losing control, a "diversionary war" used to secure support from the North Korean military for a near-failed regime.

At that point, the regime may even have some evidence of military plotting to overthrow the regime. Facing serious survival risks if it does nothing, the North Korean regime may decide that a general war will restore military support for the regime and give it a chance for survival, despite all the other risks.

Such a North Korean decision to invade the ROK would not be easy. North Korea has been deterred from invading the ROK since 1953, suggesting that the North Korean leadership already doubts its prospects in a major war. Indeed, the current U.S. Commander in South Korea, General Walter Sharp, has said, "I'm absolutely confident that if they [North Korea] came south, the ROK-U.S. Alliance would be able to defeat them."[43] If the North Korean regime concludes that war is necessary for political reasons, it must thus also find a way to win or achieve some kind of "draw" in the conflict.

North Korean asymmetric means — its WMD — likely provides the only option for a favorable outcome. By using WMD, North Korea may feel there is some chance it could break Japanese support of the United States, and also overcome U.S. and ROK technological advantages. It has put considerable investments into WMD capabilities: investments that could have been spent on other weapons had North Korea not truly valued WMD. This is especially true for chemical and biological weapons. It has paid the price to develop these weapons almost entirely for wartime utility.

Moreover, if the North Korean regime expects U.S. nuclear weapon use in a war regardless of North Korean actions, it may view WMD use as just part of a war with the United States. While the North Korean prospects for success in such a war would be poor, in challenging circumstances the regime may perceive the prospects of war would be better than the prospects of outright regime failure. Thus, the key to deterring North Korean WMD use is to deter a North Korean invasion of the ROK in the first place, to convince the North Korean regime war is not an alternative for handling its internal problems.

Deterring North Korean WMD Attacks by Punishment

Some military analysts argue that if North Korea ever uses a nuclear weapon (or perhaps other forms of WMD), the United States will launch a large nuclear weapon response to massively damage North Korea. Some even talk of turning North Korea into a "sea of glass," reminiscent of the Cold War assured destruction logic. Would such a threat against mainly innocent civilians deter the North Korean regime's use of WMD?

The regime has shown little value for the North Korean common people, allowing the starvation of at least hundreds of thousands, and also allowing the massive societal disruption associated with a failing North Korean economy. The regime is unlikely to perceive much cost to a Cold War-like assured destruction threat.

In addition, it is unlikely that either the ROK or the United States would want to devastate North Korean society with nuclear weapons. The ROK government wants the unification of Korea, a unification that would be immensely complicated by extensive nuclear damage. Moreover, the United States would find massive societal destruction to be morally repugnant. The 2010 *Nuclear Posture Review Report* said the United States, "... would only consider the use of nuclear weapons in extreme circumstances to defend the vital interests of the United States or its allies and partners."[44] Massive societal damage to North Korea would do relatively little to defend US and allied vital interests.

Retaliation against the North Korean military or the North Korean political leadership would be alternative punishment approaches. These targets would also provide denial effects. But a North Korean leadership worried about instability might welcome attacks on its military, attacks which would likely increase military support for the political leadership.

Thus, the best punishment approach would be to threaten the North Korean political leaders themselves. Kim Jong-Il and his other leaders must come to feel their prospects for surviving a war are much less than their prospects of surviving a failing regime. A threat to target those leaders could provide much of the leverage needed to deter a North Korean invasion if the North Korean leaders believe that: (1) the U.S./ROK can effectively target them, and (2) the U.S./ROK have the will to execute such an attack.

The greatest difficulty in effectively targeting the North Korean leadership is in locating that leadership. Indeed, Kim Jong-Il has regularly "disappeared" from public view when he has committed provocations,[45] likely hoping to avoid the possibility of being targeted. The North Korean leaders may therefore perceive they can avoid damage even from nuclear attacks, undermining deterrence of their actions. In addition, North Korean leaders would likely locate underground in a conflict situation, making it difficult to cause them damage. The United States must demonstrate to the North Korean leaders that it does regularly find them when they are "hiding" and can cause destruction even against underground facilities, seeking to erase any perception of the North Korean leaders that they could survive a retaliatory attack.

Kim Jong-Il may also wonder: "Would the United States have the will to attack me, personally?" Many in the United States talk about avoiding such targeting of adversary leaders, which may give the North Korean regime hope. The United States needs to disabuse the regime of this notion through clear strategic communications. In particular, it should consider practicing attacks on the North Korean leaders as part of its exercises in Korea, demonstrating that a decision to pursue them has already been made.

The quotes above from the 2010 *Nuclear Posture Review Report* raise the question of whether punishment for North Korean WMD use, and nuclear weapon use in particular, should be done with conventional or nuclear weapons. There are several reasons for preferring the U.S. use of nuclear weapons in such punishment:

- The North Korean leaders will likely have much greater fear of U.S. nuclear weapon use. According to an East German report in 1986, "Comrade Kim Il Sung affirmed that the Democratic People's Republic of Korea (D.P.R.K.) does not intend to attack South Korea, nor could it. More than 1,000 U.S. nuclear warheads are stored in South Korea, ostensibly for defense, and it would take only two of them to destroy the D.P.R.K."[46] To the extent that such a view persists in North Korea, U.S. nuclear weapon threats will be far more effective in deterring the North Korean leaders' use of WMD and invasion of the ROK.

- If North Korea uses nuclear weapons early in a conflict and the United States does not answer with a U.S. nuclear response, the North Korean leaders will likely conclude that they can continue to use nuclear weapons without a U.S. nuclear weapon response. This would effectively reinforce their peacetime impression of U.S. threats lacking substance, thereby undermining transwar deterrence.

- The United States has promised a nuclear umbrella to both the ROK and Japan, which is a commitment of a U.S. nuclear response to North Korean nuclear weapon use. But the purpose of the nuclear umbrella commitment is to deter adversary nuclear weapon use. Once an adversary has used nuclear weapons, the U.S. nuclear umbrella has failed, and may be questioned globally. The United States would therefore need to reestablish (or abandon) the credibility of its global nuclear umbrella commitments, commitments that many would not perceive as being met by a conventional weapon response. The U.S. nuclear umbrella commitments are intended to persuade both U.S. adversaries and U.S. allies not to pursue nuclear weapon development. A failure to act consistently with these commitments could spur both US adversaries and U.S. allies to develop their own nuclear forces, something not in the U.S. interest.

In summary, the United States should threaten nuclear attacks against the North Korean leaders as punishment for North Korean nuclear weapon use and prepare to employ those threats. The North Korean leaders need to be convinced there is no chance they would survive an invasion of the ROK and associated WMD use. Other punishment threats are much less likely to deter North Korean WMD use, while punishment threats against the North Korean military may actually aid the diversionary strategy of the North Korean leaders.

Deterring North Korea by Threat of Denial

As argued above, deterrence by denial involves primarily possessing effective capabilities for counterforce attacks, active defenses and passive defenses.

Counterforce

In wartime, U.S. and ROK counterforce efforts would be launched to attempt to destroy the North Korean WMD forces (both weapons and delivery means) and potentially the associated command and control. While the United States and the ROK have many capabilities to destroy such targets, they must first identify each target's location. Since the United States and the ROK do not even know how much WMD North Korea possesses, they likely do not know all of the locations necessary to be attacked to destroy the North Korean WMD and associated delivery means.

The ROK Minister of National Defense has indicated that, "There are about 100 sites related to the nuclear program in North Korea."[47] Many of these are likely underground and destroying each could require a large force, much more than would likely be available early in a conflict when other targets would also need to be struck and when standoff attack forces would be limited. Still, whatever North Korean WMD is destroyed by counterforce attacks reduces the burden on active and passive defenses. Unfortunately, any incomplete effort to destroy the North Korean WMD could push the North Korean leaders into a "use them or lose them" approach, prompting WMD attacks on the ROK and/or Japan, an unwanted consequence.

Better intelligence on North Korean WMD, delivery means and leaders would help facilitate counterforce efforts. North Korean defectors could provide such intelligence, much as Russian defectors from its biological program provided the United States critical intelligence on that program toward the end of the Cold War. Dissatisfaction among the North Korean elites[48] may make such defections more possible now than ever before.

Active Defenses

Active defenses seek to destroy WMD after it has been launched and before it arrives on target and detonates/or is dispersed. US ROK and

Japanese air defenses would likely deny effective WMD attacks by North Korean aircraft, and thus few experts expect North Korea to deliver WMD bombs. But ballistic missile defenses provide only limited protection in Japan and especially in the ROK today. This means some North Korean missiles could leak through the missile defenses, and the missile defenses could also be exhausted by initial North Korean missiles strikes.

Broader deployment of missile defenses around potential targets plus the addition of more broad area defenses (like the U.S. Navy SM-3 interceptor and the U.S. Army THAAD system) could increase the effectiveness of the defenses and, to the degree of North Korean leaders appreciate these capabilities, thereby enhance deterrence of North Korea's aggressive actions.

In addition, enhanced control of immigration into Korea[49] and surveillance of ROK coastal areas could reduce the ability of North Korean Special Operations Forces (potentially carrying biological weapons) to infiltrate the ROK.

Passive Defenses

Passive defenses seek to protect people and assets from the effects of WMD once those weapons detonate or are dispersed.

Because nuclear weapons are so powerful, the best passive defenses against them involve evacuation of likely target and fallout zone areas and dispersal of assets to less likely target areas. In addition, the hardening of some target areas can be helpful, using blast protected shelters and underground facilities to avoid fallout casualties. The Soviets attempted such an approach to overcome U.S. assured destruction during the Cold War, and the North Koreans have made similar efforts with vast numbers of underground facilities. But building such shelters would be prohibitively expensive in the ROK, Japan or the United States for all but modest-sized groups. And evacuation would also prove challenging and difficult to sustain.

As noted earlier, passive defenses would be far more powerful against North Korean chemical and biological weapons. The United States and the ROK should use strategic communications to convey the level of passive defenses they have developed, including advanced medical measures, to convince North Korea that these weapons will not yield the leverage the North would seek in a war. Such U.S. and ROK efforts should describe the level of protection afforded by these defenses without divulging the details of the defenses, seeking to avoid North Korean work on counters.

Conclusions on Deterring North Korean WMD Use

Deterrence of WMD use would clearly be very difficult when the North Korean leaders become desperate. The United States and its allies would need to convince the North Korean leaders that they are more likely to survive with peace (facing rebellion) than with war (facing destruction): peace is still the least miserable option.

Key would be the denial component of deterrence, the ability to prevent North Korea from perceiving any chance of achieving victory. Focusing punishment on the North Korean leaders would also be important: they must be convinced they will not survive a war, even if North Korea uses WMD for leverage. In short, the United States and the ROK should focus on deterring North Korea from invading the ROK and thereby deter North Korean WMD use.

Deterring North Korean WMD Crises/Provocations

From February through July 2009, North Korea created a number of serious crises with WMD-related provocations. These provocations were apparently motivated by the conditions in North Korea described at the beginning of this chapter, some rising to the crisis level inside North Korea even before the provocation. Such crises jeopardize regime control and could eventually imperil the regime.

The provocations appear to reflect the regime's view of its jeopardy: serious enough to take modest risks with provocations, but not so serious as to justify an invasion of the ROK or major attacks on it. The North Korean sinking of the ROK warship *Cheonan* and the artillery shelling of Yeonpyeong Island in 2010 escalated this pattern to unprovoked, limited attacks. This escalation makes North Korea appear even more dangerous.

Can the United States and the ROK deter such provocations? Thus far, the United States has failed to deter a number of North Korean provocations, but it has likely deterred others. It is important to recognize while little is known for certain about North Korea, such uncertainty should not prevent purposeful US/ROK action.

Understanding the North Korean Provocations

The underlying instability in North Korea in 2009 was Kim Jong-Il's bad health. He apparently suffered a stroke in August 2008, was slow to recover and has not fully recovered. Indeed, he may not ever fully recover. This serious illness undermined his appearance of empowerment needed for leadership in North Korea. Reports of his bad health had started even before the reported stroke, with some claims that he had heart surgery in May 2007. By the spring of 2009, there were many reports of North Korea speeding succession efforts for his third son because Kim Jong-Il's health was so serious;[50] by September 2010, Kim Jong-Il had put his son in positions that made his succession appear likely. His son's previous lack of such positions and his mid-20s age made him an unlikely ruler by North Korean leadership standards.

To solve his appearance of weakness and support potential succession, Kim Jong-Il needed to create an image that the North Korean regime is powerful, and he and his son are responsible for that power. His 2009 provocations showed North Korea is close to acquiring a space launch capability and intercontinental ballistic missiles and has produced nuclear weapons, capabilities few other countries possess.

While the North Korean regime likely anticipated U.S. efforts to implement sanctions in response, the United States made no specific sanction threats, failing to reinforce deterrence. And the previous UN sanctions had not been particularly harmful to North Korea because they were largely unimplemented.[51]

Indeed, the regime likely planned to use any sanctions to once again claim that the United States and its allies are the enemies of the North Korean people and responsible for everything wrong in North Korea. Still, the regime apparently hoped to extort further aid and recognition from the United States and the regional powers, using escalatory brinksmanship until rewarded for de-escalating tensions.

North Korea's second nuclear test in late-May 2009 was a major North Korean escalation. While many in the West had criticized the first

North Korean nuclear test in 2006 as a likely failure, the second test had a much higher yield (at least several kilotons), about 10 times the first test. North Korea apparently had mastered the basics of nuclear weapons, increasing its appearance of empowerment as well as its ability to deter action by the United States and others. It had also increased its ability to market nuclear expertise. And North Korea had reached the threshold at which it may have hoped to be considered a nuclear power. "There was a sense that every North Korean escalation was intended as a bargaining chip. Now there's an alternative view taking hold: that Kim Jong-Il wants to force the world to acknowledge it as a nuclear power before he dies."[52]

Immediately after the North's nuclear test, the ROK announced it would join those nations supporting the Proliferation Security Initiative (PSI). But before the test, the ROK had refused to threaten to join PSI in response to North Korean provocations, and thus its joining PSI likely had little impact on the North Korean decision to do a nuclear test. The UN also implemented fairly serious economic and military/nuclear test sanctions against North Korea in UN Security Council Resolution (UNSCR) 1874, but no specific sanctions threats were made prior to the nuclear test, seeking to deter the test.

Especially with a risk-taking state like North Korea, threats need to be explicitly stated before the state takes an action or the threats will have little credibility and thus little deterrent value. And the United States had already failed to take action against North Korea for its nuclear proliferation to Syria, as noted earlier; the North Korean regime likely felt there was little probability it would pay serious costs for a nuclear test. In summary, the United States and its allies did not use, or poorly used, the means they had for deterring the North Korean provocations.

This is not to say the United States totally failed in deterring North Korean provocations in 2009. Just after the North Korean second nuclear test, North Korea appears to have moved intercontinental-range missiles to both its east and west coast launch facilities.[53] It appeared to be preparing for another ICBM/space launch test, similar to its April test. North Korea was likely trying to continue its escalating brinksmanship, as done in 2006, hoping to achieve a major payoff from the United States.

Shortly after the second nuclear test, President Obama announced, "We are not intending to continue a policy of rewarding provocations. I don't think that there should be an assumption that we will simply continue down a path in which North Korea is constantly destabilizing the region and we just react in the same ways by, after they've done these things for a while, then we reward them."[54] He was joined in such comments by several other members of the U.S. administration. The consistency and strength of these statements suggested North Korea's escalatory brinksmanship campaign would not pay off like its similar campaign did in 2006/7.

It is impossible to know whether these statements changed North Korean plans, but North Korea did not launch an ICBM with its missile launches on July 4, 2009. North Korea may have chosen to launch only short- to medium-range missiles then, trying to stay below a provocation threshold that might have triggered a major U.S. response. Within North Korea, the regime could still claim it had: (1) violated the UN sanctions after its second nuclear weapon test, (2) defied the U.S./UN, and (3) deterred a significant U.S./UN response.

Then former President Bill Clinton went to Pyongyang to free a U.S. woman jailed by North Korea. According to the North Korean secret police agency, "Thanks to Commander Kim Jong-Un's cleverness, former U.S. President Clinton crossed the Pacific Ocean to apologize to the General (Kim Jong-Il)."[55] For North Korean audiences, this provided Kim Jong-Il the appearance that the United States had surrendered, and he was very much empowered; the Clinton visit also supported Kim Jong-Un's succession. The regime could accept such an outcome as a very adequate end state for the 2009 provocations.

U.S./ROK Options for Deterring North Korean Provocations

How should the United States and the ROK try to deter/counter future North Korean provocations? For example, how should they have acted to deter the North Korean sinking of the warship *Cheonan*? Threats of economic sanctions have generally proven inadequate to deter North Korean provocations, and U.S./ROK threats of military actions have very little likelihood of being carried out.

Indeed, even with fairly strong evidence of North Korean culpability in the *Cheonan* sinking, the United States and the ROK did not pursue military responses, in part because of the escalatory danger of such responses.

There are two key parts of a strategy to deter North Korean provocations, corresponding to deterrence by threat of denial or retaliation.

Deterrence by Denial

The ROK has already recognized the *Cheonan* sinking reflected gaps in its military capabilities. ROK President Lee has committed to, "…make sure such an incident does not occur again."[56] The ROK needs to fill the gaps in its military preparations against provocations and limited warfare threats, with US help, and appears to be proceeding to do so. This means not only developing capabilities to detect and counter North Korean submarines in ROK territorial waters, but also addressing North Korea missile, artillery, SOF and other limited threats. Poor ROK military capabilities on Yeonpyeong Island undoubtedly contributed to North Korea feeling it could fire artillery at the island in November 2010; the ROK has greatly reinforced the ROK Marine forces on all of the Northwest Islands since then.

The ROK has singled out North Korean asymmetric threats as a particular area of focus, within which North Korean WMD falls.[57] Thus, the earlier discussion of counterforce, active defense and passive defense against WMD is equally relevant here. North Korea is unlikely to execute provocations which it anticipates will fail, causing the regime to look weak.

Deterrence by Punishment

As with major warfare, U.S./ROK efforts to punish North Korean provocations via limited attacks on its military would be unlikely to do immediate, significant damage to North Korean military power, but would likely drive the North Korean military to be more supportive of the regime, exactly the opposite of the desired response. Instead, punishment needs to focus more on the North Korean regime's political weaknesses, where the regime would likely perceive a major cost being imposed.

This approach needs to start by recognizing that North Korea is a failing state, and that sooner or later, the North Korean government will collapse. If a collapse were to occur today, the United States and the ROK are woefully unprepared to handle the consequences[58] (as is China, the other major player in such a collapse). This lack of preparation could be extraordinarily costly to these countries if collapse were to occur in the short term. Thus, they need to prepare for a collapse and shape the North Koreans to reduce the potential negative outcomes.

Anything the United States or the ROK does to prepare for a North Korean government collapse would be offensive to the North Korean regime. These actions therefore become the perfect political threats that can be applied in trying to deter North Korean provocation. They would include simply talking about collapse and the subsequent ROK-led unification of Korea. Thus, the United States and the ROK should outline a unification strategy and plan and use some actions from them to punish North Korea for its provocations while threatening other (stronger) actions to deter further North Korean provocations.[59] Any US/ROK actions to shape North Korea for unification would impose costs on North Korea and directly undercut the benefits North Korea seeks in its provocations (a denial outcome).

But to correct earlier weaknesses in U.S./ROK deterrence efforts, the U.S./ROK would need to explicitly threaten North Korea with specific deterrent responses and then be prepared to execute them if necessary. Vagueness in making threats or showing little apparent U.S./ROK will to take these actions could thoroughly undermine deterrence of North Korea, especially as the regime feels more threatened internally and thus more willing to take risks.

For example, to respond to the shelling of Yeonpyeong Island, the United States and the ROK leaders could have announced that North Korean internal instability led to the shelling, and such instability forces the ROK to prepare for a North Korean collapse. As a first step in these preparations, the ROK president could ask the U.S. and ROK Marines to train to deliver humanitarian aid (especially food and medicine) along the North Korean coastlines.

Such an effort is needed because food and medicine are already in short supply in North Korea and would largely disappear in the aftermath of a collapse, leading to a humanitarian disaster. The roads across the demilitarized zone (DMZ) would be inadequate to transport all of the needed humanitarian aid into North Korea, making across-the-beach deliveries one appropriate option.

ROK and U.S. Marines would need to perform this task (as opposed to international humanitarian organizations--IHOs) because of the lack of security in a collapse environment and the danger posed by the North Korean military and black market criminals. IHOs could take over once a secure environment in specific areas of North Korea is achieved.

The North Korean regime would clearly hate such declarations and actions by the United States and the ROK, as these efforts would impose serious costs. The costs could be enhanced by training along the ROK coasts for humanitarian aid delivery, filming those exercises, and broadcasting those films and pictures into North Korea. The message to the North Korean people and even the elites would be clear: the United States and the ROK are not your enemies and are instead preparing to help you when the North Korean regime allows. By directly countering the propaganda of the North Korea regime leaders, a significant penalty could be imposed on them.

North Korea is likely to respond unfavorably to these U.S./ROK actions and could escalate, seeking to retain the appearance of empowerment but also to deter further ROK/U.S. actions of this kind. The potential for escalation compels the U.S./ROK into planning deterrence against a range of North Korean escalations, as well as other North Korean provocations.

The U.S./ROK actions that could be used for deterring further North Korean provocations could also be used to prepare North Korea for ROK-led unification. These measures could include: demonstrating high technology ROK military capabilities, actively seeking North Korean defectors especially from the North Korean nuclear program and senior North Korean political/military leaders, a declaration that the U.S. will attempt to shoot down any North Korean missiles launched, development of counter-fire plans against North Korean artillery use, pursuit of laser or other weapons to destroy North Korean artillery in flight,[60] selective amnesty for the elites, and a discussion of ROK plans for retirement payments to be offered to senior North Korean elites. The ROK/U.S. should prepare these and then privately threaten to take some of these actions if the North Korean regime initiates any further provocations.

Proper Terminology with Nuclear Powers

The United States and the ROK must also deny North Korean efforts to achieve its objective of becoming a recognized nuclear weapon power.

Such a designation would be a major accomplishment for the regime, strengthening its ability to deter external threats and coerce its neighbors, while demonstrating the empowerment of the regime and partially legitimizing North Korea's possession of nuclear weapons. Unfortunately, even the former "…head of the United Nations nuclear agency, has said that North Korea is a fully fledged nuclear power."[61]

It is neither accurate nor in the interest of the world to so recognize North Korea or to reward Kim Jong-Il. Eight other countries currently possess nuclear weapons, and even the country with the smallest nuclear arsenal in this group may have 10 times as many weapons as North Korea. In addition, each of these other countries has forces equipped to deliver nuclear weapons on targets. North Korea is just not in the same league. More importantly, the Nonproliferation Treaty (NPT) recognizes only five nuclear powers, and they are designated as the only states approved for possession of nuclear weapons.

To avoid rewarding North Korea and other aspiring nuclear weapon countries (like Iran or even Myanmar), the international community should develop new terminology associated with state possession of nuclear weapons. Appropriate terms might be:

- **A Compliant Nuclear Power**: One of the five countries recognized in the NPT as a nuclear power (the United States, Russia, China, Great Britain, and France).
- **A Noncompliant Nuclear Power**: Countries which have circumvented the NPT in fielding significant numbers of nuclear weapons, and organized nuclear forces for the delivery of those weapons. Today, the states in this category apparently would be India, Pakistan, and Israel.
- **A Noncompliant Nuclear Experimenter**: Countries which have circumvented the NPT and begun testing nuclear weapons but still have few such weapons and little delivery capability. Today, North Korea is the state in this category.

The U.S. 2010 *Nuclear Posture Review Report* makes a big issue of compliance with the NPT, and argues global policy should follow that precedent. But it is also important to characterize even a "noncompliant nuclear power" as a country that has done much more than just test nuclear weapons. The nuclear power designation should be reserved for those responsible states that:

- Field secure, transparent nuclear forces of a size appropriate for regional minimum deterrence.
- Establish nuclear weapon safety programs to prevent unauthorized use of nuclear weapons. These efforts would include weapon employment limits like the U.S. permissive action link (PAL).
- Limit nuclear testing and do not test nuclear weapons on delivery means like ballistic missiles

A state unwilling to meet these standards is either a non-compliant nuclear experimenter or a designation like a noncompliant nuclear rogue.

Speaking of North Korea as a non-compliant nuclear experimenter more accurately captures its nuclear weapon capabilities. It downgrades the recognition North Korea wants, which is a good thing, and discourages other states from thinking they can quickly improve their international standing by testing a nuclear weapon. While North Korea appears determined to pursue further nuclear weapon tests to demonstrate its nuclear weapon status, these terms would reduce the incentive North Korea would have with further tests and leave it permanently designated as out of compliance with the Nuclear Non-Proliferation Treaty. This would reduce a major benefit North Korea has sought with its nuclear weapon tests (thereby increasing the disincentives for North Korean provocations in the future) and might dissuade other countries seeking to gain nuclear weapon capabilities.

Conclusions

North Korea appears to pose a serious WMD threat. In particular, its nuclear weapon threat is potentially greater than normally assumed. Because North Korea is a failing state, it will have considerable incentives to employ its WMD in crises and conflict.

The United States and the ROK need a deterrence strategy against this threat, addressing both North Korean provocations and potential WMD use. This strategy will be different from the Cold War nuclear deterrence strategy because of North Korean risk taking behavior and the nature of the North Korean WMD capability (especially the small number of its nuclear weapons). The U.S./ROK deterrence strategy must thus be based on a combination of their capabilities for denial and punishment, both of which need to be increased.

To prevent significant North Korean WMD use, the United States and the ROK need to focus on the internal threats the North Korean regime faces. They need to convince the North Korean regime it has no prospects of survival in war, and thus war is not an alternative for dealing with internal threats. Moreover, they need to convince North Korea its WMD use would often be thwarted by U.S./ROK denial capabilities, reducing the North Korean incentives to use WMD.

To prevent North Korean provocations and limited attacks, potentially including WMD use, the United States and the ROK must first work to resolve the ROK gaps in defenses against limited attacks. This is not just a naval issue after the sinking of the *Cheonan*, but rather a broader issue including North Korean missile, artillery and SOF attacks. The ability to deny North Korea success in these limited attacks will significantly strengthen deterrence against a regime wishing to avoid embarrassment and the appearance of weakness. The United States and the ROK should also develop a strategy and plans for ROK-led unification of Korea and use key elements of such a strategy to punish and deter North Korean provocations. The North Korean regime is likely to see that these actions impose serious costs on the regime. And these actions will generally be within the feasible set of actions available to the United States and the ROK, thereby strengthening deterrence.

Notes

[1] North Korea needs about 5.4 million tons of grain to feed its people, and produced only about 4.1 million tons in 2009. See, for example, "Food shortage worsens in N. Korea: official," *The Korea Herald* (Feb. 10, 2010), http://www.koreaherald.com.kr/NEWKHSITE/data/html_dir/2010/02/10/201002100069.asp.
[2] "Tens of thousands of North Koreans have crossed the border seeking a better life. Some 15,000 have successfully defected to the South, while an estimated 100,000 to half a million are in China seeking asylum." Tae-hoon Lee, "NK Regards OPLAN 5029 as

Declaration of Warfare," *The Korea Times* (Nov. 8, 2009), http://www.koreatimes.com.kr/www/news/nation/2009/11/116_55089.html.

[3] "Survival of the Wickedest," Strategypage.com (June 26, 2008), http://www.strategypage.com/qnd/korea/articles/20080626.aspx.

[4] Sang-hyun Um, "N. Korea: Kim Jong-il's Distant Relative Tried to Kill Him With Chinese Blessing," *Shin-Dong-A* (S. Korean Monthly, October 2004).

[5] Blaine Harden, "Dear Leader Appears To Be Losing N. Koreans' Hearts And Minds," *The Washington Post* (March 24, 2010), 11. See also "Millions of N.Koreans Listen to Foreign Radio Broadcasts," *The Chosun Ilbo* (April 30, 2010), http://english.chosun.com/site/data/html_dir/2010/04/30/2010043001070.html.

[6] "USFK commander warns of possible N.K. instability," *The Korea Herald*, (Mar. 26, 2010), http://www.koreaherald.com.kr/NEWKHSITE/data/html_dir/2010/03/26/201003260041.asp.

[7] "North Korean Nuclear Weapons: CIA Estimate for Congress" (Nov. 19, 2002), http://www.fas.org/nuke/guide/dprk/nuke/cia111902.html,.

[8] See, for example , David Albright, and Paul Brannan, "The North Korean Plutonium Stock," Institute for Science and International Security (Feb. 20, 2007), http://www.isis-online.org/publications/dprk/DPRKplutoniumFEB.pdf.

[9] Smith, R. Jeffrey, and Joby Warrick, "Pakistani scientist depicts more advanced nuclear program in North Korea," *The Washington Post* (Dec. 28, 2009).

[10] "Hwang Jang-Yop ... said that Jong Pyong-Ho, a senior party official in charge of military matters, had told Hwang in 1996 that North Korea had five plutonium-based nuclear weapons," International Institute of Strategic Studies, *North Korea's Weapons Programmes: A Net Assessment* (Jan. 21, 2004), http://www.iiss.org/publications/strategic-dossiers/north-korean-dossier/north-koreas-weapons-programmes-a-net-asses/north-koreas-nuclear-weapons-programme.

[11] Larry A. Niksch, *North Korea's Nuclear Weapons Program*, Congressional Research Service, IB91141 (updated Aug. 27, 2003), p. 9, http://fpc.state.gov/documents/organization/24045.pdf.

[12] General Leon J. LaPorte, "Statement Before the Senate Armed Services Committee" (April 1, 2004), 5, http://www.globalsecurity.org/military/library/congress/2004_hr/040401-laporte.pdf.

[13] Ibid.

[14] GlobalSecurity.org, "North Korea: Chemical Weapons Program," http://www.globalsecurity.org/wmd/world/dprk/cw.htm.

[15] Federation of American Scientists, "North Korea: Chemical Weapons Program," http://www.fas.org/nuke/guide/dprk/cw/.

[16] Defense Intelligence Agency, *North Korea Handbook*, PC-2600-6421-94, (1994), 3-15 to 3-16.

[17] "Longer-Range Seoul Missiles In The Works," *Singapore Straits Times* (Oct. 9, 2009), 38.

[18] "N.Korea Believed to Have 200,000 Special Forces Troops," *The Chosun Ilbo* (October 11, 2010), http://english.chosun.com/site/data/html_dir/2010/10/11/2010101101081.html..

[19] Ibid.

[20] Myong Chol Kim, "Nuclear war is Kim Jong-il's game plan," *Asia Times* (June 12, 2009), http://www.atimes.com/atimes/Korea/KF12Dg01.html.

[21] U.S. Joint Chiefs of Staff, "Over-All Effect of Atomic Bomb on Warfare and Military Organization," J.C.S. 1477/1, (from the US National Archives) (Oct. 30, 1945).

[22] For example, "Korea cannot be unified in a peaceful way. They [the North Koreans] are prepared for war. If a war occurs in Korea, it will be waged by nuclear weapons, rather than by conventional ones." This quote is from a report by one of the Hungarian Foreign Ministry Staff, based on a 1976 conversation with one of the staff of the North Korean Embassy in Hungary, in Balazs Szalontai and Sergey Radchenko, "North Korea's Efforts to Acquire Nuclear Technology and Nuclear Weapons: Evidence from Russian and Hungarian Archives," Woodrow Wilson International Center for Scholars, Cold War International History Project, Working Paper #53, (August 2006), Document No. 28, 55, *www.wilsoncenter.org/topics/pubs/WP53_web_final.pdf.*

[23] "North Korea threatened Thursday to turn Japan into a 'nuclear sea of fire' if the United States launches a nuclear war against the communist country." See "Yonhap Cites DPRK Warning to Japan on U.S. Cooperation Causing 'Nuclear Sea of Fire,'" *Seoul Yonhap in English,* FBIS translation KPP20040923000069 (Sept. 23, 2004).

[24] The areas compared here are from U.S. Congress Office of Technology Assessment, *Proliferation of Weapons of Mass Destruction: Assessing the Risks* (August 1993), 53-54.

[25] Department of Defense, *Deterrence Operations Joint Operating Concept*, Version 2.0, (December 2006), 3.

[26] "This is a stylized view of deterrence often associated with rational choice/expected utility deterrence models of the Cold War era. The DO JOC expands upon rational choice considerations and incorporates elements of prospect theory in its approach." *Ibid.*, 20.

[27] Mathematically, the adversary's utility (U) of each action (j) is assessed by combining the benefits (B) and costs (C) of each outcome (i) with the probability (P) of that outcome if the action is taken:

$$U(\text{Action j}) = \Sigma \, (B_{ji} - C_{ji}) * P_{ji}$$

The utilities are then compared and "restraint" is chosen if: U(restraint)> max(U(Action 1), U(Action 2), ..., U(Action n))

[28] Robert Jervis, "The Political Effects of Nuclear Weapons," *International Security*, Vol. 13, No. 2 (Fall 1988), 80-81.

[29] By analogy, monetary gambling almost always involves a negative expected value payoff to the individual because the "house" takes a portion of the money bet. Gamblers are thus normally risk takers (unless they believe that they have a "system"), because while they may win a large amount of money, on average they will lose.

[30] These concepts were introduced in Glenn H. Snyder, *Deterrence and Defense: Toward a Theory of National Security*, (Princeton: Princeton University Press, 1961), 14-16.

[31] "Joint Vision for the Alliance of the United States of America and the Republic of Korea" (June 16, 2009), http://www.whitehouse.gov/the_press_office/Joint-vision-for-the-alliance-of-the-United-States-of-America-and-the-Republic-of-Korea/.

[32] On April 5, 2009, North Korea test launched a long-range missile that it described as a space-launch vehicle.

[33] There is, however, a risk to the United States in trying to shoot-down a North Korean missile: If the United States tries but then fails to shoot down the missile, the US missile defense capabilities would be discredited, and Kim Jong-Il would appear to be further strengthened and even more capable.

[34] On March 19, 2009, Admiral Keating, then commander of the U.S. Pacific Command, "said the U.S. is 'fully prepared' to shoot down the missile and added that the U.S. military has the capability to do it." But Secretary of Defense Gates subsequently indicated that the United States would not attempt an intercept, likely fearing the escalatory implications and perhaps anticipating that the North Korean test would have likely failed. "Does Obama Have a N.Korea Policy?" *The Chosun Ilbo* (March 31, 2009), http://english.chosun.com/w21data/html/news/200903/200903310031.html.

[35] Of course, North Korea would claim that such a missile launch was actually of a space launch vehicle, allowed by international law. Thus, the United States would have to carry out a strategic communications plan to preemptively discredit such a North Korean claim and to focus on the destabilizing implications of operational North Korean ICBMs.

[36] This is an extremely simple example for illustrative purposes. In practice, U.S. strategic planners need to be developing more sophisticated assessments, including potential escalations, and also sensitivity testing the uncertain factors, seeking robust counters to North Korea's threats.

[37] In trying to deal with the sinking of the South Korean warship Cheonan, U.S. Secretary of Defense, "Gates, who met counterparts from Japan and South Korea ... admitted Washington and its allies had limited options." Dan De Luce, "Gates warns of more N.Korea 'provocations'," *Agence France-Presse* (June 6, 2010), http://www.google.com/hostednews/afp/article/ALeqM5j2tSpWVOsgH_J-qS1H874U1CMSQg.

[38] The Soviet cities curve shown here is derived from Alain C. Enthoven and K. Wayne Smith, *How Much Is Enough?*, Harper and Row (1971), 207. The U.S. cities curve is derived from U.S. manufacturing value added data of the same era.

[39] An equivalent megaton consists of the number of weapons of any given explosive yield needed to do the same damage as a single 1-megaton weapon. Three 200 Kt weapons, seven 50 Kt weapons, or twenty-one 10 Kt weapons would constitute 1 EMT.

[40] In practice, the database used to make this assessment included only about 77 percent of Soviet industry. Thus the fact that the lines quickly peak at 77 percent does not mean that 23 percent of Soviet industry would necessarily have survived, but rather that the information needed to determine the survivability of that 23 percent was not available.

[41] This analysis was extremely simplistic and assumed, for example, that all nuclear weapons would be targeted on cities, and that weapons destroyed by counterforce attacks would be replaced by surviving weapons in attacking each target.

[42] Department of Defense, *Nuclear Policy Review Report* (April 2010), viii.

[43] "U.S. General Concerned by Threat to Seoul Posed by N. Korea's 800-Missile Arsenal," East-Asia-Intel.com (Oct. 17, 2008). General Sharp's predecessor, General Bell, said, "'I also know with some certainty that if for some reason deterrence fails and North Korea attacks South Korea in any way, that we would quickly and decisively defeat the aggression.'" Anna Fifield, "U.S. General Warns of N Korean Nuclear Test," *The Financial Times* (Oct. 30 2006).

[44] Department of Defense, *Nuclear Policy Review Report* (April 2010), viii-ix.

[45] See, for example, "Kim Jong Il Vanishes From Public Eye," *Donga Ilbo*, (Aug. 7, 2006), and more recently, Ji-hyun Kim, "Kim Jong-il lying low," *The Korea Herald* (June 2, 2010), http://www.koreaherald.com/national/ Detail.jsp?newsMLId=20100602000180.

[46] This quote is from a report on the visit of Erich Honecker to North Korea in 1986, and is included in Balazs Szalontai and Sergey Radchenko, *op. cit.,* Document No. 52, 74.

[47] "Seoul Suspects About 100 Sites in N.K. Linked to Nuclear Program," *The Korea Herald* (Oct. 5, 2009), http://www.koreaherald.co.kr/NEWKHSITE/data/html_dir/2009/10/05/200910050098.asp.

[48] The December 2009 North Korean currency revaluation took most of the wealth away from even the North Korean elites, leading to reports of North Korean social unrest that may open the door to defection for some.

[49] The author has been told stories of North Korean SOF coming into the ROK on commercial airlines, using forged passports. This kind of activity could be largely eliminated by tying the passport databases together for the regional countries, and dealing with anyone using a forged passport.

[50] See, for example, Yonhap News, "Kim's Failing Health Prompting N. Korean Power Transfer to Son: Seoul Minister," *The Korea Herald* (June 4, 2009).

[51] The North Korean leaders were likely surprised by the relative strength of the subsequent UN Security Council Resolution (UNSCR) 1874 and the sanctions it applied.

[52] David E. Sanger, Mark Mazzetti and Choe Sang-Hun, "North Korean Leader Is Said To Pick A Son As Heir," *New York Times* (June 3, 2009), 1.

[53] "N.Korean Missile Train on the Move," *The Chosun Ilbo*, (June 17, 2009), http://english.chosun.com/site/data/html_dir/2009/06/17/2009061700282.html.

[54] Jennifer Loven, "Obama Vows Tougher N. Korea Stance," *Arizona Daily Star* (June 7, 2009).

[55] So-hyun Kim, "N. Korean Agency Uses Clinton's Visit to Praise Kim Jong-un," *The Korea Herald* (Aug. 10, 2009), at http://www.koreaherald.co.kr/NEWKHSITE/data/html_dir/2009/08/10/200908100042.asp.

[56] Jeong-ju Na, "President Plans Stern Steps After Cause of Ship Sinking Revealed," *The Korea Times* (April 19, 2010), http://www.koreatimes.co.kr/www/news/nation/2010/04/116_64442.html.

[57] Sung-ki Jung, "Lee directs W3 tril. rise in arms buying: Seoul seeking to counter NK's asymmetrical warfare," *The Korea Times* (May 16, 2010), http://www.koreatimes.co.kr/www/news/nation/2010/05/205_65967.html.

[58] See, for example, Victor Cha, "We Have No Plan," *The Chosun Ilbo* (June 9, 2008), http://english.chosun.com/w21data/html/news/200806/200806090015.html.

[59] The United States and the ROK could make such threats privately to the North Korean regime to have the best chance at deterrence.

[60] A laser weapon to shoot down artillery was developed years ago in the United States and could jump-start ROK efforts.

[61] Malcolm Moore, "North Korea now 'fully fledged nuclear power'," Telegraph.co.uk (April 24, 2009), http://www.telegraph.co.uk/news/worldnews/asia/northkorea/5212630/North-Korea-now-fully-fledged-nuclear-power.html.

CHAPTER 7

Deterrence and Saddam Hussein: Lessons from the 1990-1991 Gulf War

Barry R. Schneider

War and deterrence both begin in the minds of men. Deterrence is a psychological phenomenon and begins between the ears of the adversary you try to influence. When you seek to deter a rival from doing something you do not wish him to do, you must find a way to influence his perceptions of situations, for people act not necessarily on reality but on their perception of it. As Henry Kissinger once said, "A bluff taken seriously is more useful than a serious threat interpreted as a bluff."[1]

To deter, you need to influence the rival's cost/gain evaluations. He needs to understand he has far more to lose by initiating conflict, or by escalating it to unacceptable levels, than by not doing so.

In this study, we look at President Saddam Hussein of Iraq and President George H.W. Bush of the United States and their respective governments' attempts to deter one another in the period just before Iraq invaded Kuwait in August 1990 and through the subsequent Gulf conflict that ended in February 1991. On the United States side of this deterrence effort, one must also include the deterrent effect of U.S. coalition partners in the crisis and war.

In this analysis we look at a series of deterrence questions:

1. What are the limits of deterrence theory? Are the clearly stronger military powers able to deter significantly weaker powers all or most of the time?
2. What are the elements of deterrence strategy Western strategists developed during the Cold War confrontation with the Soviet Union?
3. Why was Saddam Hussein not deterred from ordering the Iraqi invasion of Kuwait in August 1990?

4. Why was Saddam Hussein not deterred from facing vastly superior and coalition forces assembled to force him out of Kuwait between August 1990 and January 1991?
5. Why were the United States and the coalition forces not deterred by Iraq from initiating combat in January 1991?
6. Why did Saddam Hussein not resort to use of chemical and biological weapons in the war as an equalizer against more powerful coalition forces?
7. Why during this conflict was Saddam Hussein not deterred from attacking Israel, a state with a nuclear arsenal?
8. Why did the United States and the coalition not pursue Iraqi forces into their country and end the Saddam Hussein regime in Baghdad? Was the United States deterred from pursuing the war all the way to Baghdad by the residual Iraqi military capability?
9. Was the United States deterred from the use of nuclear weapons in the war by the threat of Iraqi retaliation with chemical and/or biological weapons?
10. What conclusions and lessons can be extracted from this conflict regarding deterrence as a strategy for future crises?

The Limits of Deterrence

Deterrence is based on deductive reasoning, not evidence from history. It is a rational deduction that a weaker power should not be willing to risk almost certain defeat if it starts a war with a much more powerful rival. Also, it is a logical assumption that leaders of countries should not enter into conflicts where it appears to them they would be incurring catastrophic losses or would likely lose things the leadership values most.

On the face of it, this seems very rational and almost indisputable. The problem is deterrence does not work so often and so clearly in the real world. An inductive approach that looks at the empirical evidence from past international conflicts shows a very mixed picture.

Surprisingly, reviews of case studies show history is full of occasions when demonstrably weaker opponents have initiated what appear to be absolutely irrational attacks on much stronger opponents.[2]

According to one RAND study, in 22 percent (17 of 76) of conflicts that occurred from 1816 to 1974, weaker military powers initiated wars with stronger states. This obviously can have disastrous results in some cases. For example, in the 1864-1870 War of the Triple Alliance, Paraguay's dictator, Francisco Solano Lopez, invaded Brazil. He also attacked Argentina when that state did not allow his forces free passage through the territory. Uruguay then joined these two giants in the conflict against Paraguay. By the end of this ill-advised aggression by Paraguay, that small country had 85 percent of its population killed, reduced from 1.4 million in 1864 to just 0.22 million by 1870. By the war's end, Paraguay had just 29,000 adult males left alive.[3] Such wars can be caused by crazy rulers.

They can also be initiated by those simply unwilling to live under the heel of the enemy, thereby putting honor and their cause above survival. Think, for example, of Patrick Henry's famous words in the American Revolution, "Give me liberty or give me death." The signers of the American Declaration of Independence in 1776 all were willing to risk their lives in their cause. Indeed,

> [F]ive signers were captured by the British and brutally tortured as traitors. Nine fought in the War for Independence and died from wounds or from hardships they suffered. Two lost their sons in the Continental Army. Another two had sons captured. At least a dozen of the fifty-six had their homes pillaged and burned... Seventeen of them lost everything that they owned.[4]

Weaker states also start ill-advised wars due to wishful thinking, misperception, groupthink, illogic born of stress or a stubborn refusal to confront the facts.[5] In some historical cases, decision-makers have chosen to focus primarily on their aims and own resources and have discounted those of the adversary despite clear evidence they will lose if they push further into the crisis.

Another situation that pushes weaker powers to attack much stronger states is when time is considered not to be on their side. Saddam Hussein in 1980 is thought to have attacked Iran, a larger country with more resources and three times the population of Iraq, because he feared Iran would attack in a year or so when better organized. Leaders sometimes feel forced to start a war immediately when their chances of success, while slim, would be even poorer at a later time.

Weaker indigenous groups also often launch wars against stronger opponents out of nationalist sentiment and a desire to remove foreign or rival group influences. This is an old story repeated many times as revolutions opposed colonial regimes or the domination of other ethnic groups. In many cases these revolutionaries pit their superior zeal and a greater stake in the outcome against superior rival military forces that often do not have the same commitment to victory over time. Many times these revolutions and insurgencies fail. Sometimes, however, the fortunes of the sides reverse over time such as happened in China when communist guerrilla forces challenged initially superior nationalist Chinese forces and eventually became the stronger side in winning a protracted civil war.

Others may decide to fight an enemy with superior potential rather than give up long-standing goals or a way of life. They may be willing to bet their willingness to absorb casualties is greater than the rival's, and he will tire of the war and be willing to sue for peace short of total victory, leaving the smaller state that initiated the war in possession of their goals. This appears to be the line of thought of the Japanese leadership before Pearl Harbor and of Saddam Hussein after the coalition buildup in Saudi Arabia had put a powerful army in Saudi Arabia in the fall and winter of 1990 after his invasion of Kuwait. It also appears to have been the mindset of the Confederate leaders when they challenged the much more populous and industrialized North in the American Civil War.

Moreover, deterrence assumes state leaders can control their subordinates. Leaders of weaker states might not authorize an attack on a stronger power, but it may take place anyway because some subordinates do not follow orders.

Others might decide to strike out and start a war if they believed their regime was about to fall. Some might initiate a conflict or escalate one against a hated enemy for highly emotional reasons or if they calculated it might marshal more domestic support for their leadership at home. This is the inside-outside theory of war causation, a conflict started for internal domestic reasons. This appears to have been a partial cause of the 1982 Argentine-United Kingdom war in the Falklands, where for largely domestic political reasons the ruling junta challenged British control of the islands.

Still other leaders might be religious, cultural or ideological zealots who will stop at nothing to destroy some hated adversary, leaving the consequences to chance. For example, at the height of the Cuban Missile Crisis the Castro brothers, in a fit of revolutionary zeal, urged the Soviet leadership to fire at the United States their nuclear-tipped missiles stationed in Cuba, even though it meant their own likely deaths and the wholesale destruction of their country. Some initiators of combat may care more about their place in history rather than about the immediate consequences for themselves and their people.

However, this is not to say deterrence cannot or should not work in the majority of cases. Rather, it is wise to remember deterrence of war or escalation still can fail, even when a much stronger power confronts a weaker one, or even where both sides would suffer catastrophic warfare losses if they entered into a conflict.

Cold War Deterrence Theory

Luckily this did not happen during the Cold War when a central nuclear war could have caused hundreds of millions of deaths. By 1949, both the United States and Soviet Union had nuclear weapons, and both sides held the life or death of the rival society in their hands. The peace was secured by the dual hostage situation described as mutual assured destruction.[6] If the system failed, it would have failed deadly.

Deterrence theory developed as U.S. and allied policy-makers and strategists worked to understand the implications of nuclear weapons and how they might be used to keep the peace and advance U.S. and allied security. Several elements were eventually recognized as fundamentally important to strategic deterrence.

First, it was deemed crucial that the U.S. and its allies maintain a nuclear retaliatory force that could inflict what an aggressor leadership would consider unacceptable damage to themselves and their vital interests.[7] Aggressors must be made to believe the risks of attacking the United States and its allies were clearly and significantly greater than any conceivable rewards they might gain from such action.

Second, a potential aggressor must be made to realize the U.S. and allied leaders not only must have such lethal capabilities, but also must be willing to use such retaliatory power if challenged. Adversary risk-taking leaders must be convinced, by word and deed, that our leaders are willing, not simply to threaten to use force in response to aggression, but also to act should the line be crossed. Without both the physical capability to inflict unacceptable levels of damage on an aggressor party and the evident will to use such force, the U.S. and allied deterrent would lack credibility and might risk war where an adversary adventurer misperceived the situation. For example, this might have been the cause of the October 1962 Cuban missile crisis.[8]

Third, the origin of the attack must be known if the real aggressor is to be deterred. If an adversary leader thought he could disguise the origin of his attack, perhaps making it seem as if it came from another state, he might feel he could strike and escape the consequences. This is the problem discussed by the late Herman Kahn when he talked about the possibility of what he termed catalytic war.[9] Party A might strike Party B, making it look like it came from Party C, causing B and C to fight. Thus, a vigilant early warning and tracking system and an effective forensics capability should be a fundamental part of any successful deterrent posture. Deterrence requires a return address.

Fourth, the U.S. and allied retaliatory forces must be able to ride out an adversary surprise attack and still retaliate with overwhelming and accurate force, holding hostage what rival leaders value most. This has led the United States to rely on a mix of forces in a strategic triad of nuclear-armed ICBMs deployed on U.S. soil, strategic bombers, deployed worldwide, carrying both nuclear standoff missiles and nuclear gravity bombs, as well as nuclear-tipped SLBMs carried on ballistic missile submarines that roam the world's oceans.

Even the former Soviet Union, with its very extensive nuclear forces, could not have hoped to preemptively destroy so much of the U.S. and allied nuclear forces as to escape nuclear annihilation in return. It was seen as impossible for anyone to destroy all retaliatory elements of the U.S. alliances and strategic triad to the degree necessary to escape assured destruction in return. Maintaining this "second strike" capability was deemed an essential component of a classical deterrence posture.

Finally, deterrence is based on assuming an opponent has complete knowledge of the situation and will act rationally. This sounds plausible but how do you define rationality? Are suicide bombers rational? Further, if adversary leaders are willing to die, or see most of their followers die, in order to inflict terrible wounds on the United States and/or its allies, then deterrence may fail even if you can "take them with you."

In an era where multiple personalities guide rogue states, some of them high-risk takers, deterrence could fail. If it fails, the United States and its coalition partners will need capable counterforce units and excellent missile and air defenses all the more to limit casualties and preserve the chance for a military victory. In a crisis that has not yet escalated to war, the presence of such capable offensive strike forces and effective defenses may help to deter war.

If an adversary knows there is a good chance his deployment of chemical, biological, radiological and/or nuclear (CBRN) weapons may attract U.S. counterforce strikes that could destroy his weapons before they can be employed, he might be deterred from acquisition or attempted use of them. The same logic pertains to a situation where his use of WMD in wartime would be nullified by effective active and passive defenses. Either way, through offense or defense, if U.S. and allied forces were to rob him of a potent threat, he may be more reluctant to incur the costs of building and deploying such weapons. Thus, a rogue state regime may be deterred by the threat of retaliation or by the threat of having his attack neutralized by effective defenses. He might be deterred either by the sword or the shield, or by a combination of both. Deterrence produced by possessing effective military countermeasures (i.e., deterrence by denial) and deterrence produced by the threat of an overwhelming retaliation should be mutually reinforcing.

On the other hand, we can never be absolutely sure when deterrence has worked, but it is obvious when it has failed to work. When it fails, a war begins or a conflict escalates. When a deterrence policy and posture is successful, this is a non-event since no war starts or no escalation takes place. However, correlation is not necessarily causation. Just because A precedes B, it does not prove A caused B. Indeed, B might have another cause altogether.[10]

How do you prove that without a certain deterrence policy something, otherwise, might have happened? Unless you were able to step out of the present and rerun history to see what would have happened differently without a given deterrence policy or posture, you cannot prove the deterrence stance caused the outcome. So deterrence is far from an exact science. Deterrence is an art and we can only infer when it is successful since we have not yet found a way to read an adversary's mind or re-run historical events with one or more of the variables changed.

The Faceoff: George H.W. Bush versus Saddam Hussein

The 1990-1991 Gulf War involved 34 coalition governments and leaderships all pitted against Iraq. It was not simply crisis bargaining and warfare directed by two men. Thirty-four coalition leaderships had to be coordinated and military personnel from 34 militaries had to be made into one effective fighting force with unity of command.

Things were simpler on the other side. In Iraq, all important military and diplomatic decisions were those of Saddam Hussein acting essentially alone. This was far less true of President George H.W. Bush, but in the end it was he who mobilized and led the coalition to war, and it was he who made the final decision about when to attack the Iraqi Army in Kuwait, and, after 40 days of air bombardment and 100 hours of a ground war later, it was his decision to declare and negotiate a ceasefire with Iraq that stopped short of going on to Baghdad.

It would be difficult to find two more different men facing each other in a crisis or a war. They were separated widely in their educations, exposures to the wider world, family upbringings, values, cultures, languages, regional problems and political systems. Moreover, the leader of each country inherited a different set of world, regional and domestic problems and pressures. Both inherited a different set of previous commitments and policies from their predecessors and had a different public to deal with. Saddam Hussein and George Bush, therefore, came to this 1990-1991 conflict with very different backgrounds and perspectives.

Simply put, George Herbert Walker Bush was born to privilege and power. His father was a U.S. Senator. Saddam Hussein was born in a poor Iraqi village and his father died before he was born. Bush attended Andover Preparatory School and Yale University. Hussein dropped out of school in his teenage years and did not finish high school until he was 24. At the time, he was sought in Iraq for an attempted killing of the Iraqi President, and was a fugitive living in Cairo, Egypt. Saddam never completed a college degree, although he attended several law classes while in Egypt.

The two also differed in other ways. Bush served as a pilot in the U.S. Navy in World War II, engaged in 58 air combat missions and won the Navy Cross for bravery. Saddam Hussein never served in the Iraqi military, and, when he applied as a young man, was denied entry into the Iraq Military Academy, one of the few paths available for poor Iraqis attempting upward mobility in their society.

Bush was widely traveled and had served overseas as U.S. Ambassador to China and later as Chief U.S. Ambassador to the United Nations. Hussein never has traveled outside the Middle East. Bush was very knowledgeable about the international system and worldwide threats. He served as Director of the Central Intelligence Agency. Saddam worked exclusively within the Ba'ath Party where he first served as an organizer, then as a hit man, and later as the feared head of party security responsible for thousands of executions.

Bush served in elective politics in the United States, first as a Congressman from Texas, later as Chairman of the Republican Party National Committee, and finally as Vice President and President of the United States. By 1990, Bush already had won five elections on his way to the top of the U.S. political system. On the other hand, Saddam Hussein murdered and terrorized his way to the top of the Iraqi political system. He had never won an election until after he seized the Presidency in 1978. All political contests thereafter probably were rigged as he built a terroristic police state.

His was a fearful and feared regime, and Saddam Hussein essentially was the sole foreign policy and defense policy decision-maker in Iraq. It could be said "Saddam was Iraq and Iraq was Saddam" from the standpoint of policy decisions. As Charles Duelfer later concluded in a 2004 report to the Director of Central Intelligence,"Saddam Hussein so dominated the Iraqi regime that its strategic intent was his alone."[11]

It is instructive to realize how little knowledge Saddam Hussein had of the United States or its leaders. While President Bush was no Middle East expert, he was far better informed than Saddam about the other side's capabilities. However, both leaders lacked a clear knowledge of the other. FBI interrogator George Piro, assigned the task of interrogating Saddam after his capture in 2003, concluded from months of interviews, "One striking theme that emerged was just how little we knew about Saddam and how little he knew about us."[12]

These two leaders came from opposite ends of the earth. One is reminded of the Kipling verse when considering these two: "East is East, and West is West, and never the twain should meet." Their cultures were very different as were their life experiences. Saddam was a thug and mafia-like Iraqi leader, originally born in poverty, who maneuvered and eventually killed his way into power in Iraq. In 1991, two of his biographers concluded, "In the permanently beleaguered mind of Saddam Hussein, politics is a ceaseless struggle for survival. The ultimate goal of staying alive and in power justifies all means. Plots lurk around every corner. Nobody is trustworthy. Everyone is an actual or potential enemy."[13]

Bush was an American blue blood who started from a favored position and then achieved his way to the top of the U.S. political system. When they confronted each other over Kuwait, President Bush was leader of the richest country in the world at the head of the most powerful military force ever deployed. Confronting him was President Saddam Hussein, with his million-man army, the fourth largest in the world, now sitting astride 19 percent of the world's oil supplies after his occupation of Kuwait.

The Invasion of Kuwait

After the Iran-Iraq war, very badly needing funds to rebuild and protect his regime, Saddam Hussein ordered his forces to seize oil-rich Kuwait in order to repay his creditors, recoup his wealth, and re-equip his security and armed forces.[14] At that time "Iraq had approximately $80B in debts stemming from the war with Iran, compared with a GNP of about $35B, with a hard-currency income of about $14B."[15]

If his biographers are to be believed, Saddam Hussein probably invaded Kuwait only after long and careful thought. In previous critical decisions he was a careful planner. For example, when deciding whether to nationalize the nation's oil wells in 1972, Saddam exhibited a blend of caution and boldness. His chief biographers say,

> [T]he nationalization affords yet another vivid example of Saddam's calculated risk-taking style of operation. He proved himself a cautious, yet daring decision-maker who did not flinch before a challenge. Weighing his options

carefully and taking the necessary precautions, he did not rush into a hasty decision. But, once he made up his mind, he moved swiftly and resolutely toward his target.[16]

Later, after the invasion when his aggression against Kuwait was challenged by the United States and most of the rest of the world, Saddam refused to back down as the U.S.-led coalition poured military personnel, equipment and supplies into nearby Saudi Arabia starting in August 1990 until continuing until the end of hostilities in February 1991. Early in this military buildup tensions were high at the White House because it took months to get enough firepower transferred to the theater to offset an initial Iraqi Army advantage in the theater. Meanwhile, Saudi Arabia and its oil reserves seemed at the mercy of Iraq's Army if Saddam chose to continue its operations and invade the Saudi kingdom.

Clearly, at this point the United States leadership had spelled out its determination to defend Saudi Arabia and its desire to compel Iraq to withdraw from Kuwait. To bolster this deterrence posture, the U.S. had the clear potential military might to defeat Iraq, and this was augmented by clear verbal and non-verbal signaling of U.S. and allied intentions. The U.S. began a continuing military mobilization in the Gulf, and engaged in a worldwide diplomatic campaign to enlist allies into a coalition and to condemn Iraq's invasion at the United Nations.

Why didn't Saddam Hussein realize the catastrophe he was about to suffer and withdraw his forces back to Iraq before the coalition juggernaut destroyed his armed forces in the field? There are several hypotheses. First, he might not have had situational awareness and may have believed the U.S. President and coalition leaders simply bluffed. Second, Saddam might have engaged in wishful thinking and not faced the unpleasant possibilities he had not foreseen. Third, he might not have understood the total mismatch his forces faced and how few casualties they could inflict on a technologically superior force. Fourth, Saddam might have feared a military withdrawal would undermine his leadership and status in Iraq and lead to his replacement. Fifth, Saddam may have calculated he simply could not do without Kuwait's oil revenue to finance his own depleted treasury and to rebuild his security forces and army, and, thus, perhaps he gambled on being able somehow to keep his Kuwaiti prize.[17]

As the crisis deepened and war was about to begin again, the United States sought to persuade Iraq to withdraw from Kuwait without a fight, or, if a war was inevitable, at least tried to persuade the Iraqi leader not to order the use of chemical or biological weapons by warning he would face dire consequences.

Saddam Hussein, on the other hand, may have sought to deter a coalition attack or a U.S.-U.K.-French use of nuclear weapons by threatening retaliation with his chemical and/or biological weapons. Once the war began, the U.S. hoped in vain to deter Saddam from attacking Israel, and, once that failed, acted to influence the Israelis to let the U.S. and coalition troops do the retaliating for them, rather than have Israel enter the war and split the coalition.

Saddam, facing a superior foe, misunderstood what a mismatch it was for his army and air forces to try to compete with the coalition forces and felt high U.S. casualty rates would buy him a compromise peace that would have left his regime intact. He badly miscalculated on how many casualties his forces could inflict, but his residual chemical and biological weapons, unused in the conflict, might have helped deter a U.S. invasion and occupation of Iraq after Saddam's forces had been driven from Kuwait.

Sometimes an adversary leader may operate in a world of his own, surrounded by "yes-men," and cut off from realistic intelligence about the United States, its allies, and their intentions. This appears to be the case with Saddam Hussein at the time of Desert Storm. Such an enemy leader may disregard the messages and intelligence reports he receives, preferring instead to follow his own thinking and adhere to previous stereotypes or misinformation.

U.S. Attempts to Deter Iraq from invading Kuwait (July-August 1990)

When trouble brewed over rights in the Rumaila oil fields, a disputed area along the Iraq-Kuwait border, President Bush sent his ambassador, April Glaspie, to see if the dispute could be settled peacefully. Her meeting with Saddam Hussein appeared to be cordial and gave no hint of his inclination to take military action against Kuwait. Nor did it say much about the United States interest in backing Kuwait in the dispute. Indeed, according to reports, "U.S. Ambassador April Glaspie told Saddam that 'We have no opinion on the Arab-Arab conflicts, like your border disagreement with Kuwait.'"[18] Later, the U.S. State Department followed with another message that Washington had "no special defense or security commitments to Kuwait." Saddam must have seen this as an indication he would have little to fear from the United States if he intervened in Kuwait.

Although it is likely Saddam Hussein had already decided on the invasion of Kuwait at that time, Ambassador Glaspie reported he seemed inclined to negotiate. This was communicated to President Bush who then had the U.S. State Department transmit the following message back to the Iraqi leader stating that:

> I am pleased to learn of the agreement between Iraq and Kuwait to begin negotiations in Jeddah to find a peaceful solution to the current tensions between you. The United States and Iraq both have a strong interest in preserving the peace and stability of the Middle East. For this reason we believe these responsibilities are best resolved by peaceful means and not by threats involving military force or conflict.[19]

Perhaps if this letter had included a stronger tone, one that emphasized a threat to use military power to block any move by Iraq to settle the dispute by means of the Iraqi Army taking over Kuwait, Saddam might have put the invasion plan on hold. Using 20-20 hindsight, it is easy now to conclude that President Bush's letter, though very reasonable on its face, was evidently not the warning shot across the bow the situation required. The U.S. response was too mild to influence a dictator who did not play by any agreed upon international rules and who was bent on seizing a rich prize that could solve most of his financial and security problems if his aggression went unopposed.

Saddam Hussein might have interpreted the mild U.S. response as a green light to do what he wanted to do. Certainly it was not a stern warning to cease and desist. He might well have calculated the United States was distracted elsewhere and it would not respond forcefully to a fait accompli. Kuwait might have looked like a lucrative prize that could easily be taken, an immediate benefit realized with only a distant, intangible and uncertain risk being run in undertaking to occupy it.

This would fit with the pattern of Saddam Hussein's operational code at home and abroad. Plan carefully, conceal your moves, and then strike decisively and violently to achieve your ends. Preemptively attack against your unprepared, unsuspecting, misled opponent. Moreover, Saddam did not think the United States leadership had much of an appetite for combat or battle casualties, as they had withdrawn when they had had their fill of casualties in previous conflicts in Vietnam and Lebanon.

As James Baker notes in his memoir, "With his flagrant move into Kuwait, Saddam Hussein's ambitions revealed themselves in all their grandiosity."[20] The question that comes to mind regarding this scenario is why the United States did not do more to deter this attack on Kuwait. The answer was the Bush administration leadership was distracted and simply did not anticipate such a violent move from Saddam Hussein.

Writing eight years later in his memoir, former Secretary of State James Baker explained:

> With the benefit of hindsight, it's easy to argue that we should have recognized earlier that we weren't going to moderate Saddam's behavior, and shifted our policy approach sooner to a greater degree than we did. At the least, we should have given Iraqi policy a more prominent place on our radar screen at an earlier date. I believe the reasons we didn't change our policy approach earlier and to a greater extent are myriad and complex. And while I wish we'd focused more attention on Iraq earlier, given what happened, I remain unpersuaded that anything we might have done, short of actually moving armed forces to the region, would have deterred Iraq's invasion of Kuwait.[21]

Furthermore, Baker believes there was little support at first for blocking Saddam's ambitions in Kuwait. In his "view the only realistic chance to deter Saddam would have been to introduce U.S. forces into the region – and neither the Kuwaitis, the Saudis, the Soviets, nor the Congress would have supported that course before August 2. Indeed, it was only the shock of the invasion that allowed us to intervene militarily at all."[22]

Furthermore, the United States was fully occupied with events happening inside the Soviet Bloc as the Berlin Wall came down and Eastern Europe began to revolt against communist party control in Czechoslovakia, Poland, Hungary, and East Germany and Soviet leader Mikhail Gorbachev was unwilling to implement the "Breshnev Doctrine," and use the Red Army to terrorize the Eastern Europeans back into submission. The United States foreign policy leadership was primarily focused on these events and paid too little attention to the local squabble between Iraq and Kuwait over oil rights along their border.

Saddam acted when the U.S. focus was directed elsewhere. His invasion caught everyone unprepared. As James Baker recalls,

> Without exception, our friends in the region consistently argued that Saddam was only posturing and that confrontation would simply make matters worse. Si
> mply put, the reason why nobody believed Saddam would attack is because no realistic calculation of his interests could have foreseen a full-scale invasion of Kuwait. Shevardnadze had put it correctly in Moscow on the third day following the invasion: "this was an irrational act that made no sense.[23]

Baker also recalls,

> [E]ven the Israelis believed that Saddam was bluffing to bully the Kuwaitis into economic concessions. Israel's intelligence service, the Mossad, told U.S. intelligence counterparts that Saddam's rhetoric was designed to deter an Israeli attack, not threaten one of his own. As late as July 31, King Hussein and President Mubarak reassured us that Saddam was engaged in verbal bluster, not literal threats. Ironically, most of our allies privately worried throughout the spring and summer of 1990 that the United States might overreact to Saddam's new aggressiveness![24]

However, no one who understood Saddam Hussein's volatile nature, his extreme ambition and his lifelong tendency toward violence should have been surprised. Just the fact that a strong military under his command resided next door to a poorly defended neighbor in Kuwait that was oil rich should have suggested vigilance in any crisis brewing between the two. One has the image of a Lion contemplating a Lamb with the latter about to become dinner, or in Kuwait's case, an oil prize that represented 8 percent of the world's proven oil reserves, sitting next to Saudi Arabia, another relatively defenseless state that owned another 25 percent of the world oil reserves. Coupled with Iraq's estimated 11 percent, Saddam Hussein would control much of the Middle East oil supply. However, the United States and the rest of the world were caught by surprise and were unprepared to take the deterrence steps that might have persuaded Saddam to stop short of an invasion of Kuwait.

Saddam Hussein's first name translated into Arabic means "one who confronts." He had lived up to that throughout his entire violent lifetime. The "Butcher of Baghdad" had a career filled with blood and violence. He was thought to have killed his first victim when only a young teenage boy. He was a hit man for the Ba'athist Party and tried to assassinate the leader of Iraq. Later, when his cousin ruled Iraq, he served as the head of a lethal and brutal security service that killed opponents without remorse.

He ruled with fear, and his models were Stalin and Hitler whose biographies he had read with admiration. In 1978 he forced his cousin from power and took over as leader of Iraq. The bloodbath in Iraq escalated as he exterminated tens of thousands of domestic adversaries. In one of his first acts as Iraq's supreme leader, he called a meeting of hundreds of top Ba'ath Party leaders, singled out many of them for so-called acts of disloyalty, arrested and read them their death sentences on the spot, and forced the remainder of his party leaders to serve in firing squads that shot their doomed colleagues the next day.

Not satisfied with violence against possible domestic opponents, Saddam Hussein almost immediately went to war with his neighbors. In 1980, less than two years after the coup that brought him to power, he ordered his army to attack Iran. The result was an eight-year war that bled both states and featured the extensive use of chemical weapons and ballistic missile attacks, both initiated by Saddam's commands. In retrospect, the United States and other states concerned with the security of the region and its important oil reserves should have anticipated possible violence from a dictator whose entire career was marked with a resort to violence in solving his problems or acquiring his goals.

Coalition Deterrence of Iraq from invading Saudi Arabia, 1990-91

During the initial phases of the 1990-1991 Gulf War, both sides attempted to deter the other from certain actions. Saddam sought to deter U.S. intervention into the conflict by the threat of heavy U.S. and coalition casualties. From August 1990 until January 1991, the United States and the other coalition partners sought to deter Saddam from ordering his forces, then in Kuwait, to invade Saudi Arabia before it could be adequately defended. Iraq already had 11 percent of the world's proven oil reserves when Saddam Hussein ordered his forces into Kuwait. Had he held on in Kuwait, he would have gained another 8 percent of the world's oil reserves, or 19 percent overall. Had he continued on and conquered Saudi Arabia, a country that owns 25 percent of the world's oil reserves, Saddam would have controlled 44 percent of the world's oil reserves. Clearly, he had to be stopped or U.S. and allied vital interests in the region would have been threatened.

However, it is not at all clear whether Saddam Hussein ever seriously considered invading Saudi Arabia after consolidating his hold on Kuwait. Thus, we do not know if deterrence worked or was not needed in this case.

Certainly the thin Saudi and United States forces there in August and September 1990 could not have offered much resistance. However, to invade Saudi Arabia would have shed U.S. and Arab blood and perhaps the few U.S. forces sent immediately to the Saudi kingdom served as a trip wire, a down payment on further U.S. fighters to come and give battle to the Iraqi Army should they be attacked. Thus, an Iraqi attack on Saudi Arabia almost certainly would have triggered a war with the United States, something the Iraqi dictator almost certainly should have wanted to avoid if possible. Thus, the U.S. forces trip wire force quite likely served to halt the Iraqi force at the Saudi border until a military buildup there would permit coalition offensive action in January 1991.

Saddam's Failure to Hold the Coalition at Bay

Once the U.S. began to move its own forces into the region after the Iraqi seizure of Kuwait, Saddam Hussein had one of two moves available.

First, he could order his forces to attack and occupy much of Saudi Arabia just as they had in Kuwait. If he was to do this, he would have had to act immediately, for time was not on his side. A seizure of the Saudi kingdom would have greatly complicated the United States task of introducing large forces into the region. Certainly, he could have inflicted far more casualties and been much harder to dislodge from Kuwait if he had continued his offensive in August or September 1990 on into Saudi Arabia. In retrospect, the best defense he could mount was a good offense early before Operation Desert Shield could establish a significant force in the region to oppose his forces.

His second option was to do nothing except build up his defenses along the Saudi-Kuwait border and watch as the coalition troops poured into the theater opposite his army in Kuwait. Saddam elected the second option and relied upon his large army in Kuwait to deter an attack by threatening large coalition casualties should they attack. This was a contest of wills with the U.S. President and his allies, and ultimately Saddam Hussein lost. The coalition was not deterred from war and the result was a catastrophic defeat for the Iraqi military.

Why was the coalition not deterred from attacking Saddam's forces in Kuwait? First, Iraq dealt with states and forces much greater than his own. President Bush and his advisers and the other coalition leaders had a much greater appreciation of the qualitative superiority of their forces than did Saddam. Operation Desert Shield had put an impressive, well equipped army of 543,000 U.S. troops and thousands of other coalition military personnel at the disposal of General Norman Schwarzkopf Jr. and President Bush by January 1991.

It was clear to most military experts the coalition would have control of the air and sea around Kuwait. Further, coalition ground forces had superior armor, superior artillery, superior mobility, superior training, superior protective gear against chemical and biological weapons, and superior intelligence.

Further, the United States, United Kingdom and France were states with nuclear weapons and Iraq had been warned that any use of CB weapons would possibly be met with overwhelming responses. The bottom line was it was not likely Iraq could win a war with the coalition.

Beyond this, most of the states in the region and the West would not allow Iraq to pose such a threat to their oil supplies and economies. As previously noted, Kuwait controlled 8 percent of the known world oil reserves and its neighbor, Saudi Arabia, 25 percent. Add to this Iraq's control of 11 percent, and Saddam Hussein would either have or directly threaten up to 44 percent of world oil supplies. It was deemed in no one best interest to allow this to happen. Therefore, if Iraq did not willingly quit Kuwait, it must be expelled, and the coalition had the military means to make this happen. Saddam had very weak deterrent cards to play in this scenario and he was unable to deter the coalition attack that began on Jan. 17, 1991.

Saddam's Fallback Position: Deterring a Coalition March to Baghdad

Why did Saddam Hussein refuse to withdraw from Kuwait as the coalition military buildup continued opposite his forces in Kuwait from August 1990 until January 1991? At some point, one would have thought he would have realized a military superpower and its allies would easily defeat his forces and bring catastrophic consequences to his armed forces and regime. What kept him from retreating in the face of overwhelming force before the coalition military hammer struck?

It is possible that Saddam Hussein believed his own rhetoric and believed either the coalition, despite the buildup of forces in Saudi Arabia, was bluffing or that his army could hold its own in combat with the United States.

It is likely Saddam felt he needed the resources from Kuwait to rebuild his regime and its security forces to remain in power. He might also have reasoned a forced retreat from Kuwait, coupled with the disastrous war he had just concluded with Iran, would so weaken him at home that rivals might take encouragement from his weakened position and reputation to overthrow his regime and execute him. He might have calculated it was better to fight and rally the Iraqi people against a foreign foe than to capitulate and face their censure.

Saddam Hussein appeared to believe even if Iraq failed to deter a coalition attack on his forces and country, he nevertheless calculated he could deter the U.S.-led coalition from horizontal escalation[25] of the conflict into Iraq. He believed he could mount a stout enough defense so the coalition could not overrun his forces and occupy Iraq. He felt the U.S. leadership would stop short of attempting a total victory once U.S. forces absorbed very high casualty rates. He might also have retained hopes he could hang on to some of the Kuwait oil fields if the fighting led to a stalemate.

Saddam Hussein also thought the United States was less formidable than many others believed. Six months before his invasion of Kuwait, Saddam addressed the fourth summit of the Arab Cooperation Council in Jordan and stated:

> Brothers, the weakness of a big body lies in its bulkiness. All strong men have their Achilles heel. Therefore…we saw that the United States departed Lebanon immediately when some Marines were killed… The whole U.S. administration would have been called into question had the forces that conquered Panama continued to be engaged by the Panamanian Armed Forces. The United States has been defeated in some combat arenas for all the forces it possesses, and it has displayed signs of fatigue, frustration, and hesitation when committing aggression on other people's rights and acting from motives of arrogance and hegemony…[26]

As one analyst wrote:

> Saddam was hoping for a political not military victory in the Gulf War. He believed that he would triumph if, in the course of the ground war, Iraq inflicted substantial casualties on the Americans. On one occasion he even mentioned a casualty figure that believed would break America's will to fight; "We are sure that if President Bush pushes things

toward war and wages war against us – his war of aggression which he is planning – once five thousand of his troops die, he will not be able to continue this war."[27]

As a result of this conclusion, Saddam Hussein ordered his generals to direct their forces to "inflict 'maximum casualties' on U.S. soldiers when the fighting started."[28] He believed U.S. leaders would face mounting domestic pressure to halt their war efforts as the killing continued and the numbers of U.S. dead increased.

Former Secretary of State Baker recalls, "In retrospect, the war may seem to have been a clinical and relatively straightforward affair. At the time, however, we were confronted with very sobering casualty figures, estimated by the Pentagon to be in the thousands; the specter of possible chemical and biological attacks; and a war expected to last for months not days."[29]

Baker summarized, "Moreover, Saddam may have misread history. He apparently was fixated by our experience in Vietnam and, like Hafez al-Assad, thought our pullout from Lebanon after the Beirut barracks bombing in October 1983 showed Americans were 'short of breath.' Unlike Assad, however, Saddam was willing to test that proposition in a high profile, high-risk way."[30]

As one analyst put it, Saddam Hussein was "a great believer in the eventual victory of the side willing to suffer the most."[31] To win the war politically, if not militarily, Saddam was willing to lose thousands more of Iraqi dead to inflict the requisites number of American dead to achieve his ends.

General Norman Schwarzkopf clearly was worried Iraqi chemical weapons might cause major coalition casualties. In his memoir he wrote,

> You can take the most beat-up army in the world, and if they choose to stand and fight, we are going to take casualties: if they choose to dump chemicals on you, they might even win….My nightmare was that our units would reach the barriers in the first hours of the attack, be unable to get through, and then be hit with a chemical barrage. The possibilities of mass casualties from chemical weapons was

the main reason we had sixty-three hospitals, two hospital ships, and eighteen thousand beds in the war zone.[32]

Schwarzkopf was also worried Saddam Hussein prepared to use chemical weapons on the coalition army if it tried to go around the Iraqi flanks.[33]

Indeed, Saddam Hussein was perhaps both right and wrong in his deterrence estimates in late 1990. He was clearly mistaken about his Army's ability to inflict five thousand or more coalition casualties in that war. The U.S. personnel killed in action were 148 battle-related deaths and 145 out-of-combat deaths.[34] In addition, the U.K. suffered 47 deaths, 38 from Iraqi fire. France suffered two deaths, and the Arab countries, not including Kuwait, suffered 37 deaths.[35] On the other hand it is clear President George H.W. Bush sought to minimize both coalition and Iraqi casualties and one reason he halted the war after only 100 hours of fighting was to stop the slaughter, on both sides, even at the price of not directly toppling Saddam's regime in Baghdad, despite having that possibility well within his grasp when he ordered the ceasefire.[36]

Colin Powell, then Chairman of the Joint Chiefs of Staff, worried also about the downwind effects of targeting Iraqi biological warfare laboratories and facilities. He feared for civilians and coalition military personnel operating downwind, yet felt these sites still needed to be neutralized in the air campaign if possible. Powell was even more concerned about the effects of possible biological weapons attacks on allied troops than those of chemical attacks.[37]

And who can say if the Iraqi military had been able to fight a much more protracted war, that the Bush administration might not have called a ceasefire and settled on a compromise peace as the U.S. casualty toll reached Saddam's estimate of 5,000 dead Americans? Note in the present war in Iraq, in mid-2009, U.S. casualties have yet to reach 5,000 killed, but the United States is withdrawing without having completely defeated the Iraqi insurgency, as the cost of continuing indefinitely is perceived as unacceptable.[38]

Once the shock and awe of the coalition combined arms attack sent the Iraqi forces into precipitate retreat, there was little to stand between the U.S.-led forces and Baghdad. However, eight reasons deterred President Bush from going beyond the Kuwait borders with Iraq.

First, the United States did not want Iraq to dissolve, but rather wanted it to serve as a balancer to Iranian power in the region.

Second, President Bush wished to stay within the limits of the United Nations mandate given him and feared he would lose the unity of the coalition if he widened the war beyond such legal limits. UN resolutions limited coalition actions to expelling Iraq from Kuwait.

Third, the United States did not want the war to be perceived as a war of conquest for oil. President Bush felt the continuation of the war into Iraq would cause the U.S. to be portrayed as the aggressor rather than Iraq.

Fourth, President George H.W. Bush did not want the costs of occupying, pacifying and rebuilding Iraq if the U.S.-led coalition took it over. Moreover, there was no organized Iraqi opposition to turn power over to, so the occupation would be lengthy and painful.

Fifth, President Bush wished to limit the economic and human costs of the war, not only to the coalition but to Iraq as well. He believed entering Iraq would increase the will of the Iraqi army to fight since they would be defending the homeland rather than Kuwait. President Bush and his advisers also felt they did not want to get into an urban house-to-house war, or a chemical or biological weapons war, with increased U.S. and coalition casualties.

Sixth, the U.S. leaders did not expect Saddam Hussein to be able to stay in power once the dimensions of his defeat were felt in his country. Carrying the war into Iraq might have made him a national hero in Iraq, rather than a defeated adventurer. As James Baker wrote in his memoirs, "Strategically, the real objective was to eject Iraq from Kuwait in a manner that would destroy Saddam's offensive military capabilities and make his fall from power likely."[39] President Bush and his advisers felt the U.S. political and military war aims had been obtained.

Seventh, U.S. leaders wanted to prevent Israel from intervening in the conflict and thereby undermining the Arab ally participation in the war. Also, had Saddam ordered chemical and/or biological attacks on Israel as the war continued, the Israeli leadership might have responded with a nuclear attack on Baghdad. What might have occurred after such an exchange would have been very uncertain, but it was not a problem the Bush administration wished to risk.

Finally, an invasion of Iraq might have backfired politically in the United States and triggered major political opposition to the President.

Halting at the border left the United States and the Bush Administration with ultra-high approval ratings. Keeping the U.S. military in the theater would have been unpopular with the troops and at home.

U.S. Deterrence of Iraqi Chemical and Biological Weapons Use

On the other hand, the United States and its coalition partners tried to compel the retreat of Iraqi forces from Kuwait short of war in the months from August 1990 until January 1991. Failing to deter war, President Bush, at least, was intent on deterring Saddam Hussein from ordering chemical and biological attacks on Coalition forces and from burning the Kuwaiti oil fields. He warned the Iraqi dictator in clear and forceful terms this would be a catastrophic step if enacted.

Note the Jan. 5, 1991, letter addressed to Saddam Hussein. President Bush wrote and had Secretary of State James Baker deliver to the Iraqi Government via the Iraqi Foreign Minister, Tariq Aziz, in mid-January, 1991:

> Let me state, too that the United States will not tolerate the use of chemical or biological weapons or the destruction of Kuwait's oil fields and installations. Further, you will be held directly responsible for terrorist actions against any member of the coalition. The American people would demand the strongest possible response. You and your country will pay a terrible price if you order unconscionable acts of this sort.[40]

To augment Bush's warning letter, James Baker restated to Iraqi Foreign Minister Tariq Aziz the consequences for Iraq if they were not to leave Kuwait:

> Our objective is for you to leave Kuwait. That's the only solution we will accept. And if you do not do that, then we'll find ourselves at war, and if you do go war with the coalition, you will surely lose. This will not be a war of attrition like

you fought with Iran. It will be fought with the means and weapons that play to our strengths, not to yours. We have the means to define how the battle will be fought, and yours do not.

This is not to threaten but to inform. You may choose to reject it, or not to believe what we say, but we have the responsibility to tell you that we have tremendous technological advantages in forces, and our view is that if conflict comes, your forces will face devastatingly superior firepower. In our view – and you may reject this and disagree – our forces will really destroy your ability to command your own forces.

We owe it to you to tell you there will be no stalemate, no UN ceasefire or breathing space for negotiations. If conflict begins, it will be decisive. This will not be another Vietnam. Should war begin, God forbid, it will be fought to a swift, decisive conclusion.

If the conflict involves your use of chemical or biological weapons against our forces, the American people will demand vengeance. We have the means to exact it. With regard to this part of my presentation, this is not a threat, it is a promise. If there is any use of weapons like that, an objective won't just be the liberation of Kuwait, but the liberation of the current Iraqi regime and anyone responsible for using those weapons will be held accountable.[41]

To reinforce the idea WMD might be met with WMD, Secretary of Defense Dick Cheney also stated publicly, "Were Saddam Hussein foolish enough to use weapons of mass destruction, the U.S. response would be absolutely overwhelming and it would be devastating."[42]

In cases like the Gulf War, there are certain possible advantages in dealing with an enemy leader like Saddam Hussein, who has seldom hesitated to use maximum violence to achieve his aims and solve his problems. Such a leader, in his own mind, may project his own ruthlessness upon his opponent, in this case the President of the United States.

If a Saddam-type of killer would not hesitate to use all his available weapons against a previous foe, he might expect a stronger adversary to do the same against him if he escalated to WMD use against it. [43] In such cases the very ruthlessness of a rogue chief might become the ally of U.S. ability to deter his chemical or biological weapons employment against the United States or its allies.

Since Saddam Hussein did not use chemical or biological weapons in the subsequent fighting in Kuwait, despite the fact he had previously shown no hesitation about using them against Iran in their eight-year war, or against his own Kurdish populations when they opposed him, it might fairly be concluded U.S. threats deterred his chemical and biological use. Of course, with deterrence one can never prove 100 percent that it worked. Saddam might not have wanted to use them for other reasons.[44] Clearly, the U.S. threat of retaliation did not stop him from setting fire to Kuwait's oil fields as his forces evacuated that country. That U.S. deterrent message obviously did not work.

In 1998, seven years after Operation Desert Storm, ex-President George H.W. Bush and his former National Security Adviser Brent Scowcroft published a memoir of their times in power titled *A World Transformed*. Although Saddam Hussein was still in power in Iraq at the time of the memoir and was still considered a threat to U.S. and regional allies, Scowcroft nevertheless wrote the Bush administration had only been bluffing about using nuclear weapons should Saddam Hussein order the Iraqi Army to use chemical or biological weapons. Indeed, Scowcroft wrote that:

> No one advanced the notion of using nuclear weapons, and the President rejected it even in retaliation for chemical and biological attacks. We deliberately avoided spoken or unspoken threats to use them on the grounds that it is bad practice to threaten something you have no intention of carrying out. Publicly, we left the matter ambiguous. There was no point in undermining the deterrence it might be offering.[45]

James Baker's memoir tells the same story:

> The President had decided, at Camp David in December that the best deterrent of the use of weapons of mass destruction by Iraq would be a threat to go after the Ba'ath regime itself.

He had also decided that U.S. forces would not retaliate with chemical or nuclear weapons if the Iraqis attacked with chemical munitions, there was obviously no reason to inform the Iraqis of this. In hopes of persuading them to consider more soberly the folly of war, I purposely left the impression that the use of chemical or biological agents by Iraq could invite tactical nuclear retaliations.[46]

Saddam might have believed this threat simply because he was not a person given to moral limits and had previously always used all weapons at his command, witness the merciless Iraqi chemical attacks during the Iran-Iraq War against both military and civilian personnel. He might have viewed President Bush as like himself, willing to use everything for victory.[47]

However, it could not have helped subsequent deterrence efforts to publicize the United States had bluffed and never seriously considered using its nuclear advantages in the 1990-1991 Gulf War. After all, when the various memoirs of Bush, Scowcroft, Baker and Powell were published, Saddam Hussein was still in power in Iraq and might have needed to be deterred from future adventures by succeeding U.S. Presidents. Also, it should be noted other adversary leaders in other states like North Korea, Syria and Iran can also read, and as a result, might conclude in future crises they too, were relatively safe from any U.S. nuclear retaliations.

In any case, it is not clear Saddam Hussein believed his biological weapons in particular would be effective, because it later became clear in the mid-1990s, that Iraq had not made great progress at the time of the 1990-91 Gulf campaign, in mating its experimental biological weapons program to an effective delivery system. However, chemical weapons were another thing entirely. His regime had manufactured tens of thousands of chemical weapons and had used them to deadly and strategic effect against Iran. As the CIA later concluded,

In Saddam's view, WMD helped save the regime multiple times, He believed that during the Iran-Iraq War chemical weapons had halted Iranian ground offensives and that ballistic missile attacks on Tehran had broken its political will. Similarly during Desert Storm, Saddam believed

WMD had deterred Coalition Forces from pressing their attack beyond the goal of freeing Kuwait.[48]

Indeed, Iraq's military had the most experience delivering chemical weapons in actual battle conditions of any military in the world at the time of the 1990-1991 Gulf War. On the other hand, it is not clear Saddam and his commanders believed his forces were superior to U.S. forces on a toxic battlefield where U.S. forces, unlike most of his Iraqi military, were well trained and relatively better equipped than the Iraqi forces to fight in a chemical environment. U.S. and NATO preparations against the possible onslaught of the Warsaw Pact chemical threat had equipped the U.S. forces to fight better than the Iraq Army in this realm. Thus, it might have been that U.S. forces passive defenses played a major part in Iraq's decision not to use chemical arms, perhaps as great a role as President Bush's implied nuclear threat.

At any rate, it is likely the combination of the implied U.S. nuclear retaliatory threat and the superiority of U.S. training and better protective gear against chemical effects combined to keep the Iraqi chemical weapons out of play.

Iraqi Chemical and Biological Capability: Deterrent to U.S. Nuclear Weapons?

What confidence did Saddam Hussein have that the United States would not use its superiority in nuclear arms to destroy his army in Kuwait?

First, the Iraqi dictator hoped to deter President Bush and other coalition leaders from attacking because he believed the Iraqi military, at the time the fourth largest in the world in terms of numbers in uniform, could inflict substantial casualties on what he perceived as a casualty-adverse opponent.

Second, even President Bush's direct warning letter communicated to Saddam Hussein via Secretary Baker in a meeting with Tariq Aziz on Jan. 5, 1991, could be read the United States would not use its nuclear superiority so long as Iraqi chemical and biological weapons were not used (see Appendix B of this paper). Thus, there is the question of "who was deterring whom?" Was George Bush deterring Saddam Hussein's use of chemical and biological weapons? Or was he also indicating Iraqi chemical and biological warfare capabilities would deter U.S. use of nuclear weapons on Iraq?[49]

Saddam Hussein clearly put out warnings that Iraqi chemical and biological weapons would be used in the contingency of a U.S. or U.K. use of nuclear arms. For example, in a meeting with former British Prime Minister Edward Heath in October 1990, Saddam said, "If the going gets hard then the British and Americans will use atomic weapons against me, and the chances are that Israel will as well, and the only thing I've got are chemical and biological weapons, and I shall have to use them. I have no alternative."[50] President Bush also was under no illusions on this as he had noted on more than one occasion that Saddam "has never possessed a weapon he did not use."[51]

Saddam possibly felt his biological and chemical weapons were his ace in the hole. Saddam's poison gases had played a key role in holding the stronger Iranian military at bay and had brought the Iranians to the peace table. According to one Middle East analyst, "Saddam took the experience of the war with Iran, in which gas eventually caused the Iranian military to lose its most potent weapon – its will to fight – to mean that Iraq possessed an absolute weapon capable of stopping modernized armies as well."[52]

Clearly, the U.S. leadership had serious concerns about such chemical and biological weapons use or the President would not have made it such a central issue in his warning letter to Saddam Hussein. Further, the Combatant Commander, General Schwarzkopf, was especially concerned the Iraqi Army might ruin the "Left Hook" flanking movement by his ground forces with a devastating chemical barrage. General Colin Powell, then Chairman of the Joint Chiefs of Staff, was particularly focused on the potential casualties that might come from an Iraqi biological warfare strike.

James Baker also admitted the casualties that might flow from urban warfare and from Iraqis' who would fight harder to protect their homeland would cause many more American deaths. Thus, it is plausible the chemical and biological threats and anything that had the potential to greatly escalate U.S. casualties impacted U.S. thinking and helped serve as an Iraqi deterrent to an invasion of Iraq.[53] Thus, it is possible Saddam's WMD threat, in the form of chemical and biological weapons, might have been responsible for saving his regime.

U.S. and Israeli Failure to Deter Iraq from attacking Israel

The coalition air campaign began on Jan.17, 1991. The next day, Saddam Hussein ordered the first of 48 Scud missile attacks on Israel as well as the first of 41 such attacks against the coalition forces in Saudi Arabia. Apparently, the threat of possible Israeli nuclear retaliation did not deter such a decision. This was risky for clearly Israel had enough nuclear firepower to utterly destroy Iraq. Saddam played a very dangerous game with them.

On the other hand, Saddam attempted to split the coalition by attacking Israel. Would the coalition Arab allies fight on the same side as Israel against another Arab state? This was considered highly unlikely in Washington, D.C.[54] For this reason, United States leaders were concerned an Israeli counter-attack would undermine the support of the Arab partners in the U.S. coalition against Iraq.

Thus, U.S. leaders rushed Patriot theater missile defenses to help defend Israel from Iraqi missiles, and devoted over 2,000 air sorties against the Iraqi SCUD missile launchers in an attempt to protect Israel and keep them out of the fight. Ultimately, the swift and decisive air-land-sea war unleashed by the coalition made short work of the Iraqi military forces, and the combination of theater missile defenses and U.S. diplomacy all helped dissuade Israel from participating with its armed forces.

Conclusions and Lessons Learned

Lesson 1: What deterred the Soviet Union in the Cold War will not apply to all cases.

Deterrence is a rational strategy and theory of how to prevent war or escalation of a war. However, the evidence of history is deterrence often fails. Deterrence is inexact, an art not a science. What works perfectly in one case may fail wholly in another. Indeed, it is the weaker party that attacks the stronger party in about one of every five wars. So deterrence is not a given even when your government or coalition has overwhelming military superiority over an opposing state.

The Cold War strategy the West adopted to deter a Soviet nuclear or conventional attack seems to have worked, although one can never be absolutely sure what kept the peace. Was it because the West had a retaliatory capability to destroy the U.S.S.R. and Warsaw Pact? Was it because in crises, Soviet leaders believed the U.S. leaders had the will to use their nuclear weapons if necessary? Was it because the United States and its allies had a second strike force, one not vulnerable to a surprise disarming attack? Or was it because the West faced rational leaders in Moscow who understood the logic of mutual assured destruction? Or were we simply lucky? Would war have occurred if all these factors had not been put in place? Or would both sides have maintained the peace anyway? And how much retaliatory force was enough to deter a war with the U.S.S.R.? Did we need thousands of nuclear weapons or just a few? How much was enough to deter war and the escalation of crises?[55] We can never know for sure. We are only certain that we did not have a central nuclear war with the Soviet Union and its Warsaw pact and other allies.

One thing clear from the Gulf War example is despite all the destructive power in the United States, U.K. and French nuclear arsenals, and for all the coalition's conventional might, they could not deter Saddam Hussein from seizing Kuwait, and they could not compel him to withdraw his forces without first resorting to war. One reason for this is the U.S. and coalition did not develop a firm response to Iraq prior to Saddam's decision to invade Kuwait. Had the United States delivered a strong warning and deployed forces to back this up prior to Saddam's final decision to invade Kuwait, he might have been deterred. The tardiness of the deterrence signals ruined the chances for their success.

This calls into question whether the Cold War calculus of what it takes to deter a conflict worked in the Gulf War. Apparently, the possession of nuclear weapons by his opponents did not deter Saddam Hussein or compel him to leave Kuwait or end the conflict until his forces were routed in Kuwait. He was willing to strike U.S., U.K., French and Israeli targets, risking possible nuclear annihilation. He was willing to fight a coalition of over 30 states in Kuwait rather than withdraw peacefully.

Lesson 2: States that possess WMD or other extraordinary military power may feel that they can afford to start a conflict and keep it within tolerable levels of escalation where they can achieve their aims.

Perhaps Saddam Hussein believed the threat of his chemical and biological (CB) weapons would deter any nuclear use by the coalition forces, and perhaps he even believed, under his chemical and biological deterrent umbrella, his forces in Kuwait were formidable enough to deter a coalition attack or to prevent a complete and utter defeat.

Saddam Hussein may have relied on his CB capability first to deter any coalition attack on his forces in Kuwait. This failed on Jan.17, 1991, when the coalition air attack began. Second, he may have relied on his CB threat to prevent U.S., U.K., French and Israeli nuclear attacks. There is no evidence such weapons use had ever been seriously considered by any of the four states. Indeed, memoirs of U.S. decision-makers Bush, Scowcroft, Baker and Powell, indicate this was never seriously considered, although Secretary of Defense Cheney asked the Joint Chiefs to look into the utility of nuclear strikes if the President ever changed his mind.

Finally Saddam Hussein may have assumed his CB arsenal would have made it too costly for the coalition to march to Baghdad, occupy Iraqi territory and replace his regime. Clearly, he might have been tempted to use such weapons and risk further coalition escalation to nuclear weapons, as his situation became more and more desperate. Even if he resisted the impulse to use CB weapons as the invasion of Iraq began, it is likely if it became clear to him his regime was about to fall, the CB gloves quite likely would have come off, and the coalition might have been struck with last minute chemical and biological revenge strikes.[56] Saddam Hussein probably realized coalition leaders would also understand the perils from Iraq's CB weapons of trying to achieve a total defeat of his regime. It is likely he is correct this possibility weighed heavily in the U.S. and coalition decision not to press for a total defeat of his forces and regime in Iraq.

Lesson 3: Saddam felt he was willing to sustain deeper casualties than the United States, and this would give him a political if not military victory. States willing to suffer more than their opponents may count on their adversary halting the war effort when casualities reach a certain painful threshold that tempers their war aims.

It appears Saddam was willing to gamble the United States was so casualty averse we would halt our military operations after suffering the first

5,000 deaths from the clash with Iraq. Of course, he was badly mistaken in how his forces matched up with the coalition. Since his forces were able to kill only 148 U.S. fighters in the battles that ensued, not 5,000, his deterrence theory of U.S. and coalition escalation, estimated at a threshold of 5,000 killed in action, was never tested.

It should be noted President Bush and his field commander, General Schwarzkopf, prepared for possible heavy coalition casualties. Note the United States and the coalition had transported 63 mobile field hospitals to the region before launching Operation Desert Storm, as well as two hospital ships and 18,000 hospital beds.[57]

On the other hand, while Saddam Hussein thought the United States leaders were very averse to suffering casualties, nevertheless, he still perhaps underestimated President Bush's regard for human life – Iraq lives as well as those of Americans and the rest of the coalition. Indeed, unlike Bush, it may never have occurred to Saddam Hussein to limit his military actions in order to prevent enemy combatant deaths as well as those of his own forces.

Lesson 4: If the rival leadership does not understand when it faces extreme military disadvantages, deterrence of the weaker by the stronger side is more likely to fail. Situational awareness and rationality must be joined together in the rival leadership for the deterrent effect to work.

The Cold War deterrence requirement of having a situationally aware and rational opponent was not met fully in the Gulf War. Saddam Hussein may have been logical in his thinking, but ignorant of important facts. He was not situationally aware of the magnitude of military forces arrayed against him nor was he cognizant of much of the movement on the battlefield due to faulty intelligence. For example, he did not have satellites for intelligence, surveillance and reconnaissance of the coalition forces, and much of the Iraqi air force had fled by the time the coalition ground forces attacked. Saddam never detected the "Left Hook" flanking attack General Schwarzkopf put into motion at the beginning of the land battle.

Lesson 5: Dictators who kill the messenger seldom get good intelligence and are far less effective in countering adverse possibilities.

Saddam Hussein had a decision style that produced "yes men" only, robbing him of much important information on which to inform his decisions. To disagree with him was literally to risk your life if you were in his circle. His extreme brutality gave him unrivaled power. It also gave him information that conformed only to what his advisers thought he wanted to hear. Saddam did not welcome negative news or views and thus became the prisoner of his own perceptions of reality and rarely had those views been challenged or informed by facts or interpretations counter to his preconceptions such as: (1) the view the United States would not respond to an attack on Kuwait, or (2) the belief the coalition would not attack him in Kuwait because he had chemical and biological weapons, or (3) the Iraqi force could hold its own with that of the coalition, or (4) his forces could at least inflict 5,000 U.S. casualties and save him from absolute defeat.

Lesson 6: Many variables go into whether deterrence will work: time, place, culture, politics, leadership and the personalities that make the decisions. The greater the divergence between the personalities, world views of the adversary leaders, and the leadership stakes in the outcome, the greater the chances for deterrence to fail.

In this 1990-1991 Gulf War there were two kinds of deterrence to consider: (1) deterrence of the Iraqi invasion of Kuwait and (2) deterrence of an escalation of that war once it had begun. This was a war with many players, but it is fair to begin with the two key players in this drama, President Saddam Hussein and President George H.W. Bush. On the Iraqi side, the unquestioned chief decision-maker was Saddam Hussein. Saddam was Iraq, and Iraq was Saddam in this case. He was the unrivaled Iraqi decision-maker in foreign and defense policy.[58]

Things were a bit more complicated in the U.S. and coalition side. Clearly President George H.W. Bush was the ultimate decision-maker.[59] The United States was the key state in the formation of the coalition since it was and is the world's military superpower. However, others like U.K. Prime Minister Margaret Thatcher were influential in collaborating with the United States leadership. Thatcher was considered particularly instrumental in advising President Bush to take an uncompromising policy requiring Iraq to abandon Kuwait or face war. And clearly, the instruments of power were provided by all the coalition members as they mobilized for war, sent their armed forces to Saudi Arabia and participated in Operation Desert Storm that succeeded brilliantly in routing the Iraqi Army in Kuwait.

The frequent insensitivity of enemies to each other's stakes and signals, and the all-too-often misperceptions they have of each other's aims and motives is at the core of why deterrence theory so often fails to explain interstate behavior in conflict situations.

Lesson 7: Deterrence fails frequently, and what works in one case will fail in another. Governments run largely by a single dominant individual are rare and thus deterring Saddam Hussein and Iraq will be different from most cases where power is shared. Lessons learned from this case study should be applied very cautiously to other cases.

One must also be careful in drawing deterrence lessons from a particular case. In the 1990-1991 Gulf War, Saddam Hussein ruled Iraq with an iron fist and did not have to negotiate with others in forming his decisions. Thus, Iraq was a unitary actor. This will not always be the case. In most states power and decisions are shared by a group at the top. Power is often dispersed. Deterrence becomes a group affair. One must persuade a group of decision-makers and power holders before deterrence can succeed. Thus, on the Iraqi side at least this is a special case where one man, Saddam Hussein, could speak for the entire country, and his will became Iraq's path.

On the opposing side, although he was by far the most influential decision-maker on his side of the conflict, President Bush could not have acted nearly as freely as Saddam Hussein did in Iraq. Bush and his able team first had to mobilize diverse coalition of allied states, secure the backing of the U.S. Congress, seek the support of the United Nations, and mobilize U.S. public support prior to kicking off the January 1991 counterattack against Iraq. Even so, once such efforts to mobilize support had succeeded, it took additional time to deploy and equip a sufficient military force in the region to repel the Iraqi invaders from Kuwait. Nearly six months elapsed before the coalition was ready to go to war to reclaim Kuwait.

In other cases where a government attempts to deter a war or launch one, the power to make such decisions may be shared, and policy may be a product of multiple factors that combine to take the decision or policy in a certain direction. This becomes even more complicated when the more power is shared on both sides. Thus, the 1990-1991 Gulf War may be a special case, and you must be careful about drawing general conclusions about deterrence from it.

Lesson 8: When dealing with an adversary bent on achieving a fait accompli, quick reaction time is absolutely required. Be alert and ready to act at the outset or fail to deter leaders like Saddam Hussein. When still considering the opening move, a rival leadership can be more easily turned away from an act of aggression. After a decision has been made and a plan set in motion, deterrence can be far more difficult or impossible.

Timing of the U.S. and coalition deterrence campaign was too late against Saddam to prevent Iraq's invasion of Kuwait. Right from the start, the U.S. leadership needed to use unambiguous language with a violence-prone leader like Saddam Hussein. All he respected was superior force and will. Anything less was not going to keep him from seizing his prize, particularly since it represented, in his mind, the path to financial solvency and subsequent physical security. It would be wise for the United States and other allies to first inventory their absolute vital interests, things like preventing the Middle East's oil reserves from falling under the control of a hostile dictator whose interests were opposed to peace and security in the region and whose grip on world energy supplies could not be trusted. After that, a continuous defense and deterrence policy and posture would be needed in the region to keep these vital interests secure.

Where these types of leaders and regimes are positioned to adversely impact U.S. and allied vital interests, particular high-level attention needs to be paid to them. When such a potential challenger is positioned to threaten a vital interest or vital ally, contingency plans need to be pre-formulated for deterring them from any power grabs or hostile interventions. These plans need to have forces attached to them so once a crisis begins, these forces can be rapidly mobilized and sent to the region to signal the seriousness of U.S. and allied intentions and to undergird the tough talk and warnings that U.S. and allied leaders must be prepared to give potential aggressors.

Beyond that, it would be wise to profile and pay extra close attention to all foreign leaders like Saddam Hussein who have a track record of violence and aggression, and who have shown repeated lawless behavior against domestic rivals and their international neighbors. Interdisciplinary teams of profilers who have read every word and observed every action of aggressive leadership should help inform U.S. decision-makers about the motives, situation and operational codes of these potential trouble makers. Such teams of profilers should stay with the observation of these particular leaders over years and decades rather than be rotated into other assignments and succeeded by uninformed and inexperienced intelligence officers. Moreover, it would be wise to have at least two parallel teams of profilers to compete in their assessments and provide decision-makers with alternative evaluations. It would also be useful if a representative of these competitive "Red Team" groups would give their interpretations of likely next moves and motives of that particular rival leader or leadership team.

Lesson 9: Beware of the enemy whose modus operandi is to attack preemptively and who has a track record of extreme violence and bold risk taking.

Saddam Hussein believed in careful plotting and swift and violent preemptive moves against his domestic and foreign foes. He came from a background that made him see enemies everywhere and he may have been seen as, or even actually been, paranoid. However, as the saying goes, just because he was paranoid does not mean people were not out to get him, especially after he had killed his way to the top of the Iraqi political system. He had actually made so many thousands of enemies by that time it was probably completely rational to act like a paranoid ruler. First he had killed the enemies of the Ba'ath Party in Iraq and anyone that stood in their way to power.[60] After that was secure, he killed anyone who he thought might become a rival, even if that was not yet the case. He killed anyone who grew in popularity like some of the more successful Iraqi generals who fought well in the Iran-Iraq War.

He killed to maintain Sunni power over the majority Shia sect in Iraq. He killed Kurdish leaders who represented an independent power source. Once at the pinnacle of power after 1978, he launched wars against his neighbors in Iran[61] and Kuwait and sent his forces to the doorstep of

Saudi Arabia. Tens of thousands of Iraqis, Iranians and Kuwaitis therefore died as a result of his aggressions.

Hussein constantly analyzed who might possibly become his rivals inside Iraq and planned brutal elimination campaigns to remove them by lethal means. In the summer of 1979, Saddam admitted to a colleague, "I know that there are scores of people plotting to kill me, and this is not difficult to understand. After all, did we not seize power by plotting against our predecessors? However, I am far cleverer than they are. I know they are conspiring to kill me long before they actually start planning to do it. This enables me to do it before they have the faintest chance of striking at me."[62]

Saddam's violent and ceaseless domestic purges follow the pattern of the terror campaigns of Stalin's rule in the Soviet Union, a leader whose bloody methods deeply impressed him. Saddam's endless warring foreign policy also reminds one of Adolph Hitler's ceaseless wars against all neighbors and all other ethnic groups.

Saddam Hussein never felt secure and his prophylactic arrests and executions no doubt kept him in power longer than previous Iraqi leaders who were all removed by coups. Indeed, the five previous rulers of Iraq all lost power in this way. Hussein also felt the Islamic Republic of Iran posed a potential lethal threat to his rule. Not only were they hostile, they were Shiite Muslims like nearly 60 percent of his Iraqi countrymen. Their revolution had targeted him. He felt he had to preemptively destroy them or see his regime destroyed by them, hence his decision to attack Iran in 1979 while they were still getting organized. Like his domestic purges, he struck before his enemies realized his lethal intent.

Lesson 10: Understand the situation and perspective of adversary leaders to anticipate when and where they might decide to initiate hostilities. Plan to deter and counter them with contingency plans and quick reaction forces in anticipation of such contingencies.

After the Iran-Iraq war ended in a ceasefire in 1988, Saddam was desperate to rebuild his armed forces and security forces before Iran regrouped and attacked again. Iran had come dangerously close to defeating him in the previous conflict and was a country with three times the population of Iraq, and four times the land area. Yet, his forces were spent, and because of his adventures, he was out of credit and deeply in debt. This led him to attack Kuwait as a means of recouping his fortunes and preparing for what he feared was the inevitable Iranian resumption of the war. The Bush administration in 1990 did not have its focus on the Iraq-Kuwait dispute, nor did it appreciate Saddam Hussein's dilemma and his modus operandi enough to anticipate his attack and occupation of Kuwait. Bush and his advisers were surprised and unprepared for the event although the threat could have been anticipated with better intelligence and forethought.

Lesson 11: Understand what motivates the adversary leadership in terms of retention of their personal power and survival in order to predict your chances of success or failure in attempts to deter further acts of war or escalation. Put yourselves in their shoes. See the world from their perspective when planning to counter them.

Saddam Hussein may have felt a retreat from Kuwait would have weakened him in the eyes of the Iraqi military and people and made him more vulnerable to overthrow. Already he was in a weakened position. He had just concluded a disastrous eight-year war with Iran costing hundreds of thousands of lives and billions of dollars worth of funds. He may have reasoned that this, coupled with forced humiliating retreat from Kuwait, might have given strong encouragement to his domestic and international rivals to try to remove him from power. Better, he might have thought, to take on a foreign force, rally the Iraqi people once more behind his rule against an external enemy, than to slink back to Iraq in defeat without putting up a fight. That posture could get him deposed and killed.

Saddam likely reasoned it was better to fight in Kuwait, try to get a compromise peace, keep some of the fruits of his invasion, and stay in power and alive. Thus, Saddam appears to have concluded what was best for him personally was to put his people and his military through yet another war, however painful. He was willing to lose thousands more of Iraqis in order to preserve his own regime and his own life. Thus, Saddam was not to be compelled to leave Kuwait without a fight.

Lesson 12: While it certainly helps if you are trying to deter a rational opponent rather than an irrational one, rational leaders without situation awareness can still fail to understand the likely consequences of their actions and may fail to be deterred.

Deterrence can be especially difficult when the opponent is severely lacking in situational awareness. Saddam Hussein was unfamiliar with the United States and its leadership. He had only a weak grasp of our political system.

Nor did Saddam Hussein appear to keep track of who President Bush and his key advisers met with the day he launched the invasion of Kuwait. On Aug. 2, 1990, President Bush met with British Prime Minister Margaret Thatcher, the "Iron Lady of Britain." It would not have taken much analysis to ascertain the kind of strong action she was likely to and did recommend to President Bush in response to the Iraqi invasion. Further, other top U.S. leaders met in Moscow with top Soviet leaders. Thus, it was far easier to begin to mobilize the United States and its allies with its leaders in such close proximity. This does not seem to have occurred to Saddam Hussein and his advisers.

Moreover, the Iraqi dictator was an untutored military leader who appears not to have grasped the power and capability of the U.S. and coalition forces arrayed against him once they were mobilized and deployed to the region. Saddam did not trust his own military. He launched the invasion of Iran division by division through personal calls to his commanders because he did not trust them to coordinate operations in a joint fashion. Allowing them to meet and plan operations jointly might have also given them an opportunity to conspire against him. He separated his commander and forced them to communicate only through him. As a result, when that war began, there was a day or two before some of his military leaders even were informed they were at war with Iran.[63]

General Chuck Horner, the Joint Forces Air Commander during Operation Desert Storm, observed it was probably not the wisest coalition strategy to try to target Saddam Hussein during the war. He noted had it occurred:

> [K]illing Saddam may have turned out to be as serious mistake…In his paranoia; Saddam often had his top generals executed. The threat of execution sometimes concentrates the mind, but more often it leads to paralysis. This

weakening of his military leadership could only benefit the coalition. And finally, as general Schwarzkopf pointed out after the war, Saddam was a lousy strategist, and thus a good man to have in charge of Iraqi armed forces, under the circumstances.[64]

In retrospect, it is difficult to imagine how Saddam Hussein expected to fight a war effectively against the coalition when his air forces were swept from the skies, when his armor and artillery were out-ranged, when he did not have any air and space intelligence, surveillance or reconnaissance capabilities, when his forces were poorly trained and when he lacked adequate command and control of his own forces. Saddam Hussein clearly did not appreciate the caliber of U.S. and allied forces he faced and assumed his large army could inflict thousands of casualties on the coalition. This, he planned, would win him a compromise peace and the chance to survive and fight another day after the immediate conflict had ended. He was lucky to have survived and did not do so because his forces executed his plan or because his strategy worked.

Saddam Hussein's leadership and lack of situational awareness led the Iraqi military into a catastrophic defeat. According to one summary of the war, "Iraqi military casualties, killed or wounded, totaled an estimated 25,000 to 65,000 and the United Nations destroyed some 3,200 Iraqi tanks, over 900 other armored vehicles and over 2,000 artillery weapons. Some 86,000 Iraqi soldiers surrendered. In contrast, the U.N. forces suffered combat losses of some 200 from hostile fire plus losses of four tanks, nine other armored vehicles, and one artillery weapon...; Although coalition aircraft flew a total of 109,876 sorties, the allies lost only 38 aircraft versus over 300 for Iraq...The terms of the cease-fire were designed to enable U.N. inspectors to destroy most of Iraq's remaining missiles, chemical weapons and nuclear weapons facilities."[65]

Lesson 13: Beware of situations where a potential adversary sees great immediate and easy gains to be achieved by taking military action, and where his risks are seen as remote, abstract and distant. It will be important to try to reverse these perceptions of limited and distant risk, and to do so emphatically early in a crisis situation, to improve the chances for deterrence to work.

Saddam Hussein saw an immediate prize in Kuwait where he could add 8 percent of the world's oil supply to his resources, find a way out of his massive debt situation, gain the purchasing power to re-equip his armed forces and police to protect his regime and his life, and fund future extensions of his power and influence. He got a mild disclaimer from the United States that it had no particular interest in the outcome of his dispute with Kuwait over the Rumailia oil fields. There appeared to be no immediate strong opposition to his unspoken aspiration to add Kuwait to his realm. This could have been foreseen if the United States and other interested regional powers had been more alert and perceived the danger sooner. Clearly, in mid-1990 a violent and ambitious Saddam Hussein considered seizing a rich trophy, one that appeared could to be had for the taking, without any immediate or significant costs.

Richard Ned Lebow and Janet Gross Stein have examined over 20 cases of deterrence failures and concluded their studies "support the conclusion that policy makers who risk or actually start wars pay more attention to their own strategic and domestic political interests than they do to the interests and military capabilities of their adversaries."[66] Indeed, such aggressors "may discount an adversary's resolve even when the state in question has gone to considerable lengths to demonstrate that resolve and to develop the military capabilities needed to defend its commitment."[67] Thus, a government can do everything right to deter an adversary and still fail because the rival does not estimate the outcome the same way.

Lesson 14: Until a sizeable deterrent force can be sent to a region of potential conflict, it is a useful stopgap to send a tripwire force to signal U.S. intent to fight any attempt at aggression from the beginning.

Such a U.S. tripwire force was sent early to Saudi Arabia in the fall of 1990 to show Saddam Hussein an attack on Saudi Arabia would spill U.S. blood and draw the United States into a conflict with Iraq. This action may have saved Saudi Arabia from an invasion in the period between the August 1990 invasion and occupation of Kuwait and the initiation of the coalition air war in January 1991 and the ground war in February 1991. Like the U.S. army forces stationed in Berlin, Germany, during the Cold

War, these tripwire forces would not have been able to stop the enemy forces from seizing that territory immediately, but it would have been a down payment on a future U.S. military escalation and counterattack. Being drawn into a war with the world's military superpower should serve as a considerable reason for rethinking an aggressive move.

Lesson 15: In cases where both sides possess some form of mass casualty weapons, deterrence can work in both directions. Both can be deterred from use of the chemical, biological, radiological or nuclear (CBRN) weapons by the threat of the other. On the other hand, both may still feel free to prosecute a limited conventional war, feeling secure that their CBRN deterrent will shield them from a similar enemy attack.

Saddam Hussein attacked the forces of the coalition that included three nuclear weapons states: The United States, United Kingdom and France. Moreover, he ordered his force to launch ballistic missile attacks against Israel, reputed to be another nuclear weapons state. This probably would not have happened if Saddam Hussein had not possessed chemical or biological weapons he thought could deter possible nuclear responses.

Further, it is reasonable to assume Iraq's possession of chemical and biological weapons may have been one of several factors that persuaded President Bush and other coalition members not to follow up their rout of Iraqi forces in Kuwait with a march all the way to Baghdad. Clearly, the U.S. military and political leaders were fully aware of the potential harm that might have come to U.S. and coalition personnel from a massive chemical or biological attack by Iraq.

Indeed, it is possible massive medical problems were simply generated by allied bombing of chemical weapons storage and production facilities. Some 183,000 U.S. military personnel were victims of symptoms referred to as Gulf War syndrome, more than a quarter of the U.S. men and women sent to fight in the war were declared permanently disabled, and some speculate these casualties were resulted from coalition air attacks on Iraqi CW facilities that caused downwind fallout and contamination.[68]

In summary, it is not possible to prove without doubt that deterrence works since it is not feasible to prove war would have occurred in the absence of deterrence signals. On the other hand, it is clear when deterrence actions fail. War and conflict escalation are clear signals of a degree of deterrence failure. Even here, it is not possible to know how much further up the escalation ladder the conflict would have climbed if deterrent actions been taken and signals had not been sent.

In the 1990-1991 Gulf War, no one successfully deterred the Iraqi invasion of Kuwait or successfully compelled the Iraqi Army to leave peacefully. U.S. deterrent signals were too weak at the beginning and too late to stop him. U.S. tripwire forces sent to early to Saudi Arabia in the late summer and fall of 1990 possibly deterred Saddam Hussein from sending his army through Kuwait and into Saudi Arabia, although it is not clear whether he was willing to risk such a gamble had U.S. reinforcements not been sent to assist the Saudi Kingdom.

It seems likely Saddam Hussein was deterred from using chemical and biological weapons in the stern warning communicated to the Iraqi leadership by President Bush and the nuclear forces at his command. Saddam could not be sure the United States would not use nuclear weapons in response to a CB attack, especially if the United States and its allies suffered mass casualties from such attacks.

We now know there was no serious consideration of employing U.S. or allied nuclear weapons during the conflict. The Bush policy team felt that U.S. nuclear superiority should deter Iraqi chemical and biological weapons use and coalition conventional superiority was so pronounced as to make victory very likely.

Saddam Hussein was willing to let his forces and population bleed to whatever degree to inflict the level of losses that might make his opponents limit their war aims. Indeed, Saddam might have been correct. The potential threat of mass casualties may partly account for President Bush's decision to end the war 100 hours after the ground campaign had routed the Iraqi army in Kuwait. Saddam may have considered Bush's actions as an exercise in "snatching defeat from the jaws of victory" since he survived and retained power after the ceasefire took place.

The 5,000-death threshold Saddam Hussein predicted would cause the coalition leaders to sue for peace talks never was reached, and his theory of deterrence was therefore untested. However, it appears the coalition forces were prepared to suffer large losses to achieve their war aims, but since this threshold was never even approached, it is impossible to say when the allies would have considered discussing peace terms due to mounting casualties.

Clearly, the Iraqi dictator took risks far beyond what Soviet leaders were willing to risk in the Cold War when confronted with overwhelming U.S. military power and a dedicated deterrent posture. The risk-taking and violent personality of the Iraqi leader, coupled with the mild deterrent signals the U.S. sent at the beginning of the Iraq-Kuwait confrontation, led Saddam Hussein to gamble on seizing an oil-rich treasure that could bail him out of the financial problems caused by the huge costs of the Iran-Iraq war. He sought to recoup his losses in Kuwait.

Thus, every crisis and conflict has different elements and players, Deterrence lessons from one case study may or may not apply to another. Deterrence is clearly an art and can fail despite the best practices of the state attempting it, since it takes two sides stepping to the same tune to have it work. Unfortunately, deterrence is a two-sided affair. Ultimately, it will work only if the potential aggressor concludes that the outcome will likely result in a price they are unwilling to risk. Those attempting to deter them can do everything possible to signal why a war would be too costly, but the ultimate decision is up to the Saddam Husseins of the world.

Appendix A

Desert Shield/Desert Storm Timeline[69]

August 1990

2	Iraq invades Kuwait.
6	U.S. forces gain permission to base operations in Saudi Arabia.
7	F-15s depart for Persian Gulf.
7	USS Independence battle group arrives in south of Persian Gulf.
8	First TFW and 82nd Airborne arrive in Persian Gulf.

November 1990

8	The United States sends 200,000 additional troops.
29	United Nations authorizes force against Iraq.

January 1991

9	Baker delivers Bush warning letter to Saddam via Aziz.
12	Congress approves offensive use of U.S. troops.
15	United Nations withdrawal deadline passes.
17	D day. Coalition launches airborne assault.
18	Iraq launches Scud missiles at Israel and Saudi Arabia.
25	Air Force begins attacking Iraqi aircraft shelters.
26	Iraqi aircraft begin fleeing to Iran.
29	Battle of Khafji begins. Airpower destroys Iraqi force.

February 1991

24	Ground War begins. Start of 100 hour battle.
26	Fleeing Iraqi forces destroyed along "Highway of Death."
28	Cease-fire becomes effective at 0800 Kuwait time.

Appendix B

A Warning Letter to Saddam Hussein
From President George H.W. Bush

Mr. President,

We stand today at the brink of war between Iraq and the world. This is a war that began with your invasion of Kuwait; this is a war that can be ended only by the Iraq's full and unconditional compliance with U.N. Security Council Resolution 678.

I am writing you now, directly, because what is at stake demands that no opportunity be lost to avoid what would be a certain calamity for the people of Iraq. I am writing, as well, because it is said by some that you do not understand just how isolated Iraq is and what Iraq faces as a result. I am not in a position to judge whether this impression is correct: what I can do, though is try in this letter to reinforce what Secretary of State Baker told your Foreign Minister and eliminate any uncertainty or ambiguity that might exist in your mind about where we stand and what we are prepared to do.

The international community is untied in its call for Iraq to leave all of Kuwait without condition and without further delay. This is not simply the policy of the United States: it is the position of the world community as expressed in no less than twelve Security Council resolutions.

We prefer a peaceful outcome. However, anything less than full compliance with UN Security Council Resolution 678 and its predecessors are unacceptable. There can be no reward for aggression. Nor will there be any negotiation. Principle cannot be compromised. However, by its full compliance Iraq will gain the opportunity to rejoin the international community. More immediately, the Iraqi military establishment will escape destruction. But unless you withdraw from Kuwait completely and without condition, you will lose more than Kuwait. What is at issue here is not the future of Kuwait – it will be free, its government will be restored – but rather the future of Iraq. The choice is yours to make.

The United States will not be separated from its coalition partners. Twelve Security Council resolutions, 28 countries providing military units to enforce them, more than one hundred governments complying with sanctions – all highlight the fact that it is not Iraq against the United States but Iraq against the world. That most Arab and Muslim countries are arrayed against you as well should reinforce what I am saying. Iraq cannot and will not be able to hold on to Kuwait or exact a price for leaving.

You may be tempted to find solace in the diversity of opinion that is American democracy. You should resist any such temptation. Diversity ought not to be confused with division. Nor should you underestimate, as others have before you, America's will.

Iraq is already feeling the effects of the sanctions mandated by the United Nations. Should war come, it will be far greater tragedy for you and your country. Let me state, too that the United States will not tolerate the use of chemical or biological weapons or the destruction of Kuwait's oil fields and installations. Further, you will be held directly responsible for terrorist actions against any member of the coalition. The American people would demand the strongest possible response. You and your country will pay a terrible price if you order unconscionable acts of this sort.

I write this letter not to threaten, but to inform. I do so with no sense of satisfaction, for the people of the United States have no quarrel with the people of Iraq. Mr. President, UN Security Council Resolution 678 establishes the period before January 15 of this year as a "pause of good will" so that this crisis may end without further violence. Whether this pause is used as intended, or merely becomes a prelude to further violence, is in your hands, and yours alone, I hope you weigh your choice carefully and choose wisely, for much will depend upon it.

George Bush[70]

Appendix C

Iraq Launches Missile Strikes[71]

If Iraq was forced to obey UN resolutions, the Iraqi government made it no secret it would respond by attacking Israel. Before the war started, Tariq Aziz, Iraqi Foreign Minister and Deputy Prime Minister, was asked, "If war starts...will you attack Israel?" His response was, "Yes, absolutely, yes."[72] The Iraqis hoped attacking Israel would draw it into the war. It was expected this would then lead to the withdrawal of the U.S. Arab allies, who would be reluctant to fight alongside Israel. Israel did not join the coalition, and all Arab states stayed in the coalition.

The Scud missiles generally caused fairly light damage, although their potency was felt on Feb. 25 when 28 U.S. soldiers were killed when a Scud destroyed their barracks in Dhahran. The Scuds targeting Israel were ineffective due to the fact that increasing the range of the Scud resulted in a dramatic reduction in accuracy and payload. Nevertheless, the total of 39 missiles that landed on Israel caused extensive property damage and two direct deaths, and caused the United States to deploy two Patriot missile battalions in Israel, and the Netherlands to send one Patriot Squadron, in an attempt to deflect the attacks. Allied air forces were also extensively exercised in "Scud hunts" in the Iraqi desert, trying to locate the camouflaged trucks before they fired their missiles at Israel or Saudi Arabia.

Three Scud missiles, along with a coalition Patriot that malfunctioned, hit Ramat Gan in Israel on Jan. 22, 1991, injuring 96 people, and indirectly causing the deaths of three elderly people who died of heart attacks. Israeli policy for the previous 40 years had always been retaliation, but at the urging of the U.S. and other commanders, the Israeli government decided discretion was the better part of valor in this instance. After initial hits by Scud missiles, Israeli Prime Minister Yitzhak Shamir hesitantly refused any retaliating measures against Iraq, due to increasing pressure from the United States to remain out of the conflict. The U.S. government was concerned any Israeli action would cost it allies and escalate the conflict, and an air strike by the IAF would have required overflying hostile Jordan or Syria, which could have provoked them to enter the war on Iraq's side or to attack Israel.

Notes

[1] Quoted in Admiral Michael G, Mullen, Chairman of the Joint Chiefs of Staff, "It's Time for a New Deterrence Model," *Joint Force Quarterly*, 4th Quarter (2008), 2.

[2] See Barry Wolf, *When the Weak Attack the Strong: Failures of Deterrence,* (Santa Monica, Calif.: Rand Report N 3262-A, 1991).

[3] Original source was Ernest R. Dupuy and Trevor N. Dupuy, *The Encyclopedia of Military History,* (New York: Harper and Row, 1970), 910-911. See also, Barry R. Schneider, *Future War and Counterproliferation* (Westport, CT: Praeger, 1999), Ch. 4.

[4] See Wikipedia, Constitution and Founding Fathers, "What Ever Happened to the Founding Fathers?" This was their promise: "For the support of this declaration, with a firm reliance on the protection of the Divine Providence, we mutually pledge to each other, our lives, our fortunes and our sacred honor."

[5] For another good discussion, see Richard Ned Lebow, "Conclusions," in Robert Jervis, Richard Ned Lebow, and Janice Gross Stein, *Psychology & Deterrence* (Baltimore, Md.: Johns Hopkins University Press, 1985), Ch. 9.

[6] Mutual Assured Destruction went by the acronym MAD. Dr. Warner Schilling later added another acronym for those who wanted to develop offensive nuclear options to disarm the other side with a counterforce strike in this heavily armed nuclear environment. He called this option Capable of Firing First If Necessary (COFFIN).

[7] Of course this still begs the question of how much U.S. and allied nuclear capability was enough to inflict that unacceptable level of damage, and what did the adversary think was an unacceptable level of damage? Further, how could we know for sure? What metrics could we use to determine this? This information or estimation of what was needed, of course, would be used to guide our deterrence strategy, our targeting policy (SIOP), our nuclear force composition, and our DOD and DOE acquisition and budget strategies.

[8] For example, during the year leading up to the Cuban Missile Crisis, it appears Nikita Khrushchev, general secretary of the Communist Party and leader of the Soviet Union, had come to the conclusion that President John F. Kennedy was a weak leader who would not act to thwart a Soviet fait accompli that put Soviet missiles into Cuba. Khrushchev had seen Kennedy's administration fail in the Bay of Pigs Crisis, fail to respond to a communist invasion of Laos and fail to respond to Soviet pressure on Berlin. Khrushchev had also engaged in bullying Kennedy at a Paris summit conference where the young President seemed not to acquit himself very forcefully. The relative youth and inexperience of Kennedy compared to Khrushchev may have also played a part in the Kremlin's risky decision to place missiles into Cuba.

[9] Herman Kahn, *On Thermonuclear War* (Princeton, N.J.: Princeton University Press, 1960).

[10] Here is an example of the logical problem. If almost all war began in the spring of the year, and the U.S. baseball season starts in the spring, does this then mean that the inception of the baseball season triggers war? No, obviously not. Just because A precedes B, does not mean it causes B. Both might be caused by another factor C. Clearly correlation (e.g., A then B) is not causation. It is very likely that another factor leads to fewer wars starting in the winter – the weather (Factor C). Clearly, military campaigns are far easier to launch in moderate weather rather than in the dead of winter when roads are clogged with ice and

snow and army movements are much more difficult. Spring is the opening of campaigning season (and baseball) in parts of the world with severe winters.

[11] Charles A. Duelfer, Special Adviser to the DCI on Iraq's WMD, See "Regime Strategic Intent," *Comprehensive Revised Report with Addendums on Iraq's Weapons of Mass Destruction* (Washington, D.C.: CIA, 2004), 1.

[12] See "Interrogator Shares Saddam's Confessions," 60 Minutes, CBS Television, (Jan. 27, 2008). Diane Sawyer of ABC News interviewed Saddam on June 24, 1990, and discovered he did not know there were no U.S. laws against joking about or criticizing the U.S. President. Nor did he fathom the working of checks and balances in the U.S. political system, where power is shared between the executive, legislative and judicial systems. Saddam asked, "Who, then, am I supposed to deal with?" See Karsh and Rautsi, *Saddam Hussein, A Political Biography* (New York: The Free Press, 1991), 178-79.

[13] Efraim Karsh and Inari Rautsi, *Saddam Hussein: A Political Biography* (New York: The Free Press, 1991), 2.

[14] See Paul K. Davis and John Arquilla, *Deterring or Coercing Opponents in Crisis: Lessons from the War with Saddam Hussein* (Santa Monica, Calif.; RAND, 1991), 7. In 1990, Saddam tried to re-arm Iraq before Iran could resume the war they had just fought to a draw. He was spending $5B per year on modernizing his military. As a result, Saddam Hussein had run out of credit and faced a mounting financial crisis. He feared this financial crisis would then result in a security crisis. To add injury, Kuwait and UAE produced and sold more oil than the limits they had agreed upon at the previous OPEC meetings. This reduced the profit margins for Iraqi oil and infuriated Saddam, who saw these declining oil prices as frustrating his expansionist dreams and as putting his regime in jeopardy. Much like the Japanese who before Pearl Harbor reacted to the U.S.-imposed oil embargo that threatened their aspirations for a Japanese co-prosperity sphere in Asia, Saddam had felt the financial noose closing on his dreams when he hit upon the idea of invading oil-rich Kuwait to solve his troubles. Thus, he was adamant about keeping the Kuwaiti prize he had just seized, the prize that was going to solve his financial and security dilemma.

[15] Ibid.

[16] Karsh and Rautsi, Op.cit. 78.

[17] Some analysts of previous deterrence failures conclude, "Policy makers who risk or actually start wars pay more attention to their own strategic and domestic political interests than they do to the interests and military capabilities needed to defend its commitment. Their strategic and political needs appear to constitute the principal motivation for a resort to force." This observation was based on 20 cases of failed deterrence. See Richard Ned Lebow, "Conclusions" in Jervis, Lebow, and Stein, *Psychology and Deterrence* (Baltimore, Md.: The Johns Hopkins University Press, 1985), 216.

[18] John J. Mearsheimer and Stephen M. Walt, "Can Saddam Be Contained? History Says Yes," *New York Times* (Feb. 2, 2003).

[19] James A. Baker III, *The Politics of Diplomacy: Revolution, War and Peace, 1989-1992* (New York: G.P. Putnam's Sons, 1995), 358-59.

[20] James A. Baker,III, *The Politics of Diplomacy: Revolution, War and Peace, 1989-1992* (New York: G.P. Putnam's Sons, 1995), 276.

[21] Ibid., 273.

[22] Ibid.

[23] Ibid., 273-74.

[24] Ibid.

[25] Herman Kahn wrote about two kinds of escalation of a conflict, vertical and horizontal. Vertical escalation involved walking up the rungs of the escalation ladder to higher and higher levels of conflict. In a war between nuclear armed states, this might begin with low-level conventional conflict and escalate into higher-level nuclear exchanges. Horizontal escalation is where the theater of a conflict is widened, by involving adjacent territories or other countries in the conflict, perhaps even extending the conflict to a different theater or region of warfare altogether. See Herman Kahn, *On Escalation: Metaphors and Scenarios* (New York: Frederick A. Praeger, 1965).

[26] From a speech given by Hussein at the fourth summit of the Arab Cooperation Council, Amman, Jordan (Feb. 24, 1990). See FBIS NESAS (Feb. 27, 1990), 1-5. Found by this author in Paul K. Davis and John Arquilla, *Deterring or Coercing Opponents in Crisis: Lessons from the War with Saddam Hussein* (Santa Monica, Calif.: RAND R-4111-JS, 1991), 56.

[27] Avigdor Haselkorn, *The Continuing Storm, Iraq's Poisonous Weapons and Deterrence* (New Haven, Conn.; Yale University Press 1999), 52. This estimate by the Iraqi dictator was made in an interview carried on German television and was released by INA, FBIS (NES) (Dec. 14, 1990), 22.

[28] Ibid.

[29] Baker, Op.Cit. 303-304.

[30] Ibid., 349. Ambassador April Glaspie "recounted a very telling story about being invited along with other diplomats to a dam construction site in Northern Iraq. Saddam had made disparaging remarks about the Vietnamese laborers who were building the dam, dismissing them as sub humans. 'And these are the people who beat the Americans,' he marveled...Iraq's leader thought that Vietnam had so traumatized the American psyche that we would never fight again." See Baker, Op.Cit., 355.

[31] Ibid. Haselkorn's research lists as his source, an article in the *Wall Street Journal* (Feb. 17, 1991), written by Rear Admiral Mike McConnell, then Director of Intelligence for the U.S. Joint Chiefs of Staff, McConnell indicated that U.S. forces found such a written order in Kuwait.

[32] H. Norman Schwarzkopf with Peter Petre, *Autobiography: It Doesn't take a Hero* (New York: Bantam Books, 1992), 439.

[33] Ibid. He wrote, "I was worried about the great empty area of southern Iraq where the (coalition) army would launch its attack. I kept asking myself, 'What does Saddam know about that flank that I don't? Why doesn't he have any forces out there?' The intelligence people suggested offhandedly, 'Maybe he plans to pop a nuke out there.' They then nicknamed the sector the 'chemical killing sack.' I flinched every time I heard it."

[34] "Gulf War," http://www.answers/cp./topic/gulf-war, 39.

[35] Ibid.

[36] Ibid., The quote is from Barry Rubin, *Cauldron of Turmoil; America in the Middle East* (New York: Harcourt Brace Javanovich, 1992), 144.

[37] Colin Powell with Joseph Persico, *My American Journey* (New York: Ballantine Books, 1995), 490-491. He said, "The biological worried me, and the impact on the public the first time the first casualty keeled over to germ warfare would be terrifying."

[38] U.S. deaths among military personnel in Operation Iraqi Freedom as of April 2009 were just over 4,200 killed over a period of six years of fighting.

[39] Baker, Op.Cit., 437.

[40] For the full text of this letter, see Appendix B of this paper.

[41] Ibid., 358-359.

[42] Richard Cheney, Secretary of Defense, *Conduct of the Persian Gulf War Final Report to Congress* (Washington, D.C.: U.S. Government Printing Office, 1992), 25.

[43] On the other hand, if a rogue state leader always expects the strong to use all its weapons against him, why not use his NBC weapons first when they could inflict maximum damage?

[44] As James Baker concluded in his book, *The Politics of Diplomacy*, "We do not really know this was the reason there appears to have been no confirmed use by Iraq of chemical weapons during the war. My own view is that the calculated ambiguity regarding how we might respond has to be part of the reason," 359.

[45] George Bush and Brent Scowcroft, *A World Transformed* (New York: Alfred A. Knopf, 1998), 463.

[46] Baker, Op Cit., 359.

[47] On the other hand, it could be argued that Saddam may have believed earlier U.S. pledges not to use nuclear weapons, even in wartime, against those non-nuclear parties in good standing with the nuclear nonproliferation treaty (NPT) regime. Iraq was considered in compliance with the NPT by the IAEA at the time of the invasion of Kuwait. Only later, after the ceasefire in February 1991, did UN inspectors prove Iraq had cheated massively on the treaty regime. In 1978, Secretary of State Cyrus Vance made a unilateral and nonbinding U.S. pledge prior to a NPT Review Conference in order to persuade more nonnuclear states to back the treaty extension. This was a policy statement of the Carter administration, but not a treaty or legally binding commitment. However, by 1990, the United States had adopted a legal interpretation and doctrine called "belligerent reprisal" that got the U.S. out of that legal box. It announced the U.S. government interpreted its NPT pledge not to use nuclear arms against non-nuclear parties to the treaty as null and void if these states were to initiate the use of either chemical or biological weapons. It is more likely Saddam did not believe the earlier U.S. pledge not to use nuclear weapons if war began simply because he would not keep such a pledge himself if he were in the place of the U.S. President.

[48] Duelfer, Op.Cit., 1.

[49] Again, review President Bush's letter of warning to Saddam Hussein, Appendix B.

[50] Haselkorn, Op.Cit., 57. The original citation is CNN, cited in AFMIC Weekly Wire 02-91 (u)," File 970613_mno2_91_0_txt_0001.txt (Washington, D.C.: DIA {?}, 1991). This plan of strategic reciprocity was confirmed in 1995 by Tariq Aziz who said that the Iraqi military had been authorized to use their biological weapons in the event that Baghdad was attacked with nuclear weapons. See Haselkorn, 53.

[51] Ibid., 93.

[52] Ibid., 31.

[53] How seriously the U.S. leadership took the Iraqi CBW threat is testified by the fact that during the run-up to the war, until its conclusion, President George H.W. Bush was accompanied by a military officer who carried a gas mask for emergency use.

[54] However, the Syrian Chief of Staff later stated in a Q&A session, when an Air War College group later visited Damascus, Syria would have stayed in the coalition despite Israeli participation in order to remove Saddam Hussein's forces from Kuwait.

[55] McGeorge Bundy, national security adviser to Presidents John Kennedy and Lyndon Johnson, has written, "There has been literally no chance at all that any sane political authority, in either the United States or the Soviet Union, would consciously choose to start a nuclear war. This proposition is true for the past, the present and the foreseeable future... In the real world of real political leaders...a decision that would bring even one hydrogen bomb on one city of one's own country would be recognized in advance as a catastrophic blunder; ten bombs on ten cities would be a disaster beyond history; and a hundred bombs on a hundred cities are unthinkable." Bundy's analysis would suggest the United States and any other state should be content with a minimum deterrence posture. On the other hand, some U.S. strategists like former Secretary of Defense James Schlesinger, once enunciated a doctrine of essential equivalence saying the United States would be safest if it matched the numbers of strategic weapons on the Soviet side no matter their number or overkill capability. This was at a time when both sides had tens of thousands of nuclear weapons. Still others have attempted to strike a balance between the retaliatory power needed and the level of damage that could be inflicted on the adversary. Two RAND analysts calculated the optimal U.S. retaliatory capability for destruction against Soviet population and industry at a given time. They sought to find a posture that gave "the most bang for the defense buck," yet suggested ways to put rational limits of the size of the nuclear forces required." For example, see Alain Enthoven and K. Wayne Smith, *How Much Is Enough? Shaping the Defense Program, 1961-1969,* (New York: Harper and Row, 1971). A reading of their analysis would lead one to conclude the optimal size of the U.S. nuclear retaliatory force was 400 equivalent megatons of explosive power. This, would, for example, give in 1971, the U.S. capability to kill 39 percent of the Soviet population and 77 percent of Soviet industry. Their calculations also indicated this would put U.S. destructive power on the "flat of the curve." Even a doubling of the U.S. equivalent mega tonnage to 800 EMT would "only" kill 5 percent more of its population and only 1 percent more of its industry. Thus, some might conclude the "optimal" solution would be to deploy enough nuclear weapons in such a fashion, in all likely scenarios, 400 EMT worth of U.S. nuclear weapons would make it through Soviet attacks and defenses to hit their targets in the USSR were the Kremlin leaders ever to launch a nuclear attack. See Enthoven and Smith, 207.

[56] Note Saddam Hussein plotted an assassination attempt against George H.W. Bush on April 13, 1993, when the retired U.S. President visited Kuwait. This revenge strike failed, but revealed much about Iraqi dictator's predilections. He was willing to risk the wrath of the United States just to kill the U.S. leader that had so soundly defeated and humiliated him in the Gulf War of 1990-1991. If he was willing to risk a renewed war and his grip on power to exact revenge it is not hard to imagine how much more willing he would have

been to use all means at hard to deal a last chemical or biological death blow if he thought his regime was about to be destroyed.

[57] Schwarzkopf, Op.cit., 439.

[58] See Charles A. Duelfer, Special Adviser to the DCI on Iraq's WMD, *Comprehensive Revised Report with Addendums on Iraq's Weapons of Mass Destruction* (Washington, D.C.: CIA, 2004).

[59] Decisions may be influenced by key decision-makers, but these, in turn, may be influenced by allies, legal restrictions, political commitment and consideration and, bureaucratic politics, and standard operating procedures, psychological factors and group dynamics. Decision-makers seldom begin decisions on issues with a blank slate. See Allison Graham with Phillip Zelikow, *Essence of Decision: Explaining the Cuban Missile Crisis,* (New York, Pearson Longman Publishers, 1999), 2nd Edition.

[60] Indeed, Saddam's earliest contribution to the Ba'ath Party was to attempt an assassination of Iraqi President General Qassem in 1958, a bungled attempt that brought him fame in the Ba'ath Party and exile in Syria and Egypt for three years. His later climb to the presidency of Iraq is akin to Lee Harvey Oswald becoming president of the United States 19 years after assassinating John F. Kennedy.

[61] Some estimate the total dead from the 1980-1988 Iran-Iraq War to have been in the neighborhood of 500,000 Iranians and Iraqis slain.

[62] Efraim Karsh and Inari Rautsi, *Saddam Hussein: A Political Biography* (New York: The Free Press, 1991), 2.

[63] Author's interview with an unnamed Iraqi general under contract with the CIA after leaving Iraq.

[64] Tom Clancy with General Chuck Horner (Ret.), *Every Man a Tiger* (New York: Putnam's Sons, 1999), 374-375.

[65] See "Gulf War," http://www.answers.com/topic/gulf-war, p. 6. Unfortunately, 183,000 U.S. veterans of the Gulf War, more than a quarter of all who participated in the war, have been declared permanently disabled by the U.S. Department of Veteran's Affairs as a result of "Gulf War Syndrome." "About 30 percent of the 700,000 men and women who served in U.S. forces during the Gulf War still suffered an array of serious symptoms whose causes are not fully understood," 40.

[66] Jervis, Lebow and Stein, Psychology & Deterrence (Baltimore, Md.: The Johns Hopkins University Press, 1985), 216.

[67] Ibid.

[68] "Gulf War," http://www.answers.com/topic/gulf-war.

[69] This chart is an adaptation of one found in Tom Clancy with General Chuck Horner, *Every Man A Tiger* (New York: G.P.Putnam's Sons, 1999), xii.

[70] See George Bush, *Public Papers of George Bush: Book 1* (Jan. 1 to June 30, 1991), "Statement by Press Secretary Fitzwater on President Bush's letter to President Saddam Hussein of Iraq" (Jan. 12, 1991). See also, Michael R. Gordon and General Bernard E. Trainor, *The General's War,* (Boston: Little Brown and Company, 1995), Chapter 9, "The Mailed Fist," footnote 17.

[71] "Operation Desert Shield and Operation Desert Storm," Wikipedia, www.wikipedia.com.

[72] Lawrence Freedman and Efraim Karsh, *The Gulf Conflict: Diplomacy and War in the New World Order*, 1990-1991 (Princeton, 1993), 332.

CHAPTER 8

Influencing Terrorist Acquisition and Use of Weapons of Mass Destruction: Exploring a Possible Strategy[*]

Dr. Lewis A. Dunn

The potential acquisition and use of weapons of mass destruction (WMD) by a terrorist group is one of the major security threats confronting the United States and its NATO allies in the early 21st century. At least for now, the most dangerous WMD threat is from the entities that comprise the al Qaeda-Jihadist movement, from the core leadership of Osama bin Laden and Ayman al-Zawahiri to Jihadist groups or cells affiliated with or inspired by that core leadership and its vision of global jihad.

This movement alone combines a proven past interest in acquiring WMD, arguments allegedly justifying the moral-religious legitimacy and justifiability of the use of such weapons, and writings that put forward a number of perceived strategic motivations for escalating to WMD violence. In turn, assistance by outside aiders and abettors not directly affiliated with the al-Qaeda-Jihadist movement could well be critical to its successful acquisition and use of WMD.

Efforts to prevent al-Qaeda and its Jihadist affiliates – or for that matter, any other terrorist group – from acquiring WMD are the first line of defense against this threat. Since the start of the precedent-setting Cooperative Threat Reduction program in the 1990s, many actions have been taken by the United States and other countries to enhance security and controls on nuclear weapons, nuclear weapons-related materials and other WMD-related materials, know-how, components and inputs.

A robust set of actions continue to be taken to buttress prevention, typified by cooperation among more than 60 countries under the U.S.-

[*] Originally published in the NATO Defense College book titled *NATO and 21st Century Deterrence*, edited by Karl-Heinz Kamp and David S. Yost, Rome, Italy, May 2009, pp. 126-142.

Russian Global Initiative to Combat Nuclear Terrorism. By contrast, despite periodic talk of the need to think seriously about "deterring terrorist use of WMD," the lack of a strategy to influence terrorists' thinking about whether to seek to acquire or use WMD remains a major gap in U.S. and global actions to counter the terrorist WMD threat.

Against this backdrop, this paper first sets out a framework for thinking about influencing terrorists' WMD acquisition and use calculus. It then applies that framework in two different cases: the al-Qaeda core leadership and possible state, criminal and individual aiders and abettors of WMD terrorism. The discussion concludes by briefly discussing the way ahead.

Before proceeding, however, three prefatory points are in order. First, an influencing strategy should be viewed as only one element of an overall U.S. and global strategy to counter the threat of terrorist escalation to the use of WMD – but a potentially important and as yet still under-developed element. Second, the strategy set out here assumes an element of rational calculation, a weighing of costs and benefits, in any terrorist decision to attempt to acquire or eventually use WMD. That element of rationality may be more or less, depending on the group and its individual members. It also will be influenced by the particular lenses through which a group or its leaders view the world.

Nonetheless, past terrorist behavior, including that of the most dangerous threat, al-Qaeda, warrants making this assumption. Third, use of the term influencing encompasses the concept of deterrence – whether by the threat of punishment or by denying terrorists the benefits sought. But the concept of influencing is intended to point toward a broader set of actions that might be pursued than simply punishment or denial. Use of the term "influencing" instead of "deterrence" also is intended to highlight a more uncertain nexus between U.S. and others' actions and terrorists' WMD calculus.

Framework for Influencing Terrorist WMD Acquisition and Use Calculus

The most important concepts of the framework set out here can be summarized by a series of propositions. These propositions are:

Disaggregate the terrorist "whom" to be influenced;

- Disaggregate the aider and abettor "whom" to be influenced;
- Identify the specific leverage points that could be used in an attempt to influence each of the different groups and their component entities as well as specific aiders and abettors;
- Think broadly in terms of "who" does the influencing – not simply governments; and
- Be prepared to use both soft and hard power, words and deeds.

Consider each of these concepts in turn.

Disaggregate the Terrorists.

There are many different *terrorist groups and entities*. With regard only to the most dangerous threat of the al Qaeda-Jihadist movement, that movement comprises: the al-Qaeda core leadership of Bin Laden and al-Zawahiri; directly affiliated organizations such as al-Qaeda in Mesopotamia and al-Qaeda in the Maghreb; inspired or more loosely-linked groups such as Jemaah Islamiyah in southeast Asia; inspired cells such as those that have carried out terrorist attacks in the United Kingdom; and individuals often linked together and with other al-Qaeda entities via the Internet. Potential future recruits to any of these entities also are an important category of people to influence.

More generally, it is useful to distinguish al-Qaeda and its Jihadist affiliates from the many non-al-Qaeda terrorist groups. Prominent among the latter are such Islamist groups as Hamas and Hezbollah and non-Islamist groups such as the Liberation Tigers of Tamil Eelam (LTTE) and the Revolutionary Armed Forces of Colombia (FARC).

At least for now, these non-al-Qaeda terrorist groups do not appear interested in escalating to WMD violence, most likely reflecting a judgment that WMD use would alienate their supporters, antagonize their opponents and make it more difficult to achieve their goals.

By contrast, the entities that make up the al-Qaeda-Jihadist movement have sought to acquire WMD. Prominent Jihadists also have argued WMD use and mass killing would be consistent with the Koran and the teachings of the Prophet – howsoever falsely.

Disaggregate the Aiders and Abettors

Three major categories of potential aiders and abettors of terrorist acquisition or use of WMD stand out: states, criminal and other organizations, and individuals.

State involvement could be witting, involving senior-most leadership or lower-level officials or technical experts. Or state involvement could be unwitting, occurring despite best-faith efforts by a state to prevent terrorist access to WMD-related materials or know-how. There also are in-between cases. As for criminal organizations, ties already exist between some of those organizations and terrorist groups. Illicit trafficking in the former Soviet Union is a good example. In pursuit of financial or other organizational gain, there is little reason to distinguish between smuggling drugs, cigarettes, other contraband, or the small quantities of nuclear materials so far detected and seized.

Personal gain also would be the most likely motivation for individuals to provide assistance to a terrorist group seeking to acquire or use WMD. The model would be the former head of Pakistan's nuclear weapons program, A.Q. Khan, who sold nuclear know-how to Iran, North Korea and Syria. But fear and blackmail also cannot be excluded as motivating forces. In turn, some individuals could well provide assistance unknowingly, whether due to the disregard of established procedures to control sensitive information, through unguarded conversations, or in other ways.

Many different types of support could be provided by aiders and abettors. Some examples include: financial backing; insider access to facilitate diversion or to defeat detection and interdiction actions; direct supply of needed inputs; provision of technical information; and logistics and transportation. The provision of so-called technical know-how and art may be the most important type of assistance – that is, the often-unwritten knowledge needed to make a particular WMD-related production process work effectively or to carry out a given operational step in a WMD attack.

The critical importance of technical art is best exemplified by the unsuccessful 1993 attempt by the Japanese cult group, Aum Shinrikyo, to kill hundreds of thousands of people by releasing anthrax in downtown Tokyo. The group mistakenly released a non-lethal vaccine strain of anthrax, thereby having no impact. More generally, lack of access to technical art has been a repeated source of terrorist WMD attack failure.

Identify Potential Leverage Points.

At least in principle, there is a spectrum of potential leverage points that might be used to influence the calculations of different terrorist groups as well as their aiders and abettors. Is the use of WMD – and quite possibly the killing of innocent civilians – justifiable and legitimate in the terms of the religious or moral teachings adhered to by the group and equally so by its wider public audience of potential supporters? What is the prospect of technical success whether in acquiring WMD or in carrying out a successful attack – the feasibility? Are there better ways to use the group's technical, organizational, financial, operational and other resources than seeking to acquire and then use WMD? More broadly, how smart would be the use of WMD as a means to achieve the goals that animate the group and its members? Finally, how much risk would be involved in attempting to acquire and use these weapons – or in aiding and abetting such acquisition and use? Depending on the particular group or on the specific aiders and abettors, the answers to these questions will vary.

Think Broadly Regarding "Who" Does the Influencing.

Many different players will need to be involved in implementing an influencing strategy. At one level, the United States should seek the support of like-minded governments among traditional U.S. friends and allies. In addition, support could be sought from moderate governments throughout the Muslim world. Despite differences with the United States on certain issues, these Muslim governments share an interest in preventing the ascendance of the al-Qaeda-Jihadist movement.

Moreover, neither traditional U.S. friends and allies nor other governments should assume that the victim of a terrorist WMD attack would necessarily be the United States. They, too, could be struck – whether due to an accident, loss of control, or deliberate intention.

Somewhat differently, international, non-governmental and community organizations also can contribute, from a traditional entity such as the United Nations to professional, scientific, industry and academic organizations. Other players would be Islamic as well as non-Islamic religious councils and associations, non-violent wings of domestic political-separatist movements across different countries, and prominent groupings of individuals with religious, social action, or other affiliations. Certain types of individuals alone, e.g., a highly-respected clerical authority, also could be sources of influence. Moderate Muslims in NATO nations and elsewhere also may be able to exert some impact on the thinking of the wider Muslim community around the globe that is the ultimate audience as well as the source of recruits for the Jihadist movement inspired by al Qaeda.

Use Soft and Hard Power, Words and Deeds

Influencing terrorists' WMD acquisition and use calculus – and of aiders and abettors – will partly entail use of soft power. In particular, efforts are essential to foster a wider public debate to influence perceptions of the legitimacy and justifiability of WMD use. In that regard, the lack of widespread outrage across the Islamic world at al Qaeda's use of chlorine-explosive bombs in Iraq during 2006-2007 may have been a lost opportunity. Perhaps more controversially, the declaratory policies of the nuclear weapons states can shape more diffuse perceptions of the legitimacy of nuclear use.

By way of example, consider a joint affirmation by the P-5 nuclear powers – the United States, Russia, France, the United Kingdom and China – that given any use of a nuclear weapon would be a calamity, they will act individually and together to ensure that nuclear weapons are never used again.

Closely related, decisive engagement by the P-5 in pursuing the goal of nuclear abolition also could de-legitimize nuclear use, though it would require them to make the case for their continued possession of nuclear weapons as a regrettable but necessary interim status pending the conditions for ultimate abolition. Declaratory policy is a means as well to influence perceptions of the risks of becoming involved in WMD terrorism.

For its part, the threatened use of hard power may be particularly important to influence perceptions of risk – whether on the part of certain terrorist entities or their aiders and abettors. Hard power encompasses but goes beyond military operations. It also includes economic and financial sanctions, covert operations and law enforcement actions.

Influencing in Action: Applying the Framework

Turning to specific cases, this section illustrates how the "influencing framework" could be implemented. The discussion focuses first on influencing the al-Qaeda core leadership and then on possible state, criminal, and individual aiders and abettors.

The al-Qaeda Core Leadership

Efforts to influence the WMD calculus of the al-Qaeda core leadership – Osama bin Laden, Ayman al-Zawahiri, and their close associates in al-Qaeda center presumed to be located on the Pakistan-Afghanistan border – are the toughest case. As already noted, their writings and statements as well as those of individuals closely linked to them make clear in their view, even indiscriminate killing using nuclear or biological weapons is seen as fully *legitimate and justifiable*. Howsoever falsely, their writings contend WMD use is fully consistent with the Koran and the teachings of the Prophet.

Thus, once in possession of WMD, the core leadership would have no moral or religious compunctions concerning use. For them, there is no controversy about the legitimacy or morality of using WMD against all enemies even if it results in loss of life among Muslims.[1] This leverage point simply does not apply.

Actions to influence the leaders' *perceptions of the risk* of escalating to WMD violence would have somewhat greater but still limited applicability. For the past decade, the United States has sought unsuccessfully either to capture or kill both bin Laden and al-Zawahiri. Particularly during the period when they were "on the run," they would likely have discounted any additional threats of capture or death. Now that the al-Qaeda core leadership appears to be recreating a base of operations on the Pakistan-Afghanistan border – and now that the Taliban is gaining strength in Afghanistan – the two leaders could be more concerned about the risks of WMD use.

For such use could well provide a powerful argument for the United States to use with its NATO allies that these countries should step up greatly their on-the-ground military commitment to defeating the Taliban. After WMD use, Pakistan also could well come under irresistible U.S. and international pressure to take effective measures against al Qaeda-Taliban safe-havens – or to turn a blind eye to stepped-up U.S. special operations in those regions.

By contrast, a much more promising leverage point would be the core leadership's perception of whether acquisition and escalation to WMD use would be *smart*. In part, smartness is tied to the leadership's assessment of whether WMD acquisition and use would be a feasible and effective use of the organization's resources as well as whether WMD use would shatter American resolve and lead to the elimination of U.S. influence from the Muslim world. Smartness also entails the leadership's calculation of whether escalation to WMD violence would alienate al-Qaeda's wider Islamic audience and make it all the more difficult to achieve its goals of an Islamic renewal and a new Islamic Caliphate. In different ways, each of these dimensions of "smartness" is subject to potential influence.

Influencing Actions

With regard to perceptions of *feasibility and use of resources*, many denial actions already are taken to make it much harder for any terrorist group to acquire or use WMD successfully. The Cooperative Threat Reduction program and its wider counterpart the G-8 Global Initiative, the newer Global Initiative to Combat Nuclear Terrorism, and implementation of United Nations Resolution 1540 (which obligates all states to put in place controls against WMD access by non-state actors) are but a few highly-visible examples.

There are, of course, gaps in these prevention efforts which still need to be addressed. Even so, U.S. and global pursuit of these types of prevention, interdiction and consequence management actions all would create uncertainties in the al-Qaeda leadership about the feasibility and impact of WMD acquisition and use. As such, they all send the message to the core leadership that it would be smarter to invest its scarce resources in the more proven "bombs and bullets" modes of attacks that have long been at the core of its operational code.

Still other actions would be intended to influence the core leadership's perception of whether escalation to WMD use would shatter *U.S. political will and resolve.* Continued actions to build habits of global cooperation against WMD terrorism would be one way to signal the core leadership that WMD use would not defeat the United States and its allies. Indeed, visible global cooperation would suggest that escalation to WMD violence could well rally other countries to the American side, much as occurred after the Sept. 11 attacks on the World Trade Center and the Pentagon.

Enhanced consequence management capabilities also would be important. Plans, procedures and capabilities to manage successfully the physical, psychological, social and economic consequences of a WMD attack – and more generally to foster public resiliency – are desirable in their own right. But they, too, could contribute to influencing the core leadership's WMD calculus.

Again, for influencing purposes, these actions need to be made highly visible. Not least, the outcome of the Iraq War is likely to be a key factor in shaping perceptions of U.S. resolve for better or for worse. If al-Qaeda in Mesopotamia is defeated and a measure of stability restored, it will be a major al-Qaeda defeat and a demonstration of American resolve.

Finally, actions also should be taken to heighten concerns that WMD use would *provoke a backlash among the wider Muslim audience* that the al-Qaeda core leadership seeks to rally to its cause. One way to do so would be to encourage more moderate Muslims at all levels to condemn WMD use. Across the global Muslim community, as reflected in recent public opinion data, there is widespread rejection of Jihadist attacks on innocent civilians, including American civilians.[2]

Though it would be difficult and probably counter-productive for U.S. officials to do so directly, the United States should work with friendly Muslim governments to encourage Islamic religious associations and prominent clerics to speak out against al Qaeda's escalation to WMD violence. In turn, a wider theological debate on the issues of the justifiability and legitimacy of WMD use should be encouraged, again with the aim of creating uncertainty in the minds of the core leadership about their audience's response to mass killing using WMD.

This last set of actions to influence the core leadership's perceptions of smartness is perhaps the most controversial. Some U.S. experts argue bin Laden and al-Zawahiri ultimately arrogate to themselves the right to act on behalf of the right-thinking Muslim community. Thus, they would not be influenced by any such concerns about Islamic public attitudes. Instead, they would assume if WMD use had the desired decisive impact, their Muslim audience would rally behind al Qaeda's decision.[3]

Nonetheless, there are good reasons to believe the core leadership is concerned about how its wider Muslim audience would respond to mass killing and use of WMD. Its investment of considerable energies in arguing for the legitimacy of WMD use is but one indication that there has been push-back on this question. Indeed, the most authoritative Jihadist religious discourse on this subject, the May 2003 *fatwa* by a Saudi cleric linked to bin Laden, Nasir bin Hamd al-Fahd, acknowledges such questions about killing innocent civilians. Al-Fahd refers explicitly to "specious arguments" against the use of WMD before seeking to counter each of those arguments.[4]

In addition, in his Oct. 11, 2005 letter to Musab al-Zarqawi, Ayman al-Zawahiri expressed concern about the excessive violence of al-Qaeda in Iraq and went on to emphasize: "If we are in agreement that the victory of Islam and the establishment of a caliphate in the manner of the Prophet will not be achieved except through jihad against the apostate rulers and their removal, then this goal will not be accomplished by the mujahed movement while it is cut off from public support. . . ."

Al-Zawahiri continued"[t]herefore, the mujahed movement must avoid any action that the masses do not understand or approve, if there is no contravention of Sharia in such avoidance, as long as there are other options to resort to."[5] Somewhat similarly, Osama bin Laden in his Oct. 23, 2007 audiotape against the "fanaticism" of the "mujahidin in Iraq," stressed "[t]he strength of the faith is the strength of the bond between Muslims and not that of a tribe or nationalism," and urged "the interest of the Umma should be given priority."[6]

This message again highlights the extent to which the al-Qaeda core leadership is sensitive to the impact of its actions on the wider Muslim community. For all of these reasons, therefore, seeking to reinforce concerns that WMD use would backfire should be part of an influencing strategy aimed at that leadership.

Other al-Qaeda and Non-Al Qaeda Terrorist Entities

Space precludes a comparable discussion of influencing either the other entities that make up the al-Qaeda-Jihadist movement or the many non-Al-Qaeda terrorist groups (whether Islamist or not).[7] Suffice it only to state here that across these other different terrorist groups and their component entities, perceptions of the more instrumental aspects or "smartness" of WMD acquisition and use again appear to be the most promising leverage point. In turn, most of the specific influencing actions identified above – from denial measures to creating uncertainties about the possible blowback from their supporters – also offer means to influence these other groups' calculus.

In addition, particularly for those non-al-Qaeda groups and entities that in the future could come to think about WMD acquisition and use, e.g., Hamas or Hezbollah among Islamist groups or the Tamil Tigers among non-Islamist groups, actions to influence their own perceptions not simply of the "smartness" but also of the justifiability and legitimacy of WMD use should not be dismissed out of hand. At least for now, unlike al-Qaeda, these non-al-Qaeda groups have not developed a line of argument to square WMD use and mass killing with their core religious, moral and political beliefs.

Aiders and Abettors

Turning to aiders and abettors, consider first possible state supporters. Two objectives stand out: on the one hand, the United States and like-minded countries should continue to take steps to encourage actions by state officials to prevent unauthorized or unwitting support to terrorist WMD acquisition and use and on the other, to dissuade official, authorized and witting support by a state's leadership to a terrorist WMD attack. As above, what leverage points and associated influencing actions stand out?

State Supporters

Leaders' perceptions that direct support for terrorist acquisition of WMD (or indirect support by not acting to put in place effective controls against diversion) would not serve their personal or national goals are one potential leverage point. Equally so, concern about the possible personal risks, especially of witting rather than unwitting support, is another leverage point.

A belief that assistance to WMD terrorism is neither justifiable nor legitimate state behavior – and conversely, that it is international "good behavior" to take actions to prevent unintended or unintentional support from within their countries – also could shape the policies of leaders and elites in most if not virtually all states.

Given these leverage points, the May 2008 statement by U.S. National Security Advisor Stephen Hadley stated "the United States will hold any state, terrorist group, or other non-state actor or individual fully accountable for supporting or enabling terrorist efforts to obtain or use weapons of mass destruction -- whether by facilitating, financing, or providing expertise or safe haven for such efforts"[8] is an important initial step. The United States should now seek other countries' support for this type of *"holding accountable"* declaratory policy and posture.

Going a step further, it could be desirable to seek a United Nations Security Council Resolution stating the international community's readiness to hold accountable aiders and abettors – or supporters and enablers, to use the Hadley formulation – of terrorist acquisition or use of WMD. Short of a Security Council resolution, the five permanent members of the Security Council –the United States, Russia, the United Kingdom, France and China – could make a common holding accountable declaration.

How the United States and like-minded countries would implement an accountability policy would need to be determined in the specific situation. Sufficient flexibility should be retained to adapt the response to different degrees of witting or unwitting state leadership involvement, the relative certainty with which a particular terrorist WMD attack or attempted attack could be tracked back to those leaders, the outcome of the attack, and other unique situational dimensions. The credibility and wider acceptability of a holding accountable policy, moreover, calls for making clear that there is a very wide range of means to use to implement it – and not simply or exclusively military means.

In a situation entailing unwitting state support for an unsuccessful terrorist WMD attack, for example, the response might be to demand the state's leadership join with the United States and others to take needed security measures to prevent any repetition as well as to punish the perpetrators. By contrast, in the case of clearly established, witting involvement by a state's highest leadership, military action proportional to the damage inflicted by the terrorist WMD attack could be warranted.[9]

Continued actions to build up habits, institutions and mechanisms of international cooperation against WMD terrorism are another important influencing action. The International Convention for the Suppression of Acts of Nuclear Terrorism and United Nations Security Council Resolution 1540 – as well as the Global Initiative to Combat Nuclear Terrorism – are three such examples. Building these habits of cooperation would help to create a presumption in the minds of possible state supporters that the international community would act against them. It also would make it easier for all states to take needed actions to prevent unintentional assistance.

The relative effectiveness of these types of efforts to influence state leaders' calculations clearly would depend on the perceived ability of the United States and other countries, possibly in collaboration with international organizations, to track a terrorist WMD attack back to the source. Unless the aiders and abettors can be identified, it will not be possible to hold that state's leaders accountable. Attribution will depend partly on technical forensics. It also would entail cooperation among intelligence and law enforcement authorities both in the United States and abroad.

Attribution already is being emphasized as part of U.S. counter-terrorism actions and a Working Group on the subject exists under the U.S.-Russian Global Initiative to Combat Nuclear Terrorism. In support of an influencing strategy, it would be desirable to publicize advances in the attribution capabilities and cooperation of the United States and other nations, to the extent possible without compromising sensitive technical information. Additional exercises and table-top games on the subject of attribution also would showcase and build habits of cooperation in this area.

Criminal Organizations

For criminal organizations, perceptions of risk stand out as the most compelling potential leverage point to convince them that the dangers of aiding and abetting a terrorist organization's acquisition or use of WMD far outweigh possible financial or other gains – whether risk to the organization as a whole or to specific members. Continued actions to build habits of global cooperation against WMD terrorism would be one means to signal the risks of helping a terrorist organization to acquire or use WMD.

Strengthening national legal mechanisms as well as procedures for international legal collaboration against WMD smuggling would be another such means. Here, both the International Convention to Suppress Acts of Nuclear Terrorism and United Nations Security Council Resolution 1540 provide a framework for accelerated action. Highly publicized actions could be taken against criminal organizations tied to terrorist pursuit of WMC, whether legal prosecutions or more direct action.

More unconventionally, likely informal if unacknowledged back-channels could be used to tell criminal organizations and their membership that the authorities would not tolerate aiding and abetting terrorist WMD acquisition and use – even if corrupt officials might have been prepared to look the other way at other types of smuggling.

In turn, background briefings to the press as well as other means could be used to manipulate fears that personal injury to the smugglers themselves might result from engaging in this type of illicit trafficking even if they were not caught, e.g., from exposure to radiation in the case of nuclear smuggling or lethal disease from biological agents.

Individual Aiders and Abettors[10]

Particularly for those individuals that might become unintentionally involved, a desire not to have innocent blood on their hands could be a potential leverage point. Perceptions of feasibility also could provide leverage, particularly the prospects for successfully trading WMD-related materials, know-how or access for financial or other personal gain. Nonetheless, given likely motivations, actions aimed at influencing individuals' perceptions of risk may be the most promising leverage point.

Turning to specific influencing actions, steps to enhance national controls and to implement United Nations Security Council Resolution 1540 in that area would be one means to shape perceptions of the likelihood of success. Encouraging different technical communities, especially in the biological sciences area, to develop their own codes of conduct could help strengthen individual awareness and responsibility. Not least, actions are needed to *influence individuals' perceptions of the personal risk* of indirectly or directly aiding or abetting terrorists' acquisition or use of WMD.

Here, too, a place to start is explicit declaratory policy statements by the United States and other countries they would join together to hold individuals accountable for such WMD-related activities. Highly publicized actions by states to put in place needed legal authorities and other mechanisms to allow cooperation to apprehend and/or extradite or prosecute WMD aiders and abettors also would signal heightened risks.

Going a step further, states could cooperate to make examples of publicly known figures involved in helping non-state actors seek or gain access to WMD materials or know-how – or in other WMD-related smuggling or illicit networks. Well-publicized prosecutions would be one means to do so; more direct covert action against such individuals could be another. Again the purpose would be to cause other potential aiders and abettors to reassess the risks of such action.

A Concluding Thought

Many different U.S. and international actions to counter the threat of WMD terrorism by preventing terrorist access to WMD-related materials or weapons are currently being pursued. These prevention activities are the first line of defense against WMD terrorism – and should be vigorously pursued and where needed, strengthened.

This paper has set out a complementary strategy for deterring – or better put, influencing – terrorists' acquisition and use of WMD. It has also sketched how that strategy could be applied in two key cases: that of the al-

Qaeda core leadership and that of possible aiders and abettors of any terrorist WMD attack.

More important, though differences in their susceptibility to influence clearly exist, for all of today's terrorist groups and entities, one or more potential leverage points can be identified – along with associated influencing actions. This includes the toughest case of the al-Qaeda core leadership.

In turn, potential leverage points and actions can also be identified for influencing those aiders and abettors that could tip the balance between a failed and a successful terrorist WMD attack, including state supporters, criminal organizations and individuals. Thus, the prospects for successfully influencing terrorists' WMD acquisition and use calculus – as well as aiders and abettors – could well be considerably greater than might be initially assumed.

Application in practice of such an influencing strategy will call for a number of enabling actions, from developing more detailed knowledge of the thinking and workings of particular terrorist groups to enhanced technical-political capabilities for attribution of the source of a terrorist WMD attack – including possible involvement of aiders and abettors. The task will be a challenging one. However, pursuit of such an influencing strategy also can leverage the many other efforts to counter the threat of WMD terrorism, not least prevention and denial writ large.

By way of conclusion, the argument of this paper is quite clear. Put most simply, the time has come to pursue a strategy to influence the WMD calculus of terrorist groups and their aiders and abettors. An influencing strategy can be a valuable adjunct to the overall set of U.S. and global actions to counter WMD terrorism. Influencing actions is part of the answer to dealing with the threat of a terrorist WMD attack against the United States, one of its friends or allies or any other country around the globe.

Notes

[1] See the discussion in Rebecca Givner-Forbes, "To Discipline the Savage Cowboys – An Analysis of Weapons of Mass Destruction in Jihadist Primary Documents," in Lewis A. Dunn (ed.), "Next Generation Weapons of Mass Destruction and Weapons of Mass Effect Terrorism," *op. cit.*

---

[2] See Steven Kull, Principal Investigator, "Muslim Public Opinion on U.S. Policy, Attacks on Civilians and al-Qaeda," WorldPublicOpinion.ORG, University of Maryland (April 24, 2007), 9-13, *passim*.

[3] These points were emphasized to the author by an expert in an earlier not-for-attribution discussion of influencing terrorists' WMD acquisition and use calculus.

[4] See, Nasir bin Hamd al-Fahd, "A Treatise on the Legal Status of Using Weapons of Mass Destruction against Infidels" (May 2003).

[5] "Letter from al-Zawahiri to al-Zarqawi" (Oct. 11, 2005), released by the Office of the Director of National Intelligence, ODNI New Release No. 2-05, 4, 5.

[6] "Osama bin Laden, "A Message to the People of Iraq" (Oct. 22, 2007). Translation of bin Laden's message, Aljazeera.net (Oct. 23, 2007).

[7] For elaboration see Dunn, "Influencing Terrorists' WMD Acquisition and Use Calculus" in "Next Generation WMD and WME Terrorism," Section 3 – Part 2.

[8] Remarks by National Security Advisor Stephen J. Hadley at the Proliferation Security Initiative Fifth Anniversary Senior Level Meeting, Washington, D.C., (May 28, 2008).

[9] Even assuming a military response to a WMD attack, there would be many options open to the United States short of responding with nuclear weapons. Though obvious given U.S. conventional capabilities, this point needs to be made because some persons have already asserted that the U.S. declaratory policy of "holding accountable" is tantamount to threatening a nuclear response against enablers and supporters of a terrorist WMD attack on the United States.

[10] This category partly overlaps with the two preceding ones to the extent that states and criminal organizations are made up of individuals. Nonetheless, it warrants separate treatment because potential individual aiders and abettors need not be either senior state officials or members of a criminal organization.

Part Two

Deterrence Issues and Challenges: A Topical Approach

CHAPTER 9

U.S. Extended Deterrence: How Much Strategic Force Is Too Little?

David J. Trachtenberg

"The objective of nuclear-weapons policy should not be solely to decrease the number of weapons in the world, but to make the world safer – which is not necessarily the same thing."
-- Herman Kahn

At the dawn of the 21st century's second decade, America finds itself on the cusp of what may be called the third atomic age. The first atomic age coincided with the period of the Cold War, which saw the United States transition from having a nuclear weapons monopoly to a superpower seeking to restore parity to the strategic balance in the wake of the Soviet Union's development and deployment of a massive, powerful and extensive nuclear weapons capability.

The second atomic age emerged with the disintegration of the Soviet Union and the end of the Cold War. It was characterized by a period of reassessment and restructuring of U.S. nuclear policies and forces to adapt them to a security environment that had changed dramatically and unexpectedly.

Today, a third atomic age emerges in which the role of nuclear weapons in U.S. national security strategy continues to diminish and the nuclear forces supporting that strategy shrink to historically low levels. However, the global proliferation of nuclear weapons and technologies has led others to move in the opposite direction – seeking to acquire the very nuclear weapons that many in the West view as increasingly irrelevant to contemporary security challenges. The potential ramifications of this development have led some analysts to suggest the world is now at a nuclear "tipping point."

Throughout both the Cold War and post-Cold War periods, the United States has relied ultimately on its nuclear potential to deter aggression. During the Cold War, the primary mission of U.S. nuclear forces was to deter the Soviet Union. In the early days of this period, U.S. policy makers calculated deterrence could be effectively maintained with a nuclear capability sufficient to inflict a certain level of damage to the Soviet Union's industrial capacity and population, which would be deemed unacceptable. This "deterrence by punishment" calculus formed the basis of force sizing and planning for the U.S. nuclear arsenal for years to come. Yet a central fallacy in this approach was that it relied on *American perceptions* of what the Soviets would find "unacceptable," rather than on definitive knowledge of what the Soviets themselves would consider sufficient to deter them.

The debate over extended deterrence is similarly challenged by a need to understand that its effectiveness depends on how both allies and adversaries perceive the credibility of American commitments. American views of how others *should* perceive the credibility of U.S. nuclear threats are less relevant than how others actually perceive them. Moreover, the views of allies and adversaries can vary widely based on historical, cultural, and other unique circumstances.

As the nature of nuclear threats evolved, the U.S. nuclear force structure and size also evolved. With the end of the Cold War and the demise of the Soviet Union, the missions and purposes of U.S. nuclear forces were increasingly called into question. This included not only the utility of nuclear forces for deterring direct attack on the United States, but the efficacy of extending a nuclear deterrent to third parties as a means of preventing aggression by others.

The Bush administration's 2001 Nuclear Posture Review (NPR) postulated a world of extant and emerging nuclear powers posing qualitatively different nuclear threats to the United States and its allies than existed during the Cold War. While deterrence of nuclear attack remained a central goal of U.S. nuclear forces, the U.S. nuclear arsenal was considered to play a broader role in ensuring global security.

Along with traditional deterrence, the 2001 NPR articulated a role for nuclear weapons in "assurance," "dissuasion," and "defeat." (These concepts were previously posited in the 2001 Quadrennial Defense Review.) In other words, the NPR acknowledged that American nuclear forces play a major role in providing security guarantees to friends and allies that lack their own nuclear weapons and face challenges from hostile neighbors or adversaries (i.e., assurance). The U.S. nuclear potential was also seen as having a dissuasive effect on adversaries who might contemplate actions contrary to American interests. And, of course, should deterrence fail – an increasingly plausible prospect in a world of rogue states and terrorist actors – U.S. nuclear forces must have the capacity to defeat any aggressor. Without this capacity, the credibility of the U.S. nuclear deterrent may be called into question, undermining the central deterrence goal of American nuclear forces.

This chapter focuses on the assurance aspect of U.S. nuclear forces, i.e., helping to assure friends and allies of the American commitment to their security. There are many ways to assure friends and allies and not all rely on threatening potential aggressors with nuclear destruction. These can include declaratory policy, creating or strengthening mutual defense agreements and military alliances, fostering broader political relationships, bolstering reliance on missile defenses and the forward deployment of conventional forces.[1]

None of these means is mutually exclusive, and a sound policy of assurance will deploy all of them, as appropriate, tailored to specific circumstances. Nevertheless, it is the nuclear deterrence aspect of assurance that is being questioned more widely as nuclear force levels are reduced and which is the focus of this chapter.

Importantly, the requirements for extended deterrence and assurance may not be identical. An adversary may be deterred from attacking an ally even though that ally does not perceive his security has been adequately "assured." Therefore, in certain cases, the requirements for assurance may exceed those of deterrence. Clearly, the answer to the question of "how much is enough (or too little)?" depends on the perception of both allies and adversaries.

In light of growing threats to the United States posed by the proliferation of nuclear and other weapons of mass destruction (WMD) capabilities to potential adversaries, the efficacy of American security guarantees also depends on how allies perceive the willingness of the United States to defend their security if doing so risks exposing the U.S. homeland to direct attack.

By extending its nuclear deterrent to other countries, the United States has historically provided a "nuclear umbrella" to others under which the United States sought to ensure their security. The prospect of a nuclear response by the United States to a third-party attack on a U.S. ally using nuclear or other weapons of mass destruction has for decades added a degree of uncertainty to the calculations of potential adversaries who may have contemplated such aggression. However, in a world of proliferating nuclear powers, a renewed American emphasis on arms control and further nuclear reductions, and a growing tension between American policies that support the elimination of nuclear weapons entirely and American adversaries who increasingly seek them, the continued viability and credibility of the U.S. extended deterrent deserves closer examination.

Some of the questions this chapter addresses include:

- How has extended deterrence worked in the past and what are the factors that influence its viability?
- Is there a link between extended deterrence and nonproliferation?
- How do allies in Europe and Asia perceive the requirements of extended deterrence?
- Is the size of the U.S. nuclear arsenal more relevant to extended deterrence than its composition?
- Are there alternatives to the extended deterrence provided by U.S. nuclear forces that can provide the same degree of assurance to friends and allies?
- What impact do nuclear reductions have on the ability of the United States to reassure allies of the credibility of American security guarantees?
- What are the implications for extended deterrence of current U.S. nuclear policies?
- And, as U.S. nuclear forces are reduced, is there some threshold level of nuclear capability beneath which the risks of aggression exceed the U.S. ability to deter it?

History of Extended Deterrence

At the dawn of the nuclear age, the United States confronted a numerically superior conventional army that had occupied the eastern half of Europe after World War II. As Cold War attitudes hardened and Soviet expansionist objectives became clearer, the United States sought to deter

Soviet aggression by extending its nuclear deterrent abroad. The threat of an American nuclear response to a conventional invasion of Western Europe was integrated into U.S. military doctrine in the post-war era.

At a time when the United States possessed nuclear superiority over the Soviet Union, this extended deterrent was perceived as a credible threat sufficient to deter a move west by the Red Army. As the Soviets approached nuclear parity, and then surpassed the United States in the overall levels and capabilities of its nuclear forces, the credibility of U.S. threats to "go nuclear" to protect Western Europe against Soviet aggression became debatable.

Nevertheless, despite changes in the balance of nuclear forces between the two superpowers in the 1960s and 1970s, the U.S. nuclear arsenal remained sizable enough to give pause to any aggressor. At its peak, the U.S. deployed more than 10,000 "strategic" and "non-strategic" (i.e., "tactical") nuclear weapons on more than 2,000 delivery platforms. Although the Soviets maintained some significant advantages in nuclear firepower, throw weight, and other measures of nuclear capability, the sheer size of the American nuclear arsenal was thought by some to have an "existential" deterrent effect.[2]

As arms control became a central element of the bilateral superpower relationship, pressures emerged to reduce the size of nuclear stockpiles. Along with the Strategic Arms Limitations Talks (SALT) and Strategic Arms Reductions Talks (START), which resulted in treaties reducing the number of long-range nuclear weapons systems, the 1986 Intermediate-Range Nuclear Forces (INF) Treaty resulted for the first time in the negotiated elimination of an entire class of nuclear weapon delivery systems. This included the Pershing II ballistic and Ground-Launched Cruise Missiles deployed in Europe that were a visible part of the U.S. extended deterrent commitment.

Extended deterrence was not limited to protecting European allies. For example, as Japan became one of the strongest post-war allies of the United States, the emerging nuclear weapons potential first of China, and then later North Korea, concerned Japanese officials, who became acutely sensitive to the role of the U.S. nuclear umbrella in assuring Japanese security.

After the Korean armistice in 1953, South Korea also enjoyed a degree of protection accorded by the American extended nuclear deterrent.

U.S. nuclear weapons were stationed on South Korean territory. The painful shadow of Vietnam, however, and the fall of the Saigon government in 1975, led to questions about whether the United States would rather accept defeat in war than resort to the use of nuclear weapons.

Since then, the United States has deployed veiled nuclear threats in limited circumstances to bolster deterrence. For example, then-Secretary of State James Baker articulated such a threat to Saddam Hussein in an effort to deter the Iraqi dictator from using weapons of mass destruction against U.S. and coalition forces in the 1991 Gulf War. Even though Secretary Baker later admitted the United States had no intention of using nuclear weapons, the possibility they might be used was arguably a consideration in Saddam's decision not to launch chemical or biological attacks against Israel or coalition forces.

The importance of extended deterrence has been recognized even by those who favor the ultimate elimination of the nuclear capabilities on which it rests. Speaking in Prague in April 2009, President Obama reiterated his vision for a nuclear-free world, but noted "as long as these weapons exist, the United States will maintain a safe, secure and effective arsenal to deter any adversary, *and guarantee that defense to our allies....*"[3] (emphasis added) Today, however, as nuclear weapons come to be seen by some decision leaders increasingly as weapons that serve no purpose, will never be used in combat, and should be eliminated, the credibility of U.S. nuclear threats is likely to be diminished in the eyes of both potential adversaries and long-time friends and allies.

The Relationship Between Extended Deterrence and Nonproliferation

For a number of states, their own security rests on the viability and credibility of American nuclear assurances. Without the assurance – or reassurance – that the U.S. nuclear "umbrella" provides, these states may pursue their own acquisition programs for nuclear weapons. As one observer has noted, "...for allies such as Japan, South Korea and Taiwan, and some NATO states, the stability both of the U.S. deterrent and extended deterrence guarantees are a significant part of these countries' own strategic calculus."[4] Indeed, there have been numerous studies in recent years suggesting "the credibility and reliability of U.S. nuclear assurances are necessary to keep countries...from reconsidering their decisions to be nonnuclear states."[5]

In a 2007 study that linked U.S. extended deterrence with non-proliferation, the State Department's International Security Advisory Board (ISAB) concluded, "Nuclear umbrella security agreements, whether unilateral or multilateral, have been, and are expected to continue to be, effective deterrents to proliferation."[6] The ISAB report stated, "There is clear evidence in diplomatic channels that U.S. assurances to include the nuclear umbrella have been, and continue to be, the single most important reason many allies have foresworn nuclear weapons" and further suggested that "a lessening of the U.S. nuclear umbrella could very well trigger a [nuclear proliferation] cascade in East Asia and the Middle East."[7]

Secretary of Defense Robert Gates has acknowledged the importance of U.S. nuclear weapons to extended deterrence and nonproliferation. In his 2008 speech to the Carnegie Endowment for International Peace he declared, "As long as others have nuclear weapons, we must maintain some level of these weapons ourselves to deter potential adversaries and to reassure over two dozen allies and partners who rely on our nuclear umbrella for their security, making it unnecessary for them to develop their own."[8]

In 2009, the bipartisan Commission on the Strategic Posture of the United States concluded, "The U.S. nuclear posture must be designed to address a very broad set of U.S. objectives, including not just deterrence of enemies in time of crisis and war but also assurance of our allies and dissuasion of potential adversaries. Indeed, the assurance function of the force is as important as ever."[9]

By some estimates nearly 30 countries rely for their ultimate security on the extended deterrent U.S. nuclear forces provide. Some of these countries are strong U.S. allies that do not feel sufficiently threatened by neighbors or adversaries to contemplate developing nuclear weapons of their own. Others have been dissuaded from doing so as a result of formal defensive alliances with the United States (such as NATO). Still others are friends with which the United States does not have a formal defense relationship but whose security is nevertheless important to the maintenance of stability and defense of American interests; therefore, the American nuclear umbrella has been extended to them.

Many of these countries can be found in dangerous or unstable regions with potentially hostile neighbors. If the American extended nuclear deterrent loses credibility, it is most likely to have significant repercussions among those states who may determine their own security is best served through the acquisition of their own nuclear weapons capability.

Allied Views of Assurance

The role of U.S. nuclear forces in extending deterrence to NATO allies is codified in NATO's Strategic Concept, promulgated in 1999. The document states: "Nuclear forces based in Europe and committed to NATO provide an essential political and military link between the European and North American members of the Alliance. The Alliance will therefore maintain adequate nuclear forces in Europe."

What constitutes "adequate" nuclear forces is a matter to be determined by the NATO members themselves. However, the Strategic Concept is clear on the inseparability of European and American security, noting the "unique contribution" of nuclear weapons to deterrence and declaring that they "remain essential to preserve peace."[10]

At the Strasbourg/Kehl NATO Summit in April 2009, Alliance members decided to update NATO's Strategic Concept before the next summit meeting at the end of 2010. This process is expected to revisit the issue of extended deterrence and the role of U.S. nuclear forces in providing that deterrence to NATO.[11]

Nevertheless, it is clear a number of U.S. NATO and non-NATO allies consider the U.S. extended deterrent to be critical to their security. A group of former NATO military officials, including former military chiefs of the United States, Britain, France, Germany and the Netherlands, reaffirmed the importance of the extended deterrent role of U.S. nuclear forces and the credibility of nuclear escalatory threats by noting, "The first use of nuclear weapons must remain in the quiver of escalation as the ultimate instrument to prevent the use of weapons of mass destruction, in order to avoid truly existential dangers."[12]

For some, the value of the extended deterrent lies in the deployment of American nuclear weapons on their territory and the demonstration of resolve these deployments convey. In these cases, additional U.S. strategic offensive arms reductions may have less significance on allied perceptions of American credibility. For others, the value of extended deterrence lies more in the ability and willingness of the United States to maintain the effectiveness of its strategic nuclear arsenal. Therefore, additional strategic arms reductions may undermine the assurance value of American security guarantees.

In the past, some U.S. allies have expressed strong views regarding the U.S. extended deterrent. This includes non-NATO allies. For example, according to documents recently de-classified by Japanese officials, concern over a possible Sino-U.S. conflict in the mid-1960s led then-Japanese Prime Minister Sato Eisaku to press U.S. Secretary of Defense Robert McNamara for assurances the United States would be prepared to use its nuclear weapons against China.

In the wake of China's nuclear testing, Secretary McNamara subsequently expressed concern that without reassuring Japan of the American commitment to its security, Tokyo might seek its own nuclear weapons. Since then, other Japanese officials have sought to elicit similar American nuclear assurances, including comments by Foreign Minister Aso Taro after North Korea's nuclear test in 2006.[13]

South Korea also reportedly sought nuclear assurances from the United States after North Korea's nuclear test.[14] Reportedly, former South Korean defense ministers approached the United States seeking the re-deployment of U.S. nuclear weapons in South Korea that had previously been withdrawn.[15]

In June 2009, President Obama and South Korean President Lee Myung-bak reaffirmed the U.S.-Republic of Korea security relationship included the "continuing commitment of extended deterrence, including the U.S. nuclear umbrella...."[16] During a subsequent visit to Seoul, Secretary of Defense Gates declared, "The United States is committed to providing extended deterrence using the full range of American military might," to protect South Korea, including "the nuclear umbrella."[17]

Obviously, allied views of extended deterrence will be shaped not only by what the United States does with respect to its nuclear forces but by the evolving global strategic situation. Although the Cold War division of Europe ended two decades ago, some allies in Europe grow increasingly concerned over what they perceive as a renewed aggressiveness in Russia's foreign and defense policies. The Russian military action in the summer of

2008 against Georgia - a country seeking NATO membership – suggested that extending U.S. nuclear guarantees to countries on Russia's periphery might be risky business. It also raised additional uncertainties on the part of Russia's other neighbors regarding the credibility of U.S. security guarantees.

On top of this, Russia has revised its military doctrine to place increased reliance on its nuclear forces, continued to pursue an aggressive nuclear weapons modernization program, resumed Cold War style exercises of its strategic nuclear forces, threatened some of its former satellite states with nuclear attack, and publicly proposed developing new "offensive weapons systems" to counter the United States.[18]

In the wake of Russian statements and actions, the concerns of Russia's neighbors and their desire to be integrated into the security perimeter of the United States are understandable. So, too, is concern that Washington's desire to "reset" its relationship with Moscow in the wake of Russia's increasing assertiveness may actually lead others to question the attractiveness of, and confidence in, American security guarantees.

Ukraine, a former Soviet state, has been wary of Russia and has sought the security guarantees that would accrue to it from NATO membership. Yet the new Ukrainian government has changed course from its predecessor, declaring Kiev's preference for neutrality and non-alignment, rejecting the previous government's push for NATO membership, and seeking greater accommodation with Russia.[19]

Nevertheless, as more countries pursue the path to NATO membership, the United States will likely find itself extending its nuclear umbrella to additional states in what was formerly viewed as Russia's "sphere of influence." Future reductions in European-based U.S. tactical nuclear forces, along with NATO's prior assurances to Russia that new NATO members would not host U.S. nuclear weapons on their territories[20], may complicate the mission of extended deterrence. Indeed, when coupled with the movement toward significant reductions in U.S. strategic nuclear forces, it may become increasingly difficult to explain credibly how nuclear deterrence can be effectively extended to a greater number of states at a lower level of forces.

In Asia, the developing nuclear capabilities of North Korea have also sparked concern among America's regional friends and allies. Japan, in particular, has encouraged the United States not to back away from its extended nuclear deterrent. After North Korea's 2006 nuclear test, one Japanese press report stated that "Defense Minister Fumio Kyuma spoke in no uncertain terms about strengthening the deterrence of U.S. nuclear weapons. The strongest deterrence would be when the United States explicitly says, 'If you drop one nuclear bomb on Japan, the United States will retaliate by dropping 10 on you,' he said."[21]

Japan is increasingly sensitive over the credibility of U.S. security guarantees. Japan's 2004 Defense Program Outline declared "to protect its territory and people against the threat of nuclear weapons, Japan will continue to rely on the U.S. nuclear deterrent," a posture explicitly reflected in the country's official Defense Program Outline since 1976.[22] A U.S.-Japan Joint Statement issued after a meeting of the bilateral Security Consultative Committee in May 2007 reaffirmed "U.S. extended deterrence underpins the defense of Japan and regional security" and this includes "the full range of U.S. military capabilities – both nuclear and non-nuclear strike forces and defensive capabilities."[23]

Yukio Satoh, Vice Chairman of the Japan Institute of International Affairs and former Japanese diplomat recently expressed his country's views of the importance of the U.S. extended deterrent by noting:

> ...the importance for Japan of the American nuclear deterrence has increased since the end of the Cold War, as the country has become exposed to a diversity of conceivable nuclear threats, such as North Korea's progressing nuclear and missile programs, China's growing military power, and Russia's strategic reassertiveness. These developments are making Japan increasingly vulnerable to possible or potential threats by nuclear and other weapons of mass destruction (WMD). Ensuring American commitment to extend deterrence against such threats is therefore a matter of primary strategic importance for Japan....
>
> In recent years, the Japanese have become growingly sensitive to the credibility of the American commitment. Exposed to a series of dangerous actions by Pyongyang, particularly its test-shooting of a missile over Japan in 1998, its nuclear testing in 2006, and yet another test of a long-

range missile, the Japanese have come to realize anew the importance of the American extended deterrence for their security, and this has made the Japanese more sensitive than ever to Washington's attitude to North Korea.[24]

Ambassador Satoh, a supporter of the "Global Zero" movement to eliminate nuclear weapons, also recognized the potential hazards the move toward nuclear disarmament could pose for Japanese security, noting: "Even the propositions advocated by eminent American strategists to pursue 'a world free of nuclear weapons' have given rise to some anxiety about the possible negative impact on the American extended deterrence.... Furthermore, the Japanese concern about the credibility of the American extended deterrence could increase if the U.S. government were to unilaterally move to redefine the concept of nuclear deterrence, particularly to reduce dependence upon nuclear weapons in providing deterrence, without proper consultations."[25]

Satoh noted, "There have been no official consultations between Washington and Tokyo on how American extended deterrence should function, nor even any mechanism put in place for such consultations." He stated "the time has come for us to create some kind of mechanism through which we can discuss the common strategy, particularly if the United States is going to reduce dependence upon nuclear weapons in their strategy."[26]

Does Size Matter?

Assurance considerations may be affected not only by the size of the American extended nuclear deterrent, but by its composition. Some countries may not consider additional numerical reductions in U.S. strategic nuclear forces to be especially significant with respect to the credibility of American security guarantees unless those reductions impact the levels or operational utility of the types of nuclear forces those countries consider most useful to deter threats to their security.

For example, the threatened use of land-based ICBMs deployed on American soil in defense of allies may be seen as less credible than SLBMs on submarines that can deploy to crisis areas, especially since a strike using forces based in the United States may increase the risk of direct retaliation against the United States. For this reason, allies may consider the United States less willing to come to their defense by employing U.S. central strategic forces. Bombers, however, may provide the highest level of reassurance to allies, since unlike ICBMs they are mobile and unlike nuclear ballistic missile-armed submarines (SSBNs) they are visible. The bomber leg of the strategic Triad is the most flexible for signaling intentions, which can provide reassurance to allies in times of crisis.

Nevertheless, the overall level of U.S strategic nuclear forces may convey to allies a sense of how the United States views the relevance of these forces in the contemporary security environment. Strategic force reductions, if pursued for example as part of a bilateral U.S.-Russia effort to diminish reliance on nuclear weapons for strategic deterrence purposes, may have unintended negative consequences for assurance and extended deterrence.

The Role of Strategic and Non-strategic Nuclear Forces in Extended Deterrence

Discussions of "strategic" and "non-strategic" nuclear forces tend to obscure the fact that for the countries whose security depends on them, all nuclear weapons are strategic. The distinction is somewhat artificial and was derived to conform to an arms control process that focused on regulating arsenals based on the range of their delivery systems. Nevertheless, both longer-range and shorter-range systems have relevance for extended deterrence.

Today, the United States maintains a minimum number of non-strategic nuclear weapons stationed in Europe. Most European-based U.S. nuclear forces were removed as a result of the 1986 INF Treaty, which eliminated the Pershing II missile and GLCMs, or as a result of the 1991 Presidential Nuclear Initiative (PNI), which led to the withdrawal of nuclear artillery shells, naval anti-submarine nuclear weapons, and short-range ballistic missile nuclear warheads.[27]

In 1971, 11 types of nuclear weapons systems were deployed in Europe.[28] Today, the number of non-strategic nuclear weapons in NATO Europe has been reduced by more than 97 percent from 1970's levels. The only remaining U.S. nuclear weapons in Europe are air-delivered gravity bombs that reportedly can be deployed on dual-capable aircraft in Turkey, Italy, Germany, Belgium, and the Netherlands.

The deployment of these non-strategic nuclear weapons in Europe has always been seen as a means of reinforcing America's extended nuclear deterrent by providing a critical link between conventional forces in Europe and American strategic nuclear forces. This is recognized in NATO's Strategic Concept, which notes "adequate sub-strategic forces based in Europe...provide an essential link with strategic nuclear forces, reinforcing the transatlantic link."[29] They have also provided a visible and tangible expression of American solidarity with host countries, which some believe has strengthened their deterrent value.

The importance of maintaining U.S. non-strategic nuclear forces in Europe was highlighted in a 2008 report by the Secretary of Defense Task Force on DoD Nuclear Weapons Management, which noted:

> The Allies believe in the U.S. nuclear deterrent as a pillar of the Alliance. Some Allies have been troubled to learn that during the last decade some senior U.S. military leaders have advocated for the unilateral removal of U.S. nuclear weapons from Europe. These Allies are convinced that the security of the United States is 'coupled' to that of Europe. Moreover, these allies are aware of the greater symbolic and political value of allied aircraft employing U.S. nuclear weapons.... USEUCOM (U.S. European Command) argues that an "over the horizon" strategic capability is just as credible. It believes there is no military downside to the unilateral withdrawal of nuclear weapons from Europe. This attitude fails to comprehend—and therefore undermines—the political value our friends and allies place on these weapons, the political costs of withdrawal, and the psychological impact of their visible presence as well as the security linkages they provide.... DCA (dual-capable aircraft) fighters and nuclear weapons are visible, capable, recallable, reusable, and flexible and are a military statement of NATO and U.S. political will. These NATO forces provide a number of advantages to the Alliance that go far beyond USEUCOM's narrow perception of their military utility. Nuclear weapons in Europe provide a continuous deterrence element; as long as our allies value their political contribution, the United

States is obligated to provide and maintain the nuclear weapon capability.[30]

Should these forces be withdrawn completely, the willingness of the United States to "go nuclear" on Europe's behalf could be called into question. It could also place increasing stress on the U.S. strategic nuclear forces by adding additional mission responsibilities (especially if the number of NATO countries protected under the U.S. nuclear umbrella continues to increase as a result of the NATO enlargement process) at a time when those forces are also likely to decline further.

It is plausible the requirements of extended deterrence may also necessitate the retention of certain types of nuclear forces that might otherwise be withdrawn or retired. As the Congressional Commission on the Strategic Posture of the United States noted, "Assurance [of allies] that extended deterrence remains credible and effective may require that the United States retain numbers or types of nuclear capabilities that it might not deem necessary if it were concerned only with its own defense."[31]

The Commission also reported some European allies believe modernization of European-based nuclear forces is "essential to prevent nuclear coercion by Moscow" and for "restoring a sense of balance" in the face of Russia's own nuclear modernization efforts.[32]

In addition, Turkey has reportedly been concerned over the potential removal of nuclear gravity bombs that can be carried by dual-capable aircraft based on its territory. As recently as August 2009, Turkish officials reportedly expressed concern that Iran's efforts to acquire nuclear weapons would lead Turkey to do the same.[33]

Some Asian officials have expressed particular concern over the potential elimination of the U.S. TLAM-N cruise missile, one of the few non-strategic nuclear weapons remaining in the U.S. nuclear arsenal. This was noted by the Congressional Commission on the Strategic Posture of the United States.[34]

One account of the concerns expressed by a "particularly important ally" indicated should the United States decide to eliminate TLAM-N, "we would like to be consulted in advance with regard to how the loss of this capability for extended deterrence will be offset."[35] Additionally, the Commission noted the views of one ally, expressed privately, that "the credibility of the U.S. extended deterrent depends on its specific capabilities to hold a wide variety of targets at risk, and to deploy forces in a way that is either visible or stealthy, as circumstances may demand."[36]

Some analysts have suggested the TLAM-N has little military utility and its importance to countries like Japan is overstated. One challenged the Strategic Posture Commission's conclusions in this regard, calling the notion TLAM-N is critical to extended deterrence in Asia "odd."[37] In particular, the deployment of other capabilities to the Pacific region, including aircraft carriers, submarines and long-range bombers, is seen by some as a sufficient deterrent to aggression.

As one analyst noted, "Why, given these extensive U.S. forces earmarked for the Pacific region, anyone in Tokyo, Washington, Beijing or Pyongyang would doubt the U.S. capability to project a nuclear umbrella over Japan – or see the TLAM-N as essential – is puzzling."[38] Such reasoning, however, reflects a decidedly *American* perspective based on *American* views of what *should* be reassuring to allies. But clearly reassurance is in the eye of the reassured, and allied views may differ from ours, based on unique historical, cultural or other factors. These factors should be taken into account if the purpose of the U.S. extended deterrent is to reassure allies of the American commitment to their security.

Since the change in Japan's government in 2009, questions have been raised about that country's views of the importance of the TLAM-N for extended deterrence. Japan's Foreign Minister Katsuya Okada has noted, "…the Japanese government is not in a position to judge whether it is necessary or desirable for [the U.S.] government to possess particular [weapons] systems.… Nevertheless, if TLAM-N is retired, we hope to receive ongoing explanations of [the U.S.] government's extended deterrence policy, including any impact this might have on extended deterrence for Japan and how this could be supplemented."[39]

Indeed, as a result of its recent review of the U.S. nuclear posture, the Obama administration has now decided to retire the TLAM-N arguing it "serves a redundant purpose in the U.S. nuclear stockpile" and its deterrence and assurance roles "can be adequately substituted" by other means including forward-deployed aircraft and U.S. central strategic forces.[40] At the same time, however, the administration has declared "No changes to U.S. extended deterrence capabilities will be made without continued close consultation with allies and partners."[41]

With respect to the continued deployment of non-strategic nuclear forces in Europe, the Obama administration's April 2010 Nuclear Posture Review argues such decisions should be made in consultation with NATO allies and states the United States "is committed to making consensus decisions through NATO processes."[42]   Moreover, it declares, "Any changes in NATO's nuclear posture should only be taken after a thorough review within – and decision by – the Alliance."[43]

Despite the expressed U.S. commitment to consult closely with countries that benefit from America's extended deterrent, some observers have argued the views of allies should not drive the United States to maintain nuclear weapons that have little military utility. They argue doing so would essentially hold American nuclear deployments "hostage" to the whims of other countries.[44]   Nevertheless, it is clear American strategic interests are best served by considering Allied views – though these views may not be determinative – prior to any future decisions regarding the appropriate level or composition of U.S. nuclear forces.

Although a number of European and Asian allies share similar views of the importance of extended deterrence, there are also important nuances. For example, it is generally the case that European allies put great value in the deployment of U.S. non-strategic nuclear weapons on European soil, whereas a number of Asian allies would prefer to keep U.S. nuclear weapons, both strategic and non-strategic, "on call."[45]

Extending Deterrence by Other Means

Extended nuclear deterrence worked well during the Cold War. NATO's deployment of U.S. nuclear weapons on European soil, coupled with its refusal to preclude the first use of nuclear weapons in response to Soviet conventional aggression, arguably helped convince Soviet leaders of the seriousness of America's nuclear guarantees to its European allies. In the post-Cold War world, however, some have questioned the value of extended deterrence, suggesting other capabilities are capable of providing the deterrent value that U.S. nuclear forces once provided.

Third Party Nuclear Capabilities

In the European context, both the U.K. and France maintain their own independent nuclear forces and could presumably extend their nuclear deterrent to the rest of Europe. However, neither country is likely to do so for a variety of political and strategic reasons. These include the difficulty of persuading their populations they should not only use their independent nuclear deterrents to protect their own citizens but other European countries as well, especially in a post-Cold War world where pressures to reduce reliance on nuclear forces continue to mount.

UK strategic nuclear deterrent policy continues to be based on a 2006 White Paper[46] and supports a minimum nuclear deterrent, although it does recognize British nuclear weapons can play an important role in NATO's collective security. British nuclear forces have been reduced by 75 percent since the end of the Cold War and the British deterrent now consists of "no more than 160 operationally available warheads."[47] British Prime Minister Gordon Brown, in a July 2009 report to Parliament, noted a "minimum nuclear deterrent remains an essential element of our national security," and declared Britain "will continue to contribute our strategic nuclear deterrent to NATO's collective security" but noted the UK "would only consider using nuclear weapons in self-defense (including the defense of our NATO allies), and even then only in extreme circumstances."[48]

In his 2006 speech to the Strategic Air and Maritime Forces at Ile Longue, French President Jacques Chirac reiterated the importance of France's nuclear deterrent, calling it "the ultimate guarantor of our security" and declared there should be no doubt "about our determination and capacity to resort to our nuclear weapons. The credible threat of their utilization permanently hangs over those leaders who harbor hostile intentions against us." But he also suggested defending France's vital interests could extend beyond the country's borders as a result of "the growing interdependence of European countries and also by the impact of globalization."

Chirac noted, "Safeguarding our strategic supplies or the defense of allied countries are, among others, interests that must be protected." He also declared France's nuclear deterrent to be "a core element in the security of the European continent."[49]

Nevertheless, this statement was offered in the context of a NATO Strategic Concept that continues to rely on American nuclear capabilities for extended deterrence. It was not meant to suggest French nuclear forces could substitute for American capabilities. Moreover, some European countries have in the past been disinclined to stake their own security on France's nuclear deterrent.[50] This may, in part, reflect political as well as military concerns.

As a practical matter, extending deterrence to European allies through exclusive reliance on the relatively small independent UK or French nuclear deterrents is unlikely to convey the same measure of credibility as using U.S. nuclear forces. In addition, neither the British nor French nuclear capabilities are seen as sufficient to extend deterrence to Asian allies against a growing Chinese nuclear capability.[51]

Non-nuclear Capabilities

Some believe the contemporary strategic environment no longer requires American nuclear threats to be made on behalf of allies, if it ever did, and non-nuclear means can be equally effective as a deterrent to aggression. As a 2008 RAND Project paper on deterrence argued, "The United States, even when resting extended deterrence almost entirely on nuclear weapons, was always extremely circumspect about even obliquely threatening their use; this was no less the case during the 1950s when it still retained a near-monopoly on long-range nuclear weapons. In addition, at present and for the near term, U.S. conventional capabilities greatly reduce the need to rely on nuclear weapons for extended deterrence relative to the 1950s."[52]

Nuclear weapons deter by threatening severe punishment to a potential attacker. The effectiveness of this type of deterrence requires the ability to hold at risk those assets an adversary values most. Although in certain cases modern conventional weapons can accomplish military objectives once thought possible only by the use of nuclear weapons, they cannot substitute for nuclear weapons in all cases.

For example, potential adversaries like North Korea and Iran have placed their most valuable strategic assets underground, in highly protected areas, beyond the reach of conventional strike capabilities. Removing the threat of a nuclear retaliatory strike would grant sanctuary to those assets or capabilities that could no longer be held at risk. Rather than deter aggression, this might provoke it if an adversary believes his most valuable assets could be spared from destruction.

Moreover, some of the bloodiest conflicts in history, including two conventional World Wars, were fought as a consequence of the failure of pre-nuclear deterrence. In the words of one analyst, "The historical record of conventional deterrence is not encouraging."[53]

One reason to question the ability of conventional forces to substitute for nuclear forces in providing extended deterrence is sufficient conventional forces may not be forward-deployed in time to regions where they can function as an effective deterrent. Moreover, while the United States continues to seek a prompt global strike capability that would allow swift and accurate strikes anywhere on the globe using non-nuclear weapons, those potential capabilities are not sufficiently mature to expect they can credibly serve the extended deterrence function that nuclear weapons do today.

In addition to the strictly military aspects of deterrence, there are psychological ones at play as well. Nuclear weapons are perceived to be the ultimate weapons and the punishment they can exact is without equal. The psychological impact of a threat to employ a weapon with such significant damage potential may, in and of itself, bolster deterrence in ways the threat of conventional retaliation cannot.

While the effectiveness of deterrence rests on the adversary's perception of the consequences of aggression, and it is impossible to know with absolute certainty how an adversary perceives nuclear threats, it is nevertheless plausible conventional deterrence alone will carry less impact than deterrent threats that include a nuclear component. As General Kevin Chilton, former commander of U.S. Strategic Command, testified last year, "The nuclear weapon has a deterrent factor that far exceeds a conventional threat."[54]

Aside from reliance on non-nuclear weapons capabilities, it is possible that extended deterrence can be bolstered through a more robust American presence on allied territory. This can take the form of troop deployments, military facilities, or other types of visible linkages that bind friends and allies more tightly to the United States.

However, the very visibility of an expanded American presence on the territories of sovereign states may also occasion negative political repercussions, especially in times of heightened tensions. Hence, the value of this means of assurance may be more susceptible to short-term fluctuations in internal host-nation politics that impact the credibility of American security guarantees.

Missile Defenses

In addition to the threat of punishment, deterrence can also be achieved through the ability to deny a potential attacker the objectives of his attack. This "deterrence through denial" strategy can be reflected in defensive measures – either as a substitute for or adjunct to – offensive retaliatory means.

The 2001 NPR reintroduced defenses into the calculus of deterrence by advocating the deployment of ballistic missile defenses. The ability to protect and defend against attack should deterrence fail was seen as a critical element of a sound nuclear strategy and a policy that reinforced deterrence by complementing the offensive threat of "punishment" with a defensive strategy of "denial."

By adding strategic defenses to the deterrent mix, the 2001 NPR argued reliance on nuclear weapons could be reduced. This did not mean, however, it could be eliminated entirely.

Ultimately, an adversary decides what best deters him from a particular course of action. For some aggressors, the threat of denial may be less of a deterrent than the threat of punishment. But it is impossible to know with certainty what will work best in all circumstances and under all scenarios.

Therefore, a prudent strategic posture should seek to maximize the effectiveness of deterrence by maintaining the capability to both punish and deny. Like advanced conventional weapons, missile defenses can be an important adjunct to a deterrence policy that includes nuclear weapons, but defenses alone cannot be a substitute for them.

Robustness of the Nuclear Enterprise

Regardless of whether nuclear deterrence relies on offensive punitive measures, defensive systems or a combination of both, the capabilities to punish or deny must be viewed as credible to be effective. In large measure, the credibility of a nuclear deterrent arsenal lies not only in a willingness to employ it if necessary but in its perceived reliability, i.e., its ability to accomplish its mission if employed.

As the American nuclear arsenal continues to age and as the United States continues to abide by the unilateral nuclear test moratorium imposed nearly two decades ago, there has been a rising chorus of concern expressed over the continued reliability and efficacy of the U.S. nuclear weapons stockpile.

Some observers have suggested American decisions over nuclear weapons modernization and sustainment of the U.S. nuclear weapons enterprise have consequences for extended deterrence. While acknowledging the importance of the actual nuclear weapons in ensuring deterrence, the viability of the nuclear weapons complex is also seen as central to ensuring deterrence.

As two Los Alamos National Laboratory officials put it, "It is not only the capabilities of the forces themselves that assure allies and deter potential adversaries, it is also the capability to sustain and modernize these forces, while also demonstrating that ability to rapidly respond to new or emerging threats."[55] This suggests a failure to modernize and to adapt the U.S. nuclear infrastructure to contemporary security threats may cast doubt on the credibility of the U.S. extended deterrent.

A similar point was made in a recent study of extended deterrence published by the Center for Strategic and International Studies, which noted, "...perceived challenges to the credibility of U.S. deterrence capabilities in the long-term could have shorter-term consequences for assurance. Perceptions of the long-term viability of the U.S. stockpile and infrastructure and of the prospects for a national consensus on the future of the U.S. deterrent are salient factors affecting allies' confidence in the durability of the U.S. commitment. Allies are paying close attention to American nuclear policy debates. Arguments from both sides of the ideological divide can undermine assurance by skewing allies' perceptions of U.S. intentions and capabilities."[56]

There is also some evidence to suggest European allies view the continued viability of the overall U.S. nuclear enterprise to be more relevant to extended deterrence than either the levels or composition of U.S. nuclear forces.[57] Indeed, the significant decline in the U.S. strategic nuclear arsenal since the height of the Cold War, the removal of almost all non-strategic nuclear forces in Europe, the suspension of underground nuclear testing, the loss of nuclear design and engineering competence and talent in the national laboratories, the congressional prohibitions on nuclear modernization, the aversion to any "new" nuclear weapons, and the general lack of attention to nuclear matters are symptomatic of a trend that suggests a diminished overall utility for nuclear weapons. These developments may also suggest to allies there is reason for additional concern over the efficacy of America's extended deterrent.

The Impact of the Obama Administration's Nuclear Policies

The Obama administration has made the global elimination of nuclear weapons a key national security goal. In the same Prague speech in which he reiterated the importance of extending nuclear deterrence to U.S. allies, President Obama also declared the United States – as the only nation to have used nuclear weapons in anger – has a "moral responsibility" to work for their elimination. One year later, the President signed a "New START" treaty with Russia that would reduce the level of strategic nuclear offensive forces – both warheads and their associated delivery vehicles – to levels below those agreed to in the 2002 Strategic Offensive Reductions Treaty (a.k.a. Moscow Treaty). In addition, he committed the administration to pursuing significantly lower levels of nuclear forces with Russia as part of a follow-on arms control agenda.

Subsequent to the signing of "New START," the administration released its own Nuclear Posture Review. This new, congressionally-mandated NPR articulated the rationale and provided the underpinning for decisions that will affect the size and composition of the American nuclear arsenal over the next decade.

As expected, the 2010 NPR reaffirmed the importance of extended deterrence, noting, "The United States remains committed to providing a credible extended deterrence posture and capabilities."[58] And it suggested a role for U.S. central strategic forces in the extended deterrence mission. In particular, it stated "nuclear-capable bombers are important to extended deterrence of potential attacks on U.S. allies and partners. Unlike ICBMs and SLBMs, heavy bombers can be visibly forward deployed, thereby signaling U.S. resolve and commitment in crisis."[59]

The 2010 NPR's recognition of the role U.S. central strategic forces can play in extending deterrence to allies and strategic partners raises the prospect that the demands on U.S. nuclear forces may grow beyond the ability to meet them. This includes the possible extension of U.S. nuclear guarantees to countries that heretofore have remained outside the formal protection of the U.S. nuclear umbrella. In November 2008 it was reported the United States might extend an explicit nuclear guarantee to Israel in the event Iran acquired nuclear weapons.[60]

In July 2009, Secretary of State Hillary Clinton appeared to broaden that guarantee by stating the United States might consider extending "a defense umbrella" over the Middle East region as a deterrent to a nuclear-armed Iran.[61] Although she did not explicitly refer to an extended nuclear deterrent, the implication was clear and was seen as an attempt to dissuade countries in the region such as Saudi Arabia and other Gulf states from seeking nuclear weapons as a counterbalance to Iran's nuclear weapons potential.

It seems odd at a time when American nuclear forces decline the United States may consider extending its nuclear deterrent to other non-NATO states with no formal alliances with the United States. The prospect of a nuclear-armed Iran has raised concerns among Iran's immediate and regional neighbors. Countries like Saudi Arabia may feel threatened by a nuclear weapon in the hands of the leaders of the Islamic Republic. A heightened level of insecurity among countries in this volatile region may propel some toward acquisition of their own indigenous nuclear weapons capability. Such a prospect would not only be a setback to U.S. nonproliferation policy, but could ignite regional tensions that threaten American friends and interests.

Seeking an Appropriate Nuclear Threshold

Global strategic developments and U.S. policy may move the United States in a potentially risky direction. The proliferation to dangerous actors of nuclear weapons and technologies is creating conditions where U.S.

allies and friends place greater stresses on, and increasingly question the credibility of, American security guarantees. For example:

- Additional European states seek security against a resurgent Russia through NATO membership that conveys the protection of the American nuclear umbrella;
- U.S. allies in Asia are wary of China's nuclear modernization programs, as China increasingly invests in developing its regional nuclear capabilities;
- North Korea's development of nuclear weapons continues unabated, fueling concerns over how the United States will ensure regional security; and
- Iran's determined pursuit of nuclear weapons may lead Middle Eastern countries – some of whom do not even get along with one another – to quietly solicit American protection.

In all of these circumstances, the extended deterrent provided by U.S. nuclear weapons may assume greater prominence and importance. Yet, the U.S. nuclear arsenal has shrunk to its lowest levels since the Eisenhower Administration and is slated to be reduced even further consistent with an American policy whose stated objective is the complete elimination of nuclear weapons.

It may be difficult to convince those who today see their own security guaranteed by the American nuclear umbrella and those who believe their future security depends on tying themselves more tightly to the safety American nuclear weapons provide that the shift toward other measures of assurance (e.g., advanced conventional capabilities, missile defenses, etc.) is not merely an attempt to justify policy decisions made in the absence of allied consultation and without sufficient understanding of the allies' perceptions of their own vulnerabilities.

As the number of strategic nuclear weapons and delivery platforms declines, the burdens on the residual nuclear forces for implementing extended deterrence will rise. These burdens are unlikely to diminish given the strategic realities noted above. A decline in U.S. strategic nuclear forces may also impact the ability of the United States to forward deploy such forces to theaters of crisis.

For example, although it may be seen as useful to forward deploy strategic bombers or submarines to the Pacific region as a signal of U.S. resolve, pressures to reduce these forces significantly – or even to abandon the traditional Triad and move to a "Dyad" or "Monad" – may mitigate against such deployments and diminish the credibility of extended deterrence in the eyes of allies, friends, and adversaries.

In Europe, the future disposition of remaining U.S. nuclear forces will likely be addressed in NATO's revised Strategic Concept. Though NATO publics are generally receptive to the goal of nuclear disarmament, NATO governments may be increasingly reluctant to abandon those remaining U.S. nuclear weapons on European soil in light of the Alliance's enlargement, growing concerns over Russian policy and behavior directed against its neighbors to the West, and the traditionally anemic defense investment of individual NATO countries who prefer that the United States continue to assume the lion's share of the burden for their ultimate security. Having suffered the consequences of a failed conventional deterrence that led to two World Wars on the continent, Europeans may not yet be ready to abandon the implements of deterrence that have successfully prevented a third World War for more than six decades.

Any changes to America's strategic nuclear posture should not occur in the absence of detailed, robust consultations with allies and friends. Such consultations will be easier to implement with European allies, as mechanisms have long existed to involve NATO governments in the nuclear planning process. The modalities for adapting this consultative process to Asian allies and friends is more complex, however, as they have not been integrated into U.S. nuclear planning activities in the same way as NATO countries.

How Little Is Too Little?

Deterrence is an art, not a science. For these reasons, it is not possible to declare with certainty a particular level of nuclear weapons is sufficient to guarantee the effective functioning of deterrence – or extended deterrence – in all cases, at all times, against all possible adversaries. Indeed, what may be considered sufficient for deterrence today may prove insufficient tomorrow, as the strategic environment is highly dynamic.[62]

In the past, assurance considerations have factored into decisions regarding the overall size of the U.S. strategic nuclear arsenal. This was certainly true with respect to the strategic force reductions postulated in the 2001 NPR. Consistent with its guidance, U.S. strategic forces have been reduced to their lowest levels in many decades. Despite these reductions, however, the range of 1,700 – 2,200 operationally deployed strategic nuclear weapons subsequently codified in the Moscow Treaty was chosen as "an assurance-related requirement for U.S. nuclear forces that they be judged second to none."[63]

To date, there has been no explanation of whether or how the reduced nuclear force levels of 1,550 warheads on 700 deployed delivery systems agreed to in the April 2010 "New START" accord have incorporated the assurance requirements of allies. The reductions required by New START, coupled with the Obama administration's declared intent to reduce U.S. nuclear weapons even further on a path toward their eventual elimination, may complicate the long-term viability of extended deterrence. As one observer noted, "...as numbers go down extended deterrence concerns go up...."[64]

Assuming continued reductions in U.S. strategic nuclear forces, is there a threshold level beneath which the risks of aggression exceed the U.S.'s ability to deter it? There can be no definitive answer to this question, as the answer will vary depending upon the specifics of the scenario postulated. However, the ultimate answer to this question depends primarily on the perceptions of allies and adversaries, not on American calculations and theories.

Likewise, it is difficult to ascertain the appropriate level of forward-deployed non-strategic nuclear forces necessary to ensure the continued credibility of extended deterrence. For Europe, NATO's new Strategic Concept will need to address this in the context of shifting perceptions of threats, Alliance membership changes, and unique national circumstances.[65]

In some cases, allies may feel extending a purely defensive umbrella (e.g., through deployment of active missile defenses on their territory), hosting the deployment of American troops, or other measures may provide sufficient deterrence against aggression from hostile neighbors or powers.

Yet this is an untestable proposition. Deterrence may succeed, but it is not possible to know with absolute certainty what accounted for its success. On the other hand, if it fails we will know with certainty that the measures we relied upon for it to work were insufficient.

Preserving the credibility of U.S. security guarantees will always be challenging. Some of the difficulties were noted by two Lithuanian analysts who argued, "...security guarantees from third nations always suffer from credibility problem (sic.). History provides many examples when extended deterrence fails (e.g. British and French security guarantees did not deter Germany from attacking Poland in 1939). Extended *nuclear* deterrence is even more difficult to implement. For the United States, the United Kingdom or France to prove to other nations that they are ready to risk nuclear holocaust for the sake of the Baltic states is extremely difficult."[66]

Indeed, on whose behalf the United States should risk "nuclear holocaust" is a matter of considerable dispute. Some argue the U.S. nuclear umbrella should not be extended to countries that do not share fundamental values with the United States. Others believe American nuclear security guarantees should only be extended to countries whose security is considered absolutely vital to U.S. survival.

If, how and to whom the United States should extend additional nuclear guarantees should be carefully considered. As the nuclear umbrella shrinks, and the number of countries seeking protection under it grows, the implications for credible extended deterrence loom large. The benefits for deterrence must be balanced against the potential risks to the United States should it fail. This is not an easy task, and there are no simple answers. But decisions on whether to extend U.S. nuclear deterrence to other states should be decided on a case-by-case basis, taking a range of country-unique and alliance-specific military, political, diplomatic, and other variables into account.

Despite these challenges, it is clear from the statements of some allies that reliance on the U.S. extended deterrent is more important than ever, especially in light of changes in the strategic environment they perceive as directly threatening their security. It is also evident additional reductions to U.S. nuclear forces may have negative consequences for the ability to assure allies that the United States is unwavering in its commitment to their security.

Conclusions

Extended nuclear deterrence has a long and relatively successful history. But most of that history was written during the Cold War under strategic circumstances that have been fundamentally altered. The demise of the Soviet Union, the rise of other nuclear armed states, the proliferation of nuclear threats, the restructuring of alliance relationships, and continued downward pressures on nuclear weapons and force levels suggest that extended deterrence, to be effective, must operate in new and challenging conditions unlike in the past.

Despite this new strategic environment, extended deterrence remains an important element of U.S. security strategy. Its continued relevance has been recognized by the Obama administration through the statements of senior spokespersons like the Secretary of State and Secretary of Defense and including the President himself. It has also been reaffirmed in the 2010 NPR.

Yet, at the same time, the credibility of the U.S. nuclear umbrella may be strained as a result of the desire to rid the world of those weapons upon which it is based. Simultaneously, the number of states seeking or obtaining the protection offered by the U.S. extended deterrent may increase as the size of U.S. nuclear forces providing that extended deterrent diminishes.

Determinations of the appropriate size and composition of the U.S. nuclear arsenal must necessarily reflect the varied requirements of extended deterrence and assurance. Given the emergence of new threats, different regional security environments, and continuing challenges to reliance on nuclear weapons for deterrence purposes, it is not possible to posit with certainty a static level of nuclear forces that can simultaneously accomplish all necessary missions. However, it does appear plausible that additional U.S. nuclear force reductions will complicate achieving these missions. For this reason, future decisions regarding the size and composition of U.S. nuclear forces should be informed by comprehensive consultations with friends and allies whose security depends on the viability of the U.S. nuclear deterrent.

Integrating allies into the formal consultative process on these issues may also have the attendant benefit of providing a form of reassurance. In the absence of such consultations, U.S. policies intended to strengthen deterrence may actually hasten its failure. The consequences of such could be unprecedented and catastrophic for all.

Notes

[1] For a more detailed examination of options for providing assurance, see "Nuclear Guarantees, Extended Deterrence, and the Assurance of Allies," *Planning the Future U.S. Nuclear Force: Volume II: Foundation Report,* National Institute for Public Policy (October 2009), 55-58.

[2] This notion of "existential deterrence" was popularized by McGeorge Bundy in the 1980s and reflected a belief that the destructive power of nuclear weapons made them militarily useless and the possession of merely a handful of them would be a sufficient deterrent to any potential aggressor.

[3] Remarks by President Barak Obama, Hradcany Square, Prague, Czech Republic (April 5, 2009).

[4] See Josiane Gabel, "The Role of U.S. Nuclear Weapons after September 11," *The Washington Quarterly*, Volume 28:1 (Winter 2004-2005), 193.

[5] Ibid., 193-194. This includes Kurt M. Campbell, Robert J. Einhorn, and Mitchell B. Reiss, eds., *The Nuclear Tipping Point: Why States Reconsider Their Nuclear Choices*, Brookings Institution, Washington, D.C., (2004).

[6] U.S. Department of State International Security Advisory Board, *Report on Discouraging a Cascade of Nuclear Weapons States* (Oct. 19, 2007), 23.

[7] Ibid., 15.

[8] Secretary of Defense Robert M. Gates, "Nuclear Weapons and Deterrence in the 21st Century," speech before the Carnegie Endowment for International Peace (Oct. 28, 2008).

[9] William J. Perry, James R. Schlesinger, et. al., *America's Strategic Posture: The Final Report of the Congressional Commission on the Strategic Posture of the United States,* Washington, DC, U.S. Institute of Peace Press (2009), xvii.

[10] "The Alliance's Strategic Concept," approved by the Heads of State and Government participating in the meeting of the North Atlantic Council in Washington D.C., (April 23-24,1999), http://www.nato.int/cps/en/natolive/official_texts_27433.htm.

[11] For an excellent discussion of this process as it relates to extended deterrence, see David Yost, "Assurance and U.S. Extended Deterrence in NATO," *International Affairs*, volume 85:4 (2009), 755-780.

[12] General Dr. Klaus Naumann, General John Shalikashvili, Field Marshal The Lord Inge, Admiral Jacques Lanxade, and General Henk van den Breemen, *Towards a Grand Strategy for an Uncertain World: Renewing Transatlantic Partnership*, Noaber Foundation, Lunteren, the Netherlands (2007), 94.

[13] Cited by James L. Schoff, in "Does the Nonproliferation Tail Wag the Deterrence Dog?," *PacNet*, Pacific Forum CSIS, Number 9 (Feb. 5, 2009).

[14] Ibid.

[15] Recounted in Keith Payne, "On Nuclear Deterrence and Assurance," *Strategic Studies Quarterly* (spring 2009), 54-55.

[16] "Joint Vision for the Alliance of the United States of America and the Republic of Korea," Office of the Press Secretary, The White House (June 16, 2009).

[17] Speech by Secretary of Defense Robert M. Gates, Yongsan Garrison, Seoul, Republic of Korea (Oct. 21, 2009).

[18] For example, see Russian Prime Minister Vladimir Putin's statement in "Russia 'Must Counter U.S. Defenses'," BBC News (Dec. 29, 2009),
http://news.bbc.co.uk/2/hi/europe/8433352.stm.

[19] See, for example, Valentina Pop, "Ukraine Drops NATO Membership Bid," http://euobserver.com/13/30212.

[20] This assurance is often referred to as the "three no's" and reflects NATO's earlier commitment to Russia that it has "no intention, no plan, and no reason to deploy nuclear weapons on the territory of new members." See the Founding Act on Mutual Reductions, Cooperation and Security Between NATO and the Russian Federation, Paris, France (May 27, 1997).

[21] Yomiuri, "North Korea's Nuclear Threat: Reinforcing Alliance With U.S. Helps Bolster Nuclear Deterrence," JPP20070323969090 Tokyo *The Daily Yomiuri*, (Internet version-WWW) in English (March 24, 2007), cited in "Nuclear Guarantees, Extended Deterrence, and the Assurance of Allies," *Planning the Future U.S. Nuclear Force: Volume II: Foundation Report,* op. cit., 48.

[22] See comments of Yukio Satoh, "Are the Requirements for Extended Deterrence Changing," Panel Discussion at Carnegie Endowment International Nonproliferation Conference (April 6, 2009).

[23] Joint Statement of the U.S.-Japan Security Consultative Committee (May 1, 2007), http://tokyo.usembassy.gov/e/p/tp-20070502-77.html.

[24] Satoh comments, op. cit.

[25] Ibid.

[26] Ibid.

[27] Joseph F. Pilat, "Nonproliferation, Arms Control and Disarmament, and Extended Deterrence in the New Security Environment," *Strategic Insights*, Volume VIII, Issue 4 (September 2009).

[28] Vaidotas Urbelis and Kestutis Paulauskas, "NATO's Deterrence Policy – Time for Change?," *Baltic Security and Defense Review*, Volume 10 (2008), 87.

[29] "The Alliance's Strategic Concept," op. cit.

[30] James R. Schlesinger, et. al., *Report of the Secretary of Defense Task Force on DoD Nuclear Weapons Management, Phase II: Review of the DoD Nuclear Mission* (December 2008), 14-15, 59-60.

[31] Strategic Posture Commission Final Report, op. cit., 13.

[32] Ibid., 20.

[33] See, for example, Alexandra Bell's report, "Turkey's Nuclear Crossroads," http://www.good.is/post/turkeys-nuclear-crossroads/, posted on Aug. 25, 2009. This account is also referenced in Miles A. Pomper, William Potter, and Nikolai Sokov, *Reducing and Regulating Tactical (Nonstrategic) Nuclear Weapons in Europe,* Monterey Institute of International Studies, (December 2009), 22. In addition, a February 2008 report to the Senate Foreign Relations Committee cited a meeting with Turkish politicians who

argued that without strong American commitments to Turkey's security, the development by Iran of a nuclear weapons capability would make it "compulsory" for Turkey to follow suit. See *Chain Reaction: Avoiding a Nuclear Arms Race in the Middle East*, Report to the Committee on Foreign Relations, United States Senate, (February 2008), 41.

[34] Strategic Posture Commission Final Report, op. cit, 26.

[35] See "Nuclear Guarantees, Extended Deterrence, and the Assurance of Allies," in *Planning the Future U.S. Nuclear Force, Volume II: Foundation Report*, op. cit., 55.

[36] Strategic Posture Commission Final Report, op. cit, 20-21.

[37] James M. Acton, "Extended Deterrence and Communicating Resolve," *Strategic Insights,* Volume VIII, Issue 5 (December 2009).

[38] Hans M. Kristensen, "Japan, TLAM-N, and Extended Deterrence," Federation of Atomic Scientists Strategic Security Blog (July 2, 2009),
http://www.fas.org/blog/ssp/2009/07/tlam.php.

[39] Reported in Jeffrey Lewis, "Japan Hates TLAM-N,"
http://www.armscontrolwonk.com/2601/japan-hates-tlam-n.

[40] U.S. Department of Defense, *Nuclear Posture Review Report* (April 2010), 28.

[41] Ibid., 28.

[42] Ibid., 27.

[43] Ibid., 32.

[44] For example, as Jeffrey Lewis has argued: "Would you do something dumb just because the Japanese asked you to? Of course not. That some Japanese officials irrationally focus on irrelevant capabilities to measure our commitment to Japan is a symptom of a much bigger problem that needs to be addressed with more than hardware." See "Japan ♥ TLAM-N," http://www.armscontrolwonk.com/2284/japan-tlamn.

[45] A discussion of this point can be found in "Nuclear Guarantees, Extended Deterrence, and the Assurance of Allies," *Planning the Future U.S. Nuclear Force: Volume II: Foundation Report,* op. cit., 64.

[46] *The Future of the United Kingdom's Future Deterrent*, Cm6994, (December 2006).

[47] See The Road to 2010: Addressing the Nuclear Question in the Twenty First Century, U.K. Cabinet Office (July 2009), 5.

[48] Ibid., 38-39.

[49] Speech by Jacques Chirac, President of the French Republic, to The Strategic Air and Maritime Forces at Landivisiau / L'Ile Longue (Jan.19, 2006).

[50] For example, former Defense Minister of the Federal Republic of Germany Manfred Wörner stated in 1985, "France's nuclear capability is insufficient to protect the Federal Republic. We will have to continue to rely on the American nuclear umbrella." Cited in Yost, op. cit., 761.

[51] See Mark Schneider, "The Future of the U.S. Nuclear Deterrent," *Comparative Strategy,* Volume 27 (2008), 345-360.

[52] Austin Long, *Deterrence From Cold War to Long War: Lessons from Six Decades of RAND Research* (2008), 63.

[53] Pilat, op. cit.

[54] Testimony of General Kevin Chilton, Commander, U.S. Strategic Command, before the Strategic Forces Subcommittee of the House Committee on Armed Services (March 16, 2010).

[55] Joseph C. Martz and Jonathan S. Ventura, "Nuclear Deterrence in the 21st Century: The Role of Science and Engineering," a paper produced by the Principal Associate Directorate for Nuclear Weapons, Los Alamos National Laboratory, LA-UR-08-05019 (2008)

[56] Clark A. Murdock, et. al., *Exploring the Nuclear Posture Implications of Extended Deterrence and Assurance: Workshop Proceeding and Key Takeaways*, Defense and National Security Group, Center for Strategic and International Studies, Washington, D.C., (November 2009), 2.

[57] For a discussion of this point, see David Yost, op. cit, 755-780.

[58] U.S. Department of Defense, *Nuclear Posture Review Report,* op. cit., 28.

[59] Ibid., 24.

[60] Aluf Benn, "Obama's Atomic Umbrella: U.S. Nuclear Strike if Iran Nukes Israel," *Haaretz* (Nov. 12, 2008).

[61] For an interesting perspective on this statement and an analysis of U.S. efforts to extend deterrence to Middle East states, see James A. Russell, "Extended Deterrence, Security Guarantees, and Nuclear Weapons: U.S. Strategic and Policy Conundrums in the Gulf," *Strategic Insights*, Volume 8, Issue 5 (December 2009), http://www.nps.edu/Academics/centers/ccc/publications/OnlineJournal/2009/Dec/russell Dec09.pdf.

[62] Unlike previous arms control treaties that established precise numerical ceilings on nuclear force levels, the 2002 Moscow Treaty allowed both the United States and Russia to maintain a range of between 1,700 and 2,200 operationally deployed strategic nuclear weapons. This flexibility was arguably more appropriate and relevant to the variable and evolving requirements of deterrence, including extended deterrence.

[63] Responses by Secretary of Defense Donald H. Rumsfeld and General Richard B. Myers to questions submitted for the record by the Senate Foreign Relations Committee in *Treaty on Strategic Offensive Reduction: The Moscow Treaty*, S. Hrg. 107-622, 107th Congress, Second Session, GPO, Washington, D.C., (2002), http://www.gpo.gov/fdsys/pkg/CHRG-107shrg622/pdf/CHRG-107shrg622.pdf.

[64] Chris Jones, "The Shades of Extended Deterrence," Center for Strategic and International Studies (Jan. 4, 2010), http://csis.org/blog/shades-extended-deterrence.

[65] As one analyst has noted, "Because NATO has not identified targets for its nuclear forces since the 1990s, it is a challenge to specify and analyze the 1999 Strategic Concept's requirement for 'adequate nuclear forces in Europe'…. The minimum level may derive more from judgments about an appropriate level of risk- and responsibility-sharing among allies, and about what is necessary to demonstrate continuing U.S. engagement and commitment, than from a quantitative analysis of potential contingencies." Yost, op. cit., 758.

[66] Urbelis and Paulauskas, op. cit., 99.

CHAPTER 10

Deterrence Issues in a World of Very Few Or Zero Nuclear Weapons

Barry Blechman

After the astounding power of nuclear weapons was unveiled at Hiroshima and Nagasaki, a proposal to transfer control of atomic energy to a U.N. Atomic Energy Commission was backed by both the United States and Soviet Union in late 1945. The Truman administration then offered the Acheson-Lilienthal Plan in March 1946 that proposed all worldwide fissile material would be owned by an international agency to parcel out small amounts to states for the peaceful uses of atomic energy. This initial effort failed, and the nuclear arms race of the Cold War ensued.

However, the dangers of nuclear war kept alive the idea of putting the nuclear genie back into the bottle. In 1958 the U.N. Disarmament Committee discussed a treaty to control the nuclear arms race and move toward total elimination. By 1968 a multilateral treaty on the Non-Proliferation of Nuclear Weapons (NPT) had been negotiated and was open for signature, and the NPT came into force on March 5, 1970. Currently, 189 states are party to the treaty. Article VI of the NPT pledges all nuclear-armed state parties to pursue negotiations toward a world free of nuclear weapons.

In the 40 years since the NPT went into effect, the two nuclear superpowers have progressively reduced the size of their arsenals, thereby making some Article VI progress, but the continuing spread of nuclear technologies (witness Pakistan, India, Israel, Iran, North Korea, etc.) and repeated terrorist attacks on major world cities have led many current and former high-level national security officials to advocate a new dedication to achieving the world-wide elimination of nuclear weapons.

Such a radical departure from current policies would no doubt have profound political and military consequences and, thus, raises many questions. For example, what would be the consequences of such a development for the dynamics of deterrence and the risk of nuclear or conventional war? Opponents of radical reductions in nuclear arsenals predict they would provide increased incentives for states to strike first in the event of crises, as well as increase the likelihood of conventional wars. Those who favor elimination predict the opposite, arguing radical reductions in nuclear arsenals would reinforce trends toward more positive political relations, and thus reduce the risk of war.

Deterrence doctrine has a strong theoretical tradition, but only limited efforts document the phenomenon empirically. As a consequence, analyses of factors influencing deterrence in a hypothetical future will be strongly colored by the individual analyst's understanding of how it operated during the Cold War and how it works in the current multi-polar international system.

It is likely agreement to reduce nuclear arsenals to very low numbers would not occur in a political vacuum, but could only result from the emergence of a consensus in a world of improving political relations among the great powers that nuclear deterrence was incapable of preventing nuclear catastrophes. Presuming such a political context, consider two scenarios, one in which no nation has more than 100 weapons, and a second scenario in which all nuclear weapons had been eliminated. Analysis of both indicates the former might pose a greater risk of strategic instability.

With small arsenals, the key deterrent factors would be the survivability of those weapons which remain and the presence or absence of effective defenses. In the scenario envisioning the total elimination of nuclear weapons, it appears that the likelihood of great power conventional wars would not increase, even if a revisionist leadership emerged in one of the great powers, so long as the other great powers responded forcefully to any early diplomatic or military forays. In a world of zero nuclear weapons, the greater risk to deterrence would stem from the potential for one nation to break-out of the treaty and reveal a clandestine cache or start to rebuild its nuclear arsenal, steps that would trigger nuclear rebuilding efforts by other great powers and the political instabilities, tensions and risk of war that would accompany a renewed arms race.

Introduction: Deterrence and the Context of Nuclear Disarmament

Humanity has lived with the possibility of millions of deaths and massive destruction resulting from nuclear war for more than 65 years. For many, this prospect is terrifying and unacceptable. They advocate the progressive reduction and eventual elimination of these weapons of mass destruction. Indeed, on Sept. 24, 2009, the leaders of the 15 members of the United Nations Security Council, including the permanent members, the first five states to possess nuclear weapons, unanimously approved a resolution committing each of their governments to "create the conditions for a world without nuclear weapons, in accordance with the goals of the Treaty on the Non-Proliferation of Nuclear Weapons (NPT), in a way that promotes international stability, and based on the principle of undiminished security for all."[1]

Many others, however, while recognizing the risks implicit in their continuing existence, believe nuclear weapons have served the world well during these 65 years and should be preserved. There have been no wars among the great powers since 1945, they point out, asserting that fear of unleashing nuclear conflict induced U.S. and Soviet leaders to behave cautiously during the crises of the Cold War, and to find ways to resolve conflicts without bloodshed. From this perspective, the maintenance of nuclear arsenals has *deterred* major wars, both nuclear and conventional. For those holding this view, the possibility of nuclear disarmament raises the concern the elimination of nuclear threats could lead to more adventurous policies by states with aggressive agendas or historical grievances, thereby renewing the risk of major world wars.[2]

Whether or not nuclear weapons kept the peace over the past 65 years may not be knowable. While it is certainly true there have not been shooting wars among the great powers (omitting brief border skirmishes between China and the U.S.S.R.), one cannot prove war would have occurred had nuclear weapons been absent. One can only say with certainty nuclear deterrence did not fail.

A war between the Soviet Union and the United States and its West European allies may have been possible after 1945 and seemed dangerously close during the 1948, 1955, and 1961 Berlin Crises and 1962 Cuban

Missile Crisis. In all cases, both sides found ways to retreat from the precipice. Was this the result of their fear of escalation to nuclear war? Perhaps. However, it is not evident Soviet leaders ever had an appetite for a new war in Europe after 1945, given they had suffered enormous losses in manpower and industry during both world wars and had already achieved their long-sought security zone on the Soviet Union's western border through the occupation of Eastern Europe. In short, there might not have been a new great power conflict after 1945 whether or not nuclear weapons had ever been invented.

In addition, nuclear weapons clearly have not been able to deter all wars, even wars involving nuclear-armed states. North Korea and China fought the nuclear-armed United States in the 1950s, as did North Vietnam in the 1960/70s. Israeli nuclear weapons did not deter Egypt and Syria from attacking in 1973 nor prevent Iraq from firing missiles at Israeli cities during the 1991 Gulf War. Nor did British nuclear weapons deter Argentina from attacking the United Kingdom's Falkland Islands in 1982. Russian nuclear weapons were no help against the Mujahedin in Afghanistan in the 1980s, and China's nuclear weapons did not deter Vietnam from attacking China's ally, Cambodia, in 1979 and then tangling successfully with China's own armies.

Finally, and perhaps of greatest importance today, nuclear weapons have proven irrelevant in preventing deadly terrorist attacks against the capital cities of nuclear-armed Russia (1996 and later years), United States (2001), United Kingdom (2005), India (2008), and Pakistan (2008 and continuing).

Thus, it appears nuclear deterrence is an uncertain phenomenon, both historically and in today's world, one in which nine countries possess a total of more than 20,000 nuclear weapons.[3] The subject of this chapter must therefore be approached with humility and can only be discussed in general terms. Appropriately, the task is therefore to describe the broad factors that will influence the effectiveness of deterrence in a future world in which nuclear arsenals had been reduced to very low levels and, subsequently, eliminated. As different questions are raised in the two stages of this disarmament process, this analysis focuses on: (a) a world in which no nation has more than 100 weapons; and (b) a world in which all nuclear weapons have been eliminated.

Before turning to these scenarios, it is important to keep in mind the political context that likely would have emerged prior to, and as a consequence of, such deep cuts in nuclear arsenals. Arms limitation agreements historically have reflected underlying political relationships, as well as judgments about the military utility of certain types or numbers of weapons.

The first U.S.-Soviet arms control agreements -- the 1972 ABM Treaty banning strategic missile defenses and the Interim Agreement on Strategic Offensive Arms Limitations -- were negotiated following the achievement of an understanding between President Richard Nixon and Soviet leader Leonid Brezhnev of the desirability of reducing tensions between the two superpowers (détente), as well as the two sides' military leaders understanding that existing missile defense technologies could be easily overcome by increases to the other side's offensive capabilities.

In such circumstances, it made sense to agree to place extremely tight mutual limits on missile defenses and also to limit offensive weapons, thereby saving both nations expenditures on weapons that would have served no purpose and reinforcing their political détente.[4]

Similarly, the 1972 multinational agreement banning biological weapons and the 1993 multinational agreement banning lethal chemical weapons were reflections of judgments that these types of weapons were ineffective militarily.[5]

The successful 2010 completion of U.S.-Russian negotiations for a follow-on strategic arms treaty (New START), allows each to have 1,550 operational strategic nuclear warheads and additional thousands of shorter range and reserve warheads.[6] France, China and the UK are estimated to have 300, 240 and 225 total warheads, respectively; no other country is believed to have more than 200 nuclear warheads.[7]

For the United States and Russia to have agreed to reduce their arsenals to the low levels assumed in this chapter, a significant improvement in relations must have occurred. Most importantly, the two great nuclear powers would have had to have reached an understanding concerning the security architecture governing Europe.

Simply put, the two nations would never agree to eliminate virtually all nuclear weapons if either Russia still feared NATO expansion or if the United States and its allies were still concerned Russia sought to reassert influence over former Soviet Union or Warsaw Pact countries, or both.

Similarly, a U.S.-Russian agreement to reduce their arsenals to levels close to those maintained by China would require a significant improvement in Sino-Russian and Sino-U.S. relations, such that residual suspicions China might harbor long-term, aggressive aims had become irrelevant. Similar observations could be made about other nuclear weapon states.

Of course, international relationships could always deteriorate following the achievement of nuclear disarmament, hence our need to examine questions of deterrence under such circumstances. But, entering the discussion, one should presume that at least for a time, the nuclear powers had been able to reach mutual accommodations and achieve a level of political comity not yet apparent on the world stage.

For the purposes of this discussion, it should also be assumed the move toward small nuclear arsenals had been accomplished in the context of the establishment of a disarmament regime which provided effective governance, verification and enforcement of the agreed-upon steps. If countries were uncertain about whether or not other signatories cheated on the disarmament treaty, it would introduce an additional set of deterrence issues arising from this uncertainty.

To simplify the discussion, it is assumed for the purposes of this analysis, the regime provides comprehensive and intrusive governance, verification and enforcement provisions, and the disarmament process had proceeded over a sufficiently long period of time (decades), that the signatories had gained confidence that each of them, and all other states, were abiding by the stated rules.[8]

Deterrence of Great Power Conflicts at Low Levels of Nuclear Weapons

The primary deterrence issue to be addressed in a scenario envisioning the deep reduction of all states' nuclear arsenals is whether the small size of a country's offensive arsenal might tempt an adversary to strike first in the event of imminent war, believing it could either completely disarm the adversary or it could destroy enough of the adversary's offensive nuclear weapons as to minimize the damage from a retaliatory strike.

If one or more of the nuclear weapon states possessed such a disarming capability vis-à-vis a potential adversary, and if political relations deteriorated such that two or more nations slid into crisis, the deterrence of war could be weakened. A world of small nuclear arsenals, in this case, might be more dangerous than the world we live in today.

The ability of states to avoid this problem would depend on several factors including: (1) the survivability of countries' remaining offensive weapons; (2) whether defenses existed and, if so, how capable they might be; and (3) the alert status of nations' nuclear forces. Now let us examine each of these factors in turn.

Survivability: In this scenario, each nuclear weapon state could distribute its 100 nuclear weapons among launch platforms in any manner it chose. Each nation would be guided by history, technological prowess relative to potential rivals and geographical circumstances, but also would be compelled to consider the fact that more survivable forces are likely to be more costly than less survivable forces.

Take Russia, for example, which tends to favor land-based missiles over submarine-launched missiles or bomber weapons. Russia has mastered advanced missile and missile warhead technologies, has large expanses upon which to deploy mobile land-based missiles, and fears U.S. anti-submarine warfare capabilities may threaten its sea-based missiles. As a result, if only permitted 100 warheads, Russia likely would place them all on land-based, mobile missiles and would have to decide how many warheads to place on each missile.

The most survivable force would be composed of 100 missiles, each carrying one warhead. Such a force could not be attacked successfully by any other nation; no other nation would have more than 100 missiles, and no missile could be assumed to be 100 percent effective, particularly against mobile platforms.

The question then would be whether the attacking state's defenses would be capable of destroying whatever number of Russia's 100 missiles survived any preemptive attack. Given we are discussing a situation many years in the future, it is impossible to know how capable offensive missiles might be at that time when targeted against mobile land-based missiles, nor how effective missile defenses might have become.

The current Russian ICBM force tends to favor missiles with multiple warheads and Russian arms control negotiators have insisted on warhead and launcher limits in the New START Treaty that went into effect in 2011 that would favor continuing to build this type of weapon system.

Russia has limited resources and wide-ranging needs for military modernization and thus favors a posture permitting it to acquire and operate fewer missiles, each of which can deliver multiple warheads. Even in a situation in which it were permitted to deploy only 100 warheads, given that such an agreement would presume a world of greatly reduced political pressures and thus the perception of a reduced possibility of a first-strike, Russia might be tempted to save money by deploying more than one warhead on fewer than 100 missiles. At an extreme, for example, Russian leaders could put 10 warheads on 10 missiles, making their force far less expensive – if more vulnerable to attack. Fifty missiles with two warheads each might be a more likely posture.

The United States, on the other hand, while retaining land-based missiles, has tended to put greater emphasis on bombers and submarine-launched missiles. This reflects the United States' geographic situation and seagoing tradition, as well as the unique advantages attributed to each leg of the so-called "triad" of land-based missiles, sea-based missiles and bombers. With only 100 weapons, you would expect the United States to probably reduce its forces to only two components, or even to only one type of basing mode.

Deploying one missile with one warhead on each of 100 submarines is highly unlikely, given the cost of submarines, but you could imagine a U.S. force of 50 silo-based (fixed) land-based missiles with one warhead each and three submarines with the remaining warheads distributed among them.

Again, given we are speculating about capabilities some decades in the future, it is impossible to know whether potential rivals would have developed potent anti-submarine capabilities, but even if there were breakthroughs in anti-submarine technologies, such a U. S. force would likely be relatively survivable, as the 50 U.S. land-based missiles would require most of an opponent's 100 weapons to be destroyed with high confidence. Again, much would depend on the capabilities of each nation's offensive and defensive capabilities.

Defenses

As should be evident from the preceding discussion, the effectiveness of deterrence in a world of very small nuclear arsenals would depend in part on each nuclear power's defensive capabilities--not only its capabilities to defend against missiles, but also anti-submarine defenses, anti-aircraft defenses, and even homeland defenses against unconventional weapon deliveries (e.g., in shipping containers) would be a factor in determining deterrent potential.

In a world of small nuclear arsenals, deterrence would be strengthened if all defenses, or even certain kinds of defenses, could be prohibited. If such prohibitions were feasible, all nuclear weapon states would have the potential to deploy their 100 warheads in a manner such that they could not all be destroyed in a first-strike and thus would retain the ability to launch a retaliatory strike and exact considerable damage. To the degree there is merit to deterrence theory, this guaranteed retaliatory capability should thus deter any foe from attacking first

The problem is systems intended to defend against military platforms armed with nuclear weapons likely could not be distinguished from systems intended to defend against tactical, conventionally-armed weapons. Thus, navies will develop and deploy anti-submarine technologies in order to defend warships from opposing submarines, as air forces will develop and deploy means of protecting tactical aircraft from surface-to-air missiles. Even tactical missile defenses – for naval forces or ground forces - increasingly will integrate with satellite-based detection and tracking systems, and thus gain the potential for defense against strategic nuclear attacks.

Indeed, looking several decades into the future, many types of defensive systems might be entirely space-based, or utilize laser technology on various platforms, that would make distinguishing between tactical and strategic defenses virtually impossible. Assuming the reduction in nuclear arsenals had not taken place in the context of a broader disarmament agreement, it is very difficult to imagine nations limiting tactical defenses and, therefore, difficult to conceive of limitations on strategic defenses as effective and verifiable.[9]

Thus, in all likelihood, in a world of small nuclear arsenals, to maintain an effective deterrent, nations would have to depend on the capability of the vast preponderance of their small force to survive a preemptive attack, thus making it more likely the survivors would penetrate the attacker's defenses. This suggests nuclear weapon states must be willing to spend more per warhead than they do currently; avoiding placing several of their small number of warheads in single targets (e.g., multiple warheads on a single missile or multiple missiles on a single submarine).

It also suggests that to strengthen deterrence, nuclear weapon states should be willing to diversify their force to two or more launch modes, thus forcing potential adversaries to develop multiple forms of defenses if they seek a first-strike capability. Finally, it suggests nuclear weapon states should invest in continuing advances in offensive weaponry, enabling them to stay ahead of developments in defenses.

While this picture of a continuing offense/defense competition suggests an unstable deterrent picture at a time of small nuclear arsenals, several ameliorating circumstances should be kept in mind. First, as has been mentioned, the agreement to move to small arsenals could only take place within a political context in which the possibility of acute crises and, therefore, first-strike temptations, would be very low; in all likelihood, these dangers would never arise. Second, given that offensive forces would be small, the cost of maintaining survivable offenses capable of penetrating an opponent's defenses would likely not be great.

Historically, it has always been easier for offenses to stay ahead of defenses. And, finally, the existence of defenses would have positive political effects, providing reassurances to citizens concerned about cheating on the agreement, or accidental launches, or irrational leaders. Indeed, the development and deployment of defenses would almost certainly be a political requirement for the United States, at least, to agree to move to very small nuclear arsenals.

Alert status: Many analysts have suggested one way to reduce the risk of nuclear war and stabilize deterrence would be to reduce the alert status of nuclear forces.[10] Currently, Russian and U.S. missiles can be launched within minutes of a command to do so; other nuclear weapon states maintain their forces in a more relaxed day-to-day posture.

Given the potential, if remote, possibility of deterrence instability when states deploy only small nuclear forces, the argument for reducing the forces' alert level becomes more compelling. Presuming measures could be devised to ensure the steps to reduce nuclear forces' alert status could not be reversed quickly and would be readily apparent to other nations' intelligence systems, such means would add time before a crisis could deteriorate into an attempted first-strike, permitting negotiations to head off the conflict. More importantly, assuming they had confidence in the alert-status verification methods put in place, it would add to the nations' confidence that their retaliatory forces were secure, thus strengthening mutual deterrence.

The downside, of course, is if a crisis occurred and a nation acted to increase its forces' alert level – perhaps to signal seriousness to the adversary or because of fear the adversary was about to do the same – a race to increase readiness could ensue, worsening the crisis and, perhaps, leading nations to conclude that war was inevitable and, therefore, they had better strike first. This type of dilemma recurs as well in the zero weapons scenario to be analyzed next. In short, measures designed to increase the stability of deterrence could have the potential, if reversed, to aggravate an already bad situation. In implementing de-alerting measures, nations would have to judge that the immediate, positive effect on deterrence would be well worth the remote risk that a decision to re-alert could worsen some future, unknown and unexpected crisis.

Deterrence of Aggressive, Smaller Nations at Low Levels of Nuclear Weapons

Rogue states with smaller nuclear arsenals should not be an issue, even if such states had acquired a very small number of nuclear weapons (e.g., 10 or so). Presumably, the nuclear disarmament regime would not prevent the great powers from maintaining very capable conventionally armed forces. If the smaller state was not nuclear armed, such conventional forces should be adequate to either deter or, if necessary, defeat the aggression, especially if several of the larger states acted in concert.

If the smaller state had acquired a very small number of nuclear weapons, the 100 weapons retained by the larger states should be sufficient to deter any aggression or, if necessary, deter nuclear attacks while conventional forces defeated the aggressor. Again, collective military action would be even more effective in meeting this threat.

If the smaller power was to continue to build its nuclear arsenal and was unwilling to join the nuclear limitation regime, then larger powers could act either singly or collectively to compel either disarmament or acceptance of the same limitations each had already accepted. In the latter case, the great powers' superior conventional forces would ensure the deterrence of aggressive actions with conventional forces, while small, but more maneuverable, nuclear forces deterred against nuclear threats, albeit with the same uncertainties concerning survivability and defenses previously described.

If it were not possible for the great powers to either prevent the smaller power from obtaining nuclear weapons militarily or to agree to adhere to the same limitation on the size of its forces as they had accepted, then they presumably would rethink their previous agreement to restrict forces and begin to build larger arsenals (see the section on "break-out" below).

Deterrence in a World of Zero Nuclear Weapons

Presuming the total disarmament treaty had effective verification provisions and the signatories had gained confidence over the decades required to implement the treaty that all nations adhered to its provisions, the major deterrent issue would be whether or not such circumstances would make conventional wars more likely. The question is not really relevant for either internal conflicts (like the ongoing struggles in Somalia), or cross-border wars involving smaller powers (such as Saddam Hussein's occupation of Kuwait in 1991).

During the 65 years of the nuclear era, there have been at least 200 such military conflicts.[11] Clearly, nuclear weapons have not deterred such wars. As such, the absence of nuclear weapons should have no effect on frequency or lethality although, some would argue, the great powers' decision to eliminate nuclear weapons would both reflect and reinforce an era of greater international cooperation in which it might be easier for all nations to cooperate to help resolve the civil and international disputes that currently lead to such military conflicts.

The more difficult question is the effect of eliminating nuclear weapons, if any, on the deterrence of wars among the great powers. The introduction to this chapter noted that it was uncertain whether nuclear weapons had prevented great power conflicts during the Cold War. In addition, it should be assumed the great powers would not have agreed to eliminate nuclear weapons unless they had reached accommodations on central issues among themselves and had projected an era of lasting peace going forward.

Still, history is full of surprises. As former Secretary of Defense Donald Rumsfeld said, "The only surprise is that we are surprised when we are surprised."[12] Let's examine one illustrative, possible, if unlikely, scenario and how deterrence might or might not work in the absence of nuclear weapons.

The scenario envisions the emergence of a highly nationalistic regime in Beijing, determined to reassert China's hegemony in Asia and to "right" perceptions of having been mistreated during the 18th, 19th and 20th centuries by the United States and European powers. An expansionist China, seeking to gain control of resources in the region and to dominate regional political relations, could come into conflict with Russia, India and Japan. The United States also would be concerned about such developments and could have formal security commitments to any or all three of these countries. While the situation could deteriorate into a new Cold War, marked by political tensions and even military skirmishes, it need not lead to a new great power conflict, even in the absence of nuclear weapons. As China would be making claims on other states, it would be natural for them to cooperate to contain Beijing's aspirations.

Looking decades into the future, it seems likely at least Russia and India would have large and technologically advanced conventional military forces. Japan, although likely to have only small forces, would likely retain the backing of the United States. Facing such a formidable alliance, it is not clear China would pursue its aims by direct, military means, but likely would prefer instead a long-term political and economic strategy. In short, so long as China's potential enemies maintained strong, modern, conventional forces and the means of cooperating against its common foe, it seems likely China would be deterred from military aggression.

Of course, if Chinese leaders were irrational or reckless, they might gamble on a surprise attack being successful, just as Japan did in 1941. But this could be the case even if the nations in question were armed with nuclear weapons. In such circumstances, reckless Chinese leaders might believe they could win a conventional conflict while deterring nuclear responses with their own nuclear forces.

Again, the conventional balance of power would be the key factor in the deterrence equation. Given this scenario takes place decades in the future, the United States and other advanced nations may well have developed and deployed highly accurate, prompt, non-nuclear global strike capabilities. Such weapon systems could be based at sea, on land or even in space, and pose the threat, that in the event of aggression, the transgressor's key leadership and military targets could be destroyed almost immediately in retaliation.[13]

The strength of international responses to China's initial sallies would also be a key determining factor. It should be recalled that Hitler was encouraged in his aggressions not by the absence of nuclear weapons, of which the world was ignorant in the 1930s, but by the other powers' unwillingness to respond militarily to his early grabs for the Rhineland, Czechoslovakia, etc. – and by their very weak diplomatic responses.

A more difficult situation could arise if an expansionist China sought to split its potential opposition by reaching an alliance with one of the Asian great powers prior to revealing its intentions, just as Hitler did with Stalin prior to invading Poland. China's most likely ally would be Russia, particularly if Russia had not regained its economic footing during the decades necessary to eliminate nuclear weapons. One could envision a mutually beneficial relationship in which Russia provided natural resources in exchange for Chinese technological and economic support.　While Russia would seem an unlikely military partner for China, even in this circumstance, such a Sino-Russian entente would remove Russian forces from the alliance seeking to contain Chinese expansion to the south and east and greatly simplify China's strategic calculations.

In these circumstances, would war be more likely if no nation was armed with nuclear weapons? Again, the question of war and peace would seem to hinge more on the calculations and personalities of China's leaders, on the balance of conventional military capabilities, and on the responses of the states China challenged, than on the presence or absence of nuclear forces.　Quite apart from the potential damage caused by the war, conventional aggression would be at great cost to China – breaking the economic relationships and financial interdependencies which enabled it to advance so far during the past 30 years.

No sane Chinese leader would wish to jeopardize the peaceful relations which facilitated China's rapid economic development. The risk of nuclear war implied by the presence of nuclear weapons would raise the stakes even higher, but the likelihood would be, in this writer's judgment, that so long as threatened nations reacted strongly, both the potential cost of conventional war and the lingering consequences for China's economy and social well-being would be deterrence enough

Break-Out

One additional deterrence issue should be considered in a world without nuclear weapons - the risk of one nation breaking out of the disarmament regime and rebuilding its weapons arsenal. Assuming the verification regime accompanying the treaty effectively precluded rebuilding a weapons arsenal surreptitiously; one nation's decision to "break-out" would no doubt trigger similar responses by others. How quickly nations acted would depend on the strength of multinational controls in place on key civilian nuclear facilities, such as uranium enrichment facilities. Access to such facilities and the creation of weapons-grade materials are probably the most time-consuming aspects of a break-out strategy. Even without access to civilian facilities, however, it would not take very long for advanced nations to rebuild nuclear weapons. Starting with only knowledge of the basic physics, after all, the United States developed and built atomic weapons in less than four years in the Manhattan Project. Presuming the parties to the disarmament treaty would maintain a cadre of knowledgeable scientists and engineers, weapon designs, and perhaps even a stock of non-nuclear components, it should not take more than a year or two to turn out weapons at a rapid pace.[14]

Thus, if one nation decided to break-out of a disarmament regime, a race to rebuild nuclear manufacturing facilities, fissile materials, and ultimately weapons could ensue. Given the initial break-out would likely have been triggered by some new conflict or re-emergence of an old grievance, or by a new leader with nationalistic ambitions, or by the kindling of a greater sense of insecurity in one nation or another, this new arms race would likely lead to an unstable political situation, an air of crisis in international affairs, and a heightened risk of war. Deterrence would likely be highly unstable in such a situation. The risk such a situation might develop needs to be weighed when considering policies that could lead to the elimination of nuclear weapons.

Conclusions

The controversial conclusion of this analysis is the elimination of nuclear weapons, in the context as described, would not necessarily make great power conventional conflicts more likely. This, of course, is a subjective conclusion; others may reach different judgments. No one can tell what might happen in the hypothetical worlds we discuss. The future nature of political and economic relations among nations is impossible to predict. So, too, it is impossible to predict the degree to which various nations will have invested the resources necessary to develop and deploy advanced conventional military technologies, including defensive technologies and prompt global strike systems.

Even more to the point, with or without nuclear weapons, the effectiveness of deterrence depends strikingly on individuals – on perceptions of personal and national interests, on priorities, on willingness to run risks, on knowledge of the objective military situation, on judgments about other nations' leaders and the credibility of the threats or promises they may be making. Few of these factors are knowable in advance of a specific situation and many can rarely be discerned even after a crisis has passed.

The relationship between specific types of weapons and the stability of deterrence, or of the balances of specific types of military power and the stability of deterrence, is intrinsically a matter of conjecture. During the Cold War, experts and officials wove elaborate theories of deterrence. They may have been accurate depictions of real international relationships and decisions about war and peace, or they may not have been accurate.

In the much more complicated, multi-polar world that has emerged since 1989, uncertainties about the linkages between deterrence theory and reality have become even greater. Discussions about deterrence in future worlds in which drastic changes have been made to nations' military capabilities can only be speculative. But this uncertainty does not mean the issues raised in this chapter should not be debated and planned for in all possibility.

Notes

[1]   United Nations Security Council Resolution 1887, http://daccess-dds-ny.un.org/doc/UNDOC/GEN/N09/523/74/PDF/N0952374.pdf?OpenElement.

[2] Fred Ikle, "Nuclear Abolition, A Reverie," *The National Interest* (September/October 2009), http://www.nationalinterest.org/Article.aspx?id=22014.

[3] The vagaries of deterrence are discussed at length in an excellent book by Keith Payne, *The Great American Gamble: Deterrence Theory and Practice from the Cold War to the Twenty-first Century* (Fairfax, Va.: National Institute Press, 2008).

[4] Gerard Smith, *Disarming Diplomat: The Memoirs of Ambassador Gerard C. Smith, Arms Control Negotiator* (Lanham, Md.: Madison Books, 1996), and Henry Kissinger, *The White House Years* (New York: Little, Brown and Company, 1979).

[5] For more information on the BWC, see Marie Isabell Chevrier, "From Verification to Strengthening Compliance: Prospects and Challenges of the Biological Weapons Convention," *Politics and the Life Sciences,* 14, 2 (August 1995), 209-219. For more information on the CWC, see J.P. Perry Robinson, "Implementing the Chemical Weapons Convention," *International Affairs,* 72, 1 (January 1996), 73-89.

[6] An authoritative, if unofficial, source estimates that at the end of 2009 Russia had a total nuclear arsenal of 13,000 intact nuclear warheads and the U.S. had a total of 9,400. See Robert Norris and Hans Kristensen, "Nuclear Notebook: Worldwide Deployments of Nuclear Weapons, 2009," *Bulletin of the Atomic Scientists,* 6 (Nov/Dec 2009), 65. In May 2010, the USG announced that the United States maintained 5,113 operational and reserve nuclear warheads. The larger estimate given above includes warheads awaiting dismantlement.

[7] Ibid. The UK stockpile of 225 was announced officially by the British government in May 2010.

[8] For detailed discussions of how a disarmament regime might be governed, verified, and enforced, see: Barry M. Blechman and Alexander K. Bollfrass, editors, *Elements of a Nuclear Disarmament Treaty,* (Washington, D.C.: Stimson Center, 2010).

[9]This reasoning suggests if the U.S. is serious about moving to very low numbers of nuclear weapons, or even eliminating them all together, it should make the development of effective, comprehensive defenses a very high priority in defense planning. It also suggests at low numbers, states may be better off to target remaining offensive forces on population centers, rather than to deter an opponent by posing a threat to its offensive capabilities.

[10] For example, see Bruce G. Blair, *Global Zero Alert for Nuclear* Forces (Brookings Institution, Occasional Paper, 1995); Hans M. Kristensen, Robert S. Norris and Ivan Oelrich, *From Counterforce to Minimal Deterrence: A New Nuclear Policy on the Path Toward Eliminating Nuclear Weapons* (Federation of American Scientists and National Resources Defense Council, Occasional Paper No.7, April 2009).

[11] Based on information from the "Correlates of War" project and a database of military conflicts compiled by the University of Maryland. See: Meredith Reid Sarkes, "The Correlates of War Data on War: An Update to 1997," *Conflict Management and Peace*

Science, 18/1 (2000), 123-44; Joseph Hewitt, et. al, *Peace and Conflict 2010,* Center for International Development and Conflict Management (College Park, Md.: University of Maryland, 2010), http://www.correlatesofwar.org/cow2%20data/WarData/InterState/Inter-State%20War%20Format%20%28V%203-0%29.htm.

[12] Bradley Graham, *By His Own Rules: The Ambitions, Successes, and Ultimate Failures of Donald Rumsfeld* (New York: Public Affairs, 2009).

[13] Of course, the credibility of this conventional, retaliatory threat would depend on the capabilities of defensive systems. There would also be the possibility that such advanced conventional systems might be limited in number as part of a nuclear disarmament treaty.

[14] These issues are discussed at length in the chapters by Alex Glaser and Harold Feiveson in Blechman and Bollfrass, Editors, *Elements of a Nuclear Disarmament Treaty* (Washington, D.C.: Stimson Center, 2010). The Stimson Center also has developed an on-line game in which players take the guise of rogue states and seek to break out of a disarmament treaty surreptitiously. It proves to be remarkably difficult. Go to www.cheatersrisk.com to play the game.

CHAPTER 11

Deterrence, the Triad, and Dyads

Kurt Guthe

On November 15, 1960, U.S.S. *George Washington* left Charleston harbor for the first operational patrol by a nuclear-powered ballistic missile submarine (SSBN). Before then, the U.S. strategic nuclear force comprised two elements: a large fleet of long- and medium-range bombers and a small but growing number of land-based intercontinental ballistic missiles (ICBMs). In the 50 years since, the United States has maintained a mix of long-range bombers, ICBMs, and ballistic missile submarines. Today this triad is made up of 76 B-52H and 18 B-2 bombers, 450 silo-based Minuteman III ICBMs, and 14 Trident SSBNs that each can carry 24 D5 submarine-launched ballistic missiles (SLBMs). Continuation of the triad is called for by the 2010 Nuclear Posture Review, a review led by the Defense Department and approved by President Obama, that sets U.S. nuclear policy, strategy, and forces for the next five to 10 years.[1]

Though venerable, the triad is not immutable. It is not the product of a grand blueprint worked out at the start of the nuclear era, but emerged during the 1950s and 1960s from the interplay of technological developments, inter-service competition, and international events. Its size, composition, and capabilities all have changed significantly over the decades. In that time, its very necessity periodically has been called into question by proposals to dispense with one or perhaps two of the three legs. Some have argued the vulnerability of bombers to air defenses, or ICBMs to counter-silo attacks, warrants the elimination of one or both legs. Others have claimed the triad is unnecessarily redundant and could be reduced by one or two legs to achieve costs savings without diminishing the deterrence of attack. Both the 2010 Nuclear Posture Review and a similar review in 1994 considered, but ultimately rejected, options to move away from the triad.[2]

At some future point, reductions in the U.S. strategic nuclear force could make preservation of the triad difficult. The latest U.S.-Russian

Strategic Arms Reduction Treaty (New START) is unlikely to cause serious problems in this regard. The treaty sets a limit of 700 on deployed strategic delivery vehicles (SDVs)—a category that encompasses SLBMs, ICBMs, and bombers—as well as a combined limit of 800 on deployed and non-deployed SDVs.[3] The United States currently has somewhat fewer than 900 deployed delivery vehicles.[4] Under New START, it plans to retain a triad of up to 60 bombers, up to 420 ICBMs, and 14 ballistic missile submarines with a total of no more 240 missiles, all carrying an aggregate of 1,550 treaty-accountable warheads.[5] If, however, further reductions led to a force level closer to 500 SDVs, maintaining a cost-effective triad would become a greater challenge.[6]

There is, then, reason to examine again alternative strategic nuclear force configurations with fewer than three legs. Any plausible option would retain ballistic missile submarines, which offer the valuable combination of high survivability against attack (better than that of silo-based ICBMs and bombers) and the lethality to neutralize a wide variety of targets (comparable to that of ICBMs and generally better than that of bombers). Not surprisingly, Trident submarines currently carry more than half of U.S. operationally deployed strategic nuclear warheads.[7] At the same time, a force of only ballistic missile submarines would have significant limitations, including the lack of a hedge against advances in the antisubmarine warfare or ballistic missile defense capabilities of hostile powers. Consequently, a dyad composed of submarines paired with either bombers or ICBMs would be the more likely alternative to the triad.

The move from the triad to a dyad would have important implications for nuclear policy, strategy, plans, programs, and budgets. Given the chief purpose of the strategic nuclear force is to discourage major aggression against the United States and its allies, a critical question would be how the shift to a dyad might affect deterrence. Deterrence, of course, is not simply a matter of a particular military balance, force structure, or weapons system, but greatly depends on the specific political-military setting in which a confrontation occurs, the characteristics of the adversary (such as motives, beliefs, perceptions, and decision-making process), and the ways in which the adversary and the United States interact.[8] The complexity of deterrence as well as the likelihood of wild cards (miscalculation, misperception, inadvertence, and chance) preclude sure predictions about the deterrent effect of a dyad, triad, or other force configuration. Nonetheless, the central deterrent role assigned to the strategic nuclear force would necessitate some judgments about the consequences a dyad might have for deterrence.

The following discussion looks at possible effects on deterrence of a change from the present strategic nuclear triad to a dyad of either SSBNs and bombers or SSBNs and ICBMs. First, the appropriate time frame and prospective security environment germane to such an assessment are considered. Second, force qualities conducive to deterrence are defined. Third, the triad legs and the triad as a whole are evaluated against those force qualities. Finally, the two dyad options are examined in terms of the deterrence-related force qualities and possible offsets for the loss of either the ICBM or bomber leg are suggested.

Strategic Context

While the long view is always useful in defense planning, it is particularly important in charting the future of the U.S. strategic nuclear force. A new bomber, missile, or submarine can take 10 to 20 years to design, develop, and build, and still more years to deploy in full. The planned follow-on to the Trident submarine, for example, will not become operational until 2028 and will not completely replace the Trident fleet until 2040.[9] Like Trident submarines, other strategic nuclear weapons systems also are expected to remain in service for another 20 or 30 years. Current plans call for existing SLBMs, ICBMs, bombers, and bomber-delivered air-launched cruise missiles (ALCM-Bs) to be maintained and upgraded in the coming years, but not replaced before 2030 (for ICBMs and ALCM-Bs) or 2040 (for SLBMs and bombers).[10] Similarly, there are programs to extend the service lives of missile warheads and gravity bombs already in the strategic nuclear arsenal, but no plans—or capacity—to produce new weapons.[11] The lengthy acquisition cycles and long service lives for U.S. strategic nuclear arms mean any dyad alternative should be suited to the security challenges of 2030 or 2040, and not only those of 2010, 2015, or 2020 (the time horizon of the latest Nuclear Posture Review).

Obviously, much can change over two or three decades. Simply recall some of the major international developments that have affected U.S. and allied security in the last 30 years: the end of the Cold War; the rise of

China; wars in the Balkans, Iraq, and Afghanistan; the spread of weapons of mass destruction (WMD); repeated confrontations with North Korea and Iran; and the emergence of Islamic terrorism. Few of these developments were foreseen.

The next 30 years could bring changes of similar consequence, perhaps unexpectedly. For example, efforts by Moscow to reestablish its sphere of influence over former Soviet republics and ex-satellites in Europe—most of which are now NATO members—could fuel renewed military rivalry with the United States. The reliance Russia places on its nuclear forces could give any confrontation a distinct nuclear cast. Likewise, competition between China and the United States in the Asia-Pacific region could lead to conflict, notably over the status of Taiwan. Nuclear threats or use in such a conflict are conceivable, especially in light of Chinese anti-access and area-denial capabilities that diminish U.S. conventional force advantages, and growth in the size and sophistication of Chinese nuclear forces that can strike U.S. forward deployments and the United States itself. In addition, U.S. allies in Northeast Asia and the Mideast could fall prey to future aggression by North Korea or Iran, respectively, including intimidation or attacks involving WMD. Within the next decade, both countries also could deploy nuclear-armed ballistic missiles capable of hitting the United States.[12]

In each of the foregoing cases, as well as others, the U.S. strategic nuclear force would have a deterrent role. That force, whether a triad or dyad, would need considerable flexibility to deal with the diversity of potential adversaries and conflicts. It also would require the adaptability to respond to political-military changes of the sort sketched above, as well as technical difficulties, operational challenges, and technological surprises. Flexibility, adaptability, and other force traits that aid deterrence are addressed below.

Deterrence-Related Force Qualities

Deterrence prevents armed attack or coercion by threatening the would-be aggressor with unacceptable military counteraction.[13] The threatened counteraction could take the form of retaliation that imposes costs greater than the expected gains of aggression (deterrence by punishment) or a response that makes those gains too difficult to achieve (deterrence by denial).[14] Deterrent strategies often are a mix of both punitive and denial threats.

The deterrent value of the U.S. strategic nuclear force for a given crisis or conflict would be determined to a great extent by the beliefs of the adversary regarding whether, how, and with what consequence that force might be used. Deterrence would be weakened if enemy leaders believed they could escape unacceptable counteraction by destroying large numbers of U.S. missiles and bombers before launch or by protecting themselves and other vital elements of their state through active and passive defenses.[15]

Deterrence also would suffer if opponents calculated that counteraction by the United States would be inhibited by the fears U.S. leaders had regarding the dangers of uncontrolled nuclear escalation, the possibility of causing high enemy civilian casualties, or the prospect of nuclear retaliatory damage to the United States that outweighed the reasons for entering or continuing a conflict. To provide a credible deterrent, the U.S. strategic nuclear force overall must have qualities that would disabuse an adversary of such beliefs and promise counteraction that would be certain, effective, and appropriate to the act of aggression.

Those qualities are *survivability, lethality, flexibility, visibility,* and *adaptability*. The first three are needed to pose credible deterrent threats for a range of contingencies, including those in which the strategic nuclear force must withstand a first strike. Visibility refers to shows of force used to amplify deterrent threats in times of crisis. And force adaptability is the quality that maintains the effectiveness of deterrent threats under changing political, military, and technological conditions.

Survivability

A significant portion of the strategic nuclear force must be manifestly capable of surviving enemy attacks on operating bases and missile silos, operations against ballistic missile submarines at sea, and defenses for intercepting bombers and missiles. Force survivability helps frustrate enemy plans (deterrence by denial) and enables retaliatory strikes (deterrence by punishment). It also permits forces to be used in a deliberate, rather than a precipitate, manner, which contributes to flexibility. Were the United States to face a world of multiple nuclear competitors, the strategic nuclear force might require the capability to survive war with one antagonist and remain sufficiently intact, or able to reconstitute, to deter subsequent aggression by another.

For the foreseeable future, concerns about the survivability of the bases and silos of the U.S. strategic nuclear force are likely to be greatest with regard to possible nuclear-prone conflicts with Russia, a nuclear peer, or perhaps with China, which may aspire to that status. Ongoing improvements in Russian and Chinese air defenses and the proliferation of advanced air defense systems to other potential adversaries would make penetration of enemy airspace more difficult for U.S. bombers and cruise missiles. Improvements in the antisubmarine warfare and ballistic missile defense capabilities of opponents also would adversely affect force survivability, although such changes are harder to predict. New problems for the survivability of U.S. forces would arise if potent long-range, precision-guided *non*nuclear strike systems were to appear in the arsenal of a major nuclear-armed adversary.

In the Cold War, nearly 100 percent of ICBMs, 60 to 65 percent of SSBNs, and 33 to 50 percent of bombers were maintained on peacetime alert as insurance against the remote possibility of a Soviet surprise first strike. After the Cold War ended, U.S. bombers were taken off alert, but the alert rates for ICBMs and SLBMs stayed roughly the same.[16] In the future, some parts of the strategic nuclear force should be kept on peacetime alert, though not because the threat of surprise attack will be any less remote. Rather, forces on alert are a quiet reminder of the readiness of the United States, *in extremis*, to act in defense of its security and that of its allies. They also hedge against the possibility that those in authority might be reluctant to increase alert rates during a crisis, because strategic warning was ambiguous, or because a higher alert level was deemed too provocative and likely to deepen the confrontation.

Lethality

Lethality is the ability to hold at risk and, in the event of conflict, destroy or sufficiently damage designated targets. Deterrence by threat of punishment entails holding at risk those things highly valued by adversary leaders, the individuals who would make decisions regarding peace or war. For the potential confrontations likely to involve the U.S. strategic nuclear force, adversary leaders would head authoritarian regimes. Authoritarian leaders place high value on continued rule, which requires their own survival, as well as that of supporting cadres and instruments of political control (intelligence services, secret police, and certain military units). Related targets would include command posts and wartime relocation sites for ruling elites, facilities associated with security apparatuses, and communications links used by these groups.

Threats to destroy elements of enemy military power and defeat armed aggression would serve the purpose of deterrence by denial. Among the targets here might be WMD capabilities and conventional forces and their associated facilities. The ability to strike WMD targets offers the potential for limiting the damage from enemy attacks against U.S. and allied societies, which could reduce the prospective costs the United States would incur by countering aggression, and thereby strengthen the credibility of U.S. deterrent threats. The same would be true of active and passive defenses. Threats directed against defense-industrial, transportation, communications, and electrical power targets could be a means of deterrence by punishment (promising to make the adversary pay a steep economic price for an attack) or deterrence by denial (confronting the adversary with the likelihood U.S. retaliatory strikes would impede the conduct, sustainment, and success of enemy military operations).

To hold at risk the diverse targets related to deterrence, some or all elements of the strategic nuclear force require certain characteristics. One is intercontinental range, which allows strategic delivery vehicles to reach targets throughout Eurasia, where potential opponents are located.

Another is prompt weapons delivery for striking time-sensitive targets, such as missile launchers ready to fire, command-and-control centers with responsibilities for WMD use, and forces preparing to leave their bases.

A third is high accuracy for attacking point targets, like missile silos; this means weapon delivery with a circular error probable of a few hundred feet.[17] Pending future progress in sensors, data-processing systems, and munitions, only bombers with their onboard crews are likely to have the capability for accurate weapon delivery against mobile missile launchers and other targets on the move.

A fourth attribute is weapons of suitable explosive yield. High-yield weapons (yields of a few hundred kilotons), combined with high accuracy, have the destructive potential for dealing with targets hardened against attack through the use of steel-reinforced concrete or underground construction; missile silos and underground bunkers are examples. Some types of hard and deeply buried facilities, including command bunkers for key leaders, can only be destroyed by earth-penetrating weapons.

Finally, high reliability is necessary to avoid bomber or missile aborts and ensure weapons detonate at their specified yields.

Of course, conventionally armed delivery vehicles, particularly those with precision-guided weapons, also can threaten a wide range of targets. Current nonnuclear strike capabilities, however, have limitations as substitutes for nuclear arms. Against certain targets—deeply buried facilities, for example—conventional weapons would be ineffective or less effective in comparison with the destructive power of nuclear weapons. Enemy countermeasures that impeded precision delivery of conventional munitions could render those weapons incapable of destroying or damaging assigned targets. Multiple aircraft sorties or missiles strikes conducted over some period of time might be necessary to deliver enough conventional munitions to neutralize a single target. In conflicts in which targets must be eliminated with dispatch, economy of force, and lasting effect, nuclear weapons may be preferred.

While the bombers of the nuclear triad also can deliver conventional weapons, other nonnuclear strike capabilities lack the intercontinental range of the strategic nuclear force. (This would change if planned research and development work on "a conventional, global strike capability" were to yield an operational system.)[18] Perhaps most important, the widespread, rapid, and sure destruction promised by nuclear weapons has an intangible, but nonetheless real, deterrent effect on national leaders that threats posed by conventional bombs and missiles, no matter how lethal, cannot duplicate. The threat of nuclear use would greatly complicate the plans of would-be aggressors, making victory seem doubtful, if not impossible.[19]

Flexibility

The strategic nuclear force requires the flexibility to carry out strikes of varying scope, scale, and intensity, depending on the nature of the adversary and the type and level of aggression. Holding at risk certain kinds of targets might deter an adversary with one set of values, but not another with a different set. A disproportionate deterrent threat of large-scale retaliation for a lesser provocation might be discounted by an opponent. A threat to destroy enemy population centers might seem less than credible if U.S. cities were vulnerable to enemy reciprocal attacks. A threat to defeat offensive military operations might ring hollow unless backed with the requisite capabilities to strike opposing WMD-armed forces. An inability to limit damage and control escalation through constrained attacks on those forces could inhibit a U.S. military response to acts of aggression against allies, and thus weaken deterrent threats made on their behalf.

For these and other reasons, the strategic nuclear force must be capable of supporting a variety of attack options suited for assorted combinations of opponents and contingencies. This includes force elements that can target the mainstays of a hostile regime and its ability to project power, execute large or limited attacks, minimize unintended civilian damage, and conduct strikes quickly (against time-sensitive targets, for example) or at a slower pace if demanded by the character of the conflict and the direction of the command authorities. As these requirements suggest, both survivability and lethality are prerequisites for flexibility.

Visibility

Increases in the readiness levels and changes in the deployments of military forces long have been used to deter war. These measures also can help prepare for conflict or support coercive efforts aimed at compelling an adversary to do something rather than, as in the case of deterrence, not to do something. In the pre-nuclear era, European powers often employed their forces, especially naval forces, in armed demonstrations to deter or coerce opponents.[20] During the Cold War, the United States frequently used its armed forces to affect foreign perceptions and secure political objectives in confrontations short of war.[21]

In a number of Cold War confrontations, the alert level or deployment of the U.S. strategic nuclear force was changed for deterrent purposes. These included the 1948 and 1961 Berlin crises, the 1956 Suez crisis, the 1958 Taiwan Strait and Lebanese crises, the 1962 Cuban missile crisis, and the 1973 Arab-Israeli war.[22] In the last case, the United States was intent on deterring the Soviet Union from unilaterally sending forces to the Mideast. U.S. diplomatic moves to dissuade the Soviets from intervening were deliberately reinforced by an increase in the defense readiness condition of all military commands. Strategic Air Command assumed a heightened alert for a time and had bombers and aerial tankers ready for immediate takeoff. Fifty to 60 B-52s were brought back to the United States from Guam, where they had been based for conventional bombing missions in Southeast Asia. Their return, according to then-Secretary of State Henry Kissinger, was intended to "give the Soviets another indication that we were assembling our forces for a showdown."[23] Besides the increase in bomber readiness, the ICBM force went to a somewhat higher footing and a few more ballistic missile submarines put to sea.

In future circumstances, perhaps a severe crisis in which U.S. vital interests were endangered by a major nuclear power, the United States again might find reason to underscore the deterrent threat posed by its strategic nuclear force. Taking steps to gird the force for conflict can aid deterrence by making clear to the adversary the gravity with which the United States views its stakes in a confrontation and its determination and wherewithal to defend them. To have this effect, however, the steps must be visible to the adversary. A show of force must show force. This was true in all of the examples cited above. And in those crises, bombers put on most of the show.

In one or more cases, bombers increased ground-alert activities at air bases, conducted airborne alert missions, dispersed to alternate airfields, deployed to locations abroad, or flew close to enemy airspace. All of these actions were detectable by the opponent. Moreover, U.S. decision-makers wanted these actions to be detected. Bomber alerts and redeployments, then, exemplify the quality of visibility that contributes to deterrence.

The other two legs of the triad have inherent disadvantages in this regard. The stationary nature of silo-based ICBMs limits, without entirely excluding, displays of force. Ballistic missile submarines, part of the silent service, depend on stealth for their survivability, although they, too, might have a role in lending visibility to deterrent threats. It is also worth noting that any future bomber alert would attract more notice in foreign capitals simply because all bombers have been off alert for nearly 20 years, whereas at the same time almost all ICBMs and a large fraction of the ballistic missile submarine fleet have been maintained at a high state of alert.

Adaptability

Adaptability is the quality with which the strategic nuclear force can retain or regain its deterrent effectiveness despite adverse political, military, or technical developments. Unfavorable developments in the future could include a sharp deterioration in relations with Russia or China that spurred military competition with one or both countries, a serious violation of a nuclear arms agreement, a defect in a bomb or missile warhead, a significant problem (structural, mechanical, or electronic) with a delivery vehicle, or a serious decrease in the expected operational effectiveness of a force element brought about by improvement in opposing offensive or defense capabilities.

The strategic nuclear force can be adaptable in three ways. First, it can adapt through a force posture (deployed force, weapons stockpile, and readiness level) that has inherent resilience to meet new challenges without remedial changes. The diversity of delivery vehicles, weapons, and deployment modes found in the triad, for example, affords the current force a large measure of adaptability.

Second, the adaptation can be done through modifications of the force posture that respond to the dangers and difficulties that emerge. Alert rates might be increased, additional weapons uploaded on delivery vehicles, bombers dispersed or redeployed, different tactics adopted to offset improved enemy offenses or defenses, and tasks reallocated among force elements if one leg experienced problems.

And third, the force mix can adapt through retrofits of deployed systems (with upgraded electronics, modified weapons, and other hardware fixes) or, over the longer run, the addition of next-generation missiles, aircraft, submarines, and weapons. The lack of warm production lines for strategic nuclear weapons systems, however, means the adaptability of the current triad or a future dyad would depend primarily on the resilience and modification of the force posture, and the improvement of existing capabilities, rather than the manufacture of next-generation delivery vehicles and weapons.[24]

Before examining how an SSBN-bomber or SSBN-ICBM dyad would rate when judged against the force qualities related to deterrence, some key attributes of the three strategic nuclear force elements need to be understood. Familiarity with the deterrent advantages of the triad also is useful, since this force configuration offers a standard against which dyad alternatives can be compared.

Attributes of Strategic Nuclear Force Elements and the Triad

Outlined below are the characteristics of ballistic missile submarines, ICBMs, and bombers, as well as the triad overall, relevant to the force qualities that support deterrence.

Ballistic Missile Submarines

The 14 Trident submarines in the fleet operate from two bases, with eight at Bangor, Washington and six at Kings Bay, Georgia.[25] A number of submarines are in port at any given time, and of those, two usually are undergoing long-term overhauls and thus unable to leave port even in a crisis. Several submarines are on patrol. Although a typical patrol lasts 60 to 90 days, some have exceeded 100 days. Resupply could extend time at sea. The Navy conducts exercises for the resupply and repair of Trident submarines at alternative ports in the Pacific and the Atlantic.[26]

Each Trident submarine has launch tubes for 24 D5 missiles, each missile capable of delivering multiple independently targetable reentry vehicles (MIRVs). Current plans call for the number of SLBM launch tubes per submarine to be reduced to 20, with no more than 240 SLBMs deployed in the fleet at any time.[27] Each D5 SLBM can carry up to 12 Mk-4 reentry vehicles (RVs) with W76 warheads or 8 Mk-5 RVs with W88 warheads.[28]

The average number of reentry vehicles per missile is likely four.[29] W76 warheads represent the majority of those carried by SLBMs.[30] Although the W88 and W76 both have high yields, the yield of the W88 is significantly greater than that of the W76. Both warheads can be delivered with high accuracy by the D5 SLBM. The D5 missile has a range that exceeds 4,000 nautical miles (nm).[31] SLBMs can reach their targets in 30 minutes or less, depending on target location, the launch position of the submarine, and the trajectory of the missile.

ICBMs

The Minuteman III force currently has 450 silo-based ICBMs located at Air Force bases in Wyoming, Montana, and North Dakota. Each of the three bases has 150 missiles.[32] The alert rate of the force is "near 100 percent."[33] Minuteman III ICBMs initially were deployed with three reentry vehicles each, but now carry one, two, or three RVs.[34] In the future, no more than 420 missiles will be deployed and all will be equipped with only one reentry vehicle each.[35] The two types of weapons for the ICBM are the Mk-12A RV with the W78 warhead and the Mk-21 RV with the W87 warhead.[36] Both warheads are high yield and can be delivered with relatively high accuracy. The range of the Minuteman III is over 5,000 nm.[37] Time from launch to target would be roughly 30 minutes.

Bombers

Unlike SSBNs and ICBMs, bombers are dual-capable, with the ability carry out conventional as well as nuclear missions. Over the last two decades, bombers have been used extensively in the Kosovo, Iraq, and Afghanistan conflicts.[38] Of the 76 nuclear-capable B-52Hs, 44 are combat-coded, with the other bombers used for training, test, backup, and attrition reserve. Sixteen of the 18 nuclear-capable B-2s are combat-coded.[39] Under current plans, some B-52Hs will be converted to a conventional-only role and a smaller nuclear-capable fleet of up to 60 bombers will be retained, including all nuclear-capable B-2s.[40] The B-1B bomber, originally dual-capable, was removed from its nuclear role following the 1994 Nuclear Posture Review.[41]

The B-52Hs are split between two Air Force bases, Barksdale in Louisiana and Minot in North Dakota. The B-2s are located at a single base, Whiteman in Missouri.[42] The bomber force has not maintained a day-to-day alert status since 1991, but, if necessary, a portion of the force could placed on ground alert in a matter of days.[43]

The low-observable (stealth) features of the B-2 bomber aid it in penetrating opposing air defenses. This enables the aircraft to close on targets and deliver nuclear gravity bombs. The older B-52H bomber is more readily detected and thus is armed with long-range (1,300 nm) cruise missiles that can be launched from outside enemy air defense coverage.[44] The B-2 can carry up to 16 B61-7, B61-11, or B83 bombs. The B61-11 bomb, it should be noted, is the only earth-penetrating nuclear weapon in the U.S. inventory and is specifically designed for use against hard and deeply buried facilities.[45] The B-52H can be armed with up to 20 ALCM-Bs,[46] each cruise missile with a W80-1 warhead.[47] Bomber weapons provide a variety of explosive yields "from megaton to subkiloton."[48] Indeed, some of the weapon types can be employed with more than one yield. Gravity bombs can be delivered with high accuracy, while the guided ALCM-B can strike targets with even better "pinpoint accuracy."[49]

Bombers have longer intercontinental ranges than ballistic missiles—6,000 nm for the B-2 and 7,500 nm for the B-52H[50]—but their flight times are measured in hours rather than minutes.

The Triad

In combination, SSBNs, ICBMs, and bombers make for a strategic nuclear force with diverse, advantageously redundant, and mutually reinforcing capabilities. While there are shared characteristics among the three force elements, each leg of the triad has a unique and useful set of attributes. Weaknesses in one leg are offset by strengths in others. Adjustments can be made within and among the legs as conditions change. The legs together make an enemy attack especially difficult. In the event of crisis or war, the three legs offer a range of possible military responses. Though elements of the strategic nuclear force in many ways could be improved, they nonetheless have important strengths with regard to survivability, lethality, flexibility, visibility, and adaptability.

Survivability

Small in number and soft, SSBN and bomber bases are vulnerable to attack. Submarines in port and bombers not on alert would be easily destroyed by nuclear strikes and could suffer severe damage even in nonnuclear attacks. The harder and more numerous silos for ICBMs can be damaged or destroyed by high-accuracy, high-yield ballistic missile warheads, like those currently found in the Russian strategic nuclear force, but the need to expend two warheads per silo to ensure a high kill probability could make the price of such an attack prohibitive. The attack could be unprofitable as well, since many of the silos currently house Minuteman III missiles with only a single warhead, and all missiles will be single-warhead in the future.

Ballistic missile submarines on patrol are virtually undetectable, barring breakthroughs in antisubmarine warfare. In the aftermath of a nuclear conflict, surviving SSBNs could serve as a deterrent to opportunistic aggression as the United States sought to recover from the catastrophe.

SLBMs launched from submarines on patrol and ICBMs fired from silos that survived an attack would face, at worst, limited missile defenses. Because of the wide-ranging mobility of SSBNs, SLBMs could be launched from many different azimuths, complicating enemy plans.

The air defense threat confronting bombers would be greater, although the stealth of B-2s and the standoff missiles of B-52Hs would mitigate the danger. Bombers and cruise missiles also could be flown so as to attack an enemy from multiple directions, thereby stressing the opposing defenses, and to skirt parts of the defensive system. The combination of penetrating bombers and standoff bombers with cruise missiles can compel an adversary to develop and deploy not only perimeter air defenses, but also close-in defenses of high-value targets. This can complicate the attack planning of a would-be aggressor, impose costs on the adversary, dilute opposing defense efforts, and divert resources from enemy offensive forces.

Looking at the strategic nuclear force as a whole, the ballistic missile submarines on alert and the daunting number of aim points presented by silo-based ICBMs offset, at least partially, the vulnerability of submarine and bomber operating bases, individual missile silos, and unalerted bombers. Submarines and ICBMs on alert offer insurance against surprise due to lack of sufficient warning or lack of timely response. In the absence of effective enemy missile defenses, U.S. ballistic missiles once launched are likely to reach their targets, even if defense penetration by bombers and cruise missiles is more problematic. Any enemy seeking to eliminate U.S. retaliatory capabilities would be burdened within an exceedingly complex military challenge.

Lethality

SLBMs, ICBMs, and bombers all have the intercontinental range to reach targets within the territory of any hostile power in Eurasia. Ballistic missiles could strike time-sensitive targets minutes after launch. Ballistic missiles, bombers, and cruise missiles all can deliver their nuclear weapons with high accuracy. Ballistic missiles have the accuracy/yield combinations to hold at risk most types of hard targets, including missile sites and command centers that would have to be struck quickly. High-confidence neutralization of many of these targets would require the use of more than one weapon. Bombers, with the necessary targeting updates, could attack mobile targets. The B-2 could deliver the B61-11 earth-penetrating bomb against underground targets, although some hard and deeply buried facilities would be resistant even to its effects.[51]

Though not as great as in the past, the variety of delivery vehicles (D5, Minuteman III, B-52H, B-2, ALCM-B) and weapons (W76, W78, W80-1, W87, W88, B61, B83) is a hedge against problems with a vehicle or weapon type that could compromise operational effectiveness. Force diversity also allows high-priority targets to be covered by weapons from different triad legs (cross-targeting) in order to ensure their destruction. Thus, if a command bunker were slated to be hit by both a bomber-delivered weapon and an ICBM warhead, the loss of the ICBM warhead to an enemy counter-silo attack would not prevent the bunker from being hit.

This collection of capabilities within the triad gives the overall strategic nuclear force the ability to threaten a wide array of military, regime, and economic targets.

Flexibility

Force elements of the triad have a number of characteristics suited for selective nuclear attacks. Bombers could be used for limited attacks, including the delivery of just one weapon against a single target. The low-yield options for bomber weapons would be useful in limiting unintended damage. Bombers could be routed to avoid overflight of sensitive areas, redirected in flight, or recalled from their missions. Bomber aircrews could assess damage inflicted by earlier attacks and carry out or refrain from follow-on strikes. Of course, bombers and cruise missiles would have to penetrate any air defenses protecting their designated targets, a task that might be especially difficult in a small attack, where, with advance warning, the enemy could concentrate defenses (airborne sensors, fighter-interceptors, and mobile surface-to-air missiles) to shield likely targets. Long flight times could limit the utility of bombers for selective strikes against time-sensitive targets.

Another force feature that offers flexibility is the single-warhead payload of many, and eventually all, Minuteman III ICBMs. While a ballistic missile with a MIRVed payload would have to deliver all of its warheads against multiple targets located within a certain elliptical area (or "footprint"), each single-warhead Minuteman III could be employed to hit just one target located at any point within a much larger area. Single-warhead ICBMs could be used, for example, in limited attacks against a small number of targets, attack options put together quickly, or strikes against time-sensitive targets suddenly discovered by U.S. intelligence-gathering systems. Single-warhead ICBMs probably would be up against less effective defenses than those that bombers would confront in a limited attack. But their warheads would lack the low-yield options of bomber weapons. In some cases, overflight restrictions might exclude the use of ICBMs, though not the employment of bombers or SLBMs.

D5 SLBMs have the valuable ability to strike a wide range of targets, but their MIRVed payloads and high-yield W88 warheads could be disadvantageous for certain limited attack options. The high survivability of Trident submarines on patrol is one of the most important force characteristics that would enable the United States to respond in a deliberate and flexible manner to a large-scale nuclear attack on the homeland.

For flexibility, then, bombers offer low-yield weapon options and man-in-the-loop control, attributes ballistic missiles lack. A significant number of ballistic missiles, like bombers, can deliver a single weapon, but with greater speed. More survivable than bombers at their bases or ICBMs in silos, SSBNs on patrol would have greater flexibility for conducting strikes of different sorts (or withholding attacks) as a conflict evolved and the command authorities made changes in the strategic direction of U.S. operations.

Visibility

As the earlier discussion of this force quality suggests, bombers constitute the triad leg most likely to be used for shows of force to back deterrent threats. Any display now, however, would be less impressive, probably less intimidating, and perhaps less deterring than those of the past. In all but the last of the aforementioned crises in which the alert level or deployment of the strategic nuclear force was changed, bombers made up all or most of the force. In each of those dangerous episodes, the United States had hundreds of bombers, not the tens of aircraft in the inventory today. During the Cuban missile crisis, for example, more than 1,000 bombers were on alert, some 180 bombers were dispersed to roughly 30 civilian and military airfields, and the number of bombers just on airborne alert—65—was larger than the total number of combat-coded aircraft in the current nuclear-capable bomber force.[52]

In addition, the effectiveness of a future nuclear show of force by bombers could be adversely affected by lack of alert experience during the last two decades. An Air Force report in 2008 found that "[w]ithin the next few years, the USAF will no longer have a pool of bomber wing commanders who have performed extended alert duty" and "due to limited aircraft nuclear generations, aircrews have little experience interacting with operational issues involved with bringing aircraft to nuclear alert status."[53]

It also should be noted that the training program to prepare for an airborne alert was canceled in 1993 because it had, in the words of an official history, "become anachronistic and, in [U.S. Strategic Command's] view, served little purpose."[54] Changes instituted by Air Force Global Strike Command could improve the preparedness of the bomber force for alert duty. This command, which is responsible for all ICBMs and nuclear-capable bombers, was established in 2009 to provide greater attention to the nuclear mission.[55]

Adaptability

In the past, the triad has demonstrated considerable ability to adapt to unfavorable military and technical developments. For example, from the 1960s through the 1980s, the overall resilience of the triad allowed the United States to pursue a long series of remedies for deficiencies in the bomber leg caused by improvements in Soviet air defenses. During the 1970s and 1980s, the triad also afforded time to deal with the vulnerability of the ICBM force that arose from Soviet deployment of silo-busting missiles, although no fix was implemented before the Soviet Union disintegrated. And when significant problems with Polaris and Poseidon SLBM warheads emerged, the insurance provided by the ICBM and bomber legs permitted the required retrofits to be made without undue haste.[56]

Similar adjustments in the strategic nuclear force might be necessary in the future. If, for example, bomber vulnerability increases because of air defense advances, more reliance might be placed on ballistic missiles, with additional warheads loaded on SLBMs. Some number of SLBM warheads also might be allocated for the suppression of enemy air defenses. If the W88 warhead were to experience a serious technical problem, additional W76 warheads might be deployed as replacements (despite their lesser capability against some classes of hard targets) until the problem was solved.

If, for various reasons, the strategic force required greater lethality, the guidance systems for ballistic missiles, bombers, and their weapons might be improved to increase delivery accuracies. And were the United States to find itself in a stepped-up nuclear arms competition with Russia or China, part of the bomber force again might be placed on ground alert and the number of ballistic missile submarines on alert might be increased.

In addition, warheads could be uploaded on bombers and missiles. Under the planned reductions in the strategic nuclear force, bombers, ICBMs, and SLBMs all will retain the capacity to carry more warheads than the number in their standard operational payloads. Some number of non-deployed warheads that could be uploaded will be kept in the nuclear weapons stockpile as a hedge against adverse technical, military, or international developments.[57] The bomber force could be uploaded in weeks, the SLBM force in months, and the ICBM force at a rate of one squadron (50 missiles) per missile wing (150 missiles) per year.[58] Note the availability of upload options could help in deterring opponents from breaking out of nuclear arms agreements or engaging in competitive nuclear buildups with the United States.

Dyad Alternatives

For the reasons cited at the beginning of this discussion, the force qualities of survivability, lethality, flexibility, visibility, and adaptability support—but do not guarantee—the deterrence of major aggression. As detailed in the previous section, the assorted attributes of ballistic missile submarines, ICBMs, and bombers invest the current strategic nuclear triad with all of these deterrence-related qualities, although below ideal levels. If one triad leg and its capabilities were removed from the current strategic nuclear force, it is reasonable to assume the expected deterrent effectiveness of the force might diminish, unless adequate offsetting measures were adopted. In comparison to the triad, what capabilities that support deterrence would be lost or reduced? The brief assessments below look at the deterrent effectiveness of SSBN-bomber and SSBN-ICBM dyads from this perspective. Given no new strategic nuclear weapons system is likely to be deployed for 20 years or more, next-generation bombers, missiles, and submarines are not among the offsetting measures considered here.

For the submarine-bomber dyad, it is assumed the current ICBM force would be eliminated entirely. This assumption is consistent with dyad proposals that claim the ICBM leg is superfluous, vulnerable, "destabilizing," and too costly to maintain and modernize. For the submarine-ICBM dyad, however, it is assumed bombers are removed from their nuclear role, but retained for nonnuclear missions. This assumption reflects both the significant utility bombers have demonstrated in conventional conflicts and the past precedent of removing the B-1B bomber from its nuclear role, but keeping it as a conventional strike aircraft.

SSBN-Bomber Dyad (No ICBMs)

Survivability

The absence of hundreds of silo-based ICBMs would make it less difficult for an adversary to plan an attack on the U.S. strategic nuclear force. All bombers not on alert and SSBNs not on patrol could be eliminated by an attack on just five main operating bases. SSBNs at sea would represent the main deterrent to a first strike. This deterrent could be strengthened by increasing the alert rate for the Trident submarine fleet. At the same time, if ballistic missile submarines on patrol were the only survivable element of the strategic nuclear force, hostile nuclear peers might devote greater effort to antisubmarine warfare. Maintaining part of the bomber force on alert and probably dispersed, at least during crises, would reduce prelaunch vulnerability, demonstrate that bombers could not be eliminated simply through attacks on their air bases, take some of the burden off the submarine force, and vex opponents with the problem of defending against air, as well as ballistic missile, attack.

Lethality

Without ICBMs, the strategic nuclear force would lose a large fraction of its capability for prompt, accurate, and deadly strikes against various types of targets, including those that are hardened. If required, this loss might be partially offset by uploading W88 warheads on SLBMs, assuming sufficient non-deployed warheads of this type were available.

Flexibility

Removing the ICBM force from the triad would eliminate single-warhead Minuteman III missiles. To retain the flexibility offered by a single-warhead ballistic missile, some D5 SLBMs might be converted to carry single-warhead payloads. Concurrent with this change, other D5 missiles might be uploaded in order to maintain the total number of warheads carried by SSBNs. In comparison to single-warhead Minuteman III ICBMs, single-warhead D5 SLBMs would have the added advantages of greater prelaunch survivability and more flight profiles consistent with possible overflight restrictions.

Visibility

The lack of ICBMs would not affect the ability of the bomber leg to be used for shows of force that signaled U.S. resolve.

Adaptability

Retiring all ICBMs would remove an entire force element that could hedge against technical problems, operational challenges, or technological surprises that might impair bombers or ballistic missile submarines. One of the options for uploading a significant number of hard target-capable warheads for prompt strikes would be lost. The diversity of the weapons stockpile would be diminished with the elimination of two
(the W78 and W87) of the seven warhead types. The decrease in adaptability would be worse if the bomber force, because of its dual capability and conventional commitments, were only a "half leg" in a submarine-bomber dyad.

SSBN-ICBM Dyad (No Bombers)

Survivability

With a submarine-ICBM dyad, improvements in opposing missile defenses would have the potential to weaken the entire strategic nuclear force. If adversaries no longer were threatened by nuclear-armed B-52Hs and B-2s, they might reallocate resources from air defenses to missile defenses, as well as to antisubmarine warfare aimed at SSBNs. But the fact they still faced threats from B-52Hs, B-2s, and B-1Bs with conventional payloads, not to mention from shorter-range nonnuclear strike aircraft, would likely militate against such a shift.

Lethality

Ending the nuclear role for bombers would mean the loss of the only nuclear earth-penetrating weapon (the B61-11), another high-yield weapon (the B83), and the only guided strategic nuclear weapon (the ALCM-B).

The delivery vehicle currently best suited for attacking mobile targets no longer would have a nuclear mission.

With regard to offsetting measures, an earth-penetrating ballistic missile warhead might be developed and deployed to replace the B61-11. Here it is worth noting that three decades ago, engineering development of an earth-penetrating warhead for the Pershing II intermediate-range ballistic missile was completed and the design then put on the shelf.[59] In the case of the B83, the current stockpile may not include a ballistic missile warhead with the yield and other characteristics that would make it a suitable substitute. To gain delivery accuracy comparable to that of the ALCM-B, Trident Mk-4 reentry vehicles might be retrofitted with global positioning system (GPS) guidance; some work along this line already has been done.[60] At some future point, it might be possible to equip intercontinental-range ballistic missiles with small, powered unmanned combat aerial vehicles (UCAVs) that, like bombers, could be used to attack mobile targets.[61]

Flexibility

Relieving bombers of nuclear duty would deprive the strategic nuclear force of the flexibility that comes from their readily changeable payloads, weapons with low-yield options, and man-in-the-loop control. As noted, these traits are valuable for conducting limited attacks and responding to rapid changes in conflict conditions.

In the absence of bombers, the remaining strategic force still would, or could, offer some flexibility. Single-warhead ICBMs would be available for selective strikes. SLBMs would have some ability to avoid overflight of specified areas. Some ballistic missile warheads might be modified for reduced yields. Improvements in C^4ISR[62] capabilities could facilitate the shoot-look-shoot employment of ballistic missiles. Small UCAVs delivered by future ballistic missiles might have some of the same advantages as the bomber with its man-in-the-loop control. And to give a submarine-ICBM dyad something akin to the recall option for bombers, a command destruct system might be installed on some or all ballistic missiles. It should be emphasized, however, that this last measure also would create a serious vulnerability that adversaries could exploit.[63]

Visibility

If bombers were withdrawn from the strategic nuclear force, the best means for a nuclear show of force would be lost. In theory, test launches of ICBMs and SLBMs might be used to demonstrate the might and determination of the United States to stand against aggression. Given their own use of missile tests for political-military purposes, this type of signal is one potential opponents likely would understand. North Korea and Iran have test-launched ballistic missiles as part of their strategies to counter international pressure aimed at halting their nuclear programs. China has used ballistic missile tests to intimidate the leadership and populace of Taiwan and to discourage the United States from interfering with any Chinese forcible attempts to reclaim the island. And Russia conducts ICBM and SLBM tests in exercises intended to put its strategic nuclear power on display. Yet a U.S. ballistic missile test in the context of an intense crisis could be misperceived as an attack, making it a more dangerous move than alerting and dispersing the bomber force. As an alternative, the crisis deployment of additional ballistic missile submarines to patrols at sea might be announced, or made known to an adversary through diplomatic channels, but this could compromise operations security.

Adaptability

As with the submarine-bomber dyad, the hedge offered by an entire force element would be eliminated with the removal of bombers from a nuclear role. In the absence of bombers, the two remaining legs of the strategic nuclear force both would be vulnerable to improved, expanded, or proliferated ballistic missile defenses. To respond to this danger, tactics for suppressing defensive systems might be devised, tailored penetration aids might be added to ICBM and SLBM payloads, and ballistic missiles might be uploaded with more warheads for saturating opposing defenses.

The stockpile of strategic nuclear weapons would be less diverse without the bomber-delivered B61-7, B61-11, B83, and W80-1. The stockpile would retain some redundancy, however, with two ICBM warheads (the W78 and W87) and two SLBM warheads (the W76 and W88). On the other hand, if the W76 warhead, the most numerous strategic weapon, were to suffer a major technical problem that afflicted the entire type, much of the strategic nuclear force would be rendered ineffective, since there are too few W88 warheads to be used as replacements.

Without bombers, the strategic nuclear force would lose its capacity for the rapid upload of a substantial number of nuclear weapons. Bombers are armed with no weapons today, because no aircraft are on alert, but several hundred bombs and cruise missiles could be uploaded in a matter of weeks.[64] This option would be unavailable with a submarine-ICBM dyad.

Conclusions

The move from the existing triad to a dyad could be detrimental to force survivability, lethality, flexibility, visibility, and adaptability—the qualities that support deterrence. For a submarine-bomber dyad, the quality of visibility would be unaffected because bombers would remain for shows of force. Survivability, however, would be diminished because adversaries would not confront the attack problem presented by a large force of silo-based ICBMs. The submarine-ICBM dyad would lack real options for shows of force. The entire dyad also would be vulnerable to improvements in opposing missile defenses. Both dyad alternatives would be less adaptable than the triad. With regard to lethality and flexibility, adjustments in the submarine-bomber dyad could be made to offset some of the capabilities lost by the elimination of ICBMs. For the submarine-ICBM dyad, the offsets might involve development and deployment of new systems.

Notes

[1] Department of Defense (DoD), *Nuclear Posture Review Report* (Washington, D.C.: Department of Defense, April 2010), 21-24; and Statement by President Barack Obama on the Release of Nuclear Posture Review, Office of the White House Press Secretary (April 6, 2010).
[2] DoD, *Nuclear Posture Review Report*, op. cit., 21; and Janne E. Nolan, *An Elusive Consensus: Nuclear Weapons and American Security After the Cold War* (Washington, D.C.: Brookings Institution, 1999), 52-55.
[3] Treaty Between the United States of America and the Russian Federation on Measures for the Future Reduction and Limitation of Strategic Offensive Arms (signed April 8, 2010), Article II.

[4] Amy F. Woolf, *The New START Treaty: Central Limits and Key Provisions*, R41219 (Washington, D.C.: Congressional Research Service, June 18, 2010), 19.

[5] Unclassified fact sheet on the *New START Treaty Framework and Nuclear Force Structure Plans* report, submitted by the President to the Congress in response to section 1251 of the National Defense Authorization Act for Fiscal Year 2010 (May 13, 2010); and DoD, *Nuclear Posture Review Report*, op. cit., 21.

[6] See, for example, Gen. James E. Cartwright, vice chairman of the Joint Chiefs of Staff, testimony before the Senate Armed Services Committee (July 9, 2009), committee transcript, 22.

[7] "1,000 Trident Patrols: SSBNs the Cornerstone of Strategic Deterrence," Navy News Service (Feb. 24, 2009).

[8] See Department of Defense, *Deterrence Operations Joint Operating Concept*, Version 2.0 (Washington, D.C.: Department of Defense, Dec. 2006).

[9] Ronald O'Rourke, *Navy SSBN(X) Ballistic Missile Submarine Program: Background and Issues for Congress*, R41129 (Washington, D.C.: Congressional Research Service, July 27, 2010), 4, 8-9.

[10] James N. Miller, principal deputy under secretary of defense for policy, testimony before the Senate Armed Services Committee (July 20, 2010), prepared statement, 3 and committee transcript, 21; and Vice Adm. John T. Blake, deputy chief of naval operations for integration of capabilities and resources, testimony before the Senate Armed Services Committee (May 6, 2010), committee transcript, 27. According to Dr. Miller, DoD plans to sustain the B-52H through 2035 and the B-2 through 2050.

[11] On the life extension programs for warheads and bombs, see Government Accountability Office, *NNSA and DOD Need to More Effectively Manage the Stockpile Life Extension Program*, GAO-09-385 (Washington, D.C.: Government Accountability Office, March 2009). Because of deficiencies in the nuclear weapons infrastructure (labs, plants and workforce), "the United States is now the *only* nuclear weapons state party to the [Non-Proliferation Treaty] that does not have the capacity to produce a new nuclear warhead." Moreover, "[t]he United States has not designed a new nuclear warhead since the 1980s and has not built a new nuclear warhead since the early 1990s." Department of Energy and Department of Defense, *National Security and Nuclear Weapons in the 21st Century* (Washington, D.C.: Department of Energy and Department of Defense, Sept. 2008), 19 (emphasis in original).

[12] National Air and Space Intelligence Center, *Ballistic and Cruise Missile Threat*, NASIC-1031-0985-09 (Wright-Patterson Air Force Base, Ohio: National Air and Space Intelligence Center, April 2009), 19.

[13] The Defense Department formally defines deterrence as, "The prevention from action by fear of the consequences. Deterrence is a state of mind brought about by the existence of a credible threat of unacceptable counteraction." *Department of Defense Dictionary of Military and Associated Terms*, Joint Publication 1-02 (Washington, D.C.: Joint Chiefs of Staff, April 12, 2001 — as amended through April 2010), 139.

[14] For an early discussion of the distinction between deterrence by threat of punishment and deterrence by denial, see Glenn H. Snyder, *Deterrence and Defense: Toward a Theory of National Security* (Princeton, N.J.: Princeton Univ. Press, 1961), 14-16.

[15] Active defenses are military systems designed for intercepting aircraft and missiles in flight. Examples of passive defenses include command posts that are underground or mobile, redundant (duplicate) military and industrial facilities, and plans for crisis dispersal of civilian populations, all of which are intended to mitigate the consequences of an attack.

[16] Robert Standish Norris and Thomas B. Cochran, *US-USSR Strategic Offensive Nuclear Forces, 1946-1990*, NWD 90-2 (Washington, D.C.: Natural Resources Defense Council, May 15, 1990), 2; J.C. Hopkins and Sheldon A. Goldberg, *The Development of Strategic Air Command, 1946-1986 (The Fortieth Anniversary History)* (Offutt Air Force Base, Neb.: Office of the Historian, Headquarters Strategic Air Command, Sept. 1, 1986), 65, 98, 147; Dick Cheney, *Department of Defense Annual Report to the President and the Congress* (Washington, D.C.: GPO, Feb. 1992), 59; U.S. Air Force, "LGM-30G Minuteman III," fact sheet (July 26, 2010); and Hans M. Kristensen, "U.S. Strategic Submarine Patrols Continue at Near Cold War Tempo," FAS [Federation of American Scientists] Strategic Security Blog (March 16, 2009), http://www.fas.org/blog/ssp.

[17] Circular error probable is the radius of the circle within which half the weapons are expected to fall.

[18] Secretary of Defense Robert M. Gates, DoD News Briefing with Secretary Gates and [JCS Chairman] Adm. [Michael] Mullen from the Pentagon (Feb. 1, 2010), transcript, DoD release; and Department of Defense, *Quadrennial Defense Review Report* (Washington, D.C.: Department of Defense, Feb. 2010), 33.

[19] On the limitations of deterrent threats backed by conventional forces, see Edward Rhodes, "Conventional Deterrence," *Comparative Strategy*, Vol. 19, No. 3 (July-Sept. 2000), 221-253.

[20] Alfred Vagts, *Defense and Diplomacy: The Soldier and the Conduct of Foreign Relations* (New York: King's Crown Press, 1956), 232-261.

[21] Barry M. Blechman and Stephen S. Kaplan, *Force Without War: U.S. Armed Forces as a Political Instrument* (Washington, D.C.: Brookings Institution, 1978).

[22] Hopkins and Goldberg, *The Development of Strategic Air Command*, op. cit., 14, 59, 73, 108-109; Samuel R. Williamson, Jr., with the collaboration of Steven L. Rearden, *The View from Above: High-Level Decisions and the Soviet-American Strategic Arms Competition, 1945-1950* (Washington, D.C.: Office of the OSD [Office of the Secretary of Defense] Historian, Oct. 1975), (Top Secret/Restricted Data; declassified in part), 104, 106, 111, http://www.dod.mil/pubs/foi/rdroom.html; Richard K. Betts, *Nuclear Blackmail and Nuclear Balance* (Washington, D.C.: Brookings Institution, 1987), 103, 105; Robert J. Watson, *History of the Office of the Secretary of Defense, Vol. IV: Into the Missile Age, 1956-1960* (Washington, D.C.: GPO, 1997), 65, 66-67; Dwight D. Eisenhower, *The White House Years, Vol. II: Waging Peace, 1956-1961* (Garden City, N.Y.: Doubleday, 1965), Chapter 11, "Landing in Lebanon," esp. p. 59; Michael Dobbs, *One Minute to Midnight: Kennedy, Khrushchev, and Castro on the Brink of Nuclear War* (New York: Alfred A. Knopf, 2008), esp. 49-52, 94-96; Robert Kipp, Lynn Peake, and Herman Wolk, *Strategic Air Command Operations in the Cuban Crisis of 1962, Historical Study No. 90, Vol. I* (Offutt Air Force Base, Neb.: Strategic Air Command, 1963), (Top Secret/Formerly Restricted Data/ No Foreign Dissemination; declassified in part, 2008), 33-78, http://www.gwu/~nsarchiv/; and Barry M. Blechman and Douglas M. Hart, "The Political

Utility of Nuclear Weapons: The 1973 Middle East Crisis," *International Security*, Vol. 7, No. 1 (Summer 1982), 132-156.

[23] Henry Kissinger, *Years of Upheaval* (Boston: Little, Brown & Co., 1982), 591.

[24] At present, only the D5 SLBM line remains open. Department of the Navy, *Fiscal Year (FY) 2011 Budget Estimates: Justification of Estimates—Weapons Procurement* (Washington, D.C.: Department of the Navy, Feb. 2010).

[25] U.S. Navy, "Fleet Ballistic Missile Submarines," fact sheet, Navy Fact File (May 11, 2009).

[26] Kristensen, "U.S. Strategic Submarine Patrols Continue at Near Cold War Tempo," op. cit.

[27] Unclassified fact sheet on the *New START Treaty Framework and Nuclear Force Structure Plans* report, op. cit.

[28] Congressional Budget Office, *Rethinking the Trident Force* (Washington, D.C.: Congressional Budget Office, July 1993), 10. Special fittings would be required for the D5 to carry 12 Mk-4 RVs.

[29] Amy F. Woolf, *U.S. Strategic Nuclear Forces: Background, Developments, and Issues*, RL33640 (Washington, D.C.: Congressional Research Service, Jan. 20, 2010), 17.

[30] Loc. cit. There are, in fact, more W76 warheads in the strategic force as a whole than warheads of any other type. See Thomas Scheber, *Reliable Replacement Warheads: Perspectives and Issues*, United States Nuclear Strategy Forum Publication No. 0005 (Fairfax, Va.: National Institute Press, August 2007), 9.

[31] U.S. Navy, "Trident Fleet Ballistic Missile," fact sheet, Navy Fact File (Jan. 17, 2009).

[32] Woolf, *U.S. Strategic Nuclear Forces*, op. cit., 9.

[33] U.S. Air Force, "LGM-30G Minuteman III," op. cit.

[34] Woolf, *U.S. Strategic Nuclear Forces*, op. cit., 10-11.

[35] Unclassified fact sheet on the *New START Treaty Framework and Nuclear Force Structure Plans* report, op. cit.

[36] Department of Energy, *FY 2012 Congressional Budget Request, Vol. 1: National Nuclear Security Administration,* DOE/CF-0057 (Washington, D.C.: Department of Energy, Feb. 2011), 67, 69.

[37] U.S. Air Force, "LGM-30G Minuteman III," op. cit.

[38] Rebecca Grant, *Return of the Bomber: The Future of Long Range Strike* (Arlington, Va.: Air Force Association, Feb. 2007), 10-15.

[39] U.S. Air Force, *Long Range Strike Aircraft White Paper* (Washington, D.C.: U.S. Air Force, Nov. 2001), 2; Secretary of Defense Task Force on DoD Nuclear Weapons Management, *Phase I Report: The Air Force's Nuclear Mission* (Washington, D.C.: Department of Defense, Sept. 2008), D-1; Robert S. Norris and Hans M. Kristensen, "U.S. Nuclear Forces, 2010," *Bulletin of the Atomic Scientists*, Vol. 66, No. 3 (May-June 2010), 58, 65; and Woolf, *U.S. Strategic Nuclear Forces*, op. cit., 20, 21-23.

[40] DoD, *Nuclear Posture Review Report*, op. cit., 24; and Secretary of Defense Robert M. Gates, testimony before the Senate Armed Services Committee (June 17, 2010), committee transcript, 8.

[41] Kurt Guthe, *Assessments of the Bomber Force: Lessons from the Past, Directions for the Future* (Fairfax, Va.: National Institute for Public Policy, Dec. 1998), 19. The option to

"re-role" the B-1 for nuclear missions was eliminated as a result of the 2001 Nuclear Posture Review. See Adm. James O. Ellis, commander in chief, U.S. Strategic Command, in Senate Armed Services Committee, *Department of Defense Authorization for Appropriations for Fiscal Year 2003*, Part 7, 107th Cong., 2d sess. (Washington, D.C.: GPO, 2003), 169.

[42] "Air Force Global Strike Command Gains Three Bomber Bases," Air Force News Service (Feb. 2, 2010).

[43] Secretary of Defense Dick Cheney and Gen. Colin Powell, JCS chairman, news briefing (Sept. 28, 1991), transcript, DoD release; and William S. Cohen, *Department of Defense Annual Report to the President and the Congress* (Washington, D.C.: GPO, 2001), 92.

[44] U.S. Air Force, "AGM-86B/C/D Missiles," fact sheet (May 24, 2010).

[45] William B. Scott, "Test Drops of B61-11 Penetrator Weapon Continue," *Aviation Week & Space Technology* (June 9, 1997), 75-76.

[46] U.S. Air Force, *Long Range Strike Aircraft White Paper*, op. cit., 20.

[47] Office of the Deputy Assistant to the Secretary of Defense for Nuclear Matters, *Nuclear Matters: A Practical Guide* (Washington, D.C.: Office of the Deputy Assistant to the Secretary of Defense for Nuclear Matters, 2008), 37.

[48] Ibid., 39.

[49] U.S. Air Force, "AGM-86B/C/D Missiles," op. cit.

[50] U.S. Air Force, "B-52 Stratofortress," fact sheet (April 23, 2010); and U.S. Air Force, "B-2 Spirit," fact sheet (April 23, 2010). In-flight refueling can extend these ranges.

[51] U.S. Air Force, *Long Range Strike Aircraft White Paper*, op. cit., 20; and National Research Council of the National Academies, *Effects of Nuclear Earth Penetrator and Other Weapons* (Washington, D.C.: National Academies Press, 2005), 3, 13-17, 26-27, 30-51, 110-112.

[52] Kipp et al., *Strategic Air Command Operations in the Cuban Crisis of 1962*, op. cit., 33-59.

[53] Maj. Gen. Polly Peyer, chair, *Air Force Blue Ribbon Review of Nuclear Weapons Policies and Procedures* (Washington, D.C.: Headquarters U.S. Air Force, February 8, 2008), 16, 17, http://www.fas.org/blog/ssp.

[54] Command Historian's Office, U.S. Strategic Command, *History of the United States Strategic Command, June 1, 1992—October 1, 2002* (Offutt Air Force Base, Neb.: U.S. Strategic Command, Jan. 2004), 30.

[55] Lt. Gen. Frank G. Klotz, commander, Air Force Global Strike Command, prepared statement before the House Armed Services Committee (Jan. 21, 2010); and Woolf, *U.S. Strategic Nuclear Forces*, op. cit., 22-23.

[56] A Department of Energy-sponsored study done in the early 1980s reported "at times in the past, the warheads for a large part of the U.S. [fleet ballistic missile submarine] force have been found to be badly deteriorated. At different times, a large fraction of the warheads either obviously or potentially would not work; they were obvious or potential duds." Jack W. Rosengren, *Some Little-Publicized Difficulties With a Nuclear Freeze*, RDA-TR-122116-001 (Marina del Rey, Calif.: R&D Associates, Oct. 1983), 13-20 (the quote is from p. 13). See also Walter Pincus, "Scientists Bare Warhead Duds on '60s Polaris," *Washington Post* (Dec. 2, 1978).

[57] DoD, *Nuclear Posture Review Report*, op. cit., 22, 25, 38.

[58] J.D. Crouch II, assistant secretary of defense for international security policy, "Challenges of a New Capability-Based Defense Strategy: 'Transforming US Strategic Forces,'" briefing to the National Defense Industrial Association 2003 Science & Engineering Technology Conference (March 5, 2003), briefing slide 21, "Nuclear Forces and Contingencies."

[59] National Research Council, *Effects of Nuclear Earth Penetrator and Other Weapons*, op. cit., 20.

[60] Amy F. Woolf, *Conventional Warheads for Long-Range Ballistic Missiles: Background and Issues for Congress*, RL33067 (Washington, D.C.: Congressional Research Service, Jan. 26, 2009), 7-8.

[61] Defense Science Board Task Force on Future Strategic Strike Forces, *Final Report* (Washington, D.C.: Office of the Under Secretary of Defense for Acquisition, Technology, and Logistics, February 2004), 7-8, 7-18—7-19.

[62] C^{4}ISR refers to command, control, communications, computers, intelligence, surveillance, and reconnaissance.

[63] Thomas Scheber, "Whither the Triad: Considerations for a Triad, Dyad, or Monad," in Taylor Bolz, ed., *In the Eyes of the Experts: Analysis and Comments on America's Strategic Posture* (Washington, D.C.: United States Institute of Peace Press, 2009), 73.

[64] DoD, *Nuclear Posture Review Report*, op. cit., 24; U.S. Air Force, *Long Range Strike Aircraft White Paper*, op. cit., 2, 20; Secretary of Defense Task Force on DoD Nuclear Weapons Management, *Phase I Report*, op. cit., D-1; Norris and Kristensen, "U.S. Nuclear Forces, 2010," op. cit., 58, 65; Secretary of Defense Gates, testimony before the Senate Armed Services Committee (June 17, 2010), op. cit., 8; and Crouch, "Challenges of a New Capability-Based Defense Strategy," op. cit.

CHAPTER 12

The Role of Strategic Communication in Deterrence: Lesson from History

Richard H. Estes

Gone are the Cold War days of an enemy one could count on, the isometric exercise of two enormous powers leaning against each other to keep the military balance. No more alarming encounters as the nuclear clock ticked to zero, and seemingly beyond, with great nuclear forces a word away from launch, and the world an hour away from a war after which "the survivors would envy the dead." [1]

During the Cold War the United States and its primary allies relied on a policy of deterrence to prevent the Soviet Union and its allies from starting a central nuclear war and from escalating crises or regional conflicts to that level.

To maintain an effective deterrent to war and escalation of conflicts, most believe seven essential elements needed to be in place:

1. A U.S. and allied capability that could inflict an unacceptable level of damage in retaliation to an attack.
2. The will to use this retaliatory capability if the United States, its allies or vital interests were attacked or severely threatened.
3. The ability to effectively communicate both the U.S. will and its overwhelming retaliatory capability to adversary leaders so the U.S. deterrence threat was credible and understood.
4. The capability to survive an enemy attack and still retaliate with overwhelming force.
5. The capability to correctly and speedily identify the origins of any large-scale attack.
6. Knowledge of the locations of the attackers and the capability to reach their vital assets in response.

7. A rational opponent who would understand all of the above and who, in self interest, would be dissuaded from risky aggressive behavior that could lead to central nuclear war.

During the Cold War period of 1945-1991, perhaps the closest the superpowers came to nuclear war was the October 1962 Cuban Missile Crisis. Rational behavior finally prevailed, and as a result, there was "the dawning of another day" – the metaphor used for the end of the crisis in the 2000 movie *The Thirteen Days*. This came about through a series of decisions, understandings, misunderstandings and blind alleys all communicated in some form among enemies. And that communication, that *strategic communication,* was essential in *deterring* both the United States and the Soviet Union from taking action that could quite possibly have spelled an end to civilization as we know it.

We face a somewhat different challenge in the 21st century. The world has stepped back from the Armageddon threatened by the Cold War, but has moved down a different path with dangers of its own. As nuclear weapons proliferate, and tensions rise in areas of the world where nuclear weapons have spread and exist, the threat of a smaller state or terrorist organization using one or more nuclear weapons to wreak havoc on a rival regional enemy or on the United States becomes ever more likely. The nuclear club has now grown to include not only the big five (United States, Russia, China, France and the United Kingdom), but also North Korea, Pakistan, India and reportedly, Israel. The Iranian and North Korea nuclear weapons programs may well spur their regional adversaries also to seek nuclear arms.

Nuclear know-how is available. A number of states which had nuclear weapons have now given them up: South Africa, Ukraine, Kazakhstan and Belarus. Libya nearly acquired nuclear arms through the black market before giving up its pursuit under pressure. Clearly, there is a widespread knowledge today of how to create highly enriched uranium or bomb-grade plutonium, as well as how to weaponize these highly explosive materials. While mounting such weapons on missiles or delivering them by aircraft or other means is somewhat more problematic, that knowledge is available as well. Deterring such attacks requires solving a variety of different equations, some with more variables. But one of the pivotal tools for solving that deterrence of war problem will again be strategic communication.

Effective strategic communication is at the heart of effective deterrence. It is public diplomacy, public relations, declaratory policy and actions that combine to send a deterrence message. It's all the ways a country or organization presents its intentions to its audience and attempts to influence that audience. Deterrence of war, escalation or proliferation relies heavily on messages of strategic communication, and those messages have little effect if they are not credible. To demonstrate credibility in the post-Cold War world, military power is necessary, but not sufficient. For deterrence of war to work, the United States must have a coherent message, the message must be well-explained, and others in the world must understand and buy into the message, whether from an allied or adversarial point of view.

The strategic deterrence policy of the United States is among the most important for this country, and one that must be virtually perfect. In a coherent strategic communication plan, one that conveys the nuclear retaliatory power and will of the United States, the threshold for the use of nuclear weapons should be the centerpiece of the U.S. deterrence posture. For this enterprise to be successful the United States must have the absolute confidence and respect of its various audiences – and its threat of retaliation must be credible.

The 2010 Nuclear Posture Review

As this was written, the United States had just concluded its Nuclear Posture Review (NPR); a top-to-bottom look at all matters nuclear performed at the start of each administration. This review forms the foundation for the *strategic deterrence policy* and its underlying *strategic communication plan* of the United States. The 2010 NPR lays out the strategy and capability required to deter war, to deter escalation of ongoing conflict and is mated with a nuclear nonproliferation policy to reduce nuclear threats. This story, this vision the United States wishes to project, at once must be credible and at the same time be backed by policies that match the philosophical objectives.

The Nuclear Posture Review for the Obama administration had the benefit of front-end guidance from the President, namely his speech made in Prague in April of 2009.[2] The speech outlined four goals for his nuclear weapons national strategy:

1. Negotiation of a new Strategic Arms Reduction Treaty (New START)
2. United States ratification of the Comprehensive Test Ban Treaty.
3. Strengthening of the Nuclear Non-Proliferation Treaty (NPT) which was reviewed in 2010.
4. Locking down of all fissile material worldwide inside four years to prevent it from falling into hostile hands.

The Prague speech was *declaratory policy,* a clear and unambiguous statement on the record that outlines the intentions of the President and the United States.[3] Such statements are elements of strategic communication and help convey the vision of the United States. In President Obama's speech, he clearly lays out where he would like to lead the country and the world *vis a vis* nuclear weapons. But all four goals require the cooperation and approval of others. The first and third are treaties that require agreements with other countries and eventual ratification by the United States Senate. The Comprehensive Test Ban Treaty, part of the push for controlling nuclear spread, was concluded in 1996 but has not yet been ratified by Congress. The President has told the world the direction he wishes to take, but that direction is anything but sure. But his willingness to enter into and abide by treaties with respect to nuclear weapons, rather than only take unilateral actions, is a strategic communication message all by itself and signals a declaratory policy that is a departure from the policies of the George W. Bush administration.

This NPR, unlike any before it, is first and foremost a product of the front office, and the document *does* represent policies the President controls. President Obama was "making editing changes in the Nuclear Posture Review right up to the last minutes before it was to go to press," says William J. Perry, defense secretary in the Clinton administration.[4] In the past, this document was always important in the halls of the Pentagon and the scientific world, but had never risen to the level of political policy.

But this NPR is presidential declaratory policy, and such emphasis reinforces its effectiveness as strategic communication.

Among the key conclusions of the NPR:

- The United States will continue to strengthen conventional capabilities and reduce the role of nuclear weapons in deterring non-nuclear attacks, with the objective of making deterrence of nuclear attack on the United States or our allies and partners the sole purpose of U.S. nuclear weapons.
- The United States would consider the use of nuclear weapons only in extreme circumstances to defend the vital interests of the United States or its allies and partners.
- The United States will not use or threaten to use nuclear weapons against non-nuclear states party to the NPT and is in compliance with their non-proliferation obligations.[5]

The language in the report concerned some the United States had not foresworn the first use of nuclear weapons. It concerned others the United States had been too transparent with non-nuclear states that may use chemical or biological weapons against it knowing in advance the penalty would not be nuclear, provided they were toeing the line with regard to the NPT.

But no one could say the administration's policy was not clearly communicated. And a reasonable case could be made the policy was credible. In the document, the administration made no claims not backed up. For instance, in the case of stating publicly the United States would not use nuclear weapons against a non-nuclear country in compliance with the NPT, it merely stated the obvious. The threat of nuclear attack against a non-nuclear state as a policy may have excited some hard-liners in the past, but in fact almost no one believed the United States would have lowered the nuclear-use threshold to that level if the survival of the country were not in question; the threat of "nuking them back to the stone age" was simply not credible.

Leaving some ambiguity in the public declarations was good strategic communication as well. Allowing nuclear states, or those on the road to nuclear weapons such as Iran, to wonder just what the United States *would* do is effective strategic communication too, particularly when the target set has been narrowed significantly by eliminating the non-nuclear states as targets for possible nuclear retaliation. A state may be more deterred from acquiring its own nuclear weapons when it realizes the crosshairs of the United States and other nuclear states could be on it as a result of its acquisition.

The ambiguity implied in not stating a policy of "no first use" is also useful as a deterrent. After all, first use was an unstated policy option during most of the Cold War in Western Europe to be ready to blunt the superior numbers of a conventional Warsaw Pact attack. Not taking the option off the table now is credible and good strategic communication provided the President and his national security team is *willing,* and *seen to be willing* to use nuclear weapons in some contingencies.

If the 2010 NPR, underpinned by the President's Prague speech, is a blueprint for the future, what did strategic communication look like during the Cold War?

Communicating Deterrence Threats During the Cold War

The various deterrence strategies used by the United States and the Soviet Union are well known to those who lived through those years, particularly those who participated actively. In some respects, strategic communication for deterrence of war was much simpler during the years following World War II and before the fall of the Berlin Wall. There were two major super powers, the United States and the Soviet Union. A fabulously expensive arms race kept military capabilities at rough parity, rational leaders headed each country and both countries realized a nuclear war between them might possibly spell the end of civilization.

Despite endless variations on the theme – missile gaps, missile defenses, first use, survivable second strike, counterforce strategies, countervailing strategies, massive retaliation, flexible response and others – all focused on the same goal: not allowing the other side to gain enough of an edge that it thought it could win a nuclear war. To deter the Soviets or any other adversary from war or escalation, each side thought it important to communicate clearly to the other the existence of sufficient survivable retaliatory capability to make an attack by its rival futile at best, and, at worst, suicidal. Each side strove to communicate enough capability and will to use that capability to deter the other. This was strategic communication.

The United States and the Soviet Union deterred one another from nuclear attack by the concept of mutually assured destruction, or MAD, a term that actually came into use in the 1960s when coined by Robert McNamara. The underlying concept was each side controlled client states around the world, and the sponsor superpowers supplied arms and support to those clients. In turn, the sponsors could more or less count on those smaller states to do their bidding – particularly in time of war – and exercised extraordinary control over them in time of crisis. These smaller client states became part of the stalemate. The threat of nuclear war at the superpower level lessened the threat of conflict at the client state level out of fear such a war would escalate out of control. There were wars, to be sure – in the Middle East, Korea, Southeast Asia and others – but the superpowers kept a lid on these conflicts. This *balance of power* during the Cold War period brought a tense, stomach-churning, five-minutes-to-midnight sort of stability for close to 50 years. And stability and bi-polar alignment made strategic communication and resulting deterrence ever so much simpler than today.

Why was deterrence and its vehicle, strategic communication, easier then? Primarily, it was because each side had a single audience. Of course China was a player to some degree, and the "China Card" was a factor in some of the thinking between the two super powers over the years. But, essentially, if the Soviet Union and the United States deterred one another, stability in the largest sense reigned throughout most of the world. Interestingly, this stalemate that could end civilization if broken played out with a set of rules, underpinned by the concept an *accidental* war would be the cruelest of fates. Each side carefully monitored the activity of the other, and each side also informed the other when exercises or launches that could appear threatening took place so the opponent would not draw the wrong conclusion and *launch on warning* [6] when the circumstances were actually benign.

Further, the two powers established elaborate, direct communications methods to discuss any movements or crises that required immediate and personal contact to provide assurance to the other side or to negotiate. The famous "hot line" between the two countries, originally a teletype at the Pentagon installed after the Cuban Missile Crisis, is an example of such a communications tool.

All of the forgoing underscores the fact people on both sides were and are in the decision loop, and what looked like a reasonably straight-forward deterrence equation during the Cold War was run by "by people who [were] ignorant of many facts, people who [could] be gripped by anger or fear, people who make mistakes—sometimes dreadful mistakes."[7] These were rational actors who tended to act like human beings in time of crisis, and these same rational actors saw the need for very careful communication, both tactical and strategic, to ensure deterrence held. It almost didn't in 1962.

The Cuban Missile Crisis and Strategic Communication

President John F. Kennedy's foreign policy during the first year of his administration was a succession of failures starting with the ill-fated Bay of Pigs invasion in April 1961, followed by the June-November 1961 Berlin crisis during which the U.S.S.R. sealed off East Berlin by building a wall through the city while the United States did little but file diplomatic protests. The year was further marred by the March 1961 communist offensives in Laos that brought most of that country under their control. The year 1961 was also the year Nikita Khrushchev addressed the United Nations and pounded his shoe on the lectern to the dismay of the western world. The year 1961 also saw the Soviet Union exploding the world's largest nuclear explosion in a test estimated at 50 megatons.

Further, at the 1961 Vienna summit conference Khrushchev shouted across the negotiating table at the young American president, appearing to shake him. It seemed clear the Soviet leader's perception of John Kennedy was of an inexperienced and timid decision-maker who could be bullied. It is in this context the Soviet leader apparently decided to gamble by sneaking nuclear weapons, and missiles with which to launch them, into Cuba in the early fall of 1962.

The United States had long adhered to the Monroe Doctrine that admonished other great powers to avoid imperialistic adventures in the

Western Hemisphere. The Kennedy administration had indeed verbally warned the Soviet leadership against putting nuclear weapons or establishing a major military buildup in Cuba and had been assured it contemplated no such moves – right up to the event itself. The U.S.S.R. leadership then did just what it said it would not do, only to be discovered by U.S. intelligence before it had presented the nuclear *fait accompli* in Cuba.

Up until that point, U.S. deterrence policy had failed in terms of preventing the U.S.S.R. nuclear build-up in Cuba. U.S. strategic communication failed because, despite having superior nuclear forces and having verbally warned the Soviets against stationing nuclear arms in Cuba, the Soviet leader simply did not believe President Kennedy had the will to act against such a provocation. Khrushchev had underestimated President Kennedy, seeing in him the pattern of ineffectiveness and indecision at Vienna, Berlin, Cuba and during the Bay of Pigs disaster. U.S. verbal strategic communications were not congruent with previous U.S. actions "on the ground." U.S. words of warning did not match its deeds and JFK did not personally impress the Secretary General of the Communist Party of the Soviet Union.

However, once the missiles were discovered, President Kennedy toughened his stance, turning to clear and decisive verbal and action communications, which eventually caused the Soviet leadership to backtrack and reverse course on its policy by withdrawing the nuclear weapons and missiles from Cuba. Kennedy's public televised warning to the Soviet Union made it all but impossible for him to retreat and permit the Soviet gambit. In fact he was so committed publicly, that to retreat at that point would have likely resulted in calls for impeachment. His public and private communications during the missile crisis matched his actions – a blockade of Cuba accompanied by a massive buildup of military force opposite Cuba's.

The Soviet leaders were given absolutely crystal clear communication that the option was withdrawal or war, and that war would likely be nuclear war – at a time when the U.S.S.R. was at a military disadvantage. The U.S. strategic communication during the 13 days of the crisis was magnificent – a stark contrast from the previous 20 months where perceived weakness and lack of credibility were the hallmarks. The

Kennedy administration strategic communication package included a well coordinated media campaign.

The President's televised challenge to the Soviet missile buildup left him little public room to reverse course, a fact Khrushchev had to realize. The U.S.S.R. had been put in the position of retreating or risking a nuclear exchange. In the second week of the crisis, JFK's team took the communications initiative – mobilizing U.S. public opinion, allied public opinion, and world public opinion to back the U.S. position and isolate the Soviet Union. U.S. United Nations Ambassador Adlai Stevenson dramatically presented the U.S. intelligence results to the U.N. Security Council, an event reported by the world press. Dean Rusk, U.S. Secretary of State, called for a meeting of the Organization of American States (OAS) where U.S. representatives briefed Latin American allies on the developments and the Soviet threat in the Caribbean. U.S. officials briefed NATO allies. Meanwhile the United States and Soviet Officials exchanged diplomatic threats and possible solutions.

Outside the public eye, Attorney General Robert Kennedy and other U.S. representatives met with Soviet diplomats to search for a peaceful solution. One was eventually found and negotiated, an agreement where U.S. Jupiter Missiles were to be withdrawn from Turkey in exchange for the removal of Soviet missiles and nuclear weapons from Cuba. The bargain was sealed, and its compromise terms agreed upon by the Soviet leadership only if the United States kept the promise to remove missiles from Turkey, an undisclosed secret during the Cuban drawdown. This solution helped preserve JFK's reputation, as well as his ability to keep a lid on escalation pressures from his critics.

Strategic communication in the Cuban Missile Crisis played a large role in the build-up to the crisis. There could be no doubt it played a crucial role in its resolution. Kennedy and Khrushchev exchanged letters. Khrushchev communicated through a businessman who happened to be in Moscow, and back channels in Washington were used, including ABC reporter John Scali. Diplomats in countries far removed from the crisis floated proposals intended to reach the principals, direct diplomacy between the administration and Ambassador Dobrynin took place in Washington and confrontations occurred at the United Nations. Communications were all over the map, and an atmosphere prevailed of, if not 'try anything," at least 'let's make sure we are exploring all avenues.'

Further, communications were slow in 1962, and the delay had two implications. First, each side had a few hours to interpret messages and decide courses of action. This aspect had the obvious down side of allowing each to *misinterpret* messages and take the *wrong* action – which almost happened on more than one occasion during the crisis. Second, the crisis suffered from lack of *direct* communication at the highest level, leaving messages to be sent through lower echelons and back channels with more inherent delay and chance for inappropriate action before the decision makers were privy to the latest thinking or offer. The delays and the routing of the letters from Chairman Khrushchev allowed President Kennedy and his Executive Committee to use the tactic of ignoring a second, more intractable, letter of uncertain provenance and to respond to the first which gave some breathing room.

A case can be made the crisis was an inexorable slide into a war neither side wanted – but was saved by rational actors on both sides. An equally forceful case can be made that both sides were deterred from the start by the destructive and suicidal power that could have been triggered all too easily. In any case, a deal was struck.

The overarching implication of the whole crisis was both super powers stared down each others' gun barrels more than either would have liked. And for all of the tough talk and misinformed adventurism during that grim October 48 years ago, the Soviet Union and the United States realized they needed to be more careful in their actions and the strategic messages sent over the remainder of the Cold War.

To be sure, the arms race continued between the two diametrically opposed ways of life, and both sides spent unimaginable fortunes to maintain parity with the other. But, that the world came close to Armageddon in 1962 later made the deterrence through careful strategic communication a bit easier. Neither side wished to peer over the precipice again, and both sides were willing to communicate – and listen.

This was not a friendly arrangement – far from it. Rather, the two adversaries saw clear advantages to not blowing each other to bits and proceeded on that basis. The first of a series of arms control agreements, SALT I, came in 1972, and while honest men can argue the efficacy of arms control over the next 20 or so years, the process did at least signal a willingness to reduce tensions – or at a minimum – to talk. So, does that mean rationality prevailed during the Cold War? Probably so. But in retrospect, given the people involved could have been ignorant of many facts and could have been gripped by anger or fear, rationality seems like mighty thin gruel.

Robert Kennedy, writing in his memoir of the Cuban Missile Crisis, pointed to a key tenet of strategic communication (although the term was not yet coined in 1968) when he said, "The final lesson of the Cuban Missile Crisis was the importance of placing ourselves in the other country's shoes."[8] A corollary of the statement is, because of cultural differences and translation, others may not *hear* the same message being *sent*, and the sender must take care to ensure the message being heard is precisely the one intended. Robert Kennedy went on to quote his brother, the president, on the concept of leaving the other side the opportunity to retreat gracefully:

> Above all, while defending our own vital interests, nuclear powers must avert those confrontations which bring an adversary to the choice of either a humiliating defeat or a nuclear war.[9]

A New and Dangerous World

A combination of effective deterrence and some "plain dumb luck" allowed the Cold War to end without a central nuclear war. But 10 years after the Soviet Union came apart, a new kind of threat emerged to challenge the U.S. and its allies. The attacks of Sept. 11, 2001, showed the world terrorist ability to commit mayhem on a grand scale. The salient questions in many quarters became: what if terrorists get their hands on a nuclear weapon? If they acquire such a weapon could they be deterred? Could they build one if they had the right materials? Could they buy a complete weapon? If they somehow came into possession of one, could they smuggle the weapon into the United States or an allied country and detonate it?

Two developments amplified these concerns. First, the detection of a nuclear technology smuggling and distribution network created and operated by Dr. A.Q. Khan, the force behind Pakistan's nuclear weapons program. Second, the crumbling of the Soviet Union and the questionable state of nuclear weapons security in the 15 republics of the former Soviet Union as the union came apart. Add the underpaid or out-of-work former

Soviet nuclear scientists who could be available to other countries or terrorist organizations, and little doubt remained why President George W. Bush declared in 2002:

> The gravest danger our nation faces lies at the crossroads of radicalism and technology. Our enemies have openly declared that they are seeking weapons of mass destruction, and evidence indicates that they are doing so with determination.[10]

Three Goals, Three Audiences

During the Cold War era, the United States had three major deterrence goals: (1) deterrence of armed attacks and major warfare; (2) deterrence of escalation of any military conflict to the level of use of weapons of mass destruction (chemical, biological, radiological or nuclear); and (3) deterrence of the proliferation of WMD from one state or group to another. All three apply today.

To pursue those goals, an effective strategic communication effort needs to be consistent, unified and plausible if it is to help the United States deter war, escalation and WMD proliferation. First, all elements of the administration need to speak with one integrated voice to the rest of the world. Second, once the U.S. deterrence policies are agreed upon, every opportunity needs to be used for broadcasting those policies to rival and allied audiences so they are clearly understood and emphasized. Third, actions and words must be coordinated to communicate the same messages:

- Military aggression against the United States, its vital interest and its allies will be so severely dealt with the aggressor could not bear the cost.
- The United States has escalation dominance making escalation of any ongoing conflict counterproductive in the extreme.
- Nuclear proliferation, either by the state acquiring or the state assisting such efforts, will be dealt with so severely that those that go down that path will suffer losses that far exceed any gains in security and prosperity.

As the United States goes about nuclear deterrence in the 21st century, it also has three distinct audiences to consider: leaders of adversary nation-states, leaders of terrorist organizations and leaders of allied countries that depend on U.S. protection from the first two. Any strategic communication campaign must carefully delineate between these three.

Deterrence of military attacks or conflict escalation by other states in the international system still relies on the seven elements that helped deter superpower war during the Cold War. However, as noted elsewhere in the essays on tailored deterrence, each rival state is different in leadership, in regional pressures, in political history, strategic culture, military capability and situational awareness. Thus, the deterrence message must be tailored so rival leaders clearly understand the likely costs of starting or escalating a war or becoming a WMD proliferator and are presented with a persuasive package of messages, verbal and kinetic, that deter and contain them.

Deterring Iran and North Korea

Deterrence of war, WMD use and WMD proliferation through strategic communication leans heavily on engagement – both with our allies (who can help bring pressure to bear on mutual adversaries and who must be convinced of U.S. backing in the face of growing dangers) and directly with those adversaries.

The USAF Counterproliferation Center has proposed increased engagement with our allies and adversaries in some of its earlier work on strategic communication.[11] The central theme at the time was the United States did not have an effective government-wide integrated strategic communication campaign in place. Further, such a campaign when built must be more than just a public relations effort, and if such a campaign were to be successful, it should have a significant component focused on telling the U.S.'s story concerning WMD.

The United States was reasonably effective with its demonstration of action when it invaded Iraq in 2003, sending the clear message it would not tolerate a rogue state with a WMD program. While the invasion took place based on faulty intelligence and may have been ill-advised, it certainly had an effect around the world. Libya may have given up its WMD programs partially as a result of that demonstration. And we may never know if other countries decided to abandon or not start a weapons program as a result.

But, "The United States turned heads with its message of willingness to use force, but failed utterly in communicating the righteousness of the cause. The critical element missing was a coherent message – using precise and planned words, together with other instruments of influence, to explain to the world why the United States was worthy of being followed – and if not followed, at least understood."[12]

Now the United States faces North Korea and Iran and their weapons programs. President Obama has indicated a willingness to engage both, but has significantly fewer cards to play than did his predecessor when he dealt with Iraq. North Korea already has detonated at least two nuclear weapons, however primitive, and is *de facto* in the nuclear club, even if its ability to deliver the weapons remains questionable. An Iraq-like invasion to preempt the use of those weapons is problematic at best and a formula for disaster at worst. Iran is not as far along in its program, but has developed the ability to enrich uranium (it is not clear North Korea has that capability) and has hardened most of its nuclear facilities, as has North Korea. Again, for that reason and others, a preemptive invasion of Iran does not seem advisable in the short term. Containment through deterrence is the fallback position of the United States if Iran acquires a nuclear weapon capability as it seems poised to do.

In both cases, strategic communication is necessary, but probably not sufficient. While engagement is clearly in order, the United States and its allies must be prepared for continued obfuscation from governments that as a minimum do not think and function as ours does and are quite possibly irrational at times. Strategic communication is probably more effectively applied with our allies, partners and those who have more influence with North Korea and Iran than does the United States. These coalitions of sorts can be used to isolate the two countries and to bring pressure to bear.

The sense of the entire world being against these rogue states should be a very effective strategic communication message in itself, but the danger always exists that the isolation could drive them to believe nuclear weapons are all the more necessary – a fine line the U.S. and its allies must walk.

Communications messages normally consist of a theme, a delivery method and the audience. In North Korea, the audience almost certainly must be the government and specifically Kim Jong Il. No civil society exists to speak of, NGOs are not trusted and the average citizen has no access to the outside world. He hears what the government wants him to hear. Pure communications directed at anyone but the highest members of the government are not likely to have much effect. Further clouding the strategic communication front is security issues tend to trump the plight of the population in dealings with North Korea.[13] Themes and delivery methods are almost moot if the only audience is a 68-year-old stroke victim with an out-sized sense of entitlement.

On the other hand, Iran seems a richer target ripe for strategic communication. There are two distinct audiences, the government and the population – and the former really has two factions. Ahmadinejad's alarming rhetoric may or may not represent the full position of the Iranian government, since the supreme leader of the country is the religious leader, Ayatollah Ali Khamene'i, himself a hard-liner, but perhaps not always in consonance with his president. The population of Iran is reasonably open and proud of its country, but is not as anti-West as its leadership. As such, it represents a potential audience, or target, for a strategic communication campaign.[14] Further, the typical man on the street in Iran has more access to the outside by far than do the people of North Korea. For example, the 2009 election uprisings in Iran were broadcast around the world thanks to the protesters' access to Twitter.

Despite being brutally put down, the protesters demonstrated information flowed in and out of Iran. And Iranians have had access to the internet for some years, although the Iranian government maintains the capability of blocking or slowing access, as it did earlier this year.[15] Methods of reaching the population are there, and the Iranian people seem to be willing to take risks to reach the outside world.

The United States and allies appear to be using all of the strategic communication avenues open to them: attempting to drive a wedge between the population and the government, trying to separate the two factions of government, isolating the country through diplomatic pressure and sanctions, engaging directly with leadership, and making direct demands. Perhaps the most likely avenue for success is a popular uprising similar to 1979, but in reverse – against the theocracy. But such a shifting of the tectonic plates in Persia will undoubtedly come well after acquisition of Iranian nuclear weapons, leaving the world left to deter their use, not their development.

Communication and Deterring Terrorist WMD Use

Deterring a terrorist organization from acquiring or using WMDs is quite another matter. Brian Jenkins of RAND says we have already failed in one sense in deterrence: two out of five people in the United States consider it likely a terrorist organization will detonate a nuclear weapon on our soil in the foreseeable future. This, despite as far as we know, no terrorist organization has a nuclear weapon, nor does it presently appear to have the means or material to build one.

Yet Jenkins makes the case al-Qaeda or some other organization already is a terrorist nuclear power since, as Alfred Hitchcock put it, "The terror is not in the bang, only in the anticipation of it."[16] That may be, but many believe if a terrorist organization is able to obtain a nuclear weapon, it will not be at all deterrable, and if it can find a way to employ it, it will do so.

Prudence dictates one assumes this worst case when trying to prevent the unimaginable from happening. But Lewis Dunn of SAIC postulates possession may not be the whole story since a detonation of a nuclear weapon by a terrorist organization could be perceived as so horrible as to be damaging to the terrorist's cause, or the weapon could be deemed too valuable as a tool of blackmail to be expended.[17] Brian Jenkins would support this latter possibility. Still, as Admiral Richard Mies, former commander of the U.S. Strategic Command, says in Jenkins' book, "How do you deter or dissuade someone whose reward is in the 'afterlife?'"[18]

The short answer is you probably don't, in the current environment. People who kill thousands at once by flying airplanes into buildings are unlikely to hesitate to detonate a nuclear weapon if they have one. Neither are terrorists who are willing to make their final act on this earth a suicide bombing.

Three avenues are open to us to stop this potential game-changer. First is to marshal all of our intelligence and law enforcement capability, and that of our allies, to stop terrorists or terrorist smuggling networks from obtaining the material to make a bomb or from getting a complete weapon itself. A subset of this approach is to ensure all weapons and materials are first *known* and then *secured*. The knowing and securing become more difficult the farther one removes himself from the first world.

The second method, and this *is* strategic communication, is to encourage, to *demand,* the nations of the world band together to isolate those who would traffic these sorts of materials and particularly to isolate those who would use the weapons. And that demand needs to be specific about actions the United States will take against a country or organization that, willingly or otherwise, supports nuclear terror. This means of deterring WMD use by terrorists threatens those that supply and support their WMD efforts. This deterrence is directed at supporters rather than the possibly undeterrable terrorists.

The third way is to change the environment. This does not imply appeasing terrorists. Rather it is a sincere campaign of confidence building, of maintaining the moral high ground (or *regaining* it if one believes the United States is somewhere below the peak at the moment) and of understanding what other cultures are hearing as it communicates. It means leadership and persuading the countries of the world to follow the United States because they see it in their own best interest to cooperate because *they want to*, not just because our country is rich and powerful. Rather, a U.S. strategic communications plan to deter war, escalation and WMD proliferation must show the United States leadership and military capability is in the best interests of all its allies and most of the world community and, hence, worthy of their support.

U.S. Nuclear Posture and the Nonproliferation Regime

As the United States continues to nudge, pull, threaten and otherwise exert influence on the rest of the world with regard to the nonproliferation of nuclear weapons, it must be able to look those other countries directly in the eye and say, "This is our position on nonproliferation, here's how we are reducing our arsenal and making the world safer, and here is how we are posturing the remainder of our forces to maximize deterrence, while minimizing the potential that these weapons will ever be used again." If the United States, the only country to ever use nuclear weapons, can make that case for the moral high ground, the United States will be effectively using strategic communication.

To berate other countries on nuclear programs without first clearly explaining why the United States has the moral authority to do so is a tricky business at best. The United States *does* have that authority, but in past years it has not made a good case for it in the theater of world opinion, choosing instead to assume the other players simply will understand because of who we are. But our audience wants to know, among other things, how the United States intends to carry out its obligations under Article VI of the NPT which states:

"Each of the Parties to the Treaty undertakes to pursue negotiations in good faith on effective measures relating to cessation of the nuclear arms race at an early date and to nuclear disarmament, and on a treaty on general and complete disarmament under strict and effective international control."[19]

At the same time, our allies around the world need to be reassured the nuclear umbrella the United States has extended over them since World War II will be there as its arsenal decreases and its posture is reduced. And our adversaries should know whether or not the United States will possess sufficient retaliatory capability in the future to make any WMD attack futile on their part. They must also be convinced by U.S. words and deeds, in a coordinated strategic communication package, that the U.S. leadership has the will to use military force to punish any attacker who strikes at them.

In this world where there is a natural tension between nuclear posture and nonproliferation, the 2010 Nuclear Posture Review (NPR), combined with the Prague speech the preceding year, the new START treaty, the Global Nuclear Summit, and the five-year review of the Nonproliferation Treaty, does a good job of laying out that case for the high ground. The policy taken as a whole allows for a continuing, but reducing, nuclear arsenals, with an ultimate goal of zero nuclear weapons in the world. But at the same time it acknowledges the *realpolitik* of current times: as long as adversaries have nuclear weapons, the United States must have a strong posture for deterrence (including the continuation of the nuclear triad of bombers, submarine launched missiles and ICBMs), as well as for security guarantees.

The 2010 NPR shores up the NPT regime by foreswearing use of nuclear weapons against non-nuclear countries in compliance with the treaty, while leaving extant the possibility of first use if necessary against threatening or attacking nuclear states. Then it moves on to state publicly our largest threat to security is terrorists with nuclear weapons, and we are moving in cooperation with the countries of the world to shut off any access to nuclear materials or weapons within four years. Pretty clear and credible stuff.

If the United States is to have a consistent policy regarding how to deter proliferation by nuclear wannabes, it needs to explain why it treats some states differently than others. For example, it needs to better explain its seemingly turning a blind eye to Israel's nuclear weapons program while demanding other states adhere to the NPT. Also, it needs to develop a convincing rationale to the world as to why it rewards India with trade that supports its nuclear power industry while India remains outside the NPT and ignores the call to a ban. These are tough issues for the United States, but ones with valid policy explanations. Any part of a coherent nuclear strategic communication plan should address the exceptions and others as they arise, and fully explain why the allowances made for the Indias and Israels of the world do not apply to Iran and North Korea, or any other questionable state that chooses to start a nuclear weapons program.

Finally, a word on the goal of total nuclear disarmament. The approach the United States has chosen in recent years is the only rational one available. That is, to work with Russia to reduce the arsenals of both countries while still maintaining enough weapons to deter the other, to offer security guarantees to each side's allies, and to offer an overwhelming counter to rogue states such as Iran and North Korea. The goal of going to zero is morally correct, since clearly so long as such weapons exist, the world faces the risk of devastation from nuclear wars.

But as long as opposing sides have them, and as long as rogue states see these weapons as the great equalizer, the United States cannot go to zero. There is no deterrence value in going to zero in an attempt to show leadership; such a move would be perceived by other nations as weakness. That is not to say over time world arsenals could not be reduced to the point zero is on the horizon.

But in the near-to-medium term, no such possibility exists, and our strategic communication plan should say so. Further it would ease the U.S. task of getting world-wide support for its nuclear nonproliferation programs and goal if the United States better explained the exceptions for Israel and

India. Its strategic communications effort on behalf of deterring WMD proliferation would be strengthened if a case for such inconsistency could be more effectively communicated.

Communicating the Nuclear-Use Threshold

Taking the moral high ground and having others follow the United States depends on having a very high and very credible nuclear-use threshold. The world must know the U.S. does not consider a nuclear weapon "just another weapon" in its warfighting tool box. It must avoid situations such as experienced in Central Europe during the Cold War where first use of nuclear weapons was almost an expected choice to blunt the attack of the superior numbers of the Warsaw Pact.

The U.S. leadership can't think in terms of using nuclear penetrators because our conventional weapons don't dig deep enough. It must not revert to the thinking of some in the past that using nuclear weapons as a radioactive barrier in North Korea (MacArthur) or against the communists in North Vietnam (Goldwater) is an acceptable warfighting doctrine. The dividing line between nuclear weapons and conventional weapons should be a yawning chasm. Those with a finger on the nuclear trigger should realize going nuclear is *not* just the next step in weapons escalation, and to cross that abyss has extraordinary security and moral implications. The only possible warfighting use of nuclear weapons should be when our back is against the wall, survival is at stake and *there are no other options.*

To put ourselves in that position, the United States must maintain a superior conventional force that can take on all potential adversaries, and one that can work its will without having to resort to nuclear weapons. Sixty-five years after the fire-bombings and destruction of Dresden and Tokyo, world opinion and self-restraint also place restraints on *conventional* efforts from causing too many civilian casualties or the euphemistic *collateral damage.*

Such restrictions militate for the ultimate in precision weapons, which the United States currently possesses, but should ensure it maintains. In 1984, Freeman Dyson, a noted physicist, actually made a case that precision guided munitions (PGMs) could obviate the need for nuclear weapons altogether.[20] Dyson was about 20 years ahead of his time, but the capability of the United States is not far removed from that ideal today, particularly with regard to smaller states. As a result, President Obama seemed comfortable in foreswearing the use of nuclear weapons against the small NPT states and rightly so.

Part of a strong conventional force must be a limited defense against ballistic missiles launched from the likes of North Korea or Iran, or from larger powers that accidentally launch a single or a very low number of missiles. The United States approaches that capability now, although some newer systems have been significantly reduced in scope by the Obama administration.[21]

To leave ourselves uncovered against small attacks would be the height of irresponsibility and abandoning the Missile Defense Treaty of 1972 was the only route to conventional insurance against those attacks. During the Cold War under that treaty, each side was limited to one local system, and many restrictions were placed on testing. Both sides relied on MAD as insurance against a missile attack – not much of a defense. As Casper Weinberger said in a speech at the U.S. Air Force Academy in the early 1990s, MAD put the United States in a position that in order "to be perfectly invulnerable, we needed to be perfectly vulnerable."

Having a high nuclear threshold allows the nuclear strategic communication plan of the United States to be credible and having an invincible conventional force permits a high nuclear threshold. The United States should never put itself in a position of making threats it would never carry out and threatening to use nuclear weapons when vital national interests are not at stake falls into that category.[22]

The other side of the coin, however, is a potential adversary must first believe there *is* a threshold beyond which the United States would use nuclear weapons against it, and to be effective, the threshold should be just a bit elusive or ambiguous.

Conclusions

As the United States struggles with its role as the only superpower left on the face of the earth, it has a set of dynamics to consider. Does it exert influence from a position of pure power, or must it be the moral leader of the world? Should it attempt to shape the nations of the world or learn to live with them as they are – but nudging a bit around the edges to ensure a safer planet? Does it lead or does it revert to a form of isolationism, eschewing the benefits of potential coalitions in its actions?

How the United States responds to those challenges is the task and essence of strategic communication, and the answers must be credible. Because without credibility, positions taken by the United States will have no deterrent effect, particularly with those states that either possess nuclear weapons or would like to have them.

President Obama has taken a clear stance with his Nuclear Posture Review in 2010 and the speech in Prague in 2009. The policy is one of engagement with the nations of the world, and in concert with the new START treaty and the NPT review, one that clearly strives to balance its strength through its nuclear posture with a desire to eventually see a world without nuclear weapons. At the same time it takes a pragmatic approach, realizing nuclear weapons are necessary in the foreseeable future to use as a deterrence tool.

With this stance, the President has taken strides toward an effective strategic communication campaign, a campaign crucial to deterrence. First, the President has realized the importance of such a campaign and the importance of his own role in demonstrating to the world the vision of the United States. And that the vision is not a public relations campaign delegated to someone in the State Department. It is the vision the administration wishes to project for this country, the vision on which policies should be based, and one he and the top officials of this nation should constantly shape. This vision and its supporting policies should aim the country at the moral high ground, toward building confidence in its leadership.

The United States, the only country to ever use nuclear weapons against another, should continue to demonstrate it is a good steward of its decreasing arsenal and a tough but reliable ally that can be counted on to use that arsenal as a deterrent for the good of the world. It should demonstrate it angers slowly, it has an extremely high threshold for the use of nuclear weapons, but there is a limit to its patience.

Further, in this post Cold War age, the focus of United States deterrence should be on rogue states such as Iran and North Korea that issue threats to their neighbors, but at the same time it should not let its guard down too much against past adversaries. And it should continue to marshal the forces of the rational world to isolate these rogue states and those that would join them, and to isolate terrorist organizations and their possible attempts to acquire nuclear materials or weapons, since the latter are not likely to be deterred in their use should they ever get their hands on a weapon.

Words matter. Actions matter. Allies and partners matter. Pulling all three together effectively and communicating a coherent, tough, and credible vision and message to adversaries and allies is the essence of deterrence, and of strategic communication. Strategic communication can have no higher calling than to prevent a nuclear war or terrorist attack.

Notes

[1] Premier Nikita Khrushchev, Pravda (July 20, 1963).

[2] Speech delivered by President Barrack Obama, Prague, the Czech Republic (April 5, 2009).

[3] Strategic communication is a general term, the application of which, obviously, is not limited to the United States. However, for the purposes of this discussion, the focus of strategic deterrence will be on the positions of the United States – unless specifically mentioned otherwise.

[4] Hoagland, Jim, "President Obama's farsighted nuclear strategy," *Washington Post* (April 18, 2010).

[5] Nuclear Posture Review Report (April 2010), Department of Defense, Washington, DC., p. ix.

[6] Since ICBMs and SLBMs can reach their targets in a scant 30 minutes, each side had an incentive to launch a retaliatory attack inside that window to avoid losing that asset which itself was probably targeted in a mass attack. In modern times, the United States has been considering a conventional ICBM to deliver a "bolt from the blue" to terrorist locations and other time-sensitive targets around the world, but has hesitated to put such a weapon in the inventory for this same reason. A launch of a conventional ICBM would look like a strategic, and possibly nuclear, launch to Russia or China, and would require extensive communication and pre-briefing to avoid misinterpretation.

[7] Dr. Robert Butterworth quoting Fred Ikle, "Out of Balance," *Aerospace Power Journal* (Fall 2001).

[8] Kennedy, Robert, *Thirteen Days: A Memoir of the Cuban Missile Crisis* (Norton, New York, 1969), 124.

[9] Ibid., 126.

[10] *The National Security Strategy of the United States of America* (Sept. 17, 2002).

[11] *Toward a National Counterproliferation Strategic Communication Plan,* USAF Counterproliferation Center, (Dec. 2007).

[12] Estes, Richard. *A Message Not Yet Sent: Using Strategic Communications to Combat Weapons of Mass Destruction,* USAF Counterproliferation Center Future Warfare Series No. 35, (July 2006).

[13] Testimony of L. Gordon Flake, executive director of the Mansfield Foundation, before the Subcommittee on Asia and Pacific, House Committee on International Relations, (April 2004).

[14] Interview with Charles Lutes, director of Counterproliferation, National Security Council, (March 2010).

[15] Fathi, Nazila, *Iran Disrupts Internet Service Ahead of Protests, New York Times* (Feb. 10, 2010).

[16] Jenkins, Brian Michael, *Will Terrorists Go Nuclear?*, Prometheus Books, Amherst, N.Y. (2008), 26

[17] Lewis A. Dunn, *Can al-Qaeda be Deterred From Using Nuclear Weapons?,* Center for the Study of Weapons of Mass Destruction, Occasional Paper 3, National University Press, Washington, DC (July 2005).

[18] Jenkins, *ob cit,* 277.

[19] The Treaty on the Nonproliferation of Nuclear Weapons (NPT), Article VI (March 5, 1970).

[20] Dyson, Freeman, *Weapons and Hope,* New York (1984).

[21] Ballistic Missile Defense Review, Department of Defense (Feb. 2010).

[22] Interview with Dr. Mitchell Reiss, Vice Provost, College of William and Mary (March 2010). Dr. Reiss is the former director of Policy Planning at the State Department, a policy advisor to presidential candidate Mitt Romney, and has been chosen as the next president of Washington College in Chestertown, Md.

CHAPTER 13

A Nation's Resilience as a Deterrence Factor

Patrick Ellis

For most Berliners, New Year's Eve 1988 was the holiday finale similar to the many eves since the wall, separating East from West, was built. Unfortunately, the ushering in of the fresh year held no real clues the world was about to change and by the end of that year the wall would collapse. Like a door hinge that sets a new direction for the door, a new course was set in the geopolitical world, a harbinger of the massive changes to come. The phantom of the old epoch passed away and a new era was on the horizon. Historians call periods like this a hinge of history.

Hence, when historians write about this period the narrative may very well begin with the fall of the wall and end with the collapse of the World Trade Center buildings. Between those two events the world was transformed from a Cold War paradigm to a more connected globalized paradigm. Consequently, with these changes came new actors who would create new challenges for the United States. Traditional forms of deterrence were set on notice as being less effective against newer non-state actors trying to procure weapons of mass destruction (WMD). This hinge of change would recast our understanding of our adversaries and the deterrence efforts against them.

In the Director of National Intelligence's February 2010 Annual Threat Assessment of the US Intelligence Community, Director Dennis Blair, states, "Traditionally WMD use by most nation states has been constrained by deterrence and diplomacy, but these constraints may be of less utility in preventing the use of mass-effect weapons by terrorist groups."[1]

He further states "the time when only a few states had access to the most dangerous technologies is over. Technologies, often dual-use, circulate easily in our globalized economy, as do the personnel with scientific expertise who design and use them. It is difficult for the United

States and its partners to track efforts to acquire WMD components and production technologies that are widely available."[2] This new threat forces us to reexamine deterrence theories and to develop new means to influence adversaries. This essay is put forth to help stimulate a dialogue on how national resilience might be an affective support to deterrence efforts.

Deterrence

Deterrence has been defined as "the actions of a state or group of states to dissuade a potential adversary from initiating an attack or conflict by the threat of retaliation. Deterrence should credibly demonstrate to an adversary the costs of an attack would be too great and would outweigh any potential gains."[3] The destructive power of nuclear weapons makes retaliatory power absolute.

Fortunately, no nuclear weapons have been used since World War II. This can be mainly attributed to rational leaders who steered away from armed conflict rather than see their nations disappear in a nuclear exchange. However, we have entered into a new era of non-state actors, rational or not, who seem willing to use nuclear weapons as an act of coercion or terror if they were to acquire them. The key task is still the same, "persuading a potential enemy that he should, in his own interest, avoid certain courses of activity..."[4] But terrorists present a new dilemma. How do you deter an enemy with no known return address?

Recent events continue to highlight the terror threat to the United States. On Dec. 25, 2009, Northwest Airlines Flight 253 left Amsterdam Airport, in the Netherlands, on its way to Detroit. On its final descent, 20 minutes before landing, a young Muslim Nigerian passenger tried to set off a plastic bag of explosives sown into his underwear. He was subdued by other passengers who brought this al-Qaeda motivated operation to an end. Then most recently, on May 1, 2010, Faisal Shahzad, born in Pakistan, but naturalized as an American citizen, attempted to detonate a car bomb in Times Square. Reported to have been trained in bomb-making in Pakistan he was caught trying to take a flight to Dubai, United Arab Emirates.

Fortunately these attempts failed; but they do show terrorists will continue to try to attack us, and their weapons will evolve. We must also not lose sight that the crown jewel of terror weapons will continue to be weapons of mass destructions, in particular nuclear and biological. So how do we deter these new terror threats and their possible use of WMDs?

To maximize deterrent effects on an adversary, it is likely that we should follow a dual strategy of deterrence by denial and by retaliations combined with positive outcome for good behavior. First, let the adversary know we can deny them the benefits they seek to obtain from an attack. Second, let them know the cost resulting from an attack will be too high for them. Third, encourage restraint by letting them know that not to attack would be better for them.[5] To be effective these three tasks must be unified as one effort at all level of our government's diplomatic, intelligence, military and economic (DIME) actions.

Affecting the Decision-Making Calculus

If deterrence is in the eye of the beholder and all deterrence activities are calculated to persuade opponents not to attack us by influencing their decision matrix,[6] how do we go about influencing that calculus? What must we focus on? As previously mentioned, we should center our attention on the three "essentials" that affect their perception and decision-making process: "(1) The benefits of a course of action; (2) The costs of a course of action; and (3) The consequences of restraint (i.e., costs and benefits of not taking the course of action we seek to deter)."[7]

Taking these same essentials, Brad Roberts distills them further and says, "Deterrence, like other tools of influence, is a strategy for creating disincentives in an adversary's mind to courses of action he might otherwise adopt." Creating these disincentives takes great effort, and grafted into the body of those disincentives must be a message that asserts our ability to withstand any attack. He continues, "Sometimes those disincentives already exist...Sometimes the primary goal of an influence strategy might be simply to reinforce those existing restraints."[8]

We must also understand that anything we do could affect the targeting dynamics of adversary planners. Roberts, referring to a quote by Robert Anthony, says, "Even suicide terrorists are willing to delay their attack until they are convinced that they have a 'good' chance of success."[9] Witnessing these types of operational changes points to how decision-makers might modify their targets, as they become harder, and look for easier ones that offer more success.

This idea is further pressed by two RAND analysts, Andrew R. Morral and Brian A. Jackson, in their study *Understanding the Role of Deterrence in Counterterrorism Security.* They believe "determined terrorists—both as *individuals* and *organizations*—may be willing to risk everything to achieve their objectives, [however] they do not wish to waste their own lives or other resources on missions that are doomed to fail or unlikely to achieve their intended results."[10]

"Many terrorist groups," according to Morral and Jackson, "may be averse to engaging in operations when the likely outcomes are shrouded by significant sources of uncertainty."[11] Thus, we can increase our deterrent capability if we communicated the message to our adversaries that to attack would mean a high chance for failure. One method for discouraging attacks is to build public resiliency so terrorist acts do not unduly bother or change the everyday life of the country. Resilience can take the "terror" out of terrorist actions by not rewarding such behavior.

As early as the 1960s governmental thinkers pointed toward the necessity of fostering public resiliency, the ability to spring back after an attack, in our national fabric. This resiliency was to be manifested as a result of civil defense (CD) efforts. Thus, in the late 1960s research was begun by the Hudson Institute on behalf of the Department of the Army's Office of Civil Defense.

When completed in 1967, the report titled *Crisis Civil Defense and Deterrence,* authored by Frederick Rockett, made the following comments about the Soviet Unions and People's Republic of China's capability to withstand a nuclear exchange with the United States. The issue was survival based on Civil Defense capabilities. Rockett said, "Nuclear deterrence is a central element in the military policy of the United States. The credibility of this deterrence has depended primarily upon our ability to wreak immense destruction. If an opponent believes that he can reduce his vulnerability, this may affect his assessment of the credibility of our nuclear deterrent. Perhaps a future crisis will demonstrate the potential effectiveness of emergency CD measures. This could profoundly affect military policies and planning in many countries."[12] In particular Russia and China come to mind.

Rockett continues by saying, "Although there is no reliable way of determining what crisis CD actions could be taken and completed successfully, it may not be unreasonable to assume that under crisis conditions a significant reduction in vulnerability is possible. It may even be that during a crisis emergency, civil defense activities would be deemed more effective than either bomber or missile defenses for reducing vulnerability."[13]

In the author's view a robust civil defense could sway an aggressor's use of nuclear weapons because he would not have the desired effects. "If a crisis demonstrated that the vulnerability of an opponent had been reduced due to effective CD measures, our ability to deter his hostile actions might suffer."[14]

During the Cold War the Soviets spent large amounts of their capital building a robust CD system. The issue was not if it was effective or not, but how it made us perceive the strategic situation.

Rockett's analyses goes a step further and points out what could happen if CD is mutually robust among all affected parties. He says, "If most countries can protect themselves better than had previously been believed, then a mutual deterrence suffers, for war is less costly for both sides."[15]

Thus far, our discussion has alluded to the notion that in conjunction with a capability to inflict great overt damage, to modify an aggressor's will, a perceived ability to withstand an attack could likewise have a persuading effect on a potential attacker's decision-making calculus. This later idea falls into the category known as deterrence by denial.

Deterrence by Denial

Deterrence by denial is a posture in which enemy "operations are discouraged because... [their expected] payoffs or success rates appear too low"[16] for the effort and risks undertaken. A nation "perceived as well prepared to prevent, defeat, and mitigate the consequences of aggression, may deter an adversary from attempting a WMD attack."[17]

No doubt, if attackers abort an attack because they perceive their efforts will incur no benefit, or even fail, they have been deterred and denied the profit from a successful attack. So a central aspect of deterrence by denial is getting into the mind of an adversary and influencing them to discount the benefits of an attack.

Morral and Jackson, who focus primarily on security countermeasures, as a means for deterrence by denial, believe the way to do this is by exploiting the large degree of uncertainty associated with terror operations. They think "understanding the sources of these uncertainties for terrorist planners can aid in the design of effective security countermeasures. If attackers are sensitive to uncertainty, security interventions might be valuable even if their only effect is to increase the width of the error bar around the outcome and cost of an operation without necessarily changing the average expected payoffs or costs of the operation."[18]

One tool available to influence adversary uncertainty is strategic communication that Brad Roberts says "has a role to play in enhancing the performance of deterrence by denial. Its function is not to lend credibility, but to lend doubt. Those targets potentially amenable to deterrence by denial include foot soldiers, professionals, and leaders." For example, Roberts writes, "If their WMD assets are few, they are unlikely to risk them in unviable operations."[19]

Resilience efforts can enhance a nation's deterrence by denial efforts by affecting the terrorist decision calculus, dissuading the terrorist use of weapons of mass destruction. Countries that appear to be able to withstand and recover quickly from terror attacks stand a greater chance of not being attacked.

Resilience

In 1998, Osama bin Laden's "World Islamic Front" fatwa laid out his intent for America: "We -- with Allah's help -- call on every Muslim who believes in Allah and wishes to be rewarded to comply with Allah's order to kill the Americans and plunder their money wherever and whenever they find it."[20] Initially viewed as just empty threats, this became all too real as numerous attacks by al-Qaeda against Americans outside the Unites States began occurring, culminating in the devastating attacks of Sept. 11.

A country that pursues resiliency in all forms makes itself more durable and less vulnerable to shocks from natural disasters or terrorism. Resilient publics are less prone to panic and over-reaction. Resilient publics are not so easily terrorized. Resilient publics can regroup rapidly and do not require ultra-costly counter-measures to reassure them. Resilient public do not abandon public transport just because a bus or train or plane is attacked.

But, what is resilience? And how do you make a nation more resilient? *Merriam-Webster's online dictionary* defines resilience as "the capability of a strained body to recover its size and shape after deformation caused especially by compressive stress."[21] *Webster's Revised Unabridged Dictionary* (1913) defines resilience as "the act of recovering, springing back, or rebounding."[22] *The Collaborative International Dictionary of English* defines resilience as the "power or inherent property of returning to the form from which a substance is bent, stretched, compressed, or twisted...The power or ability to recover quickly from a setback, depression, illness, overwork or other adversity."[23]

Specifically, resilience has a more definite definition given by the Department of Homeland Security that defines resilience, in its National Infrastructure Protection Plan, as "the ability to resist, absorb, recover from, or successfully adapt to adversity or a change in conditions."[24] In his article "Critical Infrastructure, Interdependencies, and Resilience," T.D. O'Rourke points out that "definitions vary slight, but they all link the concept of resilience to recovery after physical stress."[25]

A definition more relevant to our discussion is from Karl Weick and Kathleen Sutcliffe in their book *Managing the Unexpected: Resilient Performance in an Age of Uncertainty.* They say "resilience is the 'capability of a system to maintain its function and structure in the face of internal and external changes and to degrade gracefully when it must.' Resilience occurs when the system continues to operate despite failures in some of its parts."[26]

This idea of resiliency applied to the material world looks something like this. Metals made more resilient to withstand the pressures and strains of physics are less likely to fail at the most critical moment. So aircraft designed to withstand the forces of gravity and wind dynamics at high speeds are more resilient and will less likely fail in midflight. Likewise, a nation that is more resilient could have the ability to rebound, after a terror attack, in ways unexpected to a terrorist's anticipate desire. Brian Jackson, in his RAND paper *Marrying Prevention and Resiliency Balancing Approaches to an Uncertain Terrorist Threat,* says "the definition of *resilience* differs somewhat in the literature but generally includes measures that make it possible for key infrastructures, economic activities, and other parts of society to rapidly 'bounce back' after a disruption."[27]

This ability to "bounce back" is what many resiliency promoters want to see fostered by national education and training programs. Stephen Flynn in his book *The Edge of Disaster: Rebuilding a Resilient Nation* thinks "America needs to make building national resiliency from within as important a public policy imperative as confronting dangers from without." Flynn also believes a "society that can match its strength to deliver a punch with the means to take one makes an unattractive target."[28] Stewart Baker, the assistant secretary for Policy, Department of Homeland Security, echoing Flynn's thoughts, told the United States House of Representatives Committee on Homeland Security that "we must make every effort to prevent an attack, but we must do more. As a nation, we must be able to withstand a blow and then bounce back. That's resilience."[29]

Ever since Sept. 11, homeland security practitioners have been working hard to shore up old infrastructures while trying to protect vulnerable systems from attack. But the United States is a target rich environment and protecting everything is virtually impossible. As Dr. James Jay Carafano of the Heritage Foundation points out, it "is impossible to protect every target, and a strategy predicated on protection is bound to fall short. The enemy will find something else to attack."[30] He further adds as the lists of critical infrastructures grow, they become harder to protect. "If everything is critical, nothing is critical...

In contrast, resiliency promises something much more achievable and important: sustaining society amid known threats and unexpected disasters. Indeed, the more complex the society and the more robust the nature of its civil society, the more it should adopt a strategy of resilience."[31] We cannot protect everything, and other means must be pursued to help offset our vulnerabilities. Building resilience into our way of life is one way of doing this.

Inevitably, we will be tested. Natural and technological disasters will continue to test our ability to function as a people and country. According to Weick and Sutcliffe, "unexpected events often audit our resilience. They affect how much we stretch without breaking and then how well we recover. Some of those audits are mild. But others are brutal."[32]

So how do we rebuild resilience into our national fabric to make us more able to "bounce back" from terror attacks and other crises? There are at least three ways a nation can be made more resilient. The old adage says, "A cord of three strands is not easily broken." No doubt the sailors of old, when "ships were made of wood and men of iron," knew a multi-strand rope, woven together, was much stronger and more reliable in the middle of a wicked storm than a single strand of rope. Likewise, there are three strands that, when woven together, would make us more resilient to terror attacks, giving us more robust deterrence by denial capability. These three strands are tested and resilient leadership, defended physical infrastructure and prepared populations.

Times of great danger and uncertainty often reveal the kind of leadership we have, whether strong or weak. For a nation to survive it must have strong leadership to recover from a devastating event. Consequently, the first strand is "resilient leadership." Leaders at all levels of government and society must be resilient themselves to be able to help encourage the population to hang in there, remain calm and tough, and to be brave. Leaders must be an example of hope, telling others that we will come through this as long as we hold on and have courage. Resilient leaders can inspire a people and a nation to "bounce back" and demonstrate by example how to do it well.

The second strand is ensuring that critical infrastructures are made more resistant to failure and attacks. Much work has been done in this area since the Sept. 11 attacks to shore up vulnerabilities of our physical infrastructure by improving protection of things like power grids, communication networks, and financial systems, but much more needs to be done.

The third and final strand is to understand how to make the general population more tough-minded and resilient. A population's resilience is especially crucial for a nation's ability to withstand the effects of terror attacks as well as natural and technological disasters.

When these three strands are woven together in meaningful ways, they optimize a nation's ability to rebound. This, if appreciated, should have a deterring affect on would-be attackers. Resiliency, articulates Dr. Carafano, "is about building strong, cohesive societies that can prevail against many challenges, from the heartless whims of Mother Nature to the malicious acts of terrorists."[33] A more robust resilient leadership, infrastructure and population provide an unseen shield of strength and recovery capability.

Resilient Leadership

First of all, resilient leaders are not so easy to find, but are important to have and to develop. Good leadership strengthens communities, and, as T.D. O'Rourke says, "is a critical factor in promoting resilient communities.... and also the least predictable."[34] So what does resilient leadership look like? What are the qualities of a resilient leader and how are they made? And what happens when leaders fail at being resilient?

In their book *The Secrets of Resilient Leadership: When Failure is Not an Option*, George Everly, Douglas Strouse and George Everly III state the "mystery of resilient leadership is revealed, not in the best of times, but in the worst of times – in times of crisis, even during times of initial defeat."[35] They point out getting back on your feet requires resilience, and "adversity, especially on a large scale, requires leadership."[36] When bad things happen we naturally look for strong leaders to guide us to safety.

Normally, a resilient leader is one who has had to become resilient through many trials. Adversity is the tool that tries and reveals leaders, and, I might add, builds leaders. Hardship was their teacher. Resilient leaders do not become so overnight. Well-known leadership expert Warren Bennis says, "The leaders I met, whatever walk of life they were from, whatever institutions they were presiding over, always referred back to the same failure - something that happened to them that was personally difficult, even traumatic, something that made them feel that desperate sense of hitting bottom - as something they thought was almost a necessity. It's as if at that moment the iron entered their soul; that moment created the resilience that leaders need."[37]

Resilient leaders offer their communities hope and encouragement during turbulent times. They offer a form of stability that helps the community to hold together. Some call it adaptive capacity or hardiness. The "one competence," notes Warren Bennis, "that I now realize is absolutely essential for leaders – the key competence – is adaptive capacity. Adaptive capacity is what allows leaders to respond quickly and intelligently to relentless change....Adaptive capacity is made up of many things, including resilience or what psychologist calls 'hardiness.'"[38]

In their article "To Build Resilience: Leader Influence on Mental Hardiness," National Defense University authors Bartone, Barry and Armstrong point out leaders who are resilient, or have what they term "hardiness," can become a source of great encouragement during challenging times. They believe leaders "by their example, as well as by the explanations they give to the group, they encourage others to interpret stressful events as interesting challenges that can be met."[39] Authors Everly, Strouse and Everly III, affirm this idea and say resilient leadership "is that set of leadership qualities that motivates and inspires others during crisis. It includes those actions that help others adapt to, or rebound from, adversity."[40]

We can deduce from these comments resilient leaders can lead thru hard times because they themselves have overcome adversity in their own experiences. They may also be better positioned to radiate hope and encouragement that enables others to bear the burden of adversity. But as there is great praise to bestow on such leaders who lead well in dangerous and difficult times there is also criticism for those who fail to do so.

Hurricane Katrina was "a story of human failure, more specifically *a failure of leadership to act in a strong, decisive manner* at a time when such strength was desperately needed."[41] This comment speaks to the results of missing leadership. When a leader is perceived as weak, and unable or unwilling to lead, the blow back can often result in the loss of their moral authority and even their political office. Such leaders, perceived as non-resilient or negligible in protecting their people, lose credibility. We have all witnessed past crises where leaders who failed to take measures within their means, to safeguard their communities, invited severe criticism.

Arjen Boin and Paul't Hart in their article "Public Leadership in Times of Crisis: Mission Impossible?" speaks about a modern situation that has created a more volatile hypersensitive environment for leaders during crises. They point out that the "aftermath of today's crises tends to be as intense and contentious as the acute crisis periods are, with leaders put under pressure by streams of informal investigations, proactive journalism, insurance claims, and juridical (including criminal) proceedings against them. Leadership in the face of this sort of adversity is, in short, precarious."[42]

Boin and Hart further posit that this modern occurrence creates a predicament even for those leaders who do it right. They cite German sociologist Ulrich Beck who points out we live in a "risk society" which makes health and safety issues the focal point for all political matters. This "risk society" then creates a difficult situation for leaders. The public expects leaders to be able to take care of and prevent all kinds of emergency situations.[43] When they fail, they are greatly chastised. This creates, in their thinking, a "social-psychological and political climate [that] makes it very hard—perhaps even impossible—for leaders to emerge from crises unscathed."[44]

Therefore, negative blow back for real or perceived negligence on the part of leaders and their administrations can have serious consequences. These consequences can be at the national level, in the eyes of our allies, and or in our inability to deter our enemies. This will happen for sure at the public level. For if the public thinks their government is responding inappropriately, "that government may lose legitimacy. This in turn, may lead to increased anxiety, panic, and other forms of destructive behavior that can undermine the stability of civil society."[45] But what happens to leaders who lead well, make difficult decisions and still bring on criticism? What must they do?

Because of the potential for blow back from decisions and actions taken, leaders must always be aware of their actions and potential results. For leaders to avoid blow back and become more resilient they need to be mindful of what could happen, how they would respond before an event, and what they will say and do during an event. According to Weick and Sutcliffe, to "be resilient is to be mindful about errors that have already occurred and to correct them before they worsen and cause more serious harm."[46] One way to develop this kind of mindfulness is to learn from others who have had to lead in difficult environments.

Resilient leaders must often take unpopular actions or make difficult decisions. This often requires the ability to act courageously in ways that may be politically difficult, but are the right thing to do. For Everly, Strouse and Everly III, "resilient leadership is the courage to act, the willingness to take responsibility for decisions regardless of outcome, and the ability to engender trust and fidelity through a consistent pattern of acting with integrity."[47]

Resilient leaders must also help to build systems that connect people together. Leaders who desire to build resiliency into their communities and nation must consider how to develop social networks that can be called upon during crisis and disasters. Everly, Strouse and Everly III have noted in their research that "the single most powerful predictor of the ability to withstand and rebound from adversity is the perceived support of others."[48] This means leaders must continually strive to create a resilient culture. A culture that creates social networks of "shared identity, group cohesion and mutual support."[49]

Leaders play a key role in communicating resiliency by both word and deed. Their actions must focus on building infrastructures and associated organizations that help their people become more resilient. Leaders must help make their communities believe they are resilient. Resiliency's "decisive advantage is its psychological influence on civil society....The most resilient societies are the ones that *believe* they are resilient."[50] Good leadership helps others believe.

To better understand this kind of leadership we need to look at real examples. Let's look at two historical leaders and one contemporary: Abraham Lincoln, Winston Churchill and Rudy Giuliani.

Abraham Lincoln

Abraham Lincoln is one of America's most celebrated U.S. presidents, with an overwhelming appeal not only to Americans, but also to people around the globe. However, during the early years of the American Civil War he was under constant pressure from the unfolding national trauma and also from personal family loss. His lack of popularity in the southern secessionist states led to their breaking away from the Union and eventually war. And throughout both terms of his administration he had the great burden of leading the nation through four bloody years of rebellion. Yet, in spite of all these unbearable pressures he was a resilient leader.

In September 1859, a year before being elected president when Lincoln was only known to most Americans as an up-and-coming Republican politician, he gave a speech to the Wisconsin State Agricultural Society in Milwaukee that ended with a sentiment that revealed his attitude toward adversity and his strength to get through difficult situations. Always the master communicator he said, "An Eastern monarch once charged his wise men to invent him a sentence, to be ever in view, and which should be true and appropriate in all times and situations. They presented him the words: 'And this, too, shall pass away.' How much it expresses! How chastening in the hour of pride! -- How consoling in the depths of affliction! 'And this, too, shall pass away.'"[51] Lincoln used this kind of understanding to help guide a young nation through four terrible years of warfare and division on the hope and vision that "this, too, shall pass," and the nation would once again be whole.

Lincoln also was able to grieve with the families who had lost sons in the war. His own son William "Willie" Lincoln died from sickness during his first term in the White House. It was a devastating event in his life. But through this event he was able to console a nation. Elizbeth Keckley, a dressmaker for Mrs. Lincoln, witnessed his grief. "Mr. Lincoln came in. I never saw a man so bowed down with grief...he buried his head in his hands, and his tall frame convulsed with emotion. His grief unnerved him, and made him a weak, passive child. I did not dream that his rugged nature could be so moved."[52] However, he was not a passive weak child, as U.S. Army Lieutenant General William B. Caldwell IV, in his article "Leadership in a Time of Crisis," says, "Lincoln's anguish only made him a stronger leader. His tragic loss gave him a perspective on empathy....a strength born through adversity."[53]

His own loss paved the way for him to grieve for many others. Several years later he would write a letter to a grieving mother who had lost five of her sons in combat. In a letter to Mrs. Bixby of Boston, Mass., in November 1864, Lincoln wrote, "I feel how weak and fruitless must be any word of mine which should attempt to beguile you from the grief of a loss so overwhelming. But I cannot refrain from tendering you the consolation that may be found in the thanks of the republic they died to save."[54] It was his ability to empathize and encourage people with hope of better days and knowledge their sacrifices were not in vain, that helped to inculcate resilience into the population's will to fight on.

Lincoln's resilience as a leader can be best summed up by Donald Phillips in his book *Lincoln on Leadership: Executive Strategies for Tough Times*. "It was Abraham Lincoln who, during the most difficult period in the nation's history, almost single-handedly preserved the American concept of government. Had he not been the leader that he was, secession in 1860 could have led to further partitioning of the country into an infinite number of smaller, separate pieces, some retaining slavery, some not.... Abraham Lincoln was the essence of leadership."[55]

Winston Churchill

Winston Churchill is another example of resilient leadership. In 1940, as the German *Wehrmacht* pummeled allied forces in France, Winston Churchill gave his famous "We Shall Fight on the Beaches" speech to the House of Commons which set forth and stirred the national will to fight back against all odds and not cave in.

This voice of resilient leadership helped create a resilient nation. Churchill told his people that,

> I have, myself, full confidence that if all do their duty, if nothing is neglected, and if the best arrangements are made, as they are being made, we shall prove ourselves once again able to defend our Island home, to ride out the storm of war, and to outlive the menace of tyranny, if necessary for years, if necessary alone.... whatever the cost may be, we shall fight on the beaches, we shall fight on the landing grounds, we shall fight in the fields and in the streets, we shall fight in the hills; we shall never surrender.[56]

It was such speeches that helped to inspire a nation to fight and withstand the viciousness of war.

The early days of World War II severely tested the British people. Nightly bombings, threats of invasion and German U-boats sinking allied ships put a great strain on the British nation. In spite of this, the British people's mottoes were "business as usual" and "London can take it," who according to radio newsman Edward R. Murrow was their act of defiance towards the Germans.[57]

Toward the end of 1940, while the Blitz raged, the British government produced a film called "London Can Take It." Narrated by an American journalist, it spoke of the strength and resiliency of the British people and their resolve to fight and survive. As the film rolls the narrator says,

> There is nothing but determination, confidence and high courage among the people of Churchill's island....It is true the Nazis will be over again tomorrow night and the night after that and every night. They will drop thousands of bombs and they'll destroy hundreds of buildings and they'll kill thousands of people. But a bomb has its limitations. It can only destroy buildings and kill people. It cannot kill the unconquerable spirit and courage of the people of London. London can take it![58]

Yes, most cynics today would scoff at the terms of unconquerable spirit and courage, but in November 1940 when their world was literally being bombed back to nothing, those words rang true, and men and women like Winston Churchill were able to give an example of resiliency to their people.

Rudy Giuliani

Rudy Giuliani also knows what resilient leadership looks like. He ought to, for on Sept. 11 and the days following he was the face of New York, and his ability to bounce back while confronted with many difficulties encouraged others to hang on. What did Giuliani do that demonstrated resiliency?

For starters, Giuliani and his N.Y.C. team saw the need to build resiliency into their response systems as demonstrated by their extensive preparations before Sept. 11. They had foresight about possible future threats and took actions to meet those threats. Giuliani said, "One reason New York City was able to withstand the Sept. 11 attack was that we were prepared to meet 21st century security threats...We drilled and planned for various threats.... And while we didn't anticipate the specific scenario of Sept. 11, the constant practice, and the relentless follow-up from actual emergencies, certainly helped in its aftermath."[59] All the work done to help the city respond to catastrophic emergencies gave it the necessary capacity to spring back.

Another demonstration of resiliency was when in the midst of all the chaos and death he "was able to galvanize emergency operations" despite severe loss of emergency response personnel and command and control capabilities.[60] Not only were the buildings and people down, but valuable first responders and their leaders, charged for the protection of citizens and maintaining order in chaos, were now themselves victims all in a matter of hours. Any community that suffered a similar catastrophe proportional to its size would be devastated for decades.

Not only did New York City spring back after being tested, but so did its mayor. "Giuliani's *Zivilkourage,*" According to Arjen Boin and Paul't Hart, "the first days of the World Trade Center tragedy propelled him back into the folk-hero status he once had enjoyed when taking the mayoral office on the wings of his crime-fighting reputation; gone was his image as a weary politician wounded by scandal."[61] Business author Tom Peters writes of Giuliani's courage to be visible: Rudy "showed up" when it really mattered on Sept. 11. As one individual put it, he went from being a lame duck, philandering husband to being *Time* magazine's "Man of the Year" in 111 days. How? Not through any "strategy, well-thought-out or otherwise. But by showing his face. By standing as the embodiment of Manhattan's indomitable spirit."[62]

Whether you like him or not, you cannot call him a coward because when it counted most he showed up. And Giuliani's pro-active nature did not start on Sept. 11, but years earlier. He himself says, "While mayor, I made it my policy to see with my own eyes the scene of every crisis so I could evaluate it firsthand."[63]

When he was there at ground zero, he demonstrated something else those New Yorkers and people everywhere needed to see - a leader leading with composure and control. He points out leaders "have to control their emotions under pressure. Much of your ability to get people to do what they have to do is going to depend on what they perceive when they look at you and listen to you. They need to see someone who is stronger than they are, but human, too."[64] Giuliani says he would "ask the people of New York City to do everything that they can to cooperate, not to be frightened."[65]

Giuliani was also seen everywhere, like a Churchill, visiting dangerous areas. He says "there was a method to my day on Sept. 11. I couldn't tell people, 'be brave,' unless I was willing to walk the streets, or not to panic over anthrax unless I was willing to go to the places where it was suspected. That is what the optimism of leadership is about. Once the leader gives up, then everybody else gives up, and there's no hope."[66]

Compare that with Louisiana Gov. Kathleen Blanco's response, during Hurricane Katrina, who had a problem inspiring and leading. *Time* magazine's article "4 Places Where the System Broke Down," had this to say about Gov. Blanco, "No one would mistake Blanco, 62, for Rudy Giuliani. In the first week after the storm hit, she came across as dazed and unsteady."[67] According to John Magginnis, a newspaper publisher in Louisiana, "Blanco is not an inspiring speaker and appeared 'rattled' on TV after seeing her devastated state....She's an empathetic, nurturing kind of person," he says. "Maybe she is not the towering tower of strength that some people would hope or expect to see."[68] She was counseled by General Honore who met with her regularly to "present a tougher face to the public."[69]

On Sept. 10, 2005, CNN Security Watch's "Lessons of Hurricane Katrina,"[70] aired. This program focused on the failure of resilient leadership, or none at all, during the disaster. Of those doing interviews for the program, Candy Crowley, CNN correspondent, points out that what was missing during this disaster was "a strong guiding hand in times of tragedy." Crowley goes on and says, "In the uncertainty of Sept. 11 the surest thing was his honor, the mayor, Rudy Giuliani, tough, uncompromising, fully competent."[71] She points to this common picture of a lack of a central guiding leader in response to a great tragedy, for "many reasons foreseeable and not, Katrina is a different story. It lacks a leading man or lady."[72]

David Gergen, former presidential adviser, said, "We want somebody to fill the screen and tell us what to do, and go for it - someone who's decisive. And Rudy Giuliani had all of those qualities. They were almost Churchillian."[73] Adding to this notion, Mike Deaver, former Reagan adviser, explains the need people have for a leader to help them deal with great disasters. He said one "of the things that's needed in a situation like this is for somebody to sit down with, us and tell us and reassure us, and help us sort of fathom it and tell us that it's going to be all right eventually. That hasn't happened. That's sort of the leadership quotient that we haven't seen yet."[74]

Candy Crowley's comparison of Giuliani with former Louisiana Gov. Blanco boils down to this: Giuliani had better command of details of what was going on and that steadied a hurting city. By contrast Blanco seemed faltering about fundamental things, such as water in the city being just lake or canal water instead of possible toxic soup from hazardous materials.[75] Crowley says, "Giuliani brought calm to chaos and poetry to the unspeakable.... The truth is the story of Katrina has many heroes. What it's lacked is a leader."[76]

Resilient Infrastructures

For thousands of years most people lived on farms or in communities where they were required to be self-reliant. People produced most of their own goods and services to survive and by necessity were more resilient to life's difficulties. However, this all changed as we became more interconnected and interdependent on others for our daily livelihoods.

With the merger of new technologies to facilitate modernization we became coupled into an intricate network of complex associations. "Our society and modern way of life depend on a complex system of critical infrastructures"[77] was how the 2003 *National Strategy for the Physical Protection of Critical Infrastructures and Key Assets* framed our current state. Six years later *the National Infrastructure Protection Plan* expressed, "Protecting and ensuring the continuity of the critical infrastructure and key resources (CIKR) of the United States is essential to the Nation's security, public health and safety, economic vitality, and way of life."[78]

Our way of life has become wholly dependent on technologies and the reliability of the infrastructures they spawned. As a consequence we have become less self sufficient, hence, less resilient.

Most modern developed nations have infrastructures that basically revolve around three functions: (1) Production and delivery of essential goods and services (agriculture, food and water, public health, energy, transportation, banking and finance, chemical manufacturing, and postal and shipping); (2) Interconnectivity and operability (financial, information and telecommunication systems); and (3) Public safety and security (government institutions that provide security, defense, and emergency services such as fire and police).[79] Another way to understand these three functions is to look at them as lifeline systems.

The "concept of a "lifeline system," according to T.D. O'Rourke, "was developed to evaluate the performance of large, geographically distributed networks during earthquakes, hurricanes and other hazardous natural events. Lifelines are grouped into six principal systems: electric power, gas and liquid fuels, telecommunications, transportation, waste disposal, and water supply."[80] O'Rourke concludes "because lifelines are intimately linked to the economic well-being, security and social fabric of a community, the initial strength and rapid recovery of lifelines are closely related to community resilience."[81]

Ownership of these lifelines or infrastructures varies from country to country. Some countries provide for the entire major infrastructures. Others are a mixture of private and public ownership. In the United States, private industry owns and operates about 85 percent of the critical infrastructures.[82] These are further broken down into specific kinds of infrastructure systems. These systems of interconnected and often seamless networks have also become the most vulnerable to perturbations and must be made more resilient.

For most of America's history, we have been fortunate not to have large invading forces threatening us as has happened in other parts of the world. Two large oceans have protected our homeland, but now that has changed. Advanced technologies and communications have not only changed our boundaries, but have also created what Boin and Hart call the "modern crisis," requiring new methods of protection. According to them this "modern crisis" is the result "of several modernization processes — globalization, deregulation, information and communication technology, developments and technological advances, to name but a few. These advances promote a close-knit world that is, nonetheless, susceptible to shocks from a single crisis. Comparatively slight mishaps within these massive and intricate infrastructures can sometimes create problems in unforeseen ways."[83]

As separate infrastructures develop, they often connect to other infrastructures for support or to provide support. New technologies create new infrastructures, which interconnect to the older ones. This growth creates a density of systems, which has never been seen before. As infrastructures go from the local to global connectedness, so does the density and creates a dense global medium. This makes our systems less resilient and more vulnerable to disturbances. The 2009 *National*

Infrastructure Protection Plan alludes to this by saying critical infrastructures are "systems and assets, whether physical or virtual, so vital to the United States that the incapacitation or destruction of such systems and assets would have a debilitating impact on national security, national economic security, public health or safety, or any combination of those matters."[84]

As we rely more on technology and associated networks we have become more aware of their vulnerability. Often the weaknesses in these networks are unveiled when they fail during major accidents or disasters. This was the case with Hurricane Katrina. According to Lt. Gen. H. Steven Blum, then chief of the National Guard Bureau, when referencing the Mississippi region which took the brunt of the hurricane's force, the affected region was "plunged back 200 years, to a time when there were no cell phones, no television or radio, and no electricity. I saw antebellum homes that had withstood 150 years of storms on the Gulf Coast, and all that was left was their foundations and a few steps. The rest was gone. Gone."[85]

The destruction of key support systems in the region resulted in the loss of homes, jobs, commercial enterprises and life-support kinds of functions. The disruption to regional networks also hampered military responses. "Perhaps the single greatest impediment to a faster military response to Katrina was the nearly total destruction of the communication network in the entire Gulf Coast region. Land lines, cell phone towers and electric power lines were all down."[86] Events such as Hurricane Katrina revealed the vulnerabilities of current infrastructures and the cascading affects that result. This destruction sent a ripple through the United States.

Think about physics where it takes less force to agitate a solid medium. In effect it's like throwing a rock in a pool of water and watching the ripples move away from the disturbed area. The denser the pond the smaller the rock needed to affect it. A very dense infrastructure with all of its connections and levels of interconnectivity would act in a similar way and not be unaffected.

Indeed the two most recent events in the last decade which demonstrate what happens when the technological system is disturbed are Sept. 11 and Hurricane Katrina. The former caused the nations entire air-traffic system to shut down sending shock waves throughout the world web of air-route connections. The latter shut down an entire city and petroleum and other industrial systems feeding a nation and world.

But if you think that is old news a more recent event has demonstrated the vulnerability of our globally interconnected system. In April 2010 one of Iceland's volcanoes erupted and spewed ash all across the European skies. The effects were drastic. According to *USA Today*,

> The eruption…is causing massive dislocation across Europe. By late Sunday [April 18], more than 63,000 flights had been canceled in 23 European countries, stifling the lifeblood of the continent's economy. Because few planes are flying, travelers can't travel, machinery parts can't get to factories, food sellers can't transport their goods, and businesses are finding business increasingly difficult to conduct. The economic ripples are being felt worldwide. In the USA, air carriers canceled 310 flights to and from Europe on Sunday, according to the Air Transport Association, which represents most major U.S. airlines. Because of the volcano, Kenya's hothouse flowers — responsible for 20 percent of that African nation's exports — are rotting in warehouses rather than winging their way to Europe.[87]

These kinds of events should be eye-openers, shedding light on the fragileness of our globalized interconnected systems. Failures in any of the infrastructures due to natural disasters or technological failures could be replicated deliberately by terrorists to create similar consequences, possibly by using the effects of WMDs. An attack on any one of these webs could have a ripple or cascading effect felt around the world.

Terrorists understand these new infrastructures currently define not only how people live, but also how they will operate in the world. Consequently, this infrastructure damage or takeover could become lucrative lightning rods for gaining public and national attention. So any infrastructure vulnerability could be exploited asymmetrically against us. The 2009 Homeland Security's *National Infrastructure Protection Plan* highlights this and maintains that terror attacks, using parts of the CIKR, could cause direct or indirect impacts, resulting "in large-scale human casualties, property destruction, economic disruption and mission failure, and also significantly damage national morale and public confidence."[88]

Because of the aforementioned natural disaster and terrorist threats a lot of effort and thought has gone into learning more about infrastructure fragility and survivability. After the Sept. 11 attacks new strategies and policies emerged to improve security of the American homeland.

The National Infrastructure Advisory Council (NIAC) interprets infrastructure resilience as "the ability to reduce the magnitude and/or duration of disruptive events." To be effective we have to be able to "anticipate, absorb, adapt to and/or rapidly recover"[89] from these kinds of events. The U.S. National Strategy for the Protection of Critical Infrastructure and Key Assets identified over 18 systems, networks and assets[90] deemed extremely valuable for "life as we know it." The 2006 version says "among our most important defensive efforts is the protection of critical infrastructures and key resources....These are systems and assets so vital that their destruction or incapacitation would have a debilitating effect on the security of our Nation."[91] Later, the Homeland Security's 2009 *National Infrastructure Protection Plan* emphasized the overarching goal is to "build a safer, more secure, and more resilient America by preventing, deterring, neutralizing or mitigating the effects of deliberate efforts by terrorists to destroy, incapacitate, or exploit elements of our nation's critical infrastructure and key resources."[92]

In April 2010, the Obama administration put forth its Homeland Security guiding principle, "Promote the Resiliency of our Physical and Social Infrastructure." It focuses more on specific infrastructure concerns and states, "Ensuring the resilience of our critical infrastructure is vital to homeland security. Working with the private sector and government partners at all levels will develop an effective, holistic, critical infrastructure protection and resiliency plan that centers on investments in business, technology, civil society, government and education. We will invest in our nation's most pressing short and long-term infrastructure needs."[93]

Then in May 2010, the Obama administration released its *National Security Strategy* (NSS). In general, this document lays out the major strategic concerns of the United States and the plan to address them. Resilience was brought front stage in the section called "Strengthen Security and Resilience at Home." The administration recognizes not every threat can be stopped and resilience must be a key measure.

"We...recognize that we will not be able to deter or prevent every single threat. That is why we must also enhance our resilience — the ability to adapt to changing conditions and prepare for, withstand and rapidly recover from disruption."[94]

The NSS proposes five overarching objectives to create a more resilient homeland. One objective called "Enhance Security at Home" specifically deals with infrastructures. It put forward new initiative for protecting and reducing infrastructure vulnerabilities "at our borders, ports and airports, and to enhance overall air, maritime, transportation, and space and cyber security."[95] Of key interest is the "global systems that carry people, goods, and data around the globe [which] also facilitate the movement of dangerous people, goods, and data." "Within these systems of transportation and transaction, there are key nodes—for example, points of origin and transfer, or border crossings—that represent opportunities for exploitation and interdiction."[96]

Thus, the overall strategy is to work with partners at all levels domestically and abroad to make these systems more resilient. This is a tall order in a world of diverse interest, capabilities, resources and the complexity of systems which are not fully understood. Challenges and problems notwithstanding, building resilience into our systems, and correcting resilience deficiencies are paramount.

When it comes to terrorism, we recognized our own brittleness after Sept. 11. And most would agree with Dr. James Carafano that "strengthening most critical components of infrastructure or essential systems prevents terrorists from exploiting a society's vulnerabilities and dealing blows that could cripple it. Decentralizing and reducing the brittleness of necessary global and national systems demonstrates to terrorists the futility of attacking those systems — and thus deters."[97]

The bottom line is when infrastructures are resilient to attacks terrorists may not want to waste their limited advantage and resources on a potentially failed mission.

Resilient Populations

On March 4, 1933, the newly elected president of the United States, Franklin D. Roosevelt, facing the chief justice took his oath of office. In his first inaugural address, broadcasted across the nation by radio, he set a nation at ease with words of encouragement. In the midst of a great depression he spoke to the people,

> This is preeminently the time to speak the truth, the whole truth, frankly and boldly. Nor need we shrink from honestly facing conditions in our country today. This great Nation will endure as it has endured, will revive and will prosper. So, first of all, let me assert my firm belief that the only thing we have to fear is fear itself — nameless, unreasoning, unjustified terror which paralyzes needed efforts to convert retreat into advance. In every dark hour of our national life a leadership of frankness and vigor has met with that understanding and support of the people themselves which is essential to victory.[98]

In his address he spoke to the people's sense of resiliency and their ability to bounce back in spite of hardships. Likewise, today we are confronted by new threats, and old kinds of disasters, that require Americans to once again dig deep inside for the resilience to withstand the current and future challenges to our way of life.

The United States by the very nature of its size and constitutional freedoms creates a more permissive environment for terrorist operations than in more dictatorial countries. Those responsible for protection cannot possibly provide an effective defense of all the potential targets. Therefore, many cannot be protected and are left vulnerable to attack. Consequently, a "focus on resilience has value in part because it forces us to acknowledge the limits of government capability.... No government can respond as quickly and as creatively as individuals concerned with the well-being of their families, their businesses and their communities. That is the source of our resilience as a country."[99] If this analysis is correct, the American public must become more resilient to better handle unforeseen events.

An enemy's willingness to attack is often influenced by his sense of the possibilities of operational success. If he senses a greater chance for failure, he may be dissuaded from conducting the operation in the first place. And if a population fails to react in a way satisfying to terrorist purposes he may well cease from such operations. How a population reacts to terrorist attacks could directly influence terrorist operations. If the people are able to continue on in their daily lives and recover well from the events of an attack, they are "resilient." If they fail to recover well and if they respond in ways that negatively affects a nation's ability to govern and or changes our value systems they could be characterized as malleable, breakable and exploitable.

A report on Israel's ability to bounce back and weather attacks, states, "Victory on the home front depends on national resilience. National resilience is the capacity to recover from a crisis without breaking the social fabric or compromising core human and national values. Israel's national resilience may turn into a strategic asset and even enhance Israel's deterrence."[100]

This renewed focus on population resilience was drastically brought forward by the effects of Katrina and its aftermath. Before Katrina there was a strong focus on protecting critical infrastructures. After Katrina the focus moved toward making communities resilient.[101] To help make diverse communities more resilient requires the national government to give them kinds of support only it is capable of providing. "At the end of the day," says Steward Baker, "building a resilient homeland requires us to trust our citizens. We must inform them – and trust them to inform others. We must equip them with the right tools and technologies – and trust them to use those tools to help themselves and others."[102]

The kinds of support governments need to give are vast. The Center for the Study of Weapons of Mass Destruction gives examples of the kinds of support needed. They focused on the "before and after" of a terrorist nuclear attack. Needs included "educating the general public in advance about nuclear effects and about how individuals should respond would facilitate response efforts and save many more lives. Important technical, legal, and regulatory issues of long-term recovery and restoration initiatives… need to be addressed."[103] However, government support cannot guarantee greater population resilience. It can help, but population resilience also means individual resilience.

So what does a resilient population look like? How do people react to threats that affect every aspect of their lives? And when we are attacked how do we bounce back? Hopefully, the answer to these questions can in a very real way present a clear message to future terrorists. You can attack us, hurt us, but you can't destroy us, and we will bounce back and come after you. This ability to bounce back sends a clear message when communicated by word and deed and could be a deterring factor vis-à-vis future attackers. "Don't thread on me" because I will survive and continue on. Moreover, such attacks will galvanize our counter-terror operations against you.

One concept of resilience, previously mentioned, is the notion of "hardiness." One NDU study on the subject states, "Conceptually, hardiness was originally seen as a personality trait or style that distinguishes people who remain healthy under stress from those who develop symptoms and health problems. Hardy persons have a high sense of life and work commitment and a greater expectation of control and are more open to change and challenges in life. They tend to interpret stressful and painful experiences as a normal aspect of existence."[104]

This need for hardiness, to survive difficult situations, has been part of human history especially in times of war when civilizations often break down. During World War II, "the British, the Germans and the Russians proved resilient because they summoned the will to prevail and persevere through hardship; the acumen to organize delivery of needed goods and services; and the wherewithal to maintain an organized civil structure....Keeping the heartbeat of the nation going amid adversity is the very definition of resiliency, and national will is the key element in accomplishing this goal."[105]

How do you develop hardiness in populations? According to Bartone, Barry and Armstrong, "Hardiness levels can be increased as a result of experiences and training. So it is better to think about hardiness not as an immutable trait, but rather as a generalized style of functioning that continues to be shaped by experience and social context."[106] They continue by explaining how a person's attitude and the way he sees life or frame experiences help determine the level of his hardiness or resilience to unforeseen events. "The power of hardiness to mitigate stressful experiences is related to the positive interpretations or framings of such experiences the hardy person typically makes."[107]

Dr. (Lt Col) Michael Kindt, a U.S. Air Force psychologist, in his monograph *Building Population Resilience to Terror Attacks: Unlearned Lessons from Military and Civilian Experience,* illustrates two different experiences after two separate attacks. He observed the American response to the Sept. 11 attacks and juxtaposed it to the British public's response to its July 8, 2005, London terror attacks. He says after the attacks America went into a "circle the wagons" mentality and grounded all air traffic and increased security in all areas. The result slowed travel to a crawl, from which took months to recover, at a great economic price. However, across the Atlantic after the London bombing attacks, mass traffic moved that very afternoon of the attacks even though people were still in shock. People would continue the following days to take the same modes of transportation that had been attacked. According to Dr. Kindt the difference between the two responses was resilience.[108]

He points out England's ability to bounce back after the London attacks was in part due to its history of having to cope with previous attacks. "Resilience to trauma is increased by a number of factors, which include preparation for the trauma, perceived ability to cope with trauma, and, perhaps most important, experience of successful recovery to past trauma. Clearly, London has had more experience dealing with the effects of bombing than the United States."[109] Kindt referred to German bombing campaign of World War II, and later with the Irish Republican Army bombing campaigns.

Dr. Kindt's research concluded with ways populations can increase their resilience. First, he says, "One key to the development of resilience is having had the experience of being faced with responsibility in a threat or crisis and successfully managing that crisis."[110] As people embrace very difficult situations and pass through them successfully, they build up capacity to deal with future trials.

Further, high "resilience to stress is the combination of a positive individual perspective, strong social connectedness and effective problem solving skills, all of which allow an individual to cope positively with traumatic events such as a terror attack."[111]

In addition, taking decisive action can increase resilience which "is a way of reducing the anxiety of indecision. By taking action, individuals can focus on the action at hand, rather than feeling stuck in uncertainty.'[112]

Moreover, we need to keep "things in perspective....As individuals improve their ability to look at the big picture of events they can better direct their actions and moderate emotional reactions."[113] A part of this is developing the ability to "avoid seeing crises as too large to be managed, and by beginning to break down a crisis into more manageable pieces."[114]

Finally, and most important, is the "ability to reach out to provide support to and receive support from others in times of stress. This ability to affiliate with others during crisis or stress then appears to not only help individuals cope with a crisis, but on a large scale enables groups to avoid panic behavior."[115]

Conclusions

A resilient nation possesses deterrence by denial effects if it can introduce doubt about operational success into the calculations of a terrorist leader and thus deter an attack. Therefore, the previous analysis leads to six conclusions on resilience and deterrence.

First, as a nation we should continue to announce our efforts at making the country more resilient. The more our adversaries are made to see us as a harder target, the more their decisions will be affected. "Our future deterrence success will be a function of how well we bring all our capabilities and resources to bear to achieve decisive influence over adversary decision-making."[116]

Second, for us to ensure our resilience efforts are understood by the attended audience, terrorist decision-makers, we need to have a robust strategic communication effort. This effort must constitute all facets of the U.S. government "through the use of coordinated programs, plans, themes, messages, and products synchronized with the actions of all elements of national power."[117]

Third, our message cannot be just propaganda, but must be fundamentally true or appear as such. Resiliency must be a national effort to shore up our systems with the ability to withstand attacks from terrorist or nature. Our systems must have the following three abilities to be resilient: "(1) the ability to absorb strain and preserve functioning despite the presence of adversity... (2) An ability to recover or bounce back from untoward events...and (3) An ability to learn and grow from previous episodes of resilient action."[118] In other words we require robustness, redundancy, resourcefulness and rapidity to bounce back after being challenged.[119]

Fourth, and more specifically, one of the most devastating attacks against the United States would be from a nuclear detonation. Therefore, we need a capability to recover from a nuclear terror attack. Bartone, Barry and Armstrong believe the "United States currently lacks a robust nuclear consequence management capability, although important efforts are under way to enhance preparedness. A robust consequence management capability could save lives, facilitate restoration of critical functions, better contain social and political impacts, and more effectively manage the larger international security repercussions.

Nuclear consequence management is feasible."[120]

Fifth, there should be national- and local-level discussions on what a resilient nation is and how it can have a deterring affect. Resiliency should be a national priority, and the United States should establish "a positive, consistent, national message which says 'we as American people are all vital parts of a team, each with our own critical roles, working together to prepare to ultimately defeat terrorism.'"[121]

Finally, we should make resilience a part of our educational efforts. "Resilience requires public concern about disasters and the operation of critical infrastructure, which, in turn, requires public education…. Public education also involves media coverage via newspapers and television…. Risk communication is also important to public awareness."[122]

Following that terrible day in September, Mayor Giuliani spoke words that indicated we as a nation were going to get through this dark time and gave hope to those who needed it. He said, "I am an optimist by nature. I think things will get better, that the good people of America and New York City will overcome any challenge thrown our way. So in the face of this overwhelming disaster, standing amid 16 acres of smoldering ruins, I felt a mixture of disbelief and confidence... that Americans would rise to this challenge."[123]

Notes

[1] Dennis Blair, *Annual Threat Assessment of the US Intelligence Community for the Senate Select Committee on Intelligence*, Director of National Intelligence, (Feb. 2, 2010), 12 (accessed May 14, 2010),
 http://www.dni.gov/testimonies/20100202_testimony.pdf.
[2] Ibid.
[3] WMD 411 Glossary, The Nuclear Threat Initiative, Produced by the Monterey Institute's James Martin Center for Nonproliferation Studies (accessed March 5, 2010), http://www.nti.org/f_wmd411/glossary.html#d.

[4] Brad Roberts, *Deterrence and WMD Terrorism: Calibrating its Potential Contributions to Risk Reduction*, IDA Paper P-4231 (Institute for Defense Analyses, Alexandria, Va., June 2007), 6-7. Originally found in Thomas Schelling, *The Strategy of Conflict* (Cambridge, Mass.: Harvard University Press, 1960), 9, and Thomas Schelling, "Thinking about Nuclear Terrorism," *International Security*, Vol. 6, No. 4 (Spring, 1982), 72.

[5] Director, Plans and Policy United States Strategic Command, (USSTRATCOM), *Deterrence Operations Joint Operating Concept,* Version 2.0, United States Strategic Command, Director Plans and Policy, Offutt AFB, Omaha, Neb., Office of Primary Responsibility (December 2006), www.dtic.mil/futurejointwarfare, 24-25.

[6] USSTRATCOM, *Deterrence Operations Joint Operating Concept,* 3.

[7] Ibid., 5.

[8] Roberts, *Deterrence and WMD Terrorism,* 26.

[9] Ibid., 10.

[10] Andrew R. Morral and Brian A. Jackson, *Understanding the Role of Deterrence in Counterterrorism Security*, Occasional Paper 231, Homeland Security Program, RAND Corporation , Project supported by a RAND Investment in People & Ideas (2009), 2.

[11] Ibid., 10.

[12] Frederick C. Rockett, *Crisis Civil Defense and Deterrence.* HI-777/2-RR. Hudson Institute, Inc., Croton-on-Hudson: New York (April14, 1967), iv.

[13] Ibid., vi.

[14] Ibid., vii.

[15] Ibid.

[16] Morral and Jackson, *Understanding the Role of Deterrence in Counterterrorism Security*, 7.

[17] Center for the Study of Weapons of Mass Destruction, *Are We Prepared? Four WMD Crises That Could Transform U.S. Security,* National Defense University, Washington, D.C. (June 2009), 104.

[18] Morral and Jackson, *Understanding the Role of Deterrence in Counterterrorism Security*, 10.

[19] Roberts, *Deterrence and WMD Terrorism,* 31-32.

[20] Osama bin Laden, "World Islamic Front Statement," Jihad against Jews and Crusaders (Feb. 23, 1998), http://www.fas.org/irp/world/para/docs/980223-fatwa.htm; also can be found in Bruce Lawrence's (editor) book *Messages to the World: The Statements of Osama Bin Laden*, 61. The following statement from Osama bin Laden and his associates purports to be a religious ruling (fatwa) requiring the killing of Americans, both civilian and military.

[21] Merriam-Webster On-line Dictionary (accessed May 10, 2010), http://www.merriam-webster.com/netdict/resilience.

[22] Dictionary.net (accessed May 10, 2010), http://www.dictionary.net/resilience.

[23] Ibid.

[24] National Infrastructure Protection Plan: Partnering to enhance protection and resiliency, Department of Homeland Security (2009), Glossary of Key Terms, 111.

[25] T.D. O'Rourke, "Critical Infrastructure, Interdependencies, and Resilience," *The BRIDGE (Linking Engineering and Society),* National Academy of Engineering,

Washington, DC, Volume 37, Number 1, (Spring 2007), 22-29, (accessed March 8, 2010), http://www.nae.edu/File.aspx?id=7405, 25.

[26] Karl E. Weick and Kathleen M. Sutcliffe, *Managing the Unexpected: Resilient Performance in an Age of Uncertainty,* John Wiley& Sons, Inc.: San Francisco, Calif. (2007), 69.

[27] Brian A. Jackson, *Marrying Prevention and Resiliency Balancing Approaches to an Uncertain Terrorist Threat,* Occasional Paper, Homeland Security, RAND Corporation (2008), 3,
http://www.rand.org/pubs/occasional_papers/2008/RAND_OP236.pdf.

[28] Stephen Flynn, *The Edge of Disaster: Rebuilding a Resilient Nation,* Random House: New York, (2007), xxi.

[29] Stewart Baker, Statement for the Record, Assistant Secretary for Policy, Department of Homeland Security , Before the United States House of Representatives Committee on Homeland Security, "The Resilient Homeland: Broadening the Homeland Security Strategy," (May 6, 2008), http://homeland.house.gov/SiteDocuments/20080506102214-20293.pdf.

[30] James Jay Carafano, Ph.D., "Resiliency and Public–Private Partnerships to Enhance Homeland Security," *Backgrounder*, The Heritage Foundation, No. 2150 (June 24, 2008), www.heritage.org/Research/HomelandDefense/bg2150.cfm, 4.

[31] Ibid.

[32] Weick and Sutcliffe, *Managing the Unexpected,* 1.

[33] Carafano, "Resiliency and Public–Private Partnerships to Enhance Homeland Security," 7.

[34] O'Rourke, "Critical Infrastructure, Interdependencies, and Resilience," 27.

[35] Everly, George S., Jr., Strouse, Douglas A., and Everly, George S., III. *The Secrets of Resilient Leadership: When Failure is Not an Option*. DiaMedica Publishing: New York, N.Y. (2010), xiv.

[36] Ibid., 1.

[37] Warren Bennis, Quotes about Leadership (accessed March 5, 2010), http://thinkexist.com/quotes/with/keyword/resilience/. Also found on the following sites: http://www.khabarexpress.com/Leadership_Warren-G.-Bennis-quotes.html, and http://www.leadership-development-coaching.com/leadership-quotes.html.

[38] Warren Bennis, *On Becoming a Leader*, Basic Books: New York, First Edition (1989, 2009), xxvi-xxvii.

[39] Paul T. Bartone, Charles L. Barry, and Robert E. Armstrong, "To Build Resilience: Leader Influence on Mental Hardiness," *Defense Horizons*, Center for Technology and National Security Policy, National Defense University (Nov. 2009), 5.

[40] George S. Everly Jr., Douglas A. Strouse, and George S. Everly III. *The Secrets of Resilient Leadership: When Failure is Not an Option*, DiaMedica Publishing: New York, N.Y. (2010), 3.

[41] Ibid., 8.

[42] Arjen Boin and Paul't Hart, "Public Leadership in Times of Crisis: Mission Impossible?," *Public Administration Review*, (Sept./Oct. 2003), Volume. 63, No. 5, 544-553.

[43] Ibid., 546.

[44] Ibid.

[45] Carafano, "Resiliency and Public–Private Partnerships to Enhance Homeland Security," 3.

[46] Weick and Sutcliffe, *Managing the Unexpected,* 68.

[47] Everly, Strouse, Everly III, *The Secrets of Resilient Leadership,* 18.

[48] Ibid., 95.

[49] Ibid.

[50] Carafano, "Resiliency and Public–Private Partnerships to Enhance Homeland Security," 2

[51] Abraham Lincoln, "Address before the Wisconsin State Agricultural Society," Milwaukee, Wis., (Sept. 30, 1859), *Abraham Lincoln Online*, Speeches and Writings (accessed May 14, 2010), http://showcase.netins.net/web/creative/lincoln/speeches/fair.htm; Abraham Lincoln, "Address before the Wisconsin State Agricultural Society," Milwaukee, Wisc., (Sept. 30, 1859), *Collected Works of Abraham Lincoln. Volume 3. Lincoln, Abraham, 1809-1865*, Ann Arbor, Mich.: University of Michigan Digital Library Production Services (2001), 481-482, http://name.umdl.umich.edu/lincoln3; *Collected works, The Abraham Lincoln Association,* Springfield, Ill., Roy P. Basler, editor; Marion Dolores Pratt and Lloyd A. Dunlap, assistant editors. Lincoln, Abraham, 1809-1865. New Brunswick, N.J., Rutgers University Press (1953).

[52] LTG William B. Caldwell, IV, "Leadership in a Time of Crisis," Lincoln Lecture Series at the University of Saint Mary, Leavenworth, Kan. (Feb. 12, 2009), 4-5, (accessed from the following website on April 8, 2010), http://usacac.army.mil/cac2/Repository/SelectedSpeeches/SaintMary.pdf.

[53] Ibid.

[54] Abraham Lincoln, "To Mrs. Lydia Bixby," Milwaukee, Wis., (Sept. 30, 1859). Collected *Works of Abraham Lincoln. Volume 8. Lincoln, Abraham, 1809-1865*, Ann Arbor, Mich., University of Michigan Digital Library Production Services (2001), 117, http://name.umdl.umich.edu/lincoln8.
NOTE: The Complete Letter. "Executive Mansion, Washington, Nov 21, 1864, To Mrs. Bixby, Boston, Mass. Dear Madam, I have been shown in the files of the War Department a statement of the Adjutant-General of Massachusetts, that you are the mother of five (5) sons who have died gloriously on the field of battle. I feel how weak and fruitless must be any word of mine which should attempt to beguile you from the grief of a loss so overwhelming. But I cannot refrain from tendering you the consolation that may be found in the thanks of the republic they died to save. I pray that our Heavenly Father may assuage the anguish of your bereavement, and leave you only the cherished memory of the loved and lost, and the solemn pride that must be yours to have laid so costly a sacrifice upon the altar of freedom. Yours, very sincerely and respectfully, A Lincoln."

[55] Donald T. Phillips, *Lincoln on Leadership: Executive Strategies for Tough Times* (N.Y., Business Plus), 172-173.

[56] Winston Churchill, "We Shall Fight on the Beaches" (June 4, 1940), House of Commons, http://www.winstonchurchill.org/learn/speeches/speeches-of-winston-churchill/1940-finest-hour/128-we-shall-fight-on-the-beaches.

[57] "Part 8: England in the 20th Century, World War II," Britannia, America's Gateway to the British Isles, (accessed on April 2, 2010), http://www.britannia.com/history/nar20hist4.html. Edward Murrow's famous opening line preceding each broadcast from England into American households was "This is London Calling."

[58] Produced by the British Government in October 1940, 'London Can Take It' is narrated by American journalist Quentin Reynolds and pays tribute to London, Ministry of Information Film – The London Blitz, http://www.south-wales.police.uk/museum/worksheets/london2.pdf.

[59] Giuliani, Rudolph W., "The Resilient Society: A blueprint for homeland security," *City Journal* (Winter 2008), Vol. 18, No.1, http://www.city-journal.com/2008/18_1_homeland_security.html.

[60] O'Rourke, "Critical Infrastructure, Interdependencies, and Resilience," 27.

[61] Boin and Hart, "Public Leadership in Times of Crisis," 544.

[62] Jeff Janssen, "9/11 Leadership Lessons," *PR Intelligence Report* Volume 3, Issue 16, (Wednesday, Jan. 2, 2008), (accessed May 14, 2010), http://www.enewsbuilder.net/techimage/e_article000930036.cfm?x=b11,0,w. The article can also be found at "Team Captains Network" at
http://www.teamcaptainsnetwork.com/public/230.cfm.

[63] Rudolph Giuliani, *Leadership.* New York: Hyperion, Miramax Books (2002), 4.

[64] Janssen, "9/11 Leadership Lessons."

[65] CNN Security Watch, "Lessons of Hurricane Katrina," transcript from Broadcast, CNN.Com (aired Sept. 10, 2005 - 20:00 EST, (accessed on April 7, 2010), http://transcripts.cnn.com/TRANSCRIPTS/0509/10/cp.01.html.

[66] Giuliani, *Leadership*, pp. 297-298.

[67] "4 Places Where the System Broke Down," *Time Magazine*, Time.COM (Sunday, Sept. 11, 2005), (accessed on April 7, 2010),
http://www.time.com/time/magazine/article/0,9171,1103560-1,00.html.

[68] Jill Lawrence, "Governors handle crisis in own ways," *USA TODAY* (Sept. 12, 2005), (accessed April 7, 2010), http://www.usatoday.com/news/nation/2005-09-12-two-governors_x.htm.

[69] CNN Security Watch, "Lessons of Hurricane Katrina."

[70] Ibid.

[71] Ibid.

[72] Ibid.

[73] Ibid.

[74] Ibid.

[75] Ibid.

[76] Ibid.

[77]Department of Homeland Security (DHS), *The National Strategy for The Physical Protection of Critical Infrastructures and Key Assets* (February 2003), 35, http://www.dhs.gov/xlibrary/assets/Physical_Strategy.pdf.

[78] Department of Homeland Security (DHS), *National Infrastructure Protection Plan: Partnering to enhance protection and resiliency*, 2009, Glossary of Key Terms, 7.

[79] DHS, *The National Strategy for the Physical Protection of Critical Infrastructures and Key Assets*, 6. Note: The ideas for the three functions come from this national strategy which discusses American systems; however, these systems are found in any developed and developing nation.

[80] O'Rourke, "Critical Infrastructure, Interdependencies, and Resilience," 23.

[81] Ibid., 25.

[82] DHS, *The National Strategy for The Physical Protection of Critical Infrastructures and Key Assets,* 8.

[83] Boin and Hart, "Public Leadership in Times of Crisis," 545.

[84] DHS, *National Infrastructure Protection Plan,* 7

[85] James Kitfield, "Poor communication slowed military's hurricane response," *National Journal,* GOVEXEC.com (Sept. 19, 2005), (copied on Sept. 21, 20005), www.govexec.com/story_page.cfm?articleid=32263.

[86] Ibid.

[87] Elizabeth Weise, Dan Vergano, and Doyle Rice, "Icelandic volcano: The impact is broad, but could be worse," *USA Today* (April 20, 2010), (accessed on June 4, 2010), http://www.usatoday.com/tech/science/2010-04-19-1Avolcano19_CV_N.htm.

[88] Department of Homeland Security (DHS), *National Infrastructure Protection Plan,* 7.

[89] NIAC, *Critical Infrastructure Resilience Final Report and Recommendations*, National Infrastructure Advisory Council, Secretary of the Department of Homeland Security (Sept. 8, 2009), 8.

[90] The 18 CIKR sectors are: Agriculture and Food; Commercial Facilities; Dams; Energy; Information Technology; Postal and Shipping; Banking and Finance; Communications; Defense Industrial Base; Government Facilities; National Monuments and Icons; Transportation Systems; Chemical; Critical Manufacturing; Emergency Services; Healthcare and Public Health; Nuclear Reactors, Materials and Waste; and Water. Table S-1: Sector-Specific Agencies and Assigned CIKR Sectors, the Department of Homeland Security, *National Infrastructure Protection Plan: Partnering to enhance protection and resiliency* (2009), 3.

[91] The White House, *National Strategy for Combating Terrorism*, (September 2006), 13.

[92] Department of Homeland Security (DHS), *National Infrastructure Protection Plan,* 9.

[93] The White House, Homeland Security, "Guiding Principles" (April 5, 2010), http://www.whitehouse.gov/issues/homeland-security, NOTE: This infrastructure needs include:"modernizing our electrical grid; upgrading our highway, rail, maritime, and aviation infrastructure; enhancing security within our chemical and nuclear sectors; and safeguarding the public transportation systems that Americans use every day."

[94] The White House, *National Security Strategy* (May 2010), 18.

[95] Ibid.

[96] Ibid.

[97] Carafano, "Resiliency and Public–Private Partnerships to Enhance Homeland Security," 1.

[98] Franklin D. Roosevelt, "First Inaugural Address" (Saturday, March 4, 1933), http://www.bartleby.com/124/pres49.html.

[99] Stewart Baker, "The Resilient Homeland: Broadening the Homeland Security Strategy," Statement for the Record, Assistant Secretary for Policy, Department of Homeland Security, Before the United States House of Representatives Committee on Homeland Security (May 6, 2008),
http://homeland.house.gov/SiteDocuments/20080506102214-20293.pdf.

[100] "National Resilience' Victory on the Home Front: A Conceptual Framework," Executive Summary, *The Reut Institute,* Version A, Cheshvan 5769 (November 2008), 5.

[101] O'Rourke, "Critical Infrastructure, Interdependencies, and Resilience," 25.

[102] Baker, "The Resilient Homeland: Broadening the Homeland Security Strategy."

[103] Center for the Study of Weapons of Mass Destruction, *Are We Prepared?,* 101.

[104] Bartone, Barry, and Armstrong, "To Build Resilience: Leader Influence on Mental Hardiness," 4.

[105] Carafano, "Resiliency and Public–Private Partnerships to Enhance Homeland Security," 3.

[106] Bartone, Barry, and Armstrong, "To Build Resilience: Leader Influence on Mental Hardiness," 4.

[107] Ibid., 5.

[108] Michael T Kindt, *Building Population Resilience to Terror Attacks: Unlearned Lessons from Military and Civilian Experience.* USAF Counterproliferation Center, Future Warfare Series, No.36, Maxwell Air Force Base, Alabama (Nov. 2006), 2.

[109] Ibid.

[110] Ibid., 5.

[111] Ibid., 7.

[112] Ibid., 8.

[113] Ibid.

[114] Ibid.

[115] Ibid., 9.

[116] USSTRATCOM, *Deterrence Operations Joint Operating Concept,* 56.

[117] Ibid., p. 37.

[118] Weick and Sutcliffe, *Managing the Unexpected,* 71.

[119] O'Rourke, "Critical Infrastructure, Interdependencies, and Resilience," 25.
NOTE – O'Rourke explains the four "R" as "Robustness: the inherent strength or resistance in a system to withstand external demands without degradation or loss of functionality. Redundancy: system properties that allow for alternate options, choices, and substitutions under stress. Resourcefulness: the capacity to mobilize needed resources and services in emergencies." And "rapidity: the speed with which disruption can be overcome and safety, services, and financial stability restored."

[120] Center for the Study of Weapons of Mass Destruction, *Are We Prepared?,* 99.

[121] Kindt, *Building Population Resilience to Terror Attacks,* 27.

[122] O'Rourke, "Critical Infrastructure, Interdependencies, and Resilience,"26-27. c

[123] Janssen, "9/11 Leadership Lessons."

CHAPTER 14

Summary and Conclusions

Barry Schneider and Patrick Ellis

The purpose of a deterrence strategy as defined in this analysis is to dissuade an adversary from starting a war or escalating a conflict.[1]

The Latin word *"deterre"* means to frighten from or frighten away. Deterrence success, even if achieved, is hard to prove because you cannot know absolutely why a war or escalation was avoided. After all, the adversary might not have intended to attack or escalate a conflict in the first place. Unlike the natural sciences, history does not let you repeat the experiment and change the variables. On the other hand, it is very clear when deterrence has failed, obvious as soon as the war drums sound.

And deterrence often does fail. As noted in our chapter on deterrence in the 1990-1991 Gulf War, in roughly a third of the inter-state wars of the 20th century, wars were begun by weaker states that attacked demonstrably stronger foes. In the majority of cases, superior might when recognized by the less powerful party creates a deterrent effect. Hence, the Roman motto *"si vis pacem, para bellum"* – if you wish for peace prepare for war. This is the thought behind the famous U.S. Strategic Air Command motto of "Peace is our profession." Peace through strength works in many cases but, nevertheless, there are also a significant fraction of cases when states have launched a war despite significant comparative military weakness.

An example was the Japanese attack on Pearl Harbor destroyed much of the U.S. pacific fleet in December 1941. However, at the time of the attack the Japanese GNP was about 10 percent of the United States GNP. A long war to the finish would inevitably favor the United States, a fact not lost on Admiral Yamamoto who planned the attack and explained the problem to the Japanese war leaders. They elected to gamble that the United States would stop short of a total war to the finish, and be willing to conclude a compromise peace leaving them in possession of all or much of their conquests. The Japanese leaders failed to understand the determination in America to completely defeat them and insist on a near total surrender. Their risky Pacific War venture backfired and left Japan in ruins.

Deterrence can fail for many reasons. Some leaders can be irrational, uninformed, misinformed, and reckless; gambling on adversary behavior, more focused on immediate gains than possible long term consequences, or driven to strike first because they calculate time is not on their side. Some are also willing to risk all in a war effort rather than give up their ambitions or honor as they define it. Deterrence efforts can at times fail to inhibit war escalation once the conflict has begun, as emotions often drive policy. Sometimes, as casualties mount, determination hardens, and mission creep widens the commitment to winning, lessening the willingness to compromise and end the conflict.

In this volume we look at deterrence strategy through three lenses: (1) Classic Cold War Deterrence Strategy, (2) Tailored Deterrence Strategy, and (3) Deterrence Strategy in specific Scenarios.

Classical Cold War Deterrence Strategy

The classical Cold War strategy of deterrence is most applicable when dealing with a rival state run by rational decision-makers who value their own power and survival over other objectives. An example of this kind of leadership is the Soviet high command during the October 1962 Cuban Missile Crisis. Unlike the Cuban leaders like Fidel Castro and Che Guevara at the time, they were not willing to attack the United States because of the U.S. power to retaliate and devastate the U.S.S.R.. On the other hand the Cuban leaders were willing to become martyrs if it meant destroying the United States. Classic deterrence theory would not have worked against them in this case.

The deterrence strategy that emerged in the United States in the Cold War had seven classic elements and appeared to work to help keep the Soviet Union from war with the West:

- Having retaliatory forces capable of inflicting a level of damage considered unacceptable to the Soviet leadership;
- Possessing a second strike capability that could survive a surprise attack;

- Having a will to use this nuclear force in a confrontation, if necessary;
- Communicating the US had both the will and the capability described so the U.S. threat was credible;
- Having an intelligence, surveillance and reconnaissance system able to identify the origins of any attack, answering the "who did it?" question;
- Having the capability to identify and strike a target set of highest value to the Soviet Union and its leaders.
- Having a rational adversary leadership who preferred to live and stay in power rather than die in order to inflict destruction on the United States.

Both sides held the life of the other society in their hands. Both were a few minutes or hours away from nuclear oblivion. The U.S. SAC triad of nuclear bombers, ICBMs, and SLBMs along with NATO nuclear and conventional forces deployed across from the Warsaw Pact in Europe was what we think kept the peace. The system worked, although it is a common judgment nuclear war was narrowly averted in the October 1962 Cuban Missile Crisis.

One of the limits of classic Cold War theories of deterrence is the requirement to have a rational opponent, and one not attracted to martyrdom. There are a number of problems with this requirement. First, there may be different interpretations of rational behavior in a crisis. Poor signaling or poor reception of adversary signals can lead to misunderstandings, war and escalation. A lack of leader situational awareness can undermine deterrence as can imprecise or misleading communications. Further, some leaders may misread ambiguous signals or may miss them altogether. Adversaries may also see what they expect to see rather than what is intended by their rival's words or actions. Or they may see only what they want to see rather than the reality of a situation. All this can lead to irrational actions, sometimes better seen in hindsight rather than in the heat of the moment of decision.

As Franklin Miller notes in the early years of the Cold War the message to the Soviet leadership was simple: "attack the United States or our allies, and we will immediately launch an all-out nuclear response against the Soviet homeland and on its forward deployed military forces using all elements of our nuclear arsenal. As noted, this was neither tailored nor subtle."[2]

But the Kennedy administration began to take some first steps towards a more tailored deterrence in the early 1960s. Kennedy wanted options. He did not want to have to decide on doing nothing or to initiate thermonuclear war if the Soviet leadership decided to attack with its superior conventional forces. Some U.S. strategists were convinced that the Soviet leadership might consider risking limited conventional attacks against NATO's less powerful conventional forces unless they were confronted with tailored and more believable (as opposed to all-out) U.S. and NATO nuclear responses. Thus, the administration introduced the "Flexible Response" policy.[3]

Later, during the Carter administration, the move toward a more tailored approach towards the Soviets was further refined when U.S. Secretary of Defense Harold Brown called for a Nuclear Targeting Policy Review leading to the countervailing strategy (Presidential Decision 59) based on the view "deterrence could only be achieved when the United States focused on what the Soviet leadership valued — and then threatened to destroy those assets if war occurred."[4]

Despite the demise of the Soviet Union, U.S. strategic nuclear forces are still sized and postured to deter aggression by Russia. Between them, the two nuclear giants hold over 90 percent of the world's nuclear weapons and Russian nuclear forces still pose the greatest existential threat to the United States.

U.S. Force Structure and Deterrence: Alternative Postures

Because the Russian arsenal retains an overwhelming destructive capacity, the U.S. Strategic Command still maintains a triad of strategic bombers, ICBMs, and fleet ballistic missile submarines to deter attacks. The New START Treaty signed and ratified in 2010 has now reduced those forces significantly but any new reductions beyond those limits will pose new issues for deterrence and the U.S. force structure needed to maximize it.

Kurt Guthe looked at the implications of a deeper-cut arms control regime and evaluated the pros and cons for deterrence of alternative U.S. strategic force structures. He compared three alternative force postures: (1) a strategic dyad made up of Bombers/SLBM forces, (2) a strategic dyad of ICBM/SLBM forces, and (3) the present strategic triad of air, land and sea forces. A fourth alternative is a triad made up of ICBMs based in silos and on mobile launchers, and a fleet ballistic missile force.[5]

The U.S. strategic nuclear force structure would have to change as a result of downsizing. So the question is what nuclear force structure should the United States adopt at lower force levels?

Clearly the current triad of bombers, ICBMs and SLBMs has certain advantages over dyads forces, and perhaps over other triad configurations. Each leg of the triad contributes unique advantages. ICBMs are based on U.S. soil and an attack on them is an attack on the continental United States. Such an attack is guaranteed to trigger a massive U.S. retaliatory response and this fact should make any would-be attacker think twice. On the other hand, it is not so clear that this would be true if the United States lost a ballistic missile submarine on the high seas or a strategic bomber outside U.S. air space. ICBMs are also thought to have the most secure reliable and redundant command and control links to U.S. leaders of any element of the U.S. triad. Further, ICBMs are "fast fliers" capable of reaching targets at intercontinental ranges with high accuracy within 30 minutes of launch. An adversary military planner would likely try to destroy this land-based missile force first, since they can react the fastest and are extremely difficult to defend against once launched.

Silo-based U.S. ICBMs are hardened forces that can survive all but the most accurate enemy missile attacks. Even if attacked accurately, a fraction of them are likely to survive because of the configuration and spacing of the silo-launchers would create so-called fratricide effects, whereby one enemy warhead's detonation would destroy others aimed at adjacent U.S. targets. An adversary would be very unlikely to be able to destroy all U.S. ICBMs simultaneously and would have to attack those furthest away first to avoid fratricide effects of following incoming reentry vehicles. Otherwise an over-the-pole attack that struck the northernmost rows of U.S. missile silos would send a wall of tons of dirt into the sky thereby blocking following adversary reentry vehicles from getting to their targets.

This adversary "South-North Walk" through the missile fields would enable the northernmost U.S. ICBMs time to launch while the others were being attacked. Also, an adversary would want to strike the fast fliers of the United States first to prevent such a response or limit it. Thus, they would likely try to hit the ICBMs first, leaving a window of time for U.S. bombers to get airborne. Also an attack on all three legs of the triad will dilute the weapons that could otherwise be devoted to overwhelm a less diverse force.

The most survivable element of the triad is the SLBM forces at sea. Once submerged and sent out to deep water stations far at sea, the current submarine fleet is believed to be all but invisible and virtually undetectable. Moreover, like bombers, the fleet ballistic missile submarines can provide a 360 degree azimuth threat complicating enemy defenses and forcing them to spread their missile defenses around the entire defensive perimeter. Ballistic missile submarines also complement the other two legs of the triad by providing the most survivable launchers once deployed on the high seas. Positioned off an adversary coastline, the SLBM force could reach enemy targets in the least amount of time if given timely orders. These sea-borne forces are also good at signaling U.S. readiness if they are flushed from their home ports in a crisis. And, if sighted off an adversary coastline, they would convey a near and ominous threat that should bolster deterrence effects.

There are several deterrence advantages to maintaining a bomber leg to the retaliatory forces. Basing bombers at the end of runways during crises or sending some of them aloft at one time or another can signal readiness to strike back in more evident ways than by putting ICBMs and on-station submarines on alert. Bombers also can provide a 360 degree azimuth threat to enemies and are reusable and recallable. Bomber capability would also force a rival to spend large sums on air defense and divert such funds from missile defenses. Conversely, a bomber's path to targets can be paved by ICBM and SLBM strikes against air defenses. So all legs of the strategic triad work synergistically, complicating the plans of any enemy commanders assigned the task of attempting to negate the U.S. capability to retaliate in case of war. Such combinations of sea-land-air launchers would checkmate any such plans and this is why U.S. military planners are opposed to converting the triad to a dyad that carries somewhat more risk Guthe argues that the present triad enhances our strategic force survivability, lethality, flexibility, visibility, and adaptability -- all the components needed for strong deterrence. He concludes any move from the present triad to a dyad would diminish U.S. strategic force survivability.[6]

Nevertheless, the trend in arms control negotiations is to negotiate ever smaller nuclear forces under SALT II, START, START II, SORT, and New START. Also, with the ending of the Cold War and the focus on the fighting of wars in Afghanistan and Iraq, there is a squeeze on U.S. defense resources that leads policy makers to consider nuclear force cuts for financial cost and nuclear nonproliferation reasons. Deeper cuts in allowed nuclear warhead and strategic delivery vehicle numbers will increase the pressure for either eliminating one leg of the strategic triad and/or changing the basing modes of some of the strategic force.

One solution might be to eliminate bombers from the nuclear mission and then subdivide the ICBM force, keeping some in silos and deploying others on Hardened Mobile Launchers (HMLs). The Midgetman[7] program of the late 1980s and early 1990s was already tested in this mode and might be a cost-effective way to complicate enemy targeting at lower force levels under any new deeper cut arms control regime. Further analysis is needed to evaluate the utility of fielding a triad of a mixed ICBM force, some in silos, and others on hardened mobile launchers, alongside SLBM aboard strategic submarines. At lower numbers of strategic delivery vehicles and warheads that basing mode begins to look attractive.[8]

Alternatively, the United States could move to a bomber/SLBM or a SLBM/ICBM dyad option. The downside of the first dyad is that with no ICBM problem to solve, an adversary could concentrate on defeating the submarine-bomber force. An anti-submarine warfare breakthrough coupled with improved air defenses could reduce the deterrent effect of such a dyad.

On the other hand, a SLBM-ICBM dyad presently seems like a guaranteed retaliatory capability, even without bombers in the mix, but such a dyad would be put into jeopardy if an adversary achieved a breakthrough in anti-submarine warfare and in their ballistic missile defenses (BMD). Clearly if the adversary states did not have to build air defenses alongside their missile defenses, they could concentrate their resources on BMD improvements.

Extended Deterrence: What Is Required?

David Trachtenberg investigated the concept of extended deterrence and examines the question "How Much Capability Is Too Little?" This is an important question to ask since over 30 U.S. allies depend on the U.S. nuclear umbrella to protect them. Trachtenberg believes that extended nuclear deterrence has had a long and successful history and continues as a strong theme in U.S. security strategy. However, much has changed since the Soviet Union dissolved at the end of 1991. The Cold War ended. New states have acquired and tested nuclear weapons – India, Pakistan and North Korea. Still others are attempting to acquire them, witness Iran. Non-State actors have pursued weapons of mass destruction capability – al-Qaeda and Aum Shinrikyo. Further, the nuclear arsenal of the United States was progressively reduced under START, START II, SORT, and New START ceilings. Under the administration of President H.W. Bush, the U.S. tactical or "non-strategic" nuclear weapons have been removed from the inventory.

Further, some may come to believe the United States is less serious deterring nuclear threats at a time when it has signaled less of a reliance on nuclear weapons and has set a long term goal of eliminating them altogether if others can be made to follow the U.S. lead. On the other hand, the Obama administration has embraced maintaining a strong retaliatory capability as long as other states are threaten with nuclear weapons, and supports extended deterrence as reflected in the 2010 Nuclear Posture Review and through statements of senior leaders.

Sending such mixed signals may cause some U.S. allies presently reliant on the U.S. nuclear umbrella to wonder if one day they should not begin to create a nuclear deterrent of their own rather than trust another power to shield them. Leaders of allied states might question whether any state would be willing to risk a nuclear war, and millions of casualties, on their behalf. The reality is that not all allies are of equal importance to the United States. An attack on some is guaranteed to be met with a U.S. military response. An attack on some others might not so readily cause a U.S. response. Some allies are absolutely vital to the survival and prosperity of the United States, others are not. Some allies have U.S. armed forces on their territory. An aggressor attack that shed American blood would involve the United States immediately.

Ironically the number of states wanting to be under the U.S. nuclear umbrella may increase at the same time the size of our nuclear forces, providing that umbrella, is decreasing. This thought of a declining U.S. deterrent might lead to a new wave of nuclear proliferation by states such as Turkey, Republic of Korea, Japan, and others. In a worst case, at some point a continued and much deeper U.S. nuclear force reduction could trigger a new nuclear breakout from the NPT regime.

On the other hand, this threat may be exaggerated. The United States will long have the capacity for retaliation beyond what is needed. The real question is one of will. Does the adversary believe the U.S. government will act in a given contingency? That is the question, not U.S. retaliatory or war fighting capability. It is unclear just how many nuclear weapons the United States would need to convince a Kim Jong Il or Ayatollah Khamene'i that it would unwise to use nuclear weapons on a U.S. ally. The answer probably is very few.

Clearly, a single nuclear weapon, or no more than a few nuclear weapons, has the capability to do absolutely catastrophic damage to smaller states. Indeed, the same might be said of very large states. Some smaller states are, as one observer has noted, close to being "one-bomb states."[9] A half dozen nuclear weapons could totally devastate a country like Iran, Syria or North Korea so it would be a long time before the U.S. nuclear arsenal was so depleted it could not be used to check or destroy the military capability of such rogue regimes.

And, although the United States has over 30 allies who seek protection under the nuclear umbrella that does not mean it must maintain anything like 30 times the weapons needed for deterrence. The same nuclear arsenal can be applied to all as needed for deterrence given the extremely unlikely event that more than one or two serious nuclear threats need be confronted at one time. Indeed, the first use of a nuclear weapon against an aggressor could trigger a surrender since that regime would know more nuclear strikes could be unleashed. It would be far better to cease combat before things escalated further.

Tailored Deterrence Strategy

Today's world is different from the days of the Cold War. Our adversaries are different and more diverse, and the complexities in being able to influence each of them have gotten somewhat harder, especially when trying to deter non-state actors like al Qaeda. We cannot simply use the deterrence strategies used to deter Soviet Union in the Cold War against al-Qaeda, North Korea, Iran, Syria, China and others without making adjustments. Our potential adversaries have different strategies, personalities, cultures, languages, histories, views of rational behavior, and some have a different willingness to die for their cause. All are factors that must inform our approach to tailored deterrence strategies.

As Jerrold Post points out, "In this post-Cold War era…it is clear that deterrence must be tailored and based on nuanced actor-specific behavioral models." He would have us focus on adversary's intentions as the "locus of decision making" and concludes "when it is a leader predominant society, such as Iraq under Saddam, and the leader is judged to not be deterrable, this calls for a tailored communications program designed to drive a wedge between the leader and his followers." This strategy might also be employed against some of the factions within the Iranian leadership.

It should be emphasized that each leadership of each country is different in personalities, governmental structure, regime goals, strategic culture, political and military history, internal and external threats they face, and in how they make and implement decisions. Each is different in its relations with the United States and the history of that relationship. Thus, the United States and its allies need to tailor and customize a unique deterrence strategy to maximize its dissuasive power against each of these potential adversary states.

When designing a tailored deterrence strategy, the U.S. and its allies need to get answers to a range of questions about adversary regimes, including:

- Who makes decisions on war and peace issues for the regime?
- What do the top leaders value most? How could we leverage that value to deter them?
- What motivates these leaders most? Personal power? Regime survival? Ideology? Righting past wrongs? Religion? Desire for territorial expansion?
- What are these leaders like in personality, style, personal history and views?
- How are they influenced by their strategic culture?

- Can they be influenced most by particular threats or accommodations?
- Is there a predominant leader or is power shared? Who makes what kinds of decisions? Is decision-making centralized or dispersed?
- What is the history of risk-taking by these leaders in the past?
- Are there leadership factions? Can their leadership be split?
- What U.S. actions and deterrence messages might work best with each faction?
- How are national security decisions made? What is the process of decision?
- What influence does bureaucratic bargaining play in decisions?
- What are the regime's standard operating procedures (SOPs) and military doctrine?
- What are the influences of their culture and history on decisions made?
- What are their current foreign and defense policies?
- Who do they consider to be their domestic and international allies and rivals?
- What military capabilities and vulnerabilities do they possess?
- What is their center of gravity? Can it be exploited to enhance deterrence? What are their pressure points on which to exert deterrence leverage?
- How do they implement decisions once top leaders have decided on a course?
- What does their command and control system look like? Can it be interrupted?
- What warnings and indicators do we have when they are preparing to use force?
- How can we most effectively communicate with the rival regime?

In the case of non-state actors, the United States needs a tailored deterrence policy capable of dissuading those aiding and abetting terrorist groups like al-Qaeda from assisting that organization from acquiring and employing weapons of mass destruction. It will be important to establish clear red lines that the United States and allies will not permit to be crossed. Potential aiders, abetters, and aggressors need to be clearly informed of these thresholds and must be made to understand the extremely high costs in taking such actions.

Building a history of credible responses to threats and having strategic communications that make crystal clear the costs of crossing those red lines should be part of the important work done to shore up deterrence in the post-Cold War.

In the case of leader predominant states such as Kim Jong Il's North Korea or the former Iraqi regime under Saddam Hussein, a tailored deterrence approach is especially valuable. Where power is concentrated in just one or only a few persons, leadership profiles and personal histories are extremely important in discerning how to influence their decisions. Such tailored deterrence also becomes more important in crises than in day-to-day normal dealings with a rival regime since crisis decisions are often made at the highest levels in face-to-face groups in crises where time is short, stakes are high and there is often an element of surprise.

Because of the high stakes in acute international crises, top national leaders are under pressure to get personally involved, cutting out the normal bureaucratic layers of decision. There is a greater tendency for individual decision-makers or small face-to-face top-level decision groups to make these urgent and important decisions. Precisely at such times, logic often wars with psycho-logic. At just such junctures psychological factors may interfere with clear thinking. Profiling and understanding the tendencies of rival leaders can help predict some of these crisis outcomes.

When dealing with regimes where power is more widely shared, especially when rival factions are discerned in ruling elite, it is still important to understand the participants and what faction they belong to. Here the emphasis might be placed on attempting to empower and influence the faction that is most likely to take the decision path that is in the best interest of the United States and its allies while also attempting to avoid empowering the side bent on conflict or escalation. Hence, a sophisticated understanding of the cliques within ruling circles is a necessary element of a tailored deterrence posture vis-à-vis that state. Also, note that during crises, the dominant personality or views of a faction are magnified under stressful conditions. Those prone to aggressive actions tend to be even more aggressive in situations of duress and vice versa.

The United States leadership also needs to understand the difference in decision-making done in crises as opposed to normal times by the rival leadership. During acute international crises, the top leaders are more immediately involved in decisions and psychological factors and may have a greater role. Day-to-day decisions usually involve more bureaucratic politics, and things done through standard operating procedures (SOPs), and more players involved in policy and execution decisions. Thus, in this situation, a tailored deterrence policy should also include attempting to identify the normal time decision-processes of the regime, the wider range of bureaucratic players, and the SOPs followed as their elements interact and create outcomes.

A tailored deterrence posture also requires us to understand the rival's views of deterrence of the United States and its allies. If, as Saddam Hussein believed, the United States was a casualty adverse society and we would cut and run after a certain level of casualties, then such a ruler might be prone to take greater risks, thinking he could persuade us to retreat rather than finish the job if we were to go to war. Such adversarial thinking can possibly be reversed through a series of forceful and preparatory U.S. actions and statements counteracting the rival leader's perceptions, especially if communicated in clear and unambiguous ways.

As Jerrold Post recognizes, a "special dilemma is posed by transnational radical Islamist terrorism, many of whose members seek martyrdom."[10] He proposes that for:

> this challenging target, a four point program of tailored communications is proposed with the overall goal of reducing the ranks of terrorists by inhibiting potential terrorists from joining the group, producing dissension in the group, facilitating exit from the group, and reducing support for the group and delegitimizing its leaders. Messages designed to inhibit the development and use of weapons of mass destruction is included in the suggested program.[11]

We must customize our deterrent strategies to match the adversaries we face and the scenarios in which we might confront them. Therefore, in the tailored deterrence part of this book our authors looked at different state and non-state actors as individual challenges, each to be dealt with uniquely.

The tailored approach to deterrence[12] is particularly apt when confronting an adversary state or group that is significantly different from the United States in culture, values, perspectives, capabilities, goals, and willingness to suffer great losses to achieve their ends. Tailored deterrence is also very important when confronting a rival state or group led by a pre-dominant leader. Examples are Germany under Adolph Hitler, Iraq under Saddam Hussein, or North Korea under Kim Jong Il. Profiling the leader's personality, personal and political history, and his strategic culture can provide insights in how to deal, deter and influence that regime. Of course, some leaders may be undeterrable. Hitler, Napoleon and Saddam Hussein were pre-disposed to violence and risk-taking on a grand scale.

Many obstacles can stand in the way of an effective tailored deterrence strategy. Intelligence may be lacking on rival leaderships. We may fail to understand their personalities, histories, culture, decision process, stakes and capabilities. The factions and policy splits among them on various issues may be poorly understood. Communication may be difficult between foes with different cultures, languages, experiences and problems. Communications can be difficult because a government has multiple audiences to persuade at the same time – the rival government, allies, the press, the public and other decision-makers. Effective communications to one audience may not play well with another.

Tailored Deterrence of Iran

For at least two decades, the U.S. and allied governments have been concerned about the emerging nuclear program in Iran. As a state actor with a penchant to poke its finger into the eyes of western powers and especially the United States, Iran presents unique deterrence challenges.

Greg Giles points out that tailoring a deterrence strategy for Iran will not be easy because the Iran's leaders presents a unique set of behaviors such as "intense factionalism, belief in conspiracy theories, apocalyptic messianism and superstitious reliance on fortune telling."[13] Further, Iran is committed to spreading its radical Islamic revolution to other countries and believes the United States lacks the desire to stop it. Giles says these factors set the stage for U.S. and allied deterrence to fail and prevent future Iranian aggression.[14]

Nonetheless, Giles does believe deterrence failures could be minimized if U.S. governmental planners take four specific actions:

- First, "recognize America's track record of deterring the Islamic Republic since 1979 is rather poor, and they must understand why that has been the case."[15]
- Second, "tailor deterrence strategy and tactics to Iran's unique decision- making environment."[16]
- Third, rebuild the credibility of U.S. deterrent threats which will require a greater willingness to employ limited force against Iran even if it possesses nuclear weapons, while maintaining U.S. escalation dominance to discourage Iran from initiating nuclear use.[17]
- Fourth, "use simulations and exercises to explore various means by which a nuclear crisis with Tehran could be defused." [18]

However, in the event all of these actions fail we should be prepared to use the full force of our military capability to limit Iranian adventurism and nuclear use.

Tailored Deterrence of North Korea

In addition to Iran, a second major rogue state problem is presented by North Korea. If matters were not already tenuous enough in Korea, the March 2010 North Korean sinking of the South Korean Navy's ship *Cheonin* by torpedo, and, in November 2010, the North Korean artillery shelling on South Korea's *Yeonpyeong* Islands have escalated tensions between South and North Korea.

How we deter North Korea WMD usage is a question examined by Bruce Bennett who believes North Korea poses a serious WMD threat. He argues North Korea is a failing state and will have incentives to use its nuclear, chemical, and biological weapons in future crises and conflicts.

Bennett argues a deterrence strategy against the Pyongyang regime first must be "based on a combination of their [U.S./ROK] capabilities for denial and punishment, both of which need to be increased."[19] Second, we must "focus on the internal threats the North Korean regime faces."[20] They must be made to understand their society would come apart in any wartime environment and the regime would not survive in that case. Third, it is important to "convince North Korea its WMD use would often be thwarted by U.S./ROK denial capabilities."[21] Finally, the U.S. and "ROK should develop a strategy and plans for a ROK-led unification of Korea and use key elements of such a strategy to punish and deter North Korean provocations."[22]

Bennett says to "prevent North Korean WMD use in provocations and limited attacks, the United States and the ROK must first work to resolve the ROK gaps in defenses against limited attacks."[23] If North Korea can be denied success in limited attacks, the U.S. and South Korean deterrence effort will be strengthened.

Deterring Non-State Actors

Leaving the more easily understood deterring of states we now examine the difficulties and challenges of deterring non-state actors. Groups like al-Qaeda generally have no return addresses or traditional assets to hold hostage to reprisals. Thus, anyone planning deterrence strategies must develop newer forms of tailored deterrence for each targeted group. Lewis Dunn discussed how to influence the terrorist WMD acquisition and use calculus and focused on a strategy directed towards two groups: the al-Qaeda core leadership around Osama Bin-Ladin and their support group of aiders and abettors. Dunn points out these groups are susceptible to influence, although in various degrees. He suggests terrorist groups and their aiders and abettors might be persuaded not to acquire or employ weapons of mass destruction in attacks if they were convinced:

- such use was against the religious or ethical principles of the audience they were trying to recruit and influence;
- cheaper and more cost-effective means were available to achieve their ends;
- technical difficulties of executing a successful WMD attack were too great;

- WMD use would arouse more opposition than support for their cause;
- trying to acquire WMD capability involved too much danger and risk.

How does this apply to al-Qaeda's core leadership, and associated aiders and abettors? Dunn points out that its leaders are not easily deterred from use by the argument that weapons of mass destruction are not justifiable and legitimate according to Islamic religious doctrine. Its leaders have persuaded a few radical Islamic religious leaders to bless WMD use and to release fatwas sanctioning mass killings and WMD use against infidels.

According to Dunn a more favorable approach would be to convince that use of the weapon of mass destruction was *not* the most cost-effective means of achieving their ends, rather, other means are the s*mart to use* options.

Finally, there also might be a way to influence al-Qaeda leadership if they believe use of such weapons would alienate them from the greater Muslim world, and might not be the best use of their resources. Deterrence of al-Qaeda's use of WMD might be strengthened by using all strategic communication and partnership means to propagate and reinforce the view in the Muslim world that mass killings are outside the bounds of decent and respectable behavior.

Nuclear Attribution as Deterrence

Deterrence by the threat of punishment will fail if you do not know who to punish. It is hard to retaliate against assailants who leave no clue as to who they are. Thus, nuclear attribution is necessary to deter a rival equipped with nuclear weapons. An adversary state or group must know they will be targeted if they attack the United States or its allies. Should deterrence fail, then the United States needs to be able to attribute where that attack originated from. If it's a nuclear weapon set off by a terrorist, we need to know who gave them the bomb.

Nuclear forensics is the tool to help bring to light the likely perpetrators. The United States must let the world know that if a nuclear weapon, is used it has the ability to find out who did it and then send them a message to the return address. A strong nuclear attribution is central to this message.

Current attribution technology is developed, but is not foolproof. State and non-state actors would be more effectively deterred from nuclear weapons use if current U.S. capabilities were more widely known and if the post-blast evidence assessment process was more internationalized.

What steps could be taken to improve nuclear attribution capabilities? First, an international capability must be created to examine post-blast attribution using assets from international groups that combat nuclear smuggling and work with nuclear forensics. Second, an effort should be initiated that strengthens the science of nuclear forensics and how the world views it. Third, international capabilities for post-blast attribution should be developed and tested that provide an accurate and unprejudiced analysis leading to the source of the bomb. Fourth, speedy and accurate attribution still requires careful and full investigation and the acquisition of the right resources, before the final conclusions can be reached on the sources of the nuclear materials used and possible perpetrators of the attack. At the same time, the United States and its allies should continue to improve their databases of worldwide nuclear signatures.

Matching Deterrence Strategy to Specific Scenarios

The use of scenarios to help you think through deterrence at critical times and places can also inform U.S. and allied leaders about what actions to take and strategic communications to transmit to rivals during an ongoing crisis or conflict.

In the hypothetical future Taiwan crisis described in this book, it is important to note how an asymmetry of interests can cause the side with the most commitment to winning to take riskier decisions even if the other side has the preponderance of military capability. The United States might have superior military capability in such a crisis but China might have a greater stake in the outcome, more zeal for victory and might be willing to take greater risks.

In the case study of Saddam Hussein and deterrence in the 1990-1991 Gulf War, it is instructive to note that Hussein had a view of what would deter the United States from totally defeating him, 5,000 U.S. personnel killed in action. Likewise, U.S. leaders believed he would back out of Kuwait when faced with superior firepower. Both were wrong. The United States was prepared to incur far more casualties if necessary and Saddam was not willing to move because to retreat would pose a risk to his hold on power in Iraq.

Case studies also bring new deterrence factors to the fore – such as the need to decide and communicate early and clearly to the adversary. It is important to clearly draw lines on the map that should not be crossed, warning the adversary what steps would trigger a war. The 1990-1991 Gulf War case also indicated that the U.S. needed to send military capability early to Kuwait prior to the Iraqi invasion, even if just a trip wire force, if it wanted to convince Saddam Hussein not to start the invasion.

Several other deterrence lessons were discovered in the Gulf War case study of deterrence and Saddam Hussein. This was a case of serial deterrence steps. It shows the value of careful analysis of scenarios in identifying deterrence opportunities as the situation unfolds. Thus, scenarios help you to think through junctures in a scenario where war might be avoided or further escalation prevented. In the Gulf War case, had the United States better calculated the threat to its Middle East oil supplies if Kuwait were to fall to Iraq, it might have paid more attention to the border and oil dispute between Iraq and Kuwait prior to the Iraqi invasion.

Had the United States anticipated the Iraqi occupation of Kuwait, it might have drawn a line in the sand spelling out dire consequences for Iraq if it intervened and might have thus deterred the Iraqi invasion. Had it moved US forces into Kuwait prior to the invasion, the United States Government might have communicated better its will to use force, even if the US forces sent were only "tripwire" forces.

With regard to deterring Iraq's use of chemical and biological (CB) weapons it seems likely Saddam Hussein was deterred from using them because of a stern warning communicated to the Iraqi leadership by President H.W. Bush warning indirectly but clearly of a possible U.S. nuclear retaliation in that eventuality. Also, President H.W. Bush was deterred from occupying Iraq in 1991 by his estimates of the further costs that would entail in lives, treasure, alliance cohesion, domestic political support and pain of occupying and rebuilding a defeated country.

Profiling leaders is important if we are to understand how to influence them. Saddam essentially made all major foreign and defense policy for Iraq and he was a risk taker. Indeed, as noted earlier,

> the Iraqi dictator took risks far beyond what Soviet leaders were willing to risk in the Cold War when confronted with overwhelming U.S. military power and a dedicated deterrent posture. The risk-taking and violent personality of the Iraqi leader, coupled with the mild deterrent signals the U.S. sent at the beginning of the Iraq-Kuwait confrontation, led Saddam Hussein to gamble on seizing an oil rich treasure that could bail him out of the financial problems caused by the huge costs of the Iran-Iraq war.[24]

A study of possible flashpoints and escalation scenarios also can help decision-makers see the points where they will need to take forceful actions and send strong messages if they are to curtail crises and avoid later escalations.

Deterrence in a Future U.S. China Crisis over Taiwan

Even though the United States and China are each other's best trading partners, there is a flashpoint that could one day trigger a military conflict, Taiwan. McCready argued that the asymmetrical interests of the United States and China might tilt the outcome and cause the Chinese leadership to escalate a crisis or conflict further than we might expect

Misunderstandings and misperceptions unique to both countries seem to center on national interest for each country. McCready believes that the "most dangerous misunderstanding is the belief, prevalent in both the U.S. and China, that the U.S. has no significant national interest at stake."[25] If this is the case then it's imperative for the U.S. leadership to define why this commitment is important and clearly communicate it to the P.R.C. and to the U.S. public.

However, the problem is that for the past six decades the United States has been intentionally ambiguous as to what we would do if China invaded Taiwan. This has worked since China has not used force to take the island back, but it is questionable if this will continue to be the case in the future.

McCready identified four areas of mutual misperception that need to be corrected at the top leadership levels of both countries in order for peace to be maintained over Taiwan's status:

- First, "the nature of the national interest involved"[26] must be clarified;
- Second, "the level of commitment to that interest,"[27] should be clarified;
- Third, "the governmental decision-making process," should be better understood; [28]
- Fourth, "the attitudes that drive each nation's international behavior" must be more explicit[29]

One serious misperception according to the Chinese is the American failure to understand the seriousness of their intent to regain Taiwan. That island nation has been a source of tension ever since the communist Chinese took over control of the mainland of China almost 60 years ago. In China's view "the island now became a symbol of the incompleteness of the communist victory in the civil war."[30] This fact must continuously be factored into any U.S. deterrence strategy.

Deterrence at Near Zero or Zero Nuclear Weapons

President Obama in his 2009 Prague speech discussed an eventual goal of zero nuclear weapons if other nations could also be persuaded to follow that path. In the meantime, the President has indicated that the United States will maintain a nuclear deterrent capability to maintain the peace until such time as conditions are safe to move to zero nuclear weapons or near zero. Would a world of zero or near zero nuclear weapons make the world safer or more dangerous? Would this be a world of less conflict or would global zero make conventional combat more likely because it entailed less risk? Barry Blechman argues that complete or near total nuclear disarmament need not make conventional wars more likely.

As early as 1946, in the Acheson-Lilienthal plan, the United States, then the sole possessor of the nuclear bomb offered to give them up and advocated that nuclear weapons be banned. Truman wanted to avoid a world of nuclear weapons states. Still later, the United States pledged itself to general and complete nuclear disarmament in Article VI of the nuclear non–proliferation treaty (NPT). The reason is that U.S. and other world leaders feared a future world beset by nuclear wars and catastrophic casualties. In the view of those advocating global zero, they see it as the only means of preventing such a future.

For those who claim that nuclear weapons are the deterrent to war and nuclear disarmament is a path to more rather than fewer wars, Blechman cites some examples where possession of nuclear weapons did not deter attacks from states armed only with conventional arms. North Korea and China fought the nuclear-armed United States in the Korean War. Egypt and Syria attacked a nuclear Israel in 1973. Argentina attempted to take back the Falkland Islands from a nuclear United Kingdom, and North Vietnam fought a nuclear United States in the Vietnam War. Also terrorist attacks took place inside Russia, the United States, United Kingdom, India and Pakistan despite their nuclear weapons status. Obviously, nuclear weapons do not deter all conflict. Also, at least 200 other conflicts took place among the non-nuclear weapons states in the 65 years of the nuclear era. The absence of nuclear weapons may or may not spur more conflicts – the evidence is mixed and unclear.

In a world of zero or near zero nuclear weapons, air and missile defenses could play a much greater role in deterrence. If such defenses were prohibited or greatly limited, even small nuclear arsenals of perhaps 100 nuclear weapons could inflict major damage on any aggressors and thus could be effective deterrents to war or escalation. Small nuclear arsenals would have to be protected and made more survivable by multiple basing modes probably relying more on defense of the deterrent, mobility and position location uncertainty to maintain their retaliatory capability.

In a global zero world there would always be the possibility and problem of the clandestine cache, a regime that cheated and withheld some of its nuclear weapons for the time when others had disarmed. Obviously, verification of global zero would be a major problem, and the world is a big place. Also, any nation possessing nuclear weapons where others did not might gain a decisive nuclear advantage in a crisis confrontation.

As the saying goes, "in the valley of the blind the one-eyed man is king." Cheating and breakout and the responses to them would make a zero nuclear world possibly less safe than a world of small or large nuclear arsenals. If cheating and breakout were detected, the probability is an immediate return to the manufacture of new nuclear weapons by rivals of the cheating state.

The absence of nuclear weapons, if even achieved and sustained, could remove the threat of nuclear war. However, for the foreseeable future global zero is a distant mountaintop vision and the world has only inched toward the "base camp" where we could see any reasonable path to the top. In between that base camp position are nine nuclear weapons states run by very different people who do not seem inclined to give up their nuclear arsenals any time soon.

Strategic Communications: a Key to Deterrence

Richard Estes discussed the key role of strategic communications in deterrence. He emphasizes how important it is for the United States to deliver a coordinated and effective strategic communications to convince the world that our deterrence pledges and threats are believable. To maximize our influence, all departments and divisions of our government need to speak with one convincing voice to our allies that we will defend them and to our adversaries that aggression will be met with overwhelming force. Moreover, our words must be matched by our capabilities and actions.

It would appear that the United States government has to reconcile two contrary ideas. First it must communicate to potential rivals that U.S. nuclear forces will retaliate in kind if nuclear weapons are used against it or its allies. Second, and at the same time, the U.S. government is also trying to move the world toward non-use of nuclear weapons, reduction of existing nuclear forces, and to the eventual abandonment of nuclear weapons worldwide if it can be done safely and by all parties. To communicate this dual message to the world requires a solid strategic communications campaign.

Estes stresses that for this strategic communication campaign to be effective it must have a vision that consist of certain elements:

- First, the vision and message begins with the U.S. President. Whoever is in this position must tell the world the vision of the United States, a vision that our deterrent is credible and secure.
- Second, this vision should be consistent across the administration.
- Third, it must be solid enough that policies are based on the vision and message, but have the flexibility that allows the President and other top officials to be able to shape the vision.
- Fourth, the vision and its associated policies should always aim for the moral high ground that helps build confidence in its leadership.
- Fifth, this campaign should continue to promote the United States as a good steward of its own decreasing nuclear weapons arsenal while showing faithful commitment to its allies who rely on the U.S. nuclear deterrent.
- Sixth, it should have an element that heralds the very high threshold the U.S. has on use of nuclear weapons, but also that this threshold has limits and could be reached in very critical cases, triggering a U.S. nuclear response.
- Seventh, the vision and message should have an element that communicates our focus on rogue nations who would use their emerging nuclear programs to bully their neighbors, but also indicating that we still have an eye on past adversaries.
- Eighth, any message the U.S. sends should work to compel rational leaders of other nations to help in preventing rogue nations and terrorist from obtaining nuclear material and weapons.
- Ninth, "words matter. Actions matter. Allies and partners matter. Pulling all three together effectively and communicating a coherent, tough, and credible message to adversaries and allies is the essence of deterrence, and of strategic communication."[31]

Implications of Resilience for Deterrence Success

A very different aspect of deterrence deals with a nation's ability to absorb an attack and bounce back. This is a form of deterrence by denial. If adversaries know that any attack they plan might be deflected or may serve to provoke more than to injure, they may not conduct it at all.

Deterrence begins in the mind of the adversary and that leadership may decide it is not cost-effective to attack a target known for its resiliency. It may not be deemed worth the great effort it takes to plan and conduct an operation, wasting resources, if the plan entails a high probability of failure.

For a nation to develop resiliency they must strengthen in three key spheres: leadership, infrastructure, and population. The United States should strive to build resiliency to make it appear to our rivals as a harder much more difficult target. Once we have: (1) trained our leaders to cope better through national and regional exercises and study of future options, (2) erected greater protections of our critical infrastructures and key national assets, and (3) have organized, trained and equipped our public to cope better with future crises, then the United States will be in a better position to absorb a punishing attack and bounce back, minimize losses, and win, making such an attack a move the rivals will ultimately regret.

However, for deterrence of such attacks to succeed, preparations must be mated with strategic communications that let the adversary know that their attacks will backfire. Resiliency must be developed and then advertised and this message must be based on fact and not just propaganda. The U.S. schools and educational system may be the best medium for helping to prepare the U.S. public to be resilient against natural or man-made catastrophic events.

Where Do We Go From Here?

This study of deterrence focused on three approaches to understanding deterrence. Classical Cold War deterrence principles will probably be relevant in most state-to-state relationships but what worked in the U.S.-Soviet relationship may not fully work against every other rival state or coalition. Added to this approach, not replacing it, should be an attempt to tailor the U.S. deterrent posture to rival regimes based on a more precise understanding of such enemy leaders and their regimes. A third approach, one that can supplement but not replace the other two, is one based on analysis of influence or decision points in an ongoing or contemplated scenario to discern at what junctures what actions and communications may be required to deter war or further escalation of an ongoing conflict. Mating the elements of classic deterrence with a nuanced understanding of the enemy and combining those two approaches with detailed scenario analysis can give U.S. and allied leaders the analytic tools to craft an effective deterrent capability against rival states.

This is only part of the approach to deterring a WMD attack since terrorists and insurgents have now shown an interest in WMD capability and may be more prone to use it since they are harder to find and retaliate against. The program for deterring and preventing WMD terrorism will be improved with improved strategic communication to the Islamic world, better WMD attribution capabilities, more effective defenses and programs for building U.S. and allied public resilience. Finally, deterrence will be best facilitated by letting aiders and abettors of such terrorists know they will be identified and become targets of our retaliation if WMD is used and if they were found to be part of the chain of custody from the source to the terrorist group.

There are many means to thin out the WMD threat. The United States employs three such programs: *nonproliferation* to prevent proliferation of WMD to adversaries, *counterproliferation* to use military means to offset such capabilities where they exist, and *consequence management* capabilities to survive, recover, fight and win despite such attacks.

At the heart of the counterproliferation program is deterrence of war and escalation of war. This program promises an adversary that an attack on the United States or an allied state will be catastrophically counterproductive. Moreover, U.S. and allied active and passive defenses as well as offensive capabilities can help prevent some of the harm intended from happening even if a rival strikes.

It is well that there is a rebirth of thinking about the deterrence mission for the combination of deterrence-by-punishment and deterrence-by-denial of enemy success are the strongest U.S. and allied tools available for keeping the peace.

Notes

[1] This volume does not discuss deterrence of WMD proliferation. Instead the focus is on deterrence of military conflict or escalation of such conflict.

[2] Miller, Franklin, "Chapter 3 - Tailoring U.S. Strategic Deterrence Effects on Russia," p. 43

[3] Ibid, p. 44

[4] Ibid, p. 48

[5] Lt. Col. Marc A. Peterson, "The New Triad," Professional Studies Paper, Air War College, Maxwell AFB, Alabama, (Dec. 10, 2010).

[6] *Guthe, Kurt, "Chapter 11* - Deterrence, the Triad, and Possible Dyads."

[7] The Midgetman, MGM-134, was developed in the 1980s for the U.S. Air Force. It was a three stage solid-fueled small mobile ICBM seated on a Hardened Mobile Launcher. Designed to use a "cold launch" method for lift-off it would augment the existing Minuteman and Peacekeeper missile systems. The program was terminated in 1992 as the Cold War ended. See http://www.designation-systems.net/dusrm/m-134.htm

[8] Peterson, "The New Triad."

[9] Statement of Anthony Cordesman of CSIS about most states in the Middle East.

[10] Post, Jerrold, "Chapter 2- Actor-Specific Behavioral Models of Adversaries: A Key Requirement for Tailored Deterrence," p. 37

[11] Ibid, pp. 37-38

[12] As the May 2010 U.S. National Security Strategy states "we will draw on diplomacy, development, and international norms and institutions to help resolve disagreements, prevent conflict, and maintain peace, mitigating where possible the need for the use of force. This means credibly underwriting U.S. defense commitments with *tailored approaches to deterrence* and ensuring the U.S. military continues to have the necessary capabilities across all domains—land, air, sea, space, and cyber."

[13] Giles, Greg, "Chapter 5- Deterring a Nuclear-Armed Iran from Adventurism and Nuclear Use," p. 151

[14] Ibid.

[15] Ibid, p. 152.

[16] Ibid.

[17] Ibid.

[18] Ibid.

[19] Bennett, Bruce, "Chapter 6 - Deterring North Korea from Employment of WMD in Future Korean Conflicts and Crises," p.191.

[20] Ibid.

[21] Ibid.

[22] Ibid.

[23] Ibid.

[24] Schneider, Barry, "Chapter 7 - Deterrence & Saddam Hussein: Lessons from the 1990-1991 Gulf War," p. 241.

[25] McCready, Douglas, "Chapter 4 -Crisis Deterrence in the Taiwan Strait," p.63.

[26] Ibid, p. 66.

[27] Ibid.

[28] Ibid.

[29] Ibid.

[30] Ibid, p. 62.

[31] Estes, Richard, "Chapter 12 - The Role of Strategic Communications in Deterrence: Lesson from History," p. 380.

CONTRIBUTORS

Dr. Bruce W. Bennett is a senior defense analyst at the RAND Corporation; the research leader for strategy, force planning and counterproliferation within RAND's International Security and Defense Policy Center; and a professor of policy analysis in the Pardee RAND Graduate School (PRGS). Dr. Bennett works on military strategies, including deterrence, and the forces required by those strategies. Much of his work deals with the potential operational and strategic implications of chemical, biological and nuclear threats against the United States, Northeast Asia, and the Persian Gulf. He has performed research for the Office of the Secretary of Defense, the Republic of Korea (ROK) Army, the ROK /U.S. Combined Forces Command, and the U.S. Pacific Command. He has also facilitated many war games focused on possible conflict in Korea and elsewhere. He regularly writes on Korean security issues, and has visited the region some 75 times. Dr. Bennett received a B.S. in economics from the California Institute of Technology and a Ph.D. in policy analysis from PRGS.

Dr. Barry M. Blechman is the co-founder of the Stimson Center and a distinguished fellow focused on nuclear disarmament. He was chair of Stimson's board from 1989 to 2007. Blechman has nearly 50 years of distinguished service in national security, in both the public and private sectors. He is an expert on political and military policies, military strategy, and defense budgets and industries. Blechman has worked in the Departments of State and Defense, and at the Office of Management and Budget. Among other boards and commissions, Blechman served on the Commission to Assess the Ballistic Missile Threat to the United States (1998-99), the Defense Policy Board (2002-06), the mayor's Bioterrorism Preparedness and Response Program Advisory Committee in the District of Columbia (2004-06), and the Department of State Advisory Committee on Transformational Diplomacy (2005-08). Blechman founded DFI International Inc., a research consultancy, in 1984 and served as its CEO until 2007. Blechman holds a Ph.D. in international relations from Georgetown University, has taught at several universities, and has written extensively on national security issues. His most recent publications are

Elements of a Nuclear Disarmament Treaty and National Perspectives on Nuclear Disarmament. Both volumes, which he co-edited with Alexander Bollfrass, were published by Stimson in 2010.

Dr. Lewis A. Dunn is a Senior Vice President of Science Applications International Corporation (SAIC). At SAIC, he has been responsible for many U.S. government-sponsored projects on issues such as proliferation prevention; future threat reduction and arms control initiatives; responses to WMD terrorism threats; and deterrence planning and requirements. Dr. Dunn recently concluded a major project on the roles of Cooperative Security activities—from strategic dialogue through Joint studies and analyses, to revamp arms control negotiations and agreements—in transforming the U.S.-Russia and U.S.-China strategic relationships. He was called on by various U.S. government organizations to provide advice on preparations for the 2010 Non-Proliferation Treaty Review Conference. From 1983-1987, Dr. Dunn served as the assistant director of the U.S. Arms Control and Disarmament Agency. He was also the ambassador to the 1985 Nuclear Non-Proliferation Treaty Review Conference and the 1987 U.N. Peaceful Uses of Nuclear Energy Conference. Dr. Dunn serves as an expert advisor on the Congressional Commission on the U.S. Strategic Posture and is on the Editorial Board of the Nonproliferation Review. Dr. Dunn's most recent publications include articles entitled "Why Has the American Homeland Not Been Attacked Again?" (co-authored with Dallas Boyd and James Scouras) in *The Washington Quarterly* and "The Treaty on the Nonproliferation of Nuclear Weapons: An Assessment," in *The Nonproliferation Review*. He received his Ph.D. in political science from the University of Chicago and is a member of the International Institute for Strategic Studies and the Council on Foreign Relations.

Mr. Richard H. Estes is Associate Director of the USAF Counterproliferation Center and Principal of Estes Consulting. Mr. Estes has focused his efforts for the Center in Washington, DC from his office in Williamsburg since 2001. A command pilot, he retired from the Air Force as a colonel in 2000 with over 30 years of wide-ranging service including operational, command and staff assignments at various levels. His final assignment was as the Defense and Air Attaché to the Kingdom of Morocco.

He served also on the faculty of the Air War College as Director of Regional Studies and Deputy Department Chairman, Joint Force Employment. He is a graduate in residence of the Industrial College of the Armed Forces and Air Command and Staff College, has a Bachelor of Arts from Methodist University, and holds a Master of Arts in Government and Public Administration from the University of South Carolina. He has published several articles and monographs. An expert in public diplomacy, his most recent published works are "A Message Not Yet Sent: Using Strategic Communications to Combat Weapons of Mass Destruction Threats" and "Toward a National Counterproliferation Strategic Communication Plan." He lectures frequently on strategic communications and missile defense.

Mr. Patrick Ellis is a WMD/Homeland Security analyst at the USAF Counterproliferation Center located on Maxwell AFB. He specializes in WMD terrorism, homeland security and disaster/emergency management issues. He holds a Bachelor of Arts degree from University of Maryland in Asian studies/government and politics, a Master of Public Administration degree from the University of Oklahoma, and a Master's degree in International Relations. He completed specialized courses at the Defense Nuclear Weapons School, U.S. Army Chemical School and USAF Special Operations School. Mr. Ellis has developed and taught WMD and Asymmetric Warfare related topics for the Air Force Institute of Technology, Senior NCO Academy, and the Ira C. Eaker College for Professional Development's Air Force Incident Management course. As an Air War College faculty member he has taught elective courses such as Asymmetric Warfare Issues, International Rivals and WMD Issues for the USAF. He is currently the course director for a two term Nuclear Threats, Countermeasures and Enterprise research elective. His other interests are the study of globalization, the undeveloped world, irregular warfare and homeland security. He co-authored with Randall J. Larsen a chapter titled "Securing the Homeland: The First Decade," found in the book *Avoiding the Abyss: Progress, Shortfalls, and the Way Ahead in Combating the WMD Threat*, published by Praeger Security International, 2006.

Mr. Gregory F. Giles is a Senior Director with Science Applications International Corporation (SAIC), where he advises U.S. government decision makers on issues pertaining to Iran, nonproliferation, and deterrence. He has published widely and testified before Congress on these subjects and is a regular guest lecturer at the U.S. Air Force and Army War Colleges. Since the early-1990s, Mr. Giles has been providing various USG Departments, Agencies, and Military Commands with expert analysis of Iranian decision-making dynamics and how best to harness all elements of US national power to influence them. In this regard, he has developed an in-depth profile of the Iranian regime and how it weighs costs, benefits, and the consequences of restraint. He was the featured speaker on Iran at a recent symposium on tailored deterrence at the NATO Defense College, Rome. Mr. Giles is also advising USG clients on Iran's nuclear negotiating goals, strategies, and tactics. In this regard, he has assessed Iran's motives to pursue nuclear weapons, characterized the stance of top leaders on the nuclear issue, anticipated actual Iranian nuclear moves, and postulated likely Iranian reactions to various US courses of action. He recently assessed the risk of Iran's emergence as a nuclear supplier. Prior to joining SAIC, Mr. Giles worked as a staff assistant in the British House of Commons, the United Nations General Assembly, and the U.S. House and Senate. Mr. Giles has a Bachelor's degree in international studies and political science from Dickinson College and a Master's degree in international affairs from Columbia University.

Mr. Kurt Guthe is the Director of Strategic Studies at the National Institute for Public Policy. Before rejoining NIPP in 2005, he was a senior analyst at the Center for Strategic and Budgetary Assessments. During leave from CSBA, he contributed to the 2001 Nuclear Posture Review and served in the Office of the Deputy Assistant Secretary of Defense for Forces Policy. In 1992, during a one-year leave of absence from National Institute, Mr. Guthe served on the staff of the Gulf War Air Power Survey. From 1981-1984, Mr. Guthe was on the senior professional staff of the Hudson Institute. From 1978-1981, he was a member of the research staff of the System Planning Corporation.

Dr. Douglas McCready is a retired Army Reserve Chaplain. He is a supervisory chaplain in Pennsylvania's Department of Public Welfare. He is a graduate of the University of Pennsylvania, with degrees in international relations and Chinese studies. He has a Ph.D. from Temple University in religious studies and was an Army Senior Service College Fellow at the

Fletcher School of Law and Diplomacy. He has taught at Temple University, Alvernia University and Holy Family University. He is the author of two books and has written on military subjects for the Army's Strategic Studies Institute, Military Review, Political Theology, Studies in Christian Ethics and the Journal of Military Ethics.

Mr. Franklin C. Miller is a Principal of The Scowcroft Group, an international consulting firm based in Washington, DC. Mr. Miller served 31 years in the U.S. government, including 22 years serving under seven Secretaries in a series of progressively senior positions in the Department of Defense and four years as a Special Assistant to President George W. Bush and as Senior Director for Defense Policy and Arms Control on the National Security Council staff. Following his retirement from government in 2005, Mr. Miller joined The Cohen Group, where he served for five years, first as a Vice President and later as a Senior Counselor. For his service, Mr. Miller was awarded the Defense Department's highest civilian award, the Defense Distinguished Civilian Service Medal, five times, and has received similar high-level awards from the Department of State, the Department of the Navy, the Chairman of the Joint Chiefs of Staff, the National Nuclear Security Administration and the Defense Intelligence Agency. In addition, Mr. Miller has been awarded the Norwegian Royal Order of Merit (Grand Officer) and the French Legion of Honor (Officer). In December 2006 he was awarded an honorary knighthood -- a Knight Commander of the Order of the British Empire (KBE) -- by Queen Elizabeth II in recognition of his many contributions to U.S.-UK relations during his decades of government service. Mr. Miller currently serves on the Defense Policy Board, the U.S.-European Command Advisory Board, and the U.S. Strategic Command Advisory Group. He is a member of the Council on Foreign Relations and a Director of the Atlantic Council of the United States. He serves on the Board of Directors of EADS-North America, the Charles Stark Draper Laboratory, and History Associates Incorporated. Mr. Miller received his BA (Phi Beta Kappa) from Williams College in 1972. He received an MPA from Princeton University's Woodrow Wilson School in 1977.

Dr. Jerrold M. Post is Professor of Psychiatry, Political Psychology and International Affairs, and Director of the Political Psychology Program at the George Washington University. He came to the George Washington

University after a 21-year career at the CIA, where he was the founding director of the Center for the Analysis of Personality and Political Behavior. He received the Intelligence Medal of Merit in 1979. Among his extensive publications are *Leaders and Their Followers in a Dangerous World: The Psychology of Political Behavior* (2004), and *The Mind of the Terrorist: The Psychology of Terrorism from the IRA to al-Qaeda* (2007).

Mr. David J. Trachtenberg is an independent consultant in national security affairs and serves as President and Chief Executive Officer of Shortwaver Consulting, LLC. He has more than 30 years of public policy experience in the private sector and the Executive and Legislative branches of government. From 2005-2007 he was Vice President of CACI International and Division Manager of the Strategic Analysis Division at CACI-NSR, Inc. From 2003-2005 he was Senior Vice President for Homeland Security and Senior Vice President for Corporate Support at National Security Research, Inc. From 2001-2003, Mr. Trachtenberg was Principal Deputy Assistant Secretary of Defense for International Security Policy, where his office initiated successful efforts to restructure NATO, develop the Proliferation Security Initiative, and foster closer relationships with Russia and the former Soviet states. During this time he served concurrently as Acting Deputy Assistant Secretary of Defense for Forces Policy, overseeing the office that led the development of the Nuclear Posture Review and the New Triad concept, and provided policy rationale leading to the withdrawal from the ABM Treaty and deployment of an initial national missile defense capability. In this capacity, he led interagency delegations to discuss missile defense cooperation with the Russian Federation. For his service Mr. Trachtenberg was awarded the Department of Defense Medal for Distinguished Public Service, the highest honorary award presented by DoD to private citizens. From 1995-2001, Mr. Trachtenberg was a senior professional staff member on the House Armed Services Committee (HASC), where he developed Committee positions and provided policy oversight of export control and technology transfer issues, peacekeeping, terrorism, nuclear weapons and arms control, missile defense, non-proliferation, and cooperative threat reduction with the former Soviet Union. Prior to his work on the HASC staff, Mr. Trachtenberg was a member of the technical staff of The Analytical Sciences Corporation, a consultant to the President's General Advisory Committee on Arms Control and Disarmament, Senior Defense Analyst for the Committee on the Present Danger, and a research associate with the Institute for Foreign Policy Analysis, Inc. Trachtenberg received an A.B. degree in International Relations from the University of Southern California and a Master of Science degree in Foreign Service from Georgetown University. He is widely published and has served on various advisory boards, including task forces of the Defense Science Board.

Dr. Barry R. Schneider is the Director of the USAF Counterproliferation Center (CPC) at Maxwell AFB, and is also a Professor of International Relations at the Air War College. Dr. Schneider specializes in WMD counterproliferation and nonproliferation issues as well as the profiles of adversary leaders and their strategic cultures. He is the author of *Future War and Counterproliferation: U.S. Military Responses to NBC Proliferation Threats* (Praeger, 1999); Editor, *Middle East Security Issues, In the Shadow of Weapons of Mass Destruction Proliferation* (CPC, 1999); and contributor to and co-editor of *Know Thy Enemy II* (CPC, 2007); *The World's Most Threatening Terrorist Networks and Criminal Gangs* (Palgrave Macmillan, 2009); *Avoiding the Abyss: Progress, Shortfalls and the Way Ahead in Combating WMD* (CPC, 2005; Praeger, 2006); *Know Thy Enemy: Profiles of Adversary Leaders and Their Strategic Cultures* (CPC, 2003), *The Gathering Biological Warfare Storm* (CPC, 2002), *Pulling back from the Nuclear Brink: Reducing and Countering Nuclear Threats* (Frank Cass Ltd., 1998), *Battlefield of the Future: 21st Century Warfare Issues* (Air University Press, 1998), *Missiles for the Nineties: ICBMs and Strategic Policy* (Westview, 1984), and *Current Issues in U.S. Defense Policy* (Praeger, 1976). He has served as a Foreign Affairs Officer (GS-14) and Public Affairs Officer (GS-15) at the U.S. Arms Control and Disarmament Agency, as a Congressional staffer on arms control and defense issues, and was a Senior Defense Analyst at The Harris Group and the National Institute for Public Policy. He has taught at the Air War College since 1993. As a faculty member he has taught Air War College core courses of instruction and elective courses such as International Rivals, Homeland Security Issues, International Flashpoints, Counterproliferation Issues, 21st Century Warfare Issues, and CBW Issues for the USAF. He has taught at five other colleges and universities, and has a Ph.D. in Political Science from Columbia University.

INDEX